CONSTITUTIONS IN TIMES OF FINANCIAL CRISIS

Many constitutions include provisions intended to limit the discretion of governments in economic policy. In times of financial crises, such provisions often come under pressure as a result of calls for exceptional responses to crisis situations. This volume assesses the ability of constitutional orders all over the world to cope with financial crises, and the demands for emergency powers that typically accompany them. Bringing together a variety of perspectives from legal scholars, economists, and political scientists, this volume traces the long-run implications of financial crises for constitutional order. In exploring the theoretical and practical problems raised by the constitutionalization of economic policy during times of severe crisis, this volume showcases an array of constitutional design options and the ways they channel governmental responses to emergency.

Tom Ginsburg is Leo Spitz Professor of International Law and Professor of Political Science at the University of Chicago Law School.

Mark D. Rosen is University Distinguished Professor at Chicago-Kent College of Law, Illinois Institute of Technology.

Georg Vanberg is Professor of Political Science and Law, and current Chair of the Department of Political Science at Duke University.

Constitutions in Times of Financial Crisis

Edited by

TOM GINSBURG

University of Chicago

MARK D. ROSEN

Chicago-Kent College of Law, Illinois Institute of Technology

GEORG VANBERG

Duke University

CAMBRIDGE
UNIVERSITY PRESS

CAMBRIDGE
UNIVERSITY PRESS

University Printing House, Cambridge CB2 8BS, United Kingdom

One Liberty Plaza, 20th Floor, New York, NY 10006, USA

477 Williamstown Road, Port Melbourne, VIC 3207, Australia

314–321, 3rd Floor, Plot 3, Splendor Forum, Jasola District Centre, New Delhi – 110025, India

79 Anson Road, #06–04/06, Singapore 079906

Cambridge University Press is part of the University of Cambridge.

It furthers the University's mission by disseminating knowledge in the pursuit of education, learning, and research at the highest international levels of excellence.

www.cambridge.org
Information on this title: www.cambridge.org/9781108492294
DOI: 10.1017/9781108679404

First published 2019

Printed and bound in Great Britain by Clays Ltd, Elcograf S.p.A.

A catalogue record for this publication is available from the British Library.

Library of Congress Cataloging-in-Publication Data
NAMES: Ginsburg, Tom, editor. | Rosen, Mark D., editor. | Vanberg, Georg, 1971– editor.
TITLE: Constitutions in times of financial crisis / edited Tom Ginsburg, University of Chicago; Mark D. Rosen, Illinois Institute of Technology; Georg Vanberg, Duke University, North Carolina.
DESCRIPTION: New York : Cambridge University Press, 2019. | Series: Comparative constitutional law and policy | Includes bibliographical references and index.
IDENTIFIERS: LCCN 2019003484 | ISBN 9781108492294 (hardback)
SUBJECTS: LCSH: War and emergency legislation. | Financial crises – Government policy. | Global Financial Crisis, 2008–2009. | BISAC: LAW / Constitutional.
CLASSIFICATION: LCC K4700 .C665 2019 | DDC 342.009/0511–dc23
LC record available at https://lccn.loc.gov/2019003484

ISBN 978-1-108-49229-4 Hardback

Contents

Contributors

Patrícia André is a researcher at CEDIS–NOVA Law School and DINAMIA'CET –IUL.

Eva Brems is Professor of Law, Ghent University.

Xenophon Contiades is Professor of Public Law, Panteion University of Social and Political Sciences; Managing Director, Centre for European Constitutional Law.

Barry Cushman is the John P. Murphy Foundation Professor of Law, and Concurrent Professor of Political Science and History, University of Notre Dame.

Björn Dressel is Associate Professor, Crawford School of Public Policy, Australian National University.

Federico Fabbrini is Full Professor of EU Law, School of Law & Government, Dublin City University and Director of the DCU Brexit Institute.

John Ferejohn is Samuel Tilden Professor of Law, New York University.

Alkmene Fotiadou is Dr.iur. and a research associate, Centre for European Constitutional Law.

Tom Ginsburg is the Leo Spitz Professor of International Law and Ludwig and Hilda Wolf Research Scholar, University of Chicago Law School, and Research Professor at the American Bar Foundation.

Mitu Gulati is Professor of Law, Duke University.

Turkuler Isiksel is the James P. Shenton Associate Professor of the Core Curriculum, Columbia University.

R. Daniel Kelemen is Professor of Political Science and Law, Rutgers University.

Gonçalo Saraiva Matias is a member of the Board and Director of Research at the Francisco Manuel dos Santos Foundation, Lisbon.

Gabriel L. Negretto is Associate Professor, Division of Political Studies, CIDE.

Eric A. Posner is Kirkland and Ellis Distinguished Service Professor, University of Chicago Law School.

Mark D. Rosen is University Distinguished Professor of Law, Chicago-Kent College of Law, Illinois Institute of Technology.

Georg Vanberg is Professor of Political Science, Duke University.

Teresa Violante is a research fellow at the Goethe-University Frankfurt a.M. and visiting research fellow at the Max Planck Institute for Comparative Public Law and International Law (Heidelberg).

Foreword

It is well known that the world financial crisis of 2007 and 2008 posed several challenges to the constitutions of the affected countries. These challenges were faced not only by countries which were directly affected and had to implement austerity measures, but also by countries whose economies were compelled to rescue others from the economic turmoil. This was particularly evident in Europe. Europe became, in this sense, a constitutional laboratory, given the effects of the financial crisis on economies, especially on the sovereign debt markets, on public finance, and ultimately, on the ability of governments to sustain the welfare state.

Constitutions might be prepared to respond to emergencies, but often the relevant provisions were drafted to deal with major catastrophes, or acts of war, and focus on the suspension of rights. In the context of the financial crisis, governments and courts felt reluctant to use concepts that were designed for very different purposes.

Furthermore, the global nature of the crisis undermined the traditional local constitutional responses. Protectionism and legal parochialism could not isolate states from the impact and spillover effects of a crisis that originated transnationally. One of the first reactions was for countries to distance themselves from those contaminated: 'We are not Greece, we are not Ireland, we are not Portugal' were expressions often used until they became useless. It was clear that the crisis had a potential to affect us all, even those not directly harmed by it. Again, in the context of the European Union – and because of the eurozone, the impact on the euro, and the absence of a common European debt sovereign market – those spillover effects were much more evident.

Not only were governments not prepared for the necessity – or perhaps inevitability – of this cross-national dialogue, but courts were even less prepared for it. This does not mean that courts did not incorporate international or comparative elements in their decisions, but they were probably unable to fully consider the cross-border effects of adjudication in their decisions.

An example of that impact was the jurisprudence of the Portuguese Constitutional Court on the reduction of pensions and salaries, at the same time that the German Constitutional Court was adjudicating decisions on the Outright

Monetary Transactions (OMT) program announced by the European Central Bank. At least psychologically, the OMT program would enhance the likelihood that Portugal could return to the markets and eventually pay the pensions and salaries that the government was cutting, as it later happened. Deeply intertwined decisions, with direct impact on one another, were taken as if they were totally independent. In that sense, the German Constitutional Court was wise enough to defer the case to the Court of Justice of the European Union, thus at least acknowledging the due relevance of the application of European law. In any event, it seems clear that little or no inter-court dialogue was undertaken at the time.

Awareness of constitutional constraints was also limited. This is not to say that the drafters of the austerity programs, especially those negotiated with the European Union and the IMF, ignored the constitutional risks of such programs. But these risks became more evident as the programs were implemented and sometimes amended. It is possible that the designers were not aware of the risks to the extent of acknowledging that they could jeopardize the programs as a whole, and thus the stability of the neighboring countries.

Again, this was the case with Portugal, where several regular evaluations nearly failed due to legislative measures rejected by the Constitutional Court. Only *in extremis* decisions by the government and parliament enabled the country to comply with international demands.

Fundamental constitutional concepts such as sovereignty, fiscal autonomy, human rights, and the welfare state were disputed during the crisis. Of course, to discuss these concepts in the first place, a country must have sound finances and financial independence. The discussion alternated between those who claimed that a country could only be independent with financial stability, and those who argued that sovereignty was lost from the moment a state asked for international rescue, and accepted the implementation of an austerity program. Perhaps there was a need for a middle ground between these positions, simply recognizing the inevitable impact of sovereign decisions from one state to another, and thus the need for supranational regulation and harmonization.

***

Portugal was deeply affected by the financial crisis, having undergone a very harsh adjustment program, from which it has now been able to recover completely, having returned to the sovereign debt markets in an autonomous fashion. In that way, it can be pointed to as an example of success. But the Portuguese people suffered greatly along the way, so we must all learn from the past, not only from the achievements, but also from the difficulties.

The mission of the Francisco Manuel dos Santos Foundation is to promote and improve knowledge about Portuguese reality, thereby contributing to the development of society, the consolidation of citizens' rights and the improvement of public institutions. By supporting the publication of this book, the Foundation advances one of its goals. Not only does the book dedicate a chapter to the constitutional performance of austerity in Portugal, but it also allows for a contextualization of the constitutional reaction to the crisis in a broader sense, analyzing several aspects of its impact, through very thorough research and extremely interesting taxonomies.

I hope the book will become a reference work of the field for many years to come, so that it will help us all to better prepare for the constitutional impact of future crises. If nothing else, it will contribute to open, free and informed debate, which is so much needed in an age of toxic and fake news. Promoting such a debate is, after all, precisely the mission of the Francisco Manuel dos Santos Foundation, and we are pleased to present this volume.

Gonçalo Saraiva Matias

I

The Role of Constitutions in Dealing with Crises

1

Introduction: Liberal Constitutions During Financial Crises

Tom Ginsburg, Mark D. Rosen, and Georg Vanberg

The constitutions of most liberal democracies contain provisions that constrain governmental action in relation to economic policy. Some provisions grant citizens rights: For example, Americans enjoy a right under the US constitution's Contract Clause, prohibiting states from impairing the obligation of contracts. Most constitutions also provide individual rights protections against uncompensated and arbitrary taking of property. Structural provisions of constitutions also affect economic policy, sometimes by limiting government action directly, rather than through the claims of citizens. For example, balanced-budget rules constrain fiscal decision-making, as do legislative supermajorities required by some constitutions for financial decisions. Such structural provisions have spread in recent years, especially in response to the great recession of 2007 and 2008.

The presence of constitutional provisions that limit the discretion of governments in economic policy – as for constitutional constraints more generally – raises significant normative and positive questions in times of crisis. As has long been noted, constitutions serve two separate, though inter-related purposes. On the one hand, they establish a political process for collective decision-making, thus "constituting" political power. On the other hand, they define, and thereby limit, the scope of collective decisions, thus constraining political power. Normatively, these twin purposes raise immediate questions: Are political procedures that are appropriate to ordinary political life also appropriate in times of crisis? And do crisis times require a different (presumably enlarged) scope for political action? Many constitutions explicitly answer these questions in the affirmative – for example, by the inclusion of emergency powers, or the possibility of suspending certain civil liberties during crises. At the same time, some constitutional provisions are intended by constitutional drafters to constrain governments precisely when extraordinary times tempt them to engage in extraordinary action – suggesting that some constraints should be binding even in these circumstances. Crisis times also raise positive questions for constitutionalism. How well can different constitutional orders cope with crisis? How do constitutional provisions that are intended to be effective in crisis times fare when put to the test? And do moments of crisis have long-term repercussions for constitutional order once a crisis has passed?

This volume of essays wrestles with all of these questions by considering the role of constitutional provisions that constrain economic policy during times of severe financial crisis. A distinctive mark of this collection is that it represents a multidisciplinary approach to understanding the theoretical and practical implications of the constitutionalization of economic policy, bringing together perspectives of political scientists, economists, political theorists, and legal experts. The volume's multiple theoretical perspectives are supplemented by case studies from various regions that test propositions and illustrate themes. In so doing, the volume provides an overview of an increasingly important topic in constitutional design, expanding the literature on constitutions and crises beyond the conventional understanding of states of emergency. Given that for many countries, the economy is now more likely to generate stresses on constitutional systems than are military threats, we think this is a particularly timely contribution.

In this Introduction, we first provide an overview of the ways in which constitutions can interact with financial crisis. With this taxonomy in hand, we then introduce and summarize each of the volume's chapters. The final section identifies some broad recurring themes, lays out some disagreements among contributors, and describes avenues for future research.

***

One of the enduring debates in constitutionalism is how to grapple with unanticipated crises that test the limits of normal powers.[1] A common solution, going back to the Roman dictatorship, is to transfer powers to the executive for a discrete and limited period, after which governance will resume to the "normal" state of affairs. Emergency provisions have become quite common, being found in more than 90 percent of constitutions currently in force.[2] For the most part, these provisions anticipate an emergency in the form of manmade violence, such as wars or civil unrest, or else natural disasters. Fewer than 10 percent of constitutions with emergency provisions mention economic crises or the equivalent.[3]

This means that, confronted with a financial crisis, the constituted powers will have to either limit themselves to powers that have been granted in advance, or else improvise to try to claim new powers that are necessary.[4] This can generate pushback. One way to frame the threshold question is: How do constitutional provisions "perform" under crisis conditions? Do the pressures that come with crisis affect

1 Oren Gross, *Law in Times of Crisis*. New York: Cambridge University Press, 2006.

2 Comparative Constitutions Project data on file with authors; Christian Bjørnskov and Stefan Voigt, "The Architecture of Emergency Constitutions." *International Journal of Constitutional Law* 16(1): 101–27 (2018).

3 Comparative Constitutions Project, note 2. Most of these are found in Middle Income Countries, such as Malaysia, Thailand, Colombia, and Turkey.

4 Eric Posner, *Bailout*. Chicago: University of Chicago Press, 2018.

constitutional enforcement, or how constitutional provisions are understood? Do periods of crisis prompt constitutional changes or revisions?

In this regard, it is useful to distinguish among five potential outcomes:

1. Constitutional limits that constrain crisis responses by governments are simply ignored.
2. Ordinary constitutional restrictions are suspended during severe crisis, giving government wider latitude to act than under normal times.[5]
3. The internal resources of liberal constitutionalism, understood as the result of both formal constitutional language and the practices that give effect to constitutions, afford governments sufficient space to address financial crises while maintaining their constitutional and rule-of-law commitments.
4. A crisis spotlights deficiencies in current constitutions and/or practices, leading to alterations in the constitutional order. Such changes might for the better; for instance, they might enable liberal constitutional regimes to navigate in both crisis and non-crisis times. Or the changes conceivably could be for the worse.
5. Inflexible constitutional limits flatly disable governments from effectively responding to crisis.

The analysis in most of the chapters collected in this volume suggests that constitutional provisions governing economic policy are rarely simply ignored during severe financial crisis. Nor, it would seem, have constitutional provisions flatly disabled governments from addressing such crises. In other words, most chapters' analyses suggest that the experiences of liberal constitutional states do not fall under Categories One or Five. At the same time, a specific polity's experience is often not located exclusively in one of the remaining categories. In part, this is a function of the fact that none of the constitutions explored in this volume are among those that contain an express emergency provision that triggers special constitutional powers in times of economic crisis. Moreover, the categories are not mutually exclusive, because different constitutional provisions may be treated differently. Finally, the practices of constitutionalism that give effect to constitutions are diverse and complex, giving rise to potential interactions among our categories. Among other things, constitutional language frequently is not given literal effect even in non-crisis situations. And liberal constitutions sometimes seem to allow de facto constitutional changes to occur without formal amendment of a constitution's text.

These features imply that elements of multiple categories can be present when we consider the experiences of a particular polity in light of our

[5] In other words, this category is a form of Carl Schmitt's emergency constitutionalism, albeit in the context of financial rather than military crisis. See Carl Schmitt, *Political Theology: Four Chapters on the Concept of Sovereignty* 14. George Schwab trans., MIT Press, 1985 (1922); David Dyzenhaus, "Schmitt v. Dicey: Are States of Emergency Inside or Outside the Legal Order?" 27 Cardozo L. Rev. 2005 (2006).

taxonomy. For example, the practice of constitutionalism (Category Three) might encompass informal remediation of textual deficiencies (Category Four) so that, in times of crisis, government is allowed to exercise special powers unavailable in ordinary times, and/or be shielded from ordinarily applicable limitations (Category Two), even though the constitutional text does not so provide. Alternatively, depending upon a constitution's language and a polity's constitutional practices, added flexibility during crises may fit exclusively within Category Three.

While the taxonomy does not – nor is it intended to – provide a mutually exclusive scheme that locates the crisis response of a particular constitutional order in one category, it is nonetheless a useful indicator of the range of possibilities. As such, it provides interpretive guidance as we try to make sense of how countries have, and should, react to severe financial crises. The taxonomy also highlights both the anxieties and promises that give rise to each category. Fueling Category Two's emergency constitutionalism is the concern that special rules may be necessary for the unusual circumstances of a severe crisis, without which a regime literally may be unable to meet the challenge. Put this way, emergency constitutionalism may be the constitutional analogue to Aristotle's equitable override of rules; just as equity takes account of considerations appropriately ignored by legislation as regards the general case, but that justice demands be taken account of in the unusual circumstance,[6] emergency constitutionalism may be necessary for the extraordinary circumstances for which ordinary constitutionalism's general rules are inapt. Category Two also addresses the converse concern that, even without a recognized category of emergency constitutionalism, governments will exercise the powers necessary to meet the crisis (in a Category One fashion), but that without emergency constitutionalism's resources for containing such episodes, the exercised powers will outlast the crisis, ultimately imperiling constitutionalism and the rule-of-law.

But Category Two's emergency constitutionalism is no simple panacea. Suspension of the ordinary constitutional order requires a determination that a crisis sufficient to invoke the exceptional regime exists – raising difficult questions about the mechanism by which such a determination can be made. More fundamentally, the largely unconstrained powers of emergency rule risk undermining constitutionalism and the rule of law. Categories Three and Four respond to these concerns, as they assume that there is (or at least can be) a set of constitutional provisions and practices that allow government the powers necessary to meet exigent circumstances while still instantiating constitutional and rule-of-law commitments. Category Two rejects these hopes as Pollyannaish: the exceptionalism mandated by emergency constitutionalism assumes that there is no institutional arrangement that can operate in ordinary times and also

[6] Aristotle, Nichomachean Ethics, ch. 10.

adequately respond to the unusual and unforeseeable circumstances brought by crises.

***

A related set of questions concerns the effects of financial crises on subsequent constitutional government. Of course, financial crises have an effect on the balance of power among governmental institutions that may endure post-crisis. Several scholars have noted the strengthening of the executive branch relative to the legislature as a steady trend. Executives often have a powerful role with regard to formation of the budget, and during crises they are often called on to exercise powers through decrees, sometimes stretching or going beyond the formal powers delegated ex ante. An additional twist is that executives are the ones that represent countries at the international negotiation that sometimes determine the levels of austerity that must be adopted or whether a bailout is forthcoming at all. Parliaments, by contrast, frequently lack the capacity to research and analyze the information necessary to respond effectively to crisis, and are often reduced to a passive role of approving measures adopted by the executive. A crisis, and even the anticipation of crisis, can play a role in shifting de facto power to the executive.

Where does judicial power fit in? There are powerful forces, epistemic, jurisprudential and prudential, that lead courts to defer to political branches. Courts are not particularly strong in reacting to financial crises, but are often called on nevertheless, as some of our case studies demonstrate. In the 1990s, some scholars talked about constitutional courts as being a kind of barrier against the erosion of socio economic rights.[7] The evidence from the latest round suggests more deference on the part of the constitutional courts. The Spanish constitutional courts upheld Decree law 16/2012, which introduced co-payments into the national health system and reduced coverage for certain immigrants, as well as a statute introducing flexibility of the rental market.[8]

***

The book's first part, The Role of Constitutions in Dealing with Crises, consists of four chapters. The first two chapters, John Ferejohn's "Financial Emergencies" and Eric A. Posner's "Rule-of-Law Objections to the Lender of Last Resort," primarily devote attention to the prospects and pitfalls of Category One (ignoring constitutional limitations) and Category Two (emergency constitutionalism). Ferejohn explores the ways in which financial emergencies have been dealt with by modern governments, which he views as political/legal systems that constitutionally protect

[7] Kim Lane Scheppele, "Democracy by Judiciary (Or Why Courts Can Sometimes Be More Democratic than Parliaments)." In Wojciech Sadurski, Martin Krygier and Adam Czarnota (eds.), *Rethinking the Rule of Law in Post-Communist Europe: Past Legacies, Institutional Innovations, and Constitutional Discourses*. Central European University Press, 2005.

[8] Angel Janday Imenez-Aleman and Carmen Montesinos Padilla, "The Protection of Social Rights in Spain after the Constitutionalization of the Budgetary Discipline," paper at World Conference of Constitutional Law, Seoul Korea, June 20, 2018.

rights and privileges. Ferejohn defines a financial emergency as a financial event that is difficult or impossible to anticipate, moves so quickly that institutions have little capacity to defend against its consequences using ordinary legal procedures, and involves high stakes, such as potentially destabilizing the economy, the financial system, or the political system. The chapter examines several classic cases of financial emergencies, in which governments had to take extraordinary measures either by using constitutional emergency powers, inherent executive powers, or legislation. The cases demonstrate the potential that emergencies, as well as governments responses to them, can spill over into violence, and undermine the constitutional regime itself. Some of Ferejohn's historical examples fall close to, if not into, Category One.

Eric A. Posner's chapter asks whether a liberal democratic system can handle financial crises in the context of United States governance. One view is that it cannot. If the political system provides a crisis-response agency with the vast discretion needed to resolve the crisis, then the system loses its liberal democratic character. If the system does not, and instead relies on the legislature to resolve the crisis, the legislature will fail, resulting in recurrent crises that may undermine public support for the constitutional system itself. In contrast, Posner argues that the United States has avoided both extremes by endowing crisis-response agencies with intermediate powers. At the same time, the neither-fish-nor-fowl approach has put stresses on the system, as Posner's examination of the Savings and Loan crisis of the 1980s and the financial crisis of 2007–08 illustrates. The chapter contends that excessive legal constraints hampered the government's response to the Savings and Loan crisis, while the discretionary authority that enabled the government to resolve the second crisis weakened public support for the political system. Gesturing toward Category One, he concludes that "[d]uring the 2008 financial crisis, constitutional constraints played a limited role, possibly none at all." Posner ultimately advocates a form of Category Two emergency constitutionalism, arguing that "the government must be given more, not less, power to rescue firms" by serving as a lender-of-last-resort in times of financial crisis, and that this power must reside specifically in the executive branch because only it can act with the speed, decisiveness, and discretion that is necessary to address such crises.

The next two chapters, Tom Ginsburg's "Balanced Budget Provisions in Constitutions" and Mark D. Rosen's "Legislatures and Constitutions in Times of Severe Financial Crisis," begin the volume's deep dives into Categories Three and Four. The two chapters also exemplify an important theme that is amplified by many other of the volume's contributions: any assessment of the effects of constitutions in times of financial crisis cannot only consider courts, but must account for how constitutional provisions affect non-judicial institutions such as legislatures and executives.

Ginsburg's contribution looks at the prevalence of balanced budget provisions in constitutions over time, and provides a preliminary analysis of their efficacy. Such requirements tend to be adopted in the wake of financial crises. A cross-sectional analysis shows that they tend to be associated with lower levels of deficit spending after their adoption, but also that more serious forms of commitment do not lead to additional reductions. While the analysis is not definitive, it tends to provide support for the idea that constitutions can "work" in this area to constrain fiscal decision-making, even in crisis conditions.

Rosen's chapter takes a normative approach by considering how constitutional provisions designed to constrain economic policy should affect a legislator's decision-making during times of severe financial crisis. Rosen focuses on rights-granting constitutional provisions, though he also briefly considers the implications of the analysis for structural provisions. The chapter explains why unqualified constitutional language, which may appear to absolutely bar the legislature from undertaking a certain course of action, need not always be, and in fact is not always, given literal effect. This means that legislatures have some leeway to infringe constitutional rights. But there is a cost to this degree of freedom: when legislators contemplate infringing a constitutional right, they should not act as they are permitted to in the course of ordinary politics. Rosen argues that legislators should undertake their constitutional decision-making pursuant to a set of "Special Norms" that complement, but do not displace, whatever doctrinal test a country's courts use to adjudicate the constitutionality of legislation, such as proportionality analysis or tiered scrutiny. The chapter illustrates its argument with a pressing financial challenge presently confronting many state and local governments in the United States: massively unfunded pension liabilities for public workers. Rosen thus aims to refine, if not reform, the practices of constitutionalism so legislators can simultaneously cope with crisis and uphold foundational constitutional commitments. In so doing, the chapter reminds us that there is no reason to assume that we have reached the end-of-history as concerns the practices of constitutionalism. The chapter's claim regarding the practices' potential malleability parallels Category Four's understanding that substantive constitutional provisions are susceptible to continuing evolutionary development.

The second part of the book, Courts and Crises, comprises four chapters. While the focus is primarily on courts, each chapter's analysis also illustrates the necessity of taking account of non-judicial institutions when assessing a constitution's role during financial crisis, and determining what role courts do, and should, play. Barry Cushman's chapter, "The Place of Economic Crisis in American Constitutional Law: The Great Depression as a Case Study," considers the role that conditions of economic crisis might have played in cases involving judicial review of economic regulation in the years following the Wall Street Crash of 1929. The cases decided by the Hughes Court between March of 1932 and June of 1937 provide fertile ground for such analysis, because the Supreme Court of the United States consisted of the same nine justices during that time period. Cushman first critically examines the possibility – indeed, it is a standard argument in the academic literature – that contemporary economic conditions operated as a variable exogenous to legal doctrine that induced the justices to uphold challenged regulations. The standard account thus belongs to Category One, as it claims that the Supreme Court allowed the legislative and executive branches to ignore constitutional limits on account of financial exigencies. Cushman challenges the standard account by showing that even as the Justices upheld some legislative and executive actions during the crisis, they found others to be unconstitutional. In rejecting the view that a "crisis-constitution" overwhelmed the "normal" constitution during the American Great Depression, Cushman argues that the Court upheld legislation and executive action only when the Court regarded economic considerations to be relevant to legal doctrines. In claiming that the Hughes Court resisted claims to economic emergency powers, Cushman in effect situates the Supreme Court's approach during the Great Depression within Category Three. And in arguing that the legislative and executive branches over time conformed their actions to the constitutional limitations the Court had identified, Cushman's analysis suggests that the political branches' crisis responses also ultimately belonged to Category Three.

Georg Vanberg and Mitu Gulati's chapter, "Financial Crises and Constitutional Compromise," observes that constitutional constraints are often designed with crisis in mind: Framers wish to constrain the exercise of power precisely in those circumstances in which policymakers will be tempted to violate underlying normative commitments. They argue that these constraints, however, are only as strong as the willingness and ability of courts to enforce them, and that because judges care about both themselves and policy outcomes, they are sometimes less than willing to enforce constitutional constraints. Existing scholarship has explored this phenomenon, focusing primarily on the possibility that the weakness of courts may prevent them from effectively policing constitutional boundaries in the face of governments determined to deal with a crisis. Using a formal model, Vanberg and Gulati suggest that such strategic judicial retreat may also result from judicial strength. In times of crisis, courts that command significant authority, and are likely to garner compliance with their rulings, confront a quandary that weaker courts can escape: the enforcement of constitutional boundaries may prevent an effective governmental response to a crisis. If judges are sufficiently concerned about the practical consequences of hamstringing a government under these circumstances, they may engage in judicial self-censorship not because they are weak, but because they are strong. Vanberg and Gulati's analysis inclines toward Category One insofar as they suggest that strong courts might be unwilling to police unconstitutional-but-necessary legislative and executive actions, though their model also might be characterized as describing a constitutional practice (and hence belonging to Category Three). The chapter includes brief case studies of the United States Supreme Court's "gold clause" cases in the aftermath of the Great Depression, as well as the German Constitutional Court's decisions on the EU's "outright monetary policy" during the Greek bail-out in the aftermath of the 2008 financial crisis.

R. Daniel Kelemen's "Commitment for Cowards: Why the Judicialization of Austerity Is Bad Policy and Even Worse Politics," analyzes the EU's response to the eurozone crisis. The chapter traces EU fiscal regulation from the Maastricht Treaty to the judicialization of austerity. Kelemen argues there are essentially two strategies to credibly discourage member states from taking on unsustainable deficits: tough love and rules. The EU employed both strategies through the Maastricht Treaty. First, the Treaty established the euro as the common currency and imposed a set of fiscal rules. Second, the Treaty promised tough love in the form of a "no bailout" clause, which stipulated that neither the EU nor any Member State could bailout another Member State. However, when faced with the 2010 Greek debt crisis, the EU violated its own fiscal commitments (à la Category One) and provided Greece with a bailout. Having cast aside the Maastricht regime, the EU turned to a judicialization strategy, relying on national and European courts to enforce budget requirements that were embedded in the bailouts – what in effect might be conceptualized as a Category Four attempt to reform a flawed initial rule that absolutely forbade bailouts.

Kelemen contends that the judicialization of austerity is both bad policy and bad politics. In the realm of policy, Kelemen argues that courts are unable to enforce budget requirements when they must be balanced against competing constitutional values, and that the financial differences between the EU and Member States do not allow for credible budget enforcement. In the realm of politics, Kelemen argues that shifting fiscal policy to the courts alienates voters from mainstream politicians and further disillusions voters by suggesting the impotence of institutions (such as legislatures) that are more directly accountable to citizens. In short, Kelemen's analysis seems to suggest that the EU's quasi-constitutional limits are best enforced by its political institutions, not courts.

Eva Brems' chapter, "Protecting Fundamental Rights During Financial Crisis: Supranational Adjudication in the Council of Europe Context," turns toward human rights considerations as Europe manages the financial crises it confronts. In Europe, the ultimate guarantors of fundamental rights are situated at the supranational level. Individuals and legal persons who have failed to obtain a remedy at the domestic level can address a complaint to the European Court of Human Rights (ECtHR) concerning violations of the European Convention on Human Rights (ECHR) and its additional protocols. This Convention and its additional protocols protect mainly civil and political rights. If, however, the alleged human rights violation concerns social rights, the remedy is a collective complaint before the European Committee of Social Rights (ECSR) based on the European Social Charter (ESC). Both the ECtHR and the ECSR have addressed several cases concerning austerity measures adopted during the recent financial crisis in Europe. The chapter analyzes this case law, and assesses the role that these supranational human rights monitoring bodies are playing, or may play, in the context of financial crisis. Brems deploys comparative institutional analysis between the two bodies to illustrate the divergence between mechanisms, mandates, and outcomes. The ECtHR rules on individual cases and such rulings are binding. On the other hand, ECSR rules on collective complaints; such rulings are able to take a more structural approach and serve as recommendations rather than mandates. Brems advances the thesis that the differences in institutional design result in divergent approaches to protecting human rights: the ECtHR demonstrates restraint in judgments and grants wide domestic margins to contextualize human rights concerns, while the ECSR adopts a stricter, less forgiving approach when reviewing social rights.

Akin to Vanberg and Mitu Gulati's argument in their contribution to this volume, Brems suggests that the ECtHR's restraint in protecting human rights might be linked to the binding force of its rulings, while the ECSR's strictness may result from the fact that its rulings have the status of recommendations rather than mandates. The two chapters' parallel analyses have two interesting, though potentially mutually exclusive, implications in relation to constitutional design and constitutional practice. First, on certain assumptions concerning constitutionalism, they might count as reasons in favor of weak constitutional courts; if constitutions cannot constrain legislatures and executives during financial crises (due, for example, to Category Two-type concerns that extraordinary future circumstances cannot be adequately addressed by a constitution on account of its drafters' inevitable imaginative limitations), and yet we do not wish the norms embodied in constitutional provisions to be undermined in the medium and long term, it might be best to have weak courts that can "call out" constitutional transgressions while permitting pragmatically salubrious crisis-interventions to go forward. Second, in the other direction, these two chapters' analyses might suggest a need to reformulate constitutional practice such that it recognizes a range of necessary and appropriate political branch responses to crisis that are consistent with constitutional and rule-of-law commitments; Rosen's chapter provides a template for this. This second approach retains the benefits of strong courts as it assimilates governmental response to crisis within Category Three.

The book's third part, Supranational Governance, considers the European Union's response to recent financial crises. Part III's two chapters all view the crises as partly owing to flaws in the EU's initial constitutional structure, and both chapters suggest the need for constitutional changes. As such, each chapter can be situated under Category Four. It bears mention that the chapters treat the treaties and other constitutive documents that establish the EU as constitutional materials; they constitute proactive arguments for treating the fiscal crises as opportunities to reform the EU.

In "Constitutionalism as Limitation and License: Crisis Governance in the European Union," Turkuler Isiksel employs Lockean and Hobbesian models of constitutional rule to illustrate the EU's system of functional constitutionalism.

Lockean rule emphasizes constitutional design as a restraining power to protect liberty, while Hobbesian rule asserts constitutions are a mechanism for enabling power. Isiksel observes that constitutions incorporate both models: a constitution must first call power into being before such power can be restrained. When applied to the EU, Isiksel argues that member states delegate extensive power to the EU to in turn gain fiscal efficiency and credibility. Isiksel identifies three features to distinguish the EU from conventional domestic models. First, the EU's design does not claim sole validity to public power. Second, the EU establishes rule-like rather than open-ended constitutional norms. Finally, the EU's authority rests primarily on a claim to govern effectively, meaning that its mode of legitimacy is functionalist rather than democratic or rights-based. Given the EU's functionalist design, Isiksel proposes that the EU's eurozone crisis management demonstrated the functionalist reflex endemic to its constitutional model, rather than a radical break from its system. To put it differently, what some of the volume's other authors seem to characterize as Category One lawlessness, Isiksel treats as Category Four reform that builds on values already present in the EU's constitutive documents.

Whereas Isiksel's reforms conceivably can be grounded in extant EU materials, Federico Fabbrini's chapter proposes that the EU crisis reflects more fundamental design flaws that can be overcome only by formal amendment of the EU's constitutive documents. Fabbrini's "The Institutional Origin of Europe's Constitutional Crises: Grexit, Brexit and the EU Form of Government" advances three interconnected claims to identify structural reasons for the EU's institutional weaknesses and its failure to consider appropriate proposals for constitutional reform. He claims that the EU has failed to successfully address the recent challenges facing it because of its current institutional power structure. The architecture of governance in the fields of economic affairs, home affairs, and foreign affairs is premised on a continuing intergovernmental negotiation between member states. However, tensions between member states are assured to emerge – as are, ultimately, dynamics of domination by larger, more powerful states over smaller, less powerful ones. Fabbrini argues that as a result of the problematic nature of the current EU system of governance, the EU needs broad institutional reforms, particularly in the realm of executive power. Fabbrini suggests that the creation of a president of the EU, to be elected by the EU citizens in the EU member states, would offer a way to channel popular preferences from across the EU toward the same electoral office and simultaneously create a forum for the contestation of EU policies. Provocatively, the chapter also maintains that the UK's decision to withdraw from the EU affords an opportunity to reform EU institutions in this direction.

The book's fourth part, Implementing Austerity, consists of two chapters that examine how the eurozone crisis played out in two particularly central cases, Portugal and Greece. In the first chapter, "The Constitutional Performance of

Austerity in Portugal," Teresa Violante and Patrícia André focus on the Portuguese constitutional case law that has reviewed austerity measures to assess the constitution's constraining effects on the margin of legislative choices within an economic crisis. Violante and André define "austerity legislation" as law that was adopted to cope with budgetary deficit reduction following the great recession, and that impacts individual rights and freedoms. The chapter argues that, even under a severe economic and financial crisis, the Portuguese constitution has displayed a constraining force on the legislature's margin of political discretion, grounding the invalidation of several internationally negotiated or imposed measures and forcing the political branches to find alternatives in order to cope with the creditors' demands. Violante and Andre's analysis thus places Portugal's experience squarely within Category Three. Their chapter also illustrates the complex role that a constitution can play during financial crisis, as judicially articulated limitations and guidelines were alternately taken up by, and sometimes resisted by, Portugal's political branches.

In Part IV's second chapter, "Constitutional Resilience and Constitutional Failure in the Face of Crisis: The Greek Case," Xenophon Contiades and Alkmene Fotiadou offer an overview of the domestic constitutional changes that resulted from the financial crisis in Greece. They focus on changes and shifts in the following areas: changes in jurisprudence and in the role of the judiciary, changes in the law-making process, and changes in the function of the political system. The chapter advances three frameworks for understanding crisis-induced change: constitutional resilience, defined as the ability of a constitution to survive shock and further legal order; constitutional retrogression, defined as simultaneous incremental erosion of competitive elections, freedom of speech and association, and rule of law guarantees; and finally, the notion that rule of law may be eroded when legal professionals disagree on the boundaries of rule of law behavior. Their review shows that the Greek constitution ultimately did not undergo formal change during the financial crisis; the text endured, and the constitution continued to perform its basic functions. Greece did not experience constitutional regression, at least not to the extent that it would be possible to talk of backsliding. Still, signs of erosion are conspicuous in all three areas, and there were crucial occasions where the possibility of backsliding was high. Contiades and Fotiadou's study confirms Ferejohn's point concerning the risks to constitutionalism that crises pose. Relatedly, their study of Greece serves as a reminder that crisis-induced constitutional changes cannot be presumed to be for the better; Category Four changes might be progressive, but also might be retrogressive.

The book's fifth, and final, part consists of two regional studies that aim to assess the effects that crises have had on constitutions and constitutionalism. The first chapter is Gabriel L. Negretto's "Economic Crises, Political Fragmentation, and Constitutional Choice: The Agenda-Setting Power of

Presidents in Latin America." Negretto argues that the formal powers of presidents in Latin America have radically changed since the early decades of the twentieth century. One salient feature of this transformation is that whereas the government powers of executives have generally decreased, the executive's powers in the legislative arena (in particular to promote legislative change) have increased. The chapter argues that these changes in executive powers are explained to a significant degree by economic crises. In particular, Negretto proposes that economic crises that demanded prompt policy shifts provided reformers with an incentive to strengthen the agenda-setting powers of presidents in fragmented political environments. This argument is supported with a statistical analysis of constitutional changes in eighteen countries of Latin America from 1900 to 2014 and a comparative study of the impact of economic crisis and policy reform in Mexico and Argentina between 1982 and 1994. Negretto's analysis thus falls squarely in Category Four.

In the book's final chapter, "Constitutions, Crisis, and Regime Change: Perspectives on East and Southeast Asia," Björn Dressel looks to the experiences of states in East and Southeast Asia over the last quarter century (1990–2013) to consider the consequences of financial crisis on liberal democratic constitutions. Drawing on cross-regional quantitative and in-depth qualitative analysis, this study finds only limited evidence of an impact of the Asian and the global financial crises on formal constitutional change in the region, compared to the effects of political variables. However, across the region there have been informal effects on constitutions due to changes in other laws and judicial interventions that often have direct consequences for constitutional practice in the countries affected. Rather than highlighting the strength of constitutionalism in the region, this broader pattern, Dressel suggests, might have more to do with the recent nature of constitutional change, the external perception of an economic shock, and continuing legacies of executive dominance in the region.

***

In closing this Introduction, let us circle back to the two related sets of questions with which we began: Descriptively, what are the experiences of liberal democratic constitutions during times of severe of financial crises? And normatively, how should constitutions operate in such circumstances? While the broad categorization we introduced helpfully identifies the range of possible answers to these questions, the performance of specific constitutions examined in this volume typically involves elements that draw on multiple categories. In part, this is a function of the amorphousness of Category Three's concept of the practices of constitutionalism. Insofar as the practices through which a polity gives effect to its written constitution might permit informal amendment or even temporary suspension, Category Three can swallow Categories One, Two, and Four; not so, if the practices of constitutionalism are defined more narrowly. Even if informal amendment or suspension are out of bounds, constitutional practices that allow for substantial interpretive leeway might permit a response that could – depending on the analyst's perspective – belong to Category One, Two, or Three. Consider in this regard Isiksel's and Kelemen's competing interpretations of the EU's bailouts: What Kelemen views as lawless, Isiksel sees as an evolving realization of pre-existing constitutional commitments.

***

The fact that the categories of our taxonomy are not mutually exclusive or exhaustive should not obscure important broad themes that emerge through this volume's chapters. First, severe financial crises present a dual danger: the crisis risks destroying the political system, while the polity's self-preservation efforts risk undermining constitutionalism and its commitment to the rule-of-law (Ferejohn; Posner; Contiades and Fotiadou). Second, crisis can put severe stresses on the constitutional order, leading to the weakening – or less than vigorous enforcement – of constitutional provisions (Vanberg and Gulati; Ferejohn). That said, the analyses in these essays also make clear that constitutions can perform real work during times of crisis, guiding and constraining governmental responses (Ginsburg; Cushman; Violante and Andre; Contiades and Fotiadou). But that work is varied and complex. To begin, constitutions do meaningful work insofar as the governmental institutions that act during crises were brought into being by the constitutions (Isiksel). Beyond this, sometimes, though not always, constitutional limitations are judicially enforced to limit the political branches. Judicial enforcement is easiest to identify when courts declare the political branches' crisis-response unconstitutional, as they sometimes do (Cushman; Violate and Andre; Brems). But there are many instances where a court's blessing of the government's crisis-response properly qualifies as judicial enforcement of the constitution. This is most clearly the case when the political branches comply with conditions that the courts have identified as constitutionally required, as also sometimes occurs (Violante and Andre; Cushman). Beyond that, meaningful judicial enforcement would seem to extend to instances where courts believe that the political branches have complied with what the constitution demands, even if previously announced judicial doctrine did not guide the legislature and executive (Rosen).

Even where constitutional provisions are not judicially enforced, it does not follow that constitutional provisions are without effect. Constitutional provisions might meaningfully shape the political branches' approach, even if courts do not review their actions owing to a lack of jurisdiction or other reasons (such as laid out in the chapters by Ginsburg and Rosen). Moreover, in at least some circumstances it might be preferable for constitutional limitations to *not* be judicially enforceable, but that they be enforced by the political branches themselves.

In short, the potential impact of a constitution is not measured solely by the judicial enforcement of its provisions. Assessing the work a constitution does in times of crisis demands analysis of how the constitution affects all governmental institutions, not just an examination of judicial decisions.

***

Finally, the essays collected here suggest that constitutionalism has not reached its end-of-history. Financial crises can, and have, brought needs for constitutional reform into high relief (Fabbrini; Isiksel; Kelemen). Such reforms might take the form of formal amendments to the constitution (Fabbrini; Negretto), but changes can also be effectuated through informal mechanisms (Isiksel). Moreover, the need for reform may extend beyond the constitution's text to the practices of governmental actors (Rosen). That we have not reached constitutionalism's end-of-history can be invigorating, but also sobering, for there is no guarantee that the next steps will be forward. Severe financial crises risk undermining the conditions that support constitutionalism, and there always is the possibility that any constitutional changes catalyzed by the crisis will be retrogressive (Contiades and Fotiadou; Dressel).

2

Financial Emergencies

John Ferejohn

I. INTRODUCTION

This chapter explores ways in which financial emergencies are dealt with by modern governments, by which I mean political/legal systems that constitutionally protect rights and privileges. The key feature of such systems, from my perspective, is that they can be slow to react to shocks, even those that destabilize the government or threaten the whole legal regime. A financial emergency is, arguably, an example of such a shock. I define such an emergency as a financial event that

1. is difficult or impossible to anticipate;
2. moves so quickly that institutions have little capacity to defend against its consequences using ordinary legal procedures; and
3. carries high stakes, such as potentially destabilizing the economy, the financial system, or the political system.

Examples might include a sudden incapacity to finance government operations, a bank run, a hyperinflation, or an imploding asset price bubble. These features make financial emergencies both threatening and hard to effectively resolve using only existing governmental authority or ordinary legislative procedures. For that reason, governments may be tempted to deal with them by using emergency powers of some kind that permit the suspension of rights and the circumvention of ordinary political and legal processes.

The kinds of powers needed to address a financial emergency may, however, be quite different from those needed to confront the more conventional emergencies of an invasion or insurrection. Violent disturbances traditionally require powers to suspend rights against arbitrary searches, arrest, detention without charge, free assembly and speech, or freedom of the press, in order to take measures to maintain or restore order and public safety. Normally, these measures are temporary and have only temporary effects (except on those who are killed). Those affected are likely to be isolated regime opponents, or those under suspicion of colluding with subversive forces. Neither is likely to be politically very popular, but they may be armed and dangerous. Financial emergencies, conversely, are likely to affect wealthy and powerful interests. Remedial measures may include devaluing the currency, suspending convertibility, shutting down banks, cancelling loans, fixing prices, or defaulting on obligations in other ways. Most of these actions are in essence takings of property, and they are accomplished suddenly and in secret, without procedural protections. Such emergency measures generally have permanent effects on the distribution of wealth, as some of the other cases discussed in this volume describe.

Governments are often reluctant to invoke constitutional emergency powers even when they are available, preferring (for both political and legal reasons) to rely on ordinary law and lawmaking, even when those methods are not working well or at all. The political reason for reluctance tends to be the need perceived by the government to enlist wide political support for unpopular measures. The legal reasons are found in the government's desire to conform to the rule of law, and to prefer to use legal means to deal with problems. This reluctance may be even greater in financial emergencies. Whatever the reason, reliance on ordinary law in an emergency can be disastrous, both because it may fail to end the emergency, and because it may distort or transform the existing constitutional arrangements by incorporating emergency measures into law, or permanently shifting the institutional balance of powers.

I will examine five cases of financial emergencies where governments had to take extraordinary measures. The first three are from revolutionary France, beginning under Louis XVI, whose regime had already become a de facto constitutional one.[1] This was followed in 1789 by the constitutional monarchy which lasted until 1792, when a republic was declared. None of these regimes was able to fund its operations without defaulting on debts to powerful creditors. Next, I consider two episodes from the Weimar Republic: the impact of the hyperinflation of 1923–24, and that of the Depression (1930–33), both of which also exposed deep class divisions. Each of these

[1] By the late eighteenth century, the parlement of Paris held an effective veto over new taxes, which it used to defend traditional aristocratic privileges. While it is common to refer to the entire period of the ancien régime as an absolutist monarchy, the "absolutist" characterization is misleading when applied to the eighteenth-century monarchy. John Hurt argues that by the mid-1670s, Louis XIV brought the parlements completely to heel, having vitiated their capacity to veto or even remonstrate against his measures. Hurt argued that the Sun King did not even have to use or threaten a *lit de justice* – the traditional "emergency" measure by which a king could force the promulgation of a statute. Instead, having already sold them their offices, he imposed regulatory restrictions on parlement revenues, essentially forcing them to loan the government money to finance his wars. See John J. Hurt, *Louis XIV and the Parlements: The Assertion of Royal Authority*. Manchester: Manchester University Press, 2002, chapter 2 ("Victory over the Parliamentaires, 1671–75"). Hurt's account of Louis XIV's rule is persuasive, but I am not convinced that his successors were able to preserve these "absolutist" gains. The fact that Louis XV was driven in 1753 to abolish the parlement of Paris, only to have to recall it the following year, seems more a desperate sign of his incapacity to control the parlement than a testament of power. And the repeated and successful resistance of the parlements to Louis XVI's efforts to close chronic deficits undermines the absolutist thesis as applied to the later reigns. See John Rogister, *Louis XV and Parlement of Paris*. Cambridge: Cambridge University Press, 1995.

cases exhibited what might be called chronic gridlock, in which enacting laws proved difficult or impossible. Part of the difficulty was rooted in the fact that all these systems respected property rights in a constitutional manner. Property rights in each case were not only at the base of the chronic financial problems, but also limited the capacity of the regime to deal with them.

Each of these emergencies erupted from a chronic condition of crisis that the political/legal system had been unable to resolve. Each produced, or reflected, deep distributional conflicts, as did the policies needed to resolve them. And each generated strong political reactions that spilled over to threaten or undermine the regime. The governments handled the emergencies differently: either using constitutional emergency powers, inherent executive powers, or legislation (either by adapting existing legal instruments or by getting the legislature to enact new laws). Admittedly, these events were unusual in many respects, and I do not present them as "representative" or typical in any sense. (It is not clear what a typical emergency would be in any case.) But by examining them, we may be able to glean some broader insights into the problem of financial emergencies.

II. FINANCIAL EMERGENCY AND EMERGENCY POWERS

Whether we look to John Locke's theory of the prerogative,[2] or Alexander Hamilton's or James Madison's writings in the *Federalist*,[3] it has generally been conceded that governmental powers cannot and should not be so narrowly construed as to prevent a political regime from preserving itself and assuring the safety of its people. These thinkers argued that governments would and should (in a good regime) do what is necessary to preserve the regime, no matter what the law says and that efforts to forestall this response would only corrode the rule of law. Emergency powers can only credibly be limited by what Carl Schmitt called the "concrete" situation or by "necessity." Thus, we should understand any political/legal regime as implicitly having a Lockean prerogative power that allows someone to take necessary, even if illegal, actions to preserve the regime.[4] Sometimes that person is the executive, but it could be some other entity or, in some cases, a private person as well.

[2] John Locke, *Second Treatise of Civil Government*, "Many things there are, which the law can by no means provide for and those must necessarily be left to the discretion of him that has executive power in his hands. This power to act according to discretion, for the public good, without prescription of the law, and sometimes even against it, is that which is called *prerogative*." Chapter 14.

[3] Hamilton in *Federalist* 23 and Madison in *Federalist* 41 both argue that it is both pointless and self-defeating to try to place strict limits on what a government can do to preserve itself from existential threat. It seems clear from these and other writings that they were willing to countenance extra-legal actions in such cases. Neither, however, wants to see such necessity-driven actions as actually legal unless or until Congress passes a law immunizing or legalizing such actions. See Clement Fatovic, "James Madison and the Emergency Powers of the Legislature," *Constitutional Studies* 1(1): 67–93 (2016).

[4] The idea is, of course, much older than this and can be traced to the institution of the dictator in the Roman Republic. Republican thinkers following Machiavelli have argued that some provision for

We can illustrate how issues raised in a fiscal emergency might be answered by considering the *locus classicus* for emergency powers – the Roman Republic (until 200 BCE, when the classical emergency power lapsed). The relevance of the Republican experience to modern liberal democracies is found in the fact that the Republic was the quintessential limited government: Romans were extremely jealous to preserve their rights against the actions of officials, and their elaborate institutions and procedures reflected these concerns.

The Romans treated emergencies as facts about which there might be considerable uncertainty, and they attributed the epistemic authority to declare emergency to the Senate. Judging that the city faced an "emergency" amounted to conceding that ordinary legal processes were inadequate to deal with it. In that event, the Senate instructed the consuls to appoint a dictator to solve the problem (within a short fixed term). Ordinary rights to due process (*provocatio*) were suspended for the duration (which authorized the dictator to imprison or kill people if he thought it necessary). And the dictator was able to commandeer whatever resources were needed to do the job. The Senate, however, remained in session; it held the power of the purse, and its members were colleagues of the dictator.

Those drawing on the Roman model claim that constitutional emergency powers are existentially necessary for a republic, or at least for a government that places limits on governmental powers. The key idea found in the Roman example is that there were two constitutions: the normal constitution and the emergency constitution, and that these were each understood as legal regimes, but one was much more capable of decisive action than the other.

The rise of postwar constitutionalism among the advanced democracies has sometimes led states to put explicit emergency provisions into their written governmental constitution.[5] There are two points to such provisions: the first is to allow the regime to take action to protect itself and the people; the second is to erect a prophylactic wall between "normal" legal processes and special actions that may need to be taken in extreme circumstances in order that constitutional normality and the rule of law can

emergency rule is a necessary component of a republican constitution (whether written or not): "all republics should have some institution similar to the dictatorship" (Machiavelli, *Discourses*, chapter 34, in *The Prince and The Discourses*, New York: Modern Library, 1950: 203). A proper dictator is not self-appointed (as Caesar was), but picked by some other official or body; the dictator's powers are conferred for a short period of time and are limited to taking measures aimed at restoring the constitution which expire with the emergency. The dictator cannot enact laws or change the constitution. In that sense the dictatorship is a purely conservative institution. Essentially what Carl Schmitt called a *commissarial* rather than a *sovereign* dictator.

5 Though the Roman republican "constitution" was unwritten, the institution of the dictatorship was normatively tightly regulated at least until around 200 BCE. In addition to Machiavelli's precise description, see Wilfred Nippel, "Emergency Powers in the Roman Republic." In Pasquale Pasquino and Bernard Manin (eds.), *La theorie politico-constitutionelle du gouvernment d'exception*. Paris: Les Cahiers du CREA, 2000. See also John Ferejohn and Pasquale Pasquino, "The Law of the Exception," *ICON* 2: 210–39 (2004) .

TABLE 2.1 *Typology of legislative and constitutional emergency powers*

	Constitutional	Legislative
Epistemic and executive authority separated	(I) Roman model; Weimar Germany Article 48–2; US Congress power to declare war, French Article 16 powers	(III) Enabling Acts; AUMF; Patriot Act; TARP; Gulf of Tonkin Resolution.
Unified epistemic and executive authority	(II) Inherent presidential or Article II powers; Torture memos; Lockean Prerogative powers; Lincoln's suspension of habeas corpus	(IV) President interprets existing laws to provide authority; 1917 Espionage Act; Case precedents, such as *Quirin* or *Korematsu*; Federal Reserve actions; GM-Chrysler Bailouts

be restored.[6] Such provisions, where they exist, create two distinct powers; the epistemic authority to declare a state of emergency, and the "dictatorial" or executive authority to take actions to resolve the emergency. These powers may be exercised separately or together. Furthermore, emergency powers can be conferred either legislatively or constitutionally. Tables 2.1 sets out the options and note some examples.

There are four ways to obtain emergency powers. The first, captured in panel I, is constitutional: some constitutions have provisions that permit the government to assume extraordinary powers in certain specified circumstances. Constitutions may also confer on the executive whatever powers are needed to deal with the concrete situation (panel II), without recognizing any special state of emergency. The alternative is legislative: the government could try to get the legislature to delegate (expediently) to the government the authority to deal with the emergency (panel III). Alternatively, it could reinterpret existing laws to find the needed authority (panel IV). If we assume (as is most common) that emergency powers will be conferred on the

6 The classical judicial statement of this view is found in Justice Jackson's dissent in *Korematsu* v. *United States* (1944): "if we cannot confine military expedients by the Constitution, neither would I distort the Constitution to approve all that the military may deem expedient . . . once a judicial opinion rationalizes such an order to show that it conforms to the Constitution, or rather rationalizes the Constitution to show that the Constitution sanctions such an order, the Court for all time has validated the principle of racial discrimination in criminal procedure and of transplanting American citizens. The principle then lies about like a loaded weapon, ready for the hand of any authority that can bring forward a plausible claim of an urgent need. Every repetition imbeds that principle more deeply in our law and thinking and expands it to new purposes. All who observe the work of courts are familiar with what Judge Cardozo described as 'the tendency of a principle to expand itself to the limit of its logic.'" A similar argument favoring a strict legal/constitutional separation between normal and exceptional circumstances is developed in Ernst-Wolfgang Bockenforde, "The Repressed State of Emergency: The Exercise of State Authority in Extraordinary Circumstances" (pp. 108–32). *Constitutional and Political Theory*. Oxford: Oxford University Press, 2017.

executive, methods I and III require that some other body (whichever entity has the "epistemic" authority to declare an emergency) "declare" an emergency sufficient to warrant the delegation of emergency new powers.[7] In methods II and IV, there is no such requirement: the executive simply assumes powers by either reinterpreting older legislation or by asserting inherent executive powers.

The postwar constitutional revolution has produced additional control institutions, such as constitutional courts, with powers to legally review and control government action (including actions taken in official emergencies).[8] Indeed some of the postwar emergency provisions explicitly included such powers; Article 16 of the French constitution, for example, gives the Constitutional Council a formal role in regulating emergencies.[9] This raises the possibility that the regulation of emergency powers may actually undercut the Lockean view that a prerogative is necessary. Of course, because courts lack direct enforcement powers, this is mostly a theoretical point as, if Locke is right, under some circumstances governments will ignore restrictions on their survival powers. Political actors can always act extra-legally and dare the constitutional court to intervene or impose sanctions after the fact (as Lincoln did in suspending habeas corpus in 1861). (Chapter 7 in this volume explores this point.)

III. FINANCIAL EMERGENCY IN REVOLUTIONARY FRANCE

The analysis of the French Revolution in financial crisis by Eugene Nelson White illustrates these issues.[10] White (1995: 229) begins his analysis by noting that "There is

[7] For a constitutional emergency (I): In Rome, the Senate had the authority to declare an emergency by asking the two consuls to appoint a dictator; both would have to agree to subordinate their powers to his. The Congressional power to declare war confers (at least) the epistemic authority to declare a war. In the case of Weimar, the President could declare an emergency and confer Article 48 powers on the federal or Länder government, or some minister. In the case of legislative emergency (III) authority is conferred on government by the legislature in agreeing to delegate broad powers to resolve the issue as in the AUMF or TARP.

[8] These new constitutional courts have come to be seen as guardians of the constitution. The German jurist Carl Schmitt must have regarded this development as an abomination, as it conferred on the (Kelsenian) constitutional court "sovereign" power (to decide the exception).

[9] **Article 16 reads:** "Where the institutions of the Republic, the independence of the Nation, the integrity of its territory or the fulfilment of its international commitments are under serious and immediate threat, and where the proper functioning of the constitutional public authorities is interrupted, the President of the Republic shall take the measures required by these circumstances, after formally consulting the Prime Minister, the Presidents of the assemblies and the Constitutional Council.

He shall inform the Nation of these measures in a message.

The measures must stem from the desire to provide the constitutional public authorities, in the shortest possible time, with the means to carry out their duties. The Constitutional Council shall be consulted with regard to such measures.

Parliament shall convene as of right.

The National Assembly shall not be dissolved during the exercise of the emergency powers . . . ."

Article 36: "Martial law shall be decreed in the Council of Ministers. Its extension beyond twelve days may be authorized only by Parliament."

[10] Thomas Sargent and Francois Velde, "Macroeconomic Features of the French Revolution." *Journal of Political Economy* 103: 474–518 (1995), reconstruct ancien régime finances, illustrating the effects of

general agreement that the Crown's fiscal crisis ignited the Revolution."[11] The fiscal crisis was of very long standing and was based in the growing wedge between revenues and expenditures, and the difficulties of default. The insufficiency of royal revenues was traceable partly to the immense aid extended to the American revolutionaries in 1778, which had been substantially financed by credit provided not only by international sources but also by a wide stratum of French society. While a temporary tax had been imposed at the time, there was no way that the loans could be repaid from existing revenues. And the efforts of Jacques Necker, the finance minister, to cut royal spending came to nothing in the end. The underlying problem was structural and of long duration. White (1995: 229) summarizes:

> The monarchy's fiscal problem arose from the political economy of the Old Regime, under which authority over taxation and expenditure was split. Whereas the Crown controlled spending, any new royal tax or loan edict had to be registered by the Parlement de Paris. The noble judges ... held the view that no new permanent taxes could be decreed, except by the nation as a whole as represented by the Estates-General, which had not met since 1614.

In any case, once the austerity efforts failed, the only remaining choices were to default on the debt, raise taxes, or find some other revenue source. It is important to recall that the judges in the parlements had themselves been repeatedly pressed to make loans to the royal fisc and were, in that sense, rentiers to the state who stood to lose in a default, along with other financiers in France and abroad.

Repeated royal efforts to find a compromise without calling the Estates failed, and transformed the crisis into a full emergency: "Pressures from rentiers and taxpayers ... blocked the Crown's attempt to implement an immediate stabilization program ... Attacking the forced registration of loan edicts, the Parlement declared a tax strike, helping to de-legitimize the tax system .... " (White 1995: 233).[12] One might have thought that this was a moment for invoking constitutional emergency powers. And in fact the king actually had the power to set aside rulings of the parlement and force the registration of a royal edict as law.[13] He could have used that power to commission Necker or someone else to take necessary measures to preserve the regime. Of course, it cannot be concluded that such measures would have worked, as their success would have depended on more than the compliance of the parlement of Paris, particularly on the government's capacity to collect the new taxes.

wars on the financial system in France (compared to the United Kingdom), and tracing the underlying contradictions. They emphasize, more than White does, the growing significance of debt service as a component of government commitments, which implies of course that formal default (as opposed to inflation taxes) was rarely considered a feasible option until quite late in the Revolution.

11 Eugene Nelson White, "The French Revolution and the Politics of Government Finance, 1770-1815." *The Journal of Economic History* 55(2): 227–55 (1995).

12 White at 233.

13 Invoking a *lit du justice*.

Failing emergency action, the king's hand was forced, and the Estates-General meeting was called for May 1, 1789. Once the Estates met, however, the Crown rapidly lost control of events. On June 5, the delegates successfully challenged the composition and voting rules of the meeting (Sewell, 1994).[14] As White (1995: 234) notes, "The triumph of the Third Estate transformed the ancient body into the National Assembly, ratifying the reduced power of the king, nobility, and clergy."

The transition to a limited monarchy did nothing to resolve the fiscal crisis. The Assembly was no more able to get people to pay taxes than the Crown had been, and could not default on legacy debt if it was to have any hope of finance in the future. As in the ancien régime, the Assembly looked first to its own creatures for more revenues: "the government became increasingly dependent on borrowing from the Caisse d'Escompte, as new loans failed and tax receipts fell. Suddenly a second emergency was at hand. A run forced the Caisse d'Escompte to suspend payment on September 18, 1789, turning its banknotes into fiat money" (White 1995: 234–35). Lacking any backing for these notes, new sources of revenue were urgently needed.

White (1995: 235) goes on:

> Ruling out an increase in taxes or a default, the Assembly found a small but wealthy group that could be forced to pay. On November 2, 1789, the legislators expropriated the lands of the Church – the properties of the clergy in the town and countryside – and nationalized them as *biens nationaux*. The higher clergy, the principal beneficiary of these properties, were a very weak interest group. All other parties, including the Crown, readily agreed to impose the cost of stabilization on them.

The expropriated lands then were employed to back new bonds (assignats) issued against these properties, which then permitted the government to dispose of the *biens nationaux* in orderly auctions (which would also effectively redeem the assignats used for the purchase, which would then be burned upon redemption).

The assignats themselves inevitably became a de facto currency. However, they began to lose value immediately, as it became evident that land sales would not be sufficient to make up the deficit and, more importantly, that the government could not stop itself from issuing more assignats whenever it needed more funds. It is clear in retrospect that neither the expropriation nor the assignat system was sufficient to close the deficit. The demand for new revenues continued to increase as a result of new pressures faced by the revolutionary government, which was inevitably forced to issue more and more assignats, despite its promises not to do so. Principal among these pressures were the wars with the surrounding monarchies.

The invasion of Austrian and Prussian forces in 1792 vastly increased military spending, and the long-running tax revolt meant that revenues remained depressed. Had either of those things not occurred, the assignat scheme might have been

[14] William H. Sewell Jr., *A Rhetoric of Bourgeois Revolution The Abbé Sieyès and What Is the Third Estate?* Durham, NC: Duke University Press, 1994.

adequate to finance the debt. It seems more than plausible, however, that the expropriation itself played a role in provoking the invasion of the allied armies (which were joined by aristocratic émigrés) and in the continuing and very widespread tax revolt. That is to say, the assignat scheme cannot be easily separated from its context. Indeed "the Girondin group claimed that as long as the émigrés could promote counterrevolution abroad, the Revolution and fiscal credibility would be threatened. As early as December 31, 1791, the Jacobin Club was told that 'not to start a war is to seek to destroy the credit of our assignats'" (White 1995: 242).

Indeed, war itself seemed to offer a less painful solution to chronic deficits. Flush with the (surprising) victory over the Prussians at Valmy, the assembly decided to try to export the Revolution. French armies invaded Belgium, Germany, and Savoy, and expropriated clerical and noble properties. However, the resulting revenues were disappointing because of local resistance. And "as the transfers from abroad were limited, the domestic struggle intensified. Inflation costs fell most heavily on large segments of the urban population whose resistance to this burden created a new dimension to the economic struggle. Radicalization in the new assembly – the Convention – which had opened on September 20, 1792, led to the abolition of the monarchy and establishment of the Republic on September 22, 1793."

The Republic was, however, faced with the same problem that had brought down the ancien régime and the constitutional monarchy. Rising prices led to demands from urban constituencies for price controls (White 1995: 243). This chain of events pushed the Assembly, faced with its chronic debt problem, to more and more extreme measures, including price controls, forced tax collection and conscription, and more forced loans. In that sense, the road to the Terror was paved by repeated fiscal emergencies that moved faster and deeper than either the Crown or the subsequent revolutionary assemblies could manage.

The lesson here is that the *cause* of the repeated financial emergencies was the intractable deficit. Every competent person could see that revenues were inadequate to expenditure; replacing the king with an Assembly, or instituting a republic did not really change that imbalance. If expenditure could not be reduced, and default was impossible, taxes were needed and they could not be collected, except at the point of a bayonet. What transformed the crisis into a succession of emergencies is that each proposed solution immediately provoked distributional (class) resistance by powerful losers who threatened to bring down the regime. This need for revenues drove expropriations which, even if they were well managed, could not close the financial gap. Resistance was often hard to see or control: refusals to lend or pay taxes, demonstrations and strikes, fighting in the streets, assassinations and coups. This was so whether or not the action in question was legal. It took many forms: émigré defections to allied forces arrayed against the revolution; the revolt in the Vendée, and others. In the end, resistance prevailed as the Jacobins were overthrown in Thermidor and revolutionary policies were undermined following Napoleon's 1799 coup.[15] The creation of the National Assembly and then the Convention – actors unfettered by the constitutional restrictions of the ancien régime – did little to arrest these conflicts, as the underlying financial problems did not disappear. Indeed, the successive assemblies seem to have accelerated the flailing about for solutions, each time provoking new class-based responses.

***

Still, at various moments one could see how a dictatorship might have been useful in preserving and restoring the existing regime. What if, for example, Necker had been given the power to reform the fisc by simply ignoring the legal objections of the Parlement de Paris, and imposing (and enforcing) new taxes? Or what if the National Assembly had been able to maintain a coherent plan to end the fiscal crisis without provoking an allied invasion? In 1793 something like this happened when the National Convention created the Committee of Public Safety and eventually "permitted" it to govern in its place as a kind of constitutional dictatorship. The Committee's methods were famously bloody but it did set about systematically trying to address the underlying crisis – sending the sans culottes into the countryside to help ensure that taxes were actually collected, and attempting to restore credibility to the monetary system.

To do this, however, the Committee needed repeatedly to resort to the guillotine and, as the volume of killings increased, it was forced to suspend or abolish procedural protections such as the right to a trial. In the event none of these measures worked: taxes remained hard or impossible to collect and the government was forced to undermine its own monetary policy by issuing more assignats. These efforts, moreover, made lots of powerful enemies and in the end provoked a reaction from both left and right elements which arrested and executed the leaders of the Committee after only a year in office, and brought an end to its reign of terror.

IV. WEIMAR I: HYPERINFLATION

Following successive allied victories in World War I, increasing desertions at the front, and the prospect of a complete military collapse, Germany's leading generals (Ludendorff and Hindenburg) pushed for an armistice. The responsibility to negotiate a deal fell to a new chancellor whose political support could only be found in the center and left (by those parties already favoring peace). There was, of course, little room for the new government to obtain favorable peace terms, given the collapse of the German army. The army was reduced to 100,000 and withdrew immediately from France and Belgium across the Rhine. In other words, there was nearly a complete demobilization on German soil. Thousands of former soldiers, most of whom were unemployed and facing uncertain futures, were immediately available

[15] Napoleon did manage finally to resolve the chronic deficit problem partly by successfully extracting wealth from subordinated territories, but also by getting the French to pay taxes.

for recruiting by both left and right-wing paramilitary forces. Final treaty negotiations were no more favorable. The result at Versailles was a treaty that was generally felt to be punitive and which could easily be blamed on the (center left) politicians who were in charge of negotiations. There was a general sense (fed especially by General Ludendorff, who moved into right-wing politics) that the German people and its army had been "stabbed in back" by the leftist government.

Communist-led or inspired rebellions and takeovers soon took place in several cities, led in places by demobilized soldiers and sailors. Many other ex-soldiers enrolled in the Freikorps or other militias to battle against communists and workers, often with the moral and material support from the Reichswehr itself (which was chafing under the restrictions on the size of the regular army). The left itself was deeply divided between those who favored governing through the new workers and soldiers councils in order to implement a socialist economy, and the more moderate Social Democrats led by President Friedrich Ebert. Ebert insisted that a new government could only be formed by a constituent assembly of the German people, and could not be dictated by revolutionary vanguards such as the workers councils, as the communists and left socialists preferred. In fact, in reaction to rebellions and disorders, Ebert essentially formed an alliance with the army and gave permission to use the paramilitary Freikorps to restore order. (This decision, in turn, drove the left socialists to set up a new "independent socialist" party.)

The new center-left government, acting through the national assembly as both constituent and governing entity, managed to form a constitution in the midst of social and political chaos then reigning in the country.[16] The new constitution was accompanied by important substantive concessions to the Left, including the eight-hour work-day and an arbitration system for wage bargaining. In effect, this marked a new social contract. While the leading Weimar framers may well have preferred a centralized parliamentary system (as the French and British already enjoyed) they were persuaded to adopt a federally based presidential system – partly on the recommendation of figures like Max Weber, who thought a charismatic president, separately elected from the parliament, could best unify the country. The key features of the Weimar constitution as it emerged were these: proportional representation with a very low threshold; federalism with strong powers vested with the Länder; and a separately elected president with very strong constitutional powers. These included the powers to appoint the chancellor, dissolve parliament, and declare emergencies, as found in Article 48.

Article 48 had been put into the constitution by the centrists and social democrats who devised the Weimar constitution, and its wording suggested that its use was subject to continuing constitutional regulation.[17] Only certain constitutional rights

[16] In fact, the assembly was forced to move to Weimar to escape the street fighting in Berlin.

[17] The article reads in full:

"1. If a state (8) does not fulfil the obligations laid upon it by the Reich constitution or the Reich laws, the Reich President may use armed force to cause it to oblige.

could be suspended and the emergency could be cancelled by a majority vote of the Reichstag.[18] In his appendix to *Dictatorship*, Carl Schmitt attempted to read these restrictions out of the article, arguing the only coherent restriction on dictatorial power was "purposive" – that it be used to restore the constitution and that any and every means was available to carry out this purpose. Any other restriction, if it had real effect, could only limit the capacity of the president to achieve the purpose stated in 48–1. Schmitt argued that in practice, the proper use of Article 48 must frequently violate rights outside the enumeration in 48–2 and concluded, therefore, that its exercise respected no limits other than the requirement that government protect and restore the constitution.

Schmitt's argument for the unfettered powers of a *commissarial dictator* closely parallels John Locke's argument for the prerogative, as well as those of Hamilton and Madison. All three argued that arbitrary limits could not and should not be placed on governmental powers during emergencies. Their view was that it was the specific character of the emergency itself which "regulated" governmental powers. Of course, these earlier writers were not writing against the legal background of a specific constitutional text as Schmitt was. I am not sure that Schmitt actually persuaded anyone that Article 48 should be interpreted as he argued.

In any case, faced with the growing inflation crisis, the government found that Article 48 powers were ill-fitted for the task, needing to enlist the important social and political actors in any solution. As a result, it decided, instead, to use legislative emergency powers and seek the passage of enabling acts which would allow it to take whatever measures were needed to solve the problem. Inflation had been a chronic problem from 1914 when, in preparation for war, Germany went off the gold standard and charted a course of debt finance for what was expected to be a relatively brief war. Borrowing to finance war would have been workable if the war had been short, if it had been won, or if it had at least been settled on terms permitting acquired debt to be retired gradually. None of those things happened: the war required a total mobilization of the economy and military capacity and went on for four years, and Germany was forced to surrender without conditions. As a result, she faced crushing demands not only to service her own immense debt and somehow deal with

2. In case public safety is seriously threatened or disturbed, the Reich President may take the measures necessary to reestablish law and order, if necessary using armed force. In the pursuit of this aim he may suspend the civil rights described in articles 114, 115, 117, 118, 123, 124 and 154, partially or entirely.

3. The Reich President has to inform Reichstag immediately about all measures undertaken which are based on paragraphs 1 and 2 of this article. The measures have to be suspended immediately if Reichstag demands so.

4. If danger is imminent, the state government may, for its specific territory, implement steps as described in paragraph 2. These steps have to be suspended if so demanded by the Reich President or the Reichstag. Further details are provided by Reich law."

18 Rights that could be suspended in emergencies included those protecting speech, assembly, privacy of the home and mail, detention without cause and, for some reasons, inheritance rights. Notably, property and freedom of contract are not included.

incipient revolution, but also to pay reparations to the allies to compensate them for the fact that the war damage had been inflicted mostly on their territories.

Germany was not free to default on either foreign or domestic debt, or even to negotiate for time and refinancing. This was despite the fact that the Americans and British, having escaped wartime destruction, continued to urge more flexible terms on France and Belgium. Inflation seemed the only way the country might hope to pay its foreign debt. While domestic bondholders had to accept this (at the time), the French and Belgians saw through this maneuver and demanded payment in kind (in the form of shipments of raw materials especially from the Ruhr), rather than in devalued marks. When the German government appeared to stall on deliveries the French sent an army into the Ruhr and began extracting its payments by force.

The official German response to the French occupation was to urge – in fact, to order – "passive" resistance to the French military by, in effect, refusing to work the mines, factories or railroads. The result was that thousands of newly unemployed German workers in the Ruhr had to be supported by the Reich as they no longer drew paychecks from the mines or factories. While this policy of passive defiance was immensely popular in Germany, it only stiffened the determination of the French government, which could see that the German policy was unsustainable. In fact, the only way that workers could be paid was by printing more and more money. The result was an accelerating inflation that soon made the mark essentially worthless. Successive governments were rendered helpless.

There was plenty of spillover into violent insurrection throughout the country. The Länder governments were sharply polarized: Bavaria was in the grip of a militarist right-wing government that refused to control the rising right-wing militants, such as Hitler's National Socialists, looking the other way as these groups got control of army weapons and used them to battle their opponents in the streets and to threaten revolution as well. The governments of Saxony, Thuringia, and Prussia were oriented to the left and tried to restrain the right-wing groups and militias. The Berlin government was caught in the middle and could do little to impose political order.

By late 1923 the monetary situation had become hopeless.[19] The mark was at 3 or 4 million to the dollar in mid-August, soared to 160 million by late September, and the head of the Reichsbank reported proudly to the legislature that the bank was able to issue 46 billion new marks each day.[20] On October 13, 1923, the new (Stresemann) government proposed an enabling act that would permit it to "take all measures it

19 "The salvation of the currency marked the doom of holders of any form of asset expressed in paper marks ... Debtors were able to pay off their liabilities in depreciated paper currency. 'If only a few weeks ago it could be written that mortgages could be paid off first with the price of a pig, then with a ham,' wrote one commentator in November 1923, 'now the fraction of an egg or a litre of milk suffices to pay off even the greatest of pre-war mortgages ....'" David B. Southern, "The Revaluation Question in the Weimar Republic." *The Journal of Modern History* 51(1): D1031 (1979).

20 Erich Eyck, *A History of the Weimar Republic*. New York: Atheneum Press, 1962, 257.

deems necessary and urgent with regard to the state of emergency." Unlike Article 48, as it was widely understood (by everyone but Carl Schmitt), there were essentially no restrictions at all on the actions the government could take under an enabling act, as long as the Act was passed by a constitutional majority, and it certainly was possible (indeed, it was foreseen) that constitutional rights would be violated if that was necessary. With the support of the Social Democrats, who were then outside the government, the Act passed by the required constitutional supermajority needed to permit the infringement of constitutional rights.

The Stresemann government then moved quickly on two fronts. First, it withdrew its policy of passive resistance in the Ruhr. Then it established a new basis for a national currency by setting up a national bank (the Rentenbank) which, in the absence of gold reserves (which had fled Germany in the previous years) would have to be based on other assets. The choice was to allow the Rentenbank to hold mortgages on property throughout Germany (bypassing the constitutional rights of the Länder to control mortgages), with the authority to issue a new note, the Rentenmark. The new issue was pegged at 4.2 dollars to one (the prewar exchange rate), which amounted to a gold peg, as the dollar was on the gold standard, and each Rentenmark could be exchanged for one trillion of the old Reichsmarks. It took nearly another year for the Rentenmark to be replaced by a new Reichsmark as the reformed currency. These moves represented an enormous wealth redistribution against those who still held the old currency or debt denominated in it. Those who had accepted old Reichsmarks as debt payments were outraged.

Predictably, the massive wealth transfers effected by the new currency led to a flood of litigation contesting the dispossession of creditors and rentiers. At the same time the concessions to the French produced widespread discontent and outright rebellions from the right (in Bavaria) and the left (in Saxony and Thuringia). The Berlin government was able to use Article 48 powers to force the leftist Länder governments to step down, but it could do nothing to stop the inflamed situation in Bavaria, especially since the Bavarian government claimed the authority to direct regular army units and refused to use them against right-wing militias.

Stresemann's government fell in early November, when the Social Democrats withdrew their support, over the uneven treatment of left and right militias. A new majority could not be found. The ensuing minority government then terminated the October 13 Enabling Act prematurely, several months before it had been due to expire the following March). On November 8 Hitler launched his "beerhall putsch" in Munich, and President Ebert invoked Article 48 to give full powers to General Von Seeckt to take action against the National Socialists and their allies.[21] To say that Seeckt was lukewarm in executing his commission is an understatement. He announced, when asked what the army would do if Hitler and Ludendorff marched

[21] Von Seeckt had already hinted that he was prepared to set up a dictatorship on his own if President Ebert did not invoke Article 48.

on Berlin, that the "Reichswehr does not fire on the Reichswehr," which effectively left the defense of the city to the Berlin police. In the end it was the Munich police who suppressed the rebellion and arrested both Hitler and Ludendorff.

The lapse of the October 13 Enabling Act meant that the reformation of the currency remained incomplete and legally uncertain. It was by no means obvious that the government would be able to honor its promise to limit the Rentenmark to its collateral. This uncertainty was ratcheted up when, reacting to lawsuits from former property holders, one of the Supreme Court senates announced on November 28 that creditors were entitled to have debts owed to them recalibrated to take account of the effects of inflation (ending the general understanding by governments and courts that "a mark is a mark").[22]

The ruling was a bombshell and a shocking departure from the deferential positivist orientation of German courts. As David Southern writes, "This was judicial rebellion against the law. The judges proclaimed that the law was subordinate to the judge, not the judge to the law. For a century judges had been inculcated with the doctrine of the subordination of the judge to positive law. Now the judges purported to declare positive laws invalid by invoking a higher law of their own making."[23] The government could not allow this decision to stand, partly because of its own immense debt but also because of a great popular uproar from debtors who faced sudden and unexpected new demands for payment.

A new enabling act was enacted on December 8 with the support of the Social Democrats (who were now outside the government), providing the legal weapons for the government to overturn the Supreme Court ruling, or at least to try.[24] The result was an unprecedented constitutional showdown: "At the instigation of two of the most prominent campaigners for revaluation, Senate President Adolf Lobe and Judge Alois Zeiler, the Association of Supreme Court Judges issued a public statement on January 8, 1924, in which the judges in effect warned the government that they would refuse to recognize any law seeking to prohibit revaluation and overturn the verdict of November 28, 1923."[25] Eyck argued that such an action by an association of judges would have been inconceivable under the old regime, but "against the Republic they dared to do so."[26] The government itself was divided on the revaluation issue, as were the

[22] "Finally, the courts felt emboldened to reject the rule and declare it to be superseded by a higher law. In overriding the positive law the courts laid claim to what the Supreme Court (Reichsgericht) called 'the plenitude of power of the judge' in circumstances where both legislation and the contract made by the parties had failed to protect vital social interests." Southern, p. d1034.

[23] Southern, p. d1035.

[24] The new Act was remarkably useful. "No less than sixty-six decrees were issued under its authority, most of them on February 24th just before it went out of effect" Eyck, at 285. As might have been expected, many of these measures were pet projects that had little to do with the economic crisis. For example, it was under this Act that jury trial was abolished in Germany. So many measures were implemented that opponents referred to the 1923 Enabling Act as an instance of bureaucratic fascism.

[25] Southern, at d1037.

[26] Eyck, at 288.

Länder. While Chancellor Marx was prepared to confront the court, others in the cabinet sought to find a compromise. In the end the government was forced to concede ground: it tried several times to issue emergency decrees limiting the effect of the Supreme Court holding by putting on a ceiling of 15 percent. Several courts then declared these decrees illegal, in another departure from prior German jurisprudence. It was clear that this was not going to be the end of the matter.

At the next elections, a right-leaning government was formed and, immediately, its new cabinet lost enthusiasm for raising the complicated and emotive revaluation issue again, despite the fact that all the coalition partners had campaigned on the issue. The critical issue concerned how far back in time the legislation would apply retrospectively. The Social Democrats, now in opposition, suddenly warmed up to the idea of revaluation, and began pushing for a 40 percent cap. The move was understood as purely an effort to embarrass the right-wing parties – the Social Democratic constituency included few rentiers. In the end the government proposed and passed legislation revising the revaluation cap upwards to 25 percent.[27] The settlement satisfied no one. There was a push by the Sparebund (savers league) for a referendum, under Article 73 of the constitution, and a new political party was formed to build a united front for the referendum as well as to contest future elections.[28] The new party managed to win two seats in the 1928 elections, but ran poorly after that.

Despite the bitter struggles over its implementation, there is little doubt that the currency reform was successful from an economic viewpoint, in the sense that it put an end to the hyperinflation and soon established a stable (gold-linked) currency. There is also little doubt that emergency powers or their threat – either under Article 48 or, more often, under Enabling Acts – were critical to this accomplishment at various stages. Sometimes it is argued that the success of the currency reform made possible a new golden age for Weimar – the period from 1924 to 1929 – when it seemed as though the militias were quieter and the economy returned to "normal." This sense of normality was probably illusory. Investment remained low and growth rates were at best anemic, while unemployment remained high. Some blamed this situation on persistently high wages and on Weimar social policies, including the eight-hour day. More importantly, the political costs of the settlement were immense, especially as they undercut confidence in the legal quality of the regime

27 "The 'revaluation compromise' of July 16, 1925, was embodied in two laws: the Revaluation Law and the Public Loan Discharge Law. Notwithstanding numerous subsequent amendments and implementing decrees, these two laws represented the final form of the revaluation settlement and were adhered to by subsequent governments, both before and after 1933.'" (Southern, d1044.)

28 "The political organisation of the united revaluation leagues took the name from 1927 onwards of Die Volksrechtspartei (Reichspartei für Volksrecht und Aufwertung). This was abbreviated to VRP" (Southern, 1044). It positioned itself as the supporter of the Mittelstand, against the socialists below and capitalists above, each of which had already had their revolution.

and the good faith of its political leaders.[29] Still, at the time, the structure of the Weimar constitution may still have provided a sense that there was a reliable safety valve in the institution of the presidency.

Until the mid-1920s the presidency had been held by Fredrich Ebert, a Social Democrat who very much favored the Weimar constitution and was dedicated to using his powers to preserve it. Moreover, the "normal" Weimar governing coalition remained reliably centrist, even if there was a fair amount of coalitional turnover. Schmitt's expansive interpretation of Article 48 powers in that early period would probably have been welcome to the government, as it provided plenty of flexibility to deal with otherwise difficult issues. And certainly, President Ebert used Article 48 powers repeatedly not only to address street fighting and putsch attempts (in 1920 and 1923), but also to deal with ordinary problems of government. But Ebert's actual use of Article 48 was only part of its effect; more important were his threats to invoke the Article in order to get parliament to enact enabling acts, which were his favored means to authorize the use of emergency measures.

The prolonged crises of security and inflation in the early 1920s weakened the political center in important ways. When moderate Social Democrats reunited with the left-leaning Independent Socialists, one effect was to push the party to the left, making it a more difficult coalition partner for center-right political parties. The reformed Social Democrats kept wobbling back and forth, effectively undermining the Weimar coalition. Those wanting to form a government were increasingly forced to look to the right for partners. Moreover, the more extreme members of the independent socialists refused to join the SPD. and moved to the communists instead, strengthening the political extremes. At the same time, the conservative and nationalist parties were shifting further to the right (partly in reaction against the social democratic reforms agreed in 1919). Finally, the 1925 elections shifted control of government formation and emergency powers to the very conservative former general Paul von Hindenburg, whose support for the regime was at best lukewarm.

V. WEIMAR II: ARTICLE 48 AND PRESIDENTIALISM

President Hindenburg had the luxury of increasingly conservative cabinets in his first years in the office. But after the Social Democratic vote surged in 1928, the SDP leader, Herman Müller, had to be asked to form a government. Müller assembled a grand coalition, in which important portfolios were given to conservatives but the Social Democrats were at its core. By then it had become increasingly clear that Hindenburg and his close advisors shared the ambitions of the nationalist and Center parties not only to dismantle Social Democratic policies but also to push the Social Democrats out of their pivotal role in Weimar governments.

[29] Ben Lieberman "Luxury or Public Investment? Productivity and Planning for Weimar Recovery." *Central European History* 26(2): 195–213 (1993).

The catastrophic economic collapse that started in 1929 provided an opening on both the domestic and foreign fronts.

The Great Depression hit Germany hard, as unemployment soared from its postwar low of 6 percent to 14 percent in 1930, and 30 percent in 1932. Support for the Müller government sank. The government had barely survived a confidence motion in December on legislation concerning the deficit. It did however manage to pass the Young plan (to stretch out reparations payments) on March 11, something that both Hindenburg and the conservative coalition partners wanted and thought could only happen with Müller's government in office. It became clear at that point, however, that the main basis for coalitional agreement was gone. When Müller advanced an unemployment bill, the conservative coalition partners rebelled. As Eberhard Kolb (2006: 84) writes, "Under the influence of its trade union wing the SPD rejected a last minute compromise proposal put forward by Heinrich Brüning, the chairman of the Center group ... faced with the SDP refusal, the Cabinet decided on March 27th to resign as a body." The critical break occurred in late March 1930, when Hindenburg refused to give Article 48 powers to Social Democratic Chancellor Müller, who had failed to muster a majority for his unemployment law. Hindenburg decided instead to appoint Brüning, who had been waiting offstage for the past year for just such a chance.

As Müller's government proved unable to deal with the economic collapse, the prospect of a presidential government (in which the cabinet would be responsible to the President rather than to the Reichstag) was already far advanced. Key moves in this direction had already been taken by Hindenburg's confidants. General Schleicher had already approached Heinrich Brüning in 1929 to see if he would be willing to lead a new "presidential" cabinet in the event that the Müller government collapsed. Moreover, President Hindenburg signaled that he was prepared to move events along himself. According to Eberhard Kolb (2006: 118): "Schleicher and Meissner, Hindenburg's state secretary, told Brüning that the President had no intention of allowing the Müller cabinet to remain in office after the Young Plan legislation had been passed ... the proposed 'Hindenburg cabinet' ... was to be formed without regard to any majority in the Reichstag and without any negotiation with parties inside or outside Parliament; the President's powers under Article 48 and the power of dissolution would be placed at the new chancellor's disposal ... " As promised by General Schleicher, "Soon after Brüning took office, Hindenburg authorized the new chancellor to use Article 48, if that proved necessary, in order to institute financial reforms" (Faulkner 1989: 413).

The Brüning government was committed to weakening the unions, imposing austerity policies, and retaining a rigid adherence to gold (which had been key in Brüning's view, to the recovery after 1924). His aims became evident in his "bill for the reform of the state finances by means of rigorous deflation: cuts in public expenditure, increased taxes and levies, especially on higher incomes, and a so called 'emergency contribution' by those on fixed salaries" (Kolb 2006: 118–19).

Some argue that the austerity policy was not based on the belief that it would succeed in ending the depression but was actually aimed instead at reducing the demand for reparations payments by convincing the allies that the Germans were unable to pay.[30] Pump-priming measures were to follow as soon as the allies relented on their payment demands. Whatever its aims, the austerity bill was too big a pill for the right-wing parties that had supported Brüning's earlier initiatives. Events moved quickly from there. When the Reichstag refused to enact the austerity bill, the Cabinet decided to re-enact the bill as an emergency decree. This did not work either and, "when the Reichstag refused to cooperate with Brüning's program on July 18, the chancellor read a presidential decree dissolving that body" (Kolb 2006: 118). The government then reissued the emergency decree once again. The whole sequence was constitutionally doubtful and certainly without precedent. A contemporary commentator remarked ruefully: "with this act and on this day, there began the permanent violation of the constitutional system by the dictatorial power of the Reich President" (Kolb 2006: 119). In any case, the country had to go to elections.

The worst possible electoral results ensued: both the Nazis and Communists made huge gains, picking up 107 and 77 seats respectively, making it impossible to form a governing coalition. Bruning was forced to govern by Article 48 decrees. The Social Democrats, greatly weakened in the elections, decided on a policy of toleration; refusing to support either confidence votes or to vote to overturn decrees. With this abdication by the SDP, Brüning had a free hand and the way was clear for undiluted presidential government: "The Reichstag sat on 94 days in 1930 ... 42 in 1931 and only 13 in 1932. Ninety eight laws were passed in 1930, 34 in 1931 and only 5 in 1932. On the other hand, the number of emergency decrees rose from 5 in 1930, to 44 in 1931 and 66 in 1932" (Kolb 2006: 121).

Brüning's government was to last only two years and eventually he lost the support of Hindenburg's circle. His policies did not resolve the economic crisis (if that was their purpose) and, though reparations payments had been stretched out, they were still owed. Worse than that, Hindenburg blamed Brüning for the fact that he was not reelected by acclamation (as he had hoped and expected). Hitler decided to run against the old General, winning nearly 37 percent on the second ballot, and Hindenburg was forced to rely on SDP votes for reelection, a necessity he found to be personally humiliating. The end was complicated in one way (there were many issues that could be pointed to as reasons for Brüning's dismissal) but also simple: government depended now only on the President and

[30] Detlev Peukert, *The Weimar Republic*. New York: Hill and Wang, 1987, 256 argues that the government's policy was to let the depression takes its course: "the government behaved passively ... because it wished to use the crisis to secure its objectives in domestic and foreign policy. If Germany became insolvent, she would find it easier finally to shake off the burden of reparations." See also Eberhard Kolb, *The Weimar Republic*. New York: Routledge, 2006, 84.

therefore on the maneuvers and machinations of his inner circle – especially those of the overly clever General Schleicher – and as soon as the old man lost confidence in Brüning, there was nothing to stop his dismissal. De facto, the regime had reverted to the 1871 constitution, in which Bismarck's government answered to the Kaiser rather than parliament.[31] For those paying attention, Hindenburg's sympathies were probably clear enough in 1925 when he first stood for the presidency. He had allowed it to be said during his first election campaign that the Kaiser (then in exile) had either approved or asked him to stand for the Presidency. He then gave his support to a return to the old Reich flag, rather than the detested republican banner. Dog whistles. From there, his inclination for regime change became more and more evident.

What then was the role of economic crisis, or of emergencies, in the regime transition? I think it is harder to say in this second crisis of Weimar than in the first. Clearly there was extensive reliance on Article 48 in both cases. Whether or not there was a financial emergency after 1930, there were surely political emergencies brought about by the intractability of the depression and impossibility of forming a government. Some of the economic circumstances leading to the use of Article 48 were at least partly manufactured, if not by Hindenburg's circle then by the increasingly conservative center right parties (the Center and the DVP especially) along with the always intransigent DNVP. Electoral shocks may appear to have been more important: the explosion of support for extreme parties in 1930; Hitler's strong showing in the 1932 presidential election; and the successes of the Nazis in the 1932 Länder elections. But surely the long-running economic crisis and the government's inability or unwillingness to provide any other answer than austerity must have played a role in the growing popular support for extreme parties. But, in the end, it is hard to ignore the determination of Hindenburg and his allies to put an end both to Weimar's social policies and to its parliamentary aspects. In any case, the result was clear enough: by mid-1930 the transition to presidentialism was an accomplished fact and the newly centralized regime was ripe for a coup.

VI. DISCUSSION

The cases emphasize that the distributional effects of financial emergencies powerfully shape governmental options. These effects, or rather the anticipation of these effects by powerful interests, tend to lock up the normal political-legal system, making it hard to address them without special streamlined powers that permit the suspension or derogation of constitutional rights. But the distributional effects also raise the stakes of "emergency rule" as well, with its strong odor of extra-legality.

31 In his memoir Bruning himself argued that once his government managed to get through the economic crisis and removed the burden of reparations, he intended to restore the monarchy (Kolb 2006: 121).

The cases amply demonstrate the potential of both the emergency and its possible solutions to spill over into violence and to undermine the constitutional regime itself.

They also illustrate that recourse to legislative emergency powers, by means of enabling acts or extremely broad delegations of authority, pose special dangers to a regime. This does not amount to the claim that constitutional emergency powers should never be used. I am persuaded, however, that legislative emergencies can pose special dangers. Writing in 1978 after German experiences with several "emergencies," where attempts were made to manage the situations by ordinary laws, Ernst-Wolfgang Bockenforde opposed what he called the statutification of emergencies, by which he meant the incorporation of emergency measures into constitutional or statutory law.[32] I believe this is especially likely in the case of legislative emergency. There are two problems: measures taken under an enabling act may be very long-lasting and, indeed, may effectively transform the legal system in a permanent way. Given the haste with which such acts are enacted, these effects are rarely discussed or considered at the time of enactment. Future governments can always reinterpret the text to apply to other circumstances. The second problem with legislative emergencies is connected to the first. If the executive approaches an emergency by using older laws – possibly reinterpreted – she effectively combines epistemic and dictatorial authority in her own hands. This is a dangerous situation, made more so by the fact that it is very easy to slide into without recognizing the dangers. She will have little trouble finding legal counsel to show the way. Of course, the triggering emergency can itself become permanent in some sense. But in that case, it is a new normal situation, in which existing legal authority is insufficient under the prior constitution. In such a situation, the legislature as a constituted power is not the appropriate entity to create new authority.

[32] He appears to agree with Alexander Hamilton (and James Madison and John Locke) that the concrete nature of the specific emergency constitutes the limits on the powers of a dictator. And he rejected the idea – which he attributed to English law – that ex post statutes indemnifying excessive uses of force could be constitutionally permissible in German constitutional law, if the abuses violated constitutional provisions. Ibid.

3

Rule-of-Law Objections to the Lender of Last Resort

Eric A. Posner[*]

Did the government rescue of the financial system in 2007 and 2008 violate the US constitution or important political norms? A small number of commentators argue that it did.[1] They argue that the government broke the law in several instances; and that, even when it acted with statutory authority, the authority that it relied on was conferred on it by Congress in violation of the constitution. While legal scholars have debated whether certain crisis-response actions violated the law,[2] the bigger argument – that the entire crisis-response system violated fundamental constitutional norms – has received little attention.

The major post-crisis debates have instead focused on questions of policy – how the lender of last resort should operate during a financial crisis. Many commentators give the US government high marks on the overall response, while some of them think that the government made specific technical mistakes – for example, by failing to rescue Lehman Brothers, or by botching the homeowner rescue programs, or by failing to nationalize banks. There are also, of course, critics who believe that the agencies jumped the gun, and should not have rescued firms like Bear Stearns and AIG. This debate has concerned policy and technical issues related to the nature of the crisis and the means available for resolving it.

* Thanks to Mei Ying Barnes and Christina McClintock for helpful research assistance.

1 For purposes of this chapter, I will not distinguish their arguments and discuss them individually. Instead, I construct a rule-of-law critique that is based on common themes in their work. Interested readers should consult the originals. Lawrence White "The Federal Reserve and the Rule of Law, Testimony before the House Committee on Financial Services," Cato Institute, September 12, 2013. Available at www.cato.org/publications/testimony/federal-reserve-rule-law. John Samples, "Lawless Policy: TARP as Congressional Failure, Policy Analysis No. 660." Cato Institute, February 4, 2010. Available at www.cato.org/publications/policy-analysis/lawless-policy-tarp-congressional-failure. Todd Zywicki, "The Rule of Law During Times of Economic Crisis," George Mason Legal Studies Research Paper No. LS 15-09, August 26, 2015. Available at https://papers.ssrn.com/sol3/papers.cfm?abstract_id=2651893. Todd Zywicki, *The Auto Bailout and the Rule of Law*, 7 National Affairs 66 (2017).

2 Philip Wallach, *To the Edge: Legality, Legitimacy, and the Responses to the 2008 Financial Crisis* (Washington, DC: Brookings Institute, 2015). Eric Posner, *Last Resort: The Financial Crisis and the Future of Bailouts* (Chicago: The University of Chicago Press, 2018).

Yet, as important as this debate is, it is wrong to ignore the constitutional questions. Indeed, the technocratic policy questions are tied up with the legal and constitutional issues in complex ways. Consider, for example, the question of whether the government erred by failing to rescue Lehman. Government officials have argued in response that they were legally prohibited from rescuing Lehman. If they are right, then we ought to criticize Congress for failing to give them appropriate authority, rather than the agencies for making an incorrect policy judgment. But if constitutional constraints would have prohibited such a broad grant of authority, then the problem we face is a constitutional problem, not a legislative problem.

In this chapter, I describe the rule-of-law critique as sympathetically as I can, and then explain why it fails. The crisis response did not violate constitutional norms. The critics' argument gains surface plausibility only because the eighteenth-century constitution assumed a weak national government with limited powers. While that ideal still plays a role in certain political and legal debates, it no longer describes constitutional arrangements if it ever did. In a modern economy, the executive branch cannot realistically be deprived of the power to resolve a financial crisis; constitutional norms have evolved accordingly.

However, I also argue that the rule-of-law critique should not be too easily dismissed. While it fails as a constitutional argument, it does help illuminate the political controversy surrounding the crisis response. Many people were surprised to learn that the crisis-response agencies possessed vast powers. Even Representative Barney Frank, Congress' expert on financial matters, was "stunned" to learn how much the Fed could lend.[3] The agencies made numerous policy judgments in the course of the crisis, unavoidably picking winners and losers, and many of these judgments turned out to be politically controversial. But while the agencies had been granted broad legal authority to act, they hesitated to use it. They eventually appealed to Congress for a rescue statute because they believed that they needed political backing, not additional legal authority. Congress delivered, but it played only a superficial role in formulating policy. After the crisis, worries that the agencies possessed too much power (and abused it) led to proposals to subject the agencies to additional legal constraints, yet the result was only superficial reform. While uneasy about the powers of the agencies, Congress realized that if the agencies were subject to additional legal constraints, they would not be able to rescue the financial system in the next crisis.

The government response to the Savings and Loan (S&L) crisis of the 1980s provides an instructive comparison. While the S&L crisis was in many ways different from the 2007–08 crisis, enough similarities exist to make comparison worthwhile.[4]

3 Ben Bernanke, *The Courage to Act: A Memoir of a Crisis and Its Aftermath* (New York: W.W. Norton & Company, 2015), 285.

4 The S&L crisis was an insolvency crisis in a large but relatively limited sector of the financial industry. The problems with the S&Ls did not threaten the industry as a whole, and a panic in which depositors simultaneously withdrew funds never materialized. The 2007–08 crisis, in contrast, encompassed

In the S&L crisis, the government faced an insolvency crisis in the S&L industry. The crisis response agency – the Federal Savings and Loan Insurance Corporation (FSLIC) – lacked the legal authority and financial resources to resolve the crisis. After Congress refused its request for assistance, the agency jury-rigged a rescue plan that ultimately magnified losses by many times. Ultimately, Congress arranged an enormous bailout and abolished the agency.

A comparison of the political context of the two crises yields a lesson. In both cases, the agencies tried to resolve the crisis in a reasonable way, while Congress turned out to be an impediment. Interest-group pressures were more effective against Congress than against the agencies. And in many cases where the agencies made bad decisions or broke the law, the reason was that Congress pressured them to do so, failed to provide them with the authority or funds they needed, or imposed legal constraints on them. The rule-of-law critique fails for reasons that were familiar even to the earliest proponents of liberal democratic theory: in a crisis, Congress cannot act; only the executive can. Congress can play a valuable role by giving political backing to the government – and by refraining from the temptation to interfere – but it cannot do more than that.

I. BACKGROUND

1. *The S&L Crisis of the 1980s*

S&Ls are specialized banks that focus on consumers.[5] They take deposits from ordinary people and make money by issuing mortgages to homeowners. Before the 1990s, S&Ls dominated the consumer side of banking, while commercial banks served businesses. Because of their large and undiversified residential mortgage holdings, S&Ls were highly exposed to housing prices. Numerous regulations controlled the S&L business, while also protecting S&Ls from competition – for example, by restricting interest rates on deposit accounts. For many decades up until the 1970s, the S&L industry was stable and profitable.

In the 1970s, economic conditions turned against the industry. As inflation increased, interest-free deposits became less attractive to consumers, who began to transfer their money to money market mutual funds. These recently approved

virtually the entire financial industry, and involved classic bank-run type behavior, albeit in the shadow banking system. The institutional setting also differed. The Fed is the acknowledged lender of last resort; it enjoys considerable independence both legally and politically; it benefits from a highly competent staff; and it is self-funding. The FSLIC possessed lender-of-last resort powers of a sort (as described below); while it was legally independent, it did not enjoy as much respect and political independence as did the Fed; and it was not self-funding.

5 James Barth, S. Trimbath, and Glenn Yago, eds., *The Savings and Loan Crisis: Lessons from a Regulatory Failure* (Santa Monica, CA: The Milken Institute, 2004). Edward Kane, *The S&L Insurance Mess: How Did It Happen?* (Washington, DC: The Urban Institute, 1989). Lawrence White, *The S&L Debacle: Public Policy Lessons for Bank and Thrift Regulation* (Oxford: Oxford University Press, 1991).

institutions paid clients interest and gave them limited checking account privileges. The weak overall economic environment also did not help. S&Ls were squeezed between the low interest rates that they received on their legacy mortgages and the higher cost of funds. By the early 1980s, many S&Ls were undercapitalized or insolvent.

The FSLIC was responsible for regulating and supervising S&Ls. It also operated a deposit insurance fund, which was financed by premiums paid by S&Ls. It was an arm of the Federal Home Loan Bank Board (FHLBB), an independent agency. Like the Federal Deposit Insurance Corporation (FDIC), which regulates banks, the FSLIC was given broad power to deal with undercapitalized or insolvent S&Ls, including the power to pay off depositors from a fund to which the S&Ls contributed. It could also borrow from Treasury with approval of the FHLBB. The FSLIC was thus a kind of lender of last resort for the S&Ls.[6]

As the industry collapsed, it became clear that the FSLIC's insurance fund was insufficient to pay off depositors. Rather than bail out depositors and shut down the industry, Congress passed laws that reduced restrictions on the industry. The Garn-St. Germain Depository Institutions Act of 1982, for example, enabled S&Ls to expand by permitting them to make certain types of commercial loans. Meanwhile, the limit on interest rates for deposits was being removed, allowing S&Ls to compete for funds, but also exposing them to greater funding costs. Capital requirements were also lowered. Many states followed the federal lead. (Some S&Ls were federally chartered and regulated; others were state chartered and regulated.) The theory, or rationalization, was that if S&Ls' difficulties could be traced to legal constraints that prevented them from diversifying, the removal of those constraints would save the industry. S&Ls would be able to obtain new revenue sources. But S&Ls lacked experience and expertise in areas outside their traditional bailiwick of residential mortgages. Insolvent or near-insolvent S&Ls took advantage of these new opportunities because there was little downside, but the effect was to turn them into highly risky institutions that were gambling on an improvement in economic conditions. Many S&Ls, especially in Texas and the southwest, made highly risky loans to commercial ventures like mall construction.

As more S&Ls became insolvent, the FSLIC scrambled to find a way to protect deposits. Many weak S&Ls were bought up by healthier S&Ls and banks, but acquirers drew the line at insolvent S&Ls. To create incentives for such acquisitions,

[6] This authority can be found in various provisions of 12 U.S.C. § 1729 (repealed), e.g., § 1729(f)(1)(C), which provides that the FSLIC is authorized to make loans and purchase assets and securities from an insured S&L "if, when sever financial conditions exist which threaten the stability of a significant number of insured institutions . . ., such action is taken in order to lessen the risk to the Corporation posed by such insured institution under such threat of instability." See also ibid. § 1729(c)(3)(B), which provides that "In any case where the Corporation is appointed conservator or receiver of an insured institution pursuant to paragraph (1) or (2) — the Corporation shall have authority to liquidate such institution in an orderly manner or *to make such other disposition of the matter as it deems to be in the best interests* of the institution, its savers, and *the Corporation*" (emphasis added).

the FSLIC decided that acquirers would be granted "supervisory goodwill," an asset on the acquiring bank's balance sheet that made up for the shortfall from buying an S&L with negative value. The effect of this accounting gimmick was to allow banks or S&Ls to acquire insolvent S&Ls even when the acquirer's capital level fell as a result to what would normally be considered an unacceptable level. In substance, the regulators had figured out a way to avoid enforcing capital regulations – a practice known as "regulatory forbearance." As a result, many more S&Ls became undercapitalized, and these S&Ls in turn made risky loans that failed. By the late 1980s, this regulatory approach could no longer be sustained.

Congress finally stepped in to resolve the crisis. In the Financial Institutions Reform, Recovery, and Enforcement Act of 1989, Congress abolished the FSLIC and its parent agency, the FHLBB, replacing them with a new Office of Thrift Supervision (OTS) and a Federal Housing Finance Board. The OTS was given FSLIC's supervisory and regulatory authority; the insurance function was transferred to the FDIC. The law also created the Resolution Trust Corporation, which took over and wound up the insolvent S&Ls. And Congress abolished the supervisory goodwill regime; when their goodwill assets disappeared from their balance sheets, numerous additional S&Ls collapsed. In the Federal Deposit Insurance Corporation Improvement Act of 1991, Congress strengthened the powers of the FDIC, while also limiting its rescue powers by requiring it to resolve banks (and S&Ls) in the least costly way possible, and imposing a "prompt corrective action" regime that prohibited the FDIC from keeping alive inadequately capitalized banks and S&Ls through regulatory forbearance.

In all, thousands of S&Ls failed. The Resolution Trust Corporation sold off the assets of the insolvent S&Ls and paid back depositors. The shortfall – about $160 billion – is a rough approximation of the cost of the crisis (FDIC 2000).

2. *Financial Crisis of 2007–08*

The major source of the financial crisis of 2007–08 was financial innovation, which enabled institutions to evade regulations designed to limit risk-taking. [7] Because of the heavy regulation of the traditional banking system, creditors and debtors sought forms of financial intermediation that evaded the banking system. Their efforts gave rise to the so-called shadow banking system, in which the major roles were played by investment banks, hedge funds, pension funds, life insurance companies, sovereign wealth funds, mutual fund companies, and non-bank subsidiaries of bank holding companies.

Shadow banking took many different forms. In the repo market, creditors made very short-term loans (often just overnight) to debtors, receiving collateral in the form of liquid securities. The loans were typically rolled over for long periods of

[7] Posner, *Last Resort*.

time; the right to terminate the loan gave the creditor additional security against risk but was not normally exercised. Another important financial market was created by money market mutual funds, which bought short-term commercial paper on behalf of their customers. In both cases, lenders believed themselves highly secure, while borrowers obtained a steady, predictable source of funds at very low cost. As a result, parties preferred this system to bank deposits, which, while guaranteed by the federal government, were expensive to use.

Shadow banking has always existed. Two novel aspects of it contributed to the financial crisis. First, the sheer magnitude of shadow banking dwarfed anything that had happened earlier. By the eve of the financial crisis in 2007, shadow banking far outstripped regular banking, which had been dominant in the past. Second, as shadow banking grew, parties become more careless, or (perhaps) rationally risk-preferring, resulting in the growth of systemic risk.

The major culprit was the mortgage-backed security. When a homeowner takes out a mortgage, the bank or broker (or, generically, mortgage originator) may sell the mortgage to another institution (often an investment bank), which pools the mortgage with others. The pool will contain different kinds of mortgages – for example, from different regions – in order to minimize the effect of local shocks on total payoffs. The manager of the pool creates different risk levels for different securities by giving holders of the low-risk securities priority over the payment stream. Ratings agencies supply ratings. The highest-rated, lowest-risk securities were considered almost as safe as government debt. As the repo market grew, the parties began substituting mortgage-backed and related securities for government securities.

As demand for MBSs increased, the various parties that constructed them allowed standards to decline. Originators relaxed underwriting standards – sometimes, recklessly or fraudulently, sometimes with the explicit or tacit permission of the pool managers. Subprime mortgages played an increasingly large role in the mortgage pools. Moreover, the parties did not seem to fully understand the nature of the risk inherent in the MBS system. Based on historical data, they believed that the probability that the AAA-rated MBSs would lose value was essentially zero. For that to happen, the median national housing price would need to decline significantly – and that had never happened – and mortgage default rates would need to reach unprecedented levels.

When housing prices fell in 2006–07, homeowners defaulted on their mortgages in increasing numbers. While it was predictable that the high-risk MBSs lost value, the market was surprised when AAA-rated MBSs and related securities lost value as well. Those securities were supposed to be protected from minor variations in the default rate. Because so much of the financial system assumed that highly rated MBSs were "money good" – effectively, zero-risk – investors panicked when that assumption was proven wrong. Many of them refused to buy MBSs, or accept them as collateral. As trading ground to halt, it was no longer possible to confidently attach values to them. Companies that held them in great quantities were either insolvent (if market prices were accepted as accurate) or of indeterminate solvency (if market prices could no longer be trusted). In either case, creditors stopped lending to them.

The financial system entered freefall. Investment banks that obtained short-term funding from the repo market could no longer offer MBSs as collateral. When credit was withdrawn, they were forced to sell their MBSs and other assets at fire-sale prices, causing prices to fall even more. These firms also relied on the commercial paper market. But creditors refused to roll over commercial paper because they no longer believed that the borrowers would repay. As commercial paper lost value, mutual funds that held it could no longer redeem shares, causing people to pull out of mutual funds as well. As creditors withdrew credit and hoarded cash, debtors raised cash by selling assets at fire-sale prices, further fueling the downward spiral in prices. Because creditors and debtors were often the same entities, the collapse of a firm (like Lehman) because it could not repay its debt further reduced the availability of credit to other firms.

The government rescue was an enormous, complex undertaking. The Fed began by lowering interest rates, hoping that reducing the debt burden would enable firms to survive. When this did not work, it began offering credit on cheap terms to major financial institutions, and then to all kinds of institutions, major and minor, financial and non-financial. It also bought trillions of dollars of high-quality MBSs. The FDIC offered expanded guarantees to depositors. The Treasury used resources from its Exchange Stabilization Fund to offer guarantees to mutual funds. Congress appropriated hundreds of billions of dollars, which Treasury used to invest in banks and buy toxic assets. In the winter and spring of 2009, Treasury also conducted stress tests of major banks – giving a clean bill of health to banks with sufficient capital, and requiring the others to raise additional capital from the market or the government. Around this time, the crisis ended.

Despite the government's successful resolution of the crisis, the crisis-response agencies received a great deal of criticism – for committing errors and for favoring Wall Street. In the Dodd-Frank Act of 2010, Congress expressed its displeasure with the Fed and the other agencies by imposing some limits on their powers. It prohibited Treasury from using the Exchange Stabilization Fund to guarantee money market mutual Funds; it limited the FDIC's power to issue broad guarantees; and it prohibited the Fed from making customized loans like the AIG transaction. Many members of Congress also argued that the Fed should be subject to additional congressional oversight – in the form of an "audit" mechanism – but Congress did not act on this proposal.

Remarkably, despite the carnage caused by the financial crisis, which laid waste to thousands of financial institutions, the government made a profit on its lending activity – an amount near $80 billion.[8]

[8] ProPublica. "Bailout Tracker: Tracking Every Dollar and Every Recipient." Available at https://projects.propublica.org/bailout/.

II. THE RULE-OF-LAW CRITIQUE

1. The Argument

The rule-of-law critics argue that a commitment to liberal democracy requires a polity to obey certain norms that protect freedom and self-government. Chief among the norms is the principle that the people make law for themselves by electing representatives to the legislature. The legislators engage in public debate over policy matters, and embody their conclusions in law. The executive must enforce the law as written; it may not engage in significant policymaking itself, though it may engage in interstitial rule-making. The courts, too, must ensure that the executive as well as the public comply with the law as written.

In the 2007–08 crisis response, this norm – sometimes, called the "rule of law" – was violated. First, and most obviously, the agencies violated the law in certain instances. The most egregious examples were Treasury's use of money from the Exchange Stability Fund to guarantee money market mutual funds; certain FDIC guarantees; and a number of Fed loans that were not backed by collateral or were made in return for equity.[9] The heads of the agencies apparently saw no reason not to violate the law: they would not be personally liable, and it was unlikely that the courts would block illegal actions. Indeed, the courts did not do so when asked by affected people (Kahan and Rock 2009). These illegal actions stemmed from what might be called the problem of impunity. If agency heads are not subject to personal liability if the agency violates the law, and courts do not otherwise intervene by issuing injunctions, then the penalty for breaking the law is nil.

Second, the agencies in many cases took actions of extraordinary importance based on their own policy judgments. They did not merely "execute" policies embodied in law enacted by Congress. This can be called the problem of delegation. When the crisis began, the agencies were able to draw on existing policy-making authority that had been granted to them by Congress. As we saw, while the authority was not limitless, it was exceptionally broad. And after the 2007–08 crisis began, Congress delegated additional authority to Treasury by enacting the Emergency Economic Stabilization Act (EESA). The agencies were free to decide which firms to rescue, and on what terms; whether to help homeowners and by how much; whether responsible executives should be punished or not; and so on. This broad policy-making authority violates the rule of law because the policies are determined by appointed officials rather than elected representatives, and in secrecy rather than after public debate.

The critics argue that the agencies used their immense freedom of action to favor special interests, including Wall Street financial institutions, at the expense of the public interest. Against the mainstream view that the Fed and other crisis-response agencies acted in a reasonable technocratic fashion, some critics see evidence of

[9] Wallach, *To the Edge: Legality, Legitimacy, and the Responses to the 2008 Financial Crisis*. Posner, *Last Resort*.

political influence. Johnson and Kwak,[10] for example, argue that the agencies deliberately went easy on the banks when they could and should have demanded stricter terms for rescue loans.[11] Mian and Sufi argue that agencies preferred to aid banks rather than homeowners because of improper political influence.[12] Granted broad discretion, the crisis-response agencies could choose whether to help homeowners or financial institutions, and chose to help the latter because the financial institutions exercised political influence, thanks to connections, expertise, lobbying, and so on.[13] Neither of the two presidents – Bush or Obama – exercised real oversight over the agencies, which instead acted autonomously rather than under the guidance of elected officials.

Congress recognized that the agencies possessed excessive power. After the crisis, Congress sought to constrain the agencies. It took away power from the FDIC and Treasury, and it limited the Fed's power to make emergency loans to nonbanks. Congress also threatened to audit the Fed, a form of oversight that the Fed resisted. The abuses of power were a predictable consequence of lack of constraint, and illustrates the wisdom of forcing agencies to comply with the rule of law.

One could also argue that the S&L crisis was a failure of the rule of the law.[14] The FSLIC used its discretion to help S&Ls that it should have shut down. Moreover, the FSLIC was able to avoid significant publicity in the first years of the crisis because, like any agency, it was not required to hold public debates that might have captured the attention of the public. Many commentators believe that the FSLIC was "captured" by the S&L industry, and did its bidding, enabling many S&Ls to "gamble for resurrection."[15] Rather than shut down undercapitalized S&Ls,

10 Simon Johnson and James Kwak. 13 *Bankers: The Wall Street Takeover and the Next Financial Meltdown* (New York: Vintage Books, 2012), 154–55.

11 Ran Duchin and Denis Sosyura. "The Politics of Government Investment," 106 *J. Fin. Econ.* 24 (2012). Daron Acemoglu et al. "The Value of Connections in Turbulent Times: Evidence from the United States," 121 *J. Fin. Econ.* 368 (2013).

12 Atif Mian, and Amir Sufi. *House of Debt: How They (and You) Caused the Great Recession, and How We Can Prevent It from Happening Again* (Chicago: University of Chicago Press, 2014). See also Sumit Agarwal et al. "Policy Intervention in Debt Renegotiation: Evidence from the Home Affordable Modification Program." Working Paper Series No. 18311, National Bureau of Economic Research, Cambridge, MA, August 2012. Available at https://pdfs.semanticscholar.org/7388/af5a53f0d4e63e34335684f6e01786d49c93.pdf. Sumit Agarwal et al. "Mortgage Refinancing, Consumer Spending, and Competition: Evidence from the Home Affordable Refinancing Program." Working Paper Series No. 21512, National Bureau of Economic Research, Cambridge, MA, August 2015.

13 Acemoglu et al. *The Value of Connections in Turbulent Times*. Benjamin Blau et al., "Corporate Lobbying, Political Connections, and the Bailout of Banks," 37 *J. Banking & Finance* 3007 (2013). Duchin and Sosyura. *The Politics of Government Investment*. Todd Zywicki, "The Rule of Law During Times of Economic Crisis." Todd Zywicki, *The Auto Bailout and the Rule of Law*.

14 I have not found commentators who have put their criticisms of the FSLIC in these terms. But, in substance, their argument that the FSLIC abused its power resembles the rule-of-law critique of the Fed.

15 Thomas Romer and Barry Weingast. "The Political Foundations of the Thrift Debacle." In Alberto Alesina and Geoffrey Carliner (eds.), *Politics and Economics in the Eighties* (Washington, DC: National Bureau of Economic Research, 1991), 175–214. The truth is extremely

as public policy would dictate, the FSLIC allowed them to remain open and to expand their operations and take additional risk in the hope that an upturn in economic conditions would allow them to pay their debts. The president and other leaders of the executive branch did not attempt to exert control over the FSLIC, preferring instead to ignore the problem. The argument that the FSLIC enjoyed too much discretion apparently resonated with Congress, which abolished it and subjected the FDIC – its successor – to additional restrictions.

2. *Criticisms: Background*

The major problem with the rule-of-law critique is that it relies on an outdated and unworkable conception of liberal democracy, one that has been explicitly rejected by the US courts and implicitly abandoned by the American political system. The version assumed by the critics is sometimes attributed to James Madison, and so I will call it the Madisonian view. But the Madisonian view does not describe the way modern liberal democracies operate; it's not even clear that it describes the way the US government operated in the eighteenth and nineteenth centuries.[16]

Even in that era, the executive was not a passive executor of the law, but enjoyed significant policy-making authority. In the area of foreign relations, for example, the president was primarily responsible for making foreign policy. George Washington firmly established this principle during the neutrality debate, and it has been followed ever since. Presidents took the lead in conducting foreign relations with other countries, negotiating treaties, and directing military operations. By the twentieth century, the courts had recognized that the president was the leading figure in foreign relations. The president possesses significant if amorphous foreign-relations powers that he can use to recognize and deny recognition to countries and governments, tear up agreements even without obtaining Senate consent to a treaty, conduct military operations on his own under certain conditions, and much else.

The president's domestic relations power was more restricted at the founding, but the restrictions have eroded over time. The president was given the veto, and by the time of Andrew Jackson, presidents realized that their power to veto bills also gave them the power to set the legislative agenda. Early on, the president was given broad administrative authority – over the postal system, for example – and it turned out that it was impossible to administer a complex institution like the postal service without making policy decisions of various sorts, like where to locate post offices.

complicated. The best account I have found is Kane's. He describes the various pressures on the FSLIC, and is unsparing in his description of its mistakes, but also pronounces the administrators "honorable" – that is, they acted in what they thought was the public interest. See Edward Kane, *The S&L Insurance Mess*.

16 Eric Posner and Adriann Vermeule. *The Executive Unbound: After the Madisonian Republic* (Oxford: Oxford University Press, 2010).

The president's power to appoint became the power to bestow patronage, which presidents used to buy legislative support for their policies.

Thus, the distinction between "policy-making" by the legislature and "execution" by the president was never clean. Policy-making power was *shared* by the two institutions. Indeed, this idea can be traced back to Madison himself. He believed that the separation of powers preserved liberty by enabling the institutions to thwart each other. The executive could push back against the legislature by refusing to enforce the laws. But if the executive could refuse to enforce the laws, or certain laws, then it would necessarily participate in the determination of policy.

In the late nineteenth century and early twentieth century, circumstances called for a vast expansion of executive power. Industrialization, urbanization, and the growth of a national market necessitated the transfer of power from states to the national government, and from Congress to the president. Congress passed laws that granted the president the power to create and guide administrative agencies, which were authorized to issue and enforce regulations over many different areas of life. Among these agencies was the Federal Reserve Board, which was created in 1917, and given the power to intervene in a financial crisis by lending broadly. The New Deal would greatly expand this process by creating dozens of additional agencies and vesting them with significant powers.

The courts had generally acquiesced in these developments, but the vast expansion of the administrative state during the New Deal brought latent concerns to the surface. In 1935 the Supreme Court struck down statutes in a pair of cases on the ground that those statutes involved an unconstitutional delegation of legislative power to executive agencies. The National Industrial Recovery Act gave the president the power to adopt codes of fair competition, but otherwise gave him no guidance as to the content of those codes. The Court held that the delegation was excessive because without such guidance, the president could make policy on his own.[17] The Court cited a rule of law known as the non-delegation doctrine, which had at various times been interpreted to require that the statutory grant of authority contain an "intelligible principle" to be valid. However, that doctrine had never been used to block a federal statute – and it would not be used again for that purposes ever again.[18]

The problem, as the Court quickly recognized, is that Congress is incapable of issuing the detailed rules that are necessary to regulate a modern economy. Nor can it update them rapidly enough to address changing conditions, including the ubiquitous problem of regulatory arbitrage, where regulated parties shift their behavior to evade the rules without changing the substance of their activity. Congress is too slow, too inexpert, and too polarized; if regulation is to occur, it

[17] A.L.A. *Schechter Poultry Corp.* v. *United States*, 295 U.S. 495 (1935); *Panama Refining Co.* v. *Ryan*, 293 U.S. 388 (1935).

[18] Keith Whittington and Jason Iuliano. "The Myth of Non-Delegation Doctrine," 165 *U. Penn. L. Rev* 379 (2017).

must take place through an agency, which can act swiftly, secretly, and expertly, thanks to its hierarchical structure and mostly non-public decision-making process.

In short, the Madisonian system, such as it was, gave way to a modern system of executive primacy. The executive makes policy, while Congress and the courts play a more peripheral but still important role of oversight. The system remains true to some of the values of liberal democracy. The president is elected, after all, so the people continue to self-govern through their participation in presidential elections. Most executive action is public, or will eventually become public, when it is tested in court, as it usually is. It may well be the case that a degree of self-governance is lost compared to the Madisonian system, but that was deemed a price worth paying for living in a modern industrial economy rather than in an eighteenth-century agrarian republic.

3. *The Constitutionality of the Financial Crisis Response System*

When we turn to the rule-of-law critique of the crisis-response agencies, we can see that it reflects the outdated Madisonian vision rather than modern constitutional norms. The crisis-response agencies relied on delegated power like any other agency; they made policy because Congress authorized them to make policy. From a doctrinal standpoint, the statutes clearly provide an "intelligible principle." They direct agencies to ensure that credit flows, to resolve banks and S&Ls in ways least costly to the system, to demand collateral for loans, and so on.[19] The FSLIC, FDIC, Treasury, and the Fed all were given missions by Congress, which they carried out, albeit with varying degrees of success.

We should highlight the fact that the agencies were operating in crisis conditions. Even the classical view of Locke and other early theorists allowed the executive additional power during crises.[20] A liberal democracy, like any other system, must be able to protect itself during emergencies. While the traditional notion of emergency was limited to inter-state and civil war, there is no reason why it should be so limited. A financial crisis is an emergency in the same way that a war is: it requires very rapid and often secret action in the face of constantly changing events and radical uncertainty, in order to avoid huge costs to the public. As the classical theorists recognized, a legislature cannot operate under these conditions; only the executive can.

What of the impunity problem? As an initial matter, the critics exaggerate it. While courts did not intervene during the S&L crisis and the financial crisis, they played a role afterwards. In the *Winstar* litigation, courts found that Congress broke contracts with companies by depriving them of the supervisory goodwill that the FSLIC had used to induce them to buy up insolvent S&Ls.[21] After the financial crisis, courts have heard suits arising out of the rescues of AIG, Freddie Mac and

[19] Cf. *Whitman* v. *American Trucking Ass'n*, 531 U.S. 457 (2001).

[20] John Locke. *The Second Treatise of Civil Government* (1689). Available at www.constitution.org/jl/2ndtreat.htm.

[21] *United States* v. *Winstar*, 518 U.S. 839 (1996).

Fannie Mae, and GM and Chrysler.[22] While it is too soon to tell how these suits will conclude, complaints about agency behavior have at least received a judicial airing. The FSLIC was abolished, and it seems likely that the reputations of the government officials involved in the botched crisis response suffered as a result. By contrast, Bernanke, Geithner, and Paulson seem to have received some degree of public honor for their more competent handling of the financial crisis. This complex mix of political, social, and legal sanctions is far from optimal, but it is also different from impunity.

But the deeper point is that impunity is just another aspect of delegation. When Congress delegates authority, it does put limits on the grant of authority. But the very nature of the problem suggests that those limits may be more aspirational than real. The problem that justifies delegation in the first place is that Congress cannot anticipate the right policy response ahead of the crisis; it thus leaves policy decisions to the agencies. But if we take this problem seriously, it means that the outer limits of the delegation stipulated in the statute may turn out to be insufficient. The agency is then given the choice of respecting those limits and failing to resolve the crisis, and violating those limits in order to resolve the crisis. By granting the agency officials a degree of legal impunity, our system effectively delegates them even more power than the amount defined in the formal limits in the statutes, though how much more is ambiguous and will depend on political circumstances.

4. *A Political View*

The critics are wrong to argue that the crisis-response agencies violated the "rule of law," as the term is currently understood in the United States. The agencies' powers do not (and did not) violate the constitution, and while some of their actions were illegal, those actions did not pose constitutional questions. Yet the worries that animate the critique are not idiosyncratic to the critics; they are broadly shared. We can see how by examining the political reaction to the actions of the agencies.

As we saw, the S&L crisis was blamed in part on the FSLIC. Critics argue that the FSLIC exercised regulatory forbearance that made the crisis worse. After the crisis, Congress faced pressure to reduce the discretion of the crisis-response authority so that it could not in future engage in regulatory forbearance. In response, Congress created the prompt corrective action regime, which limited the ability of the crisis-response agency (now the FDIC) to keep firms alive, and also added a "least-cost" requirement that was meant to encourage the agency to shut down insolvent firms as cheaply as possible. In addition, Congress abolished the FSLIC and handed over its authority to the FDIC, which would be less sensitive to the S&L industry because its constituents included thousands of banks as well. Thus, the congressional response can be seen as a reaction to the presidential primacy approach to regulation.

[22] Posner, *Last Resort*.

Henceforth, the agency would be required to act within definite constraints. Madisonian values are illustrated in the hostile political reaction to the FSLIC's actions and the legislative response.

However, while there is an element of truth in this argument, the reality is more complex. For one thing, it is not clear that the prompt corrective action regime put additional constraints on the crisis-response agency.[23] It contains numerous exceptions and ambiguous terms. The least-cost provision contained an exception for systemic crises, which the FDIC would exploit during the financial crisis of 2007–08. Moreover, in a little-known move, Congress took the opportunity in the 1991 law to expand the power of the Fed to bail out financial institutions by giving it greater discretion over the collateral it could accept for emergency loans.[24] The abolition of the FSLIC itself was meaningless, since its powers were handed over to other agencies. Congress faced a dilemma. If it appeased public outrage and rule-of-law concerns by putting real constraints on the crisis-response authority, it would have undermined a needed public function. Instead, it reorganized the bureaucracy and created cosmetic restrictions.

No doubt lurking in the background was a humbling truth: that Congress, not the FSLIC, bore the primary responsibility for the failure to resolve the S&L crisis expeditiously. The FSLIC initially tried to shut down insolvent S&Ls, but was forced to stop because Congress did not appropriate sufficient funds for it to pay off depositors. The FSLIC sought additional resources from Congress but Congress refused. In the political scandals that marred the crisis response, the major culprit was Congress rather than the regulators. In the Keating 5 scandal, for example, it was learned that the FHLBB had succumbed to pressure from senators who interfered with its investigation of Lincoln Savings & Loan. It turned out that the S&L industry exerted more sway over Congress than over the FHLBB or the FSLIC.

The reason can be traced to the different institutional settings of Congress and the regulators. As Romer and Weingast relate, the S&L industry was able to use its influence over a handful of members of Congress, who were able to exploit parliamentary procedures to block reform bills that the FSLIC sought.[25] Members of Congress rely on campaign contributions, which provided the means for S&Ls to influence them. There is no similar direct route for "capturing" regulators. S&Ls can implicitly offer jobs to regulators when they leave office, but they cannot guarantee jobs without running afoul of the law. The hierarchical structure of the regulatory agency also ensures that a single person will be blamed if regulation fails.

[23] It proved unworkable during the financial crisis of 2007–08. See Albert Gilbert et al. "Federal Reserve Lending to Troubled Banks During the Financial Crisis." Working Paper 2012-006A, Federal Reserve Bank of St. Louis, St. Louis, MO, 2012.

[24] Walker Todd. "FDICIA's Emergency Liquidity Provisions," 29 *Fed. Res. Bank of Cleveland Eco. Rev* 16 (1993).

[25] Thomas Romer and Barry Weingast. "The Political Foundations of the Thrift Debacle."

By contrast, the blame for congressional failure is diffused among hundreds of members.

The lesson of the S&L crisis is not that the Madisonian system would have ensured a proper government response, but that lingering Madisonian norms subverted a rational crisis response that the system of presidential primacy, with its dependence on regulatory agencies, might otherwise have been able to accomplish. If we are to take this lesson seriously, then the proper response to the crisis was to further limit the power of Congress, not the agency. The muddled response suggests that Congress felt pressure both to create punishments and restrictions and to preserve broad discretion. In the end, Congress resolved this dilemma by imposing superficial reform.

The same point can be made about the 2007–08 rescue. The major lesson of the crisis was the hazards of congressional involvement, not of regulatory capture. Congress' initial refusal to pass EESA ushered in the most acute part of the crisis. The gridlock that almost sank the law reflected one of the major reasons for relying on crisis agencies in the first place – that Congress cannot act rapidly. Although Congress finally did pass a statute, it did not have enough time to hold substantive hearings and engage in meaningful policy debates. Mian, Sufi, and Trebbi find that Wall Street campaign contributions were correlated to voting by members of Congress,[26] while the huge amount of pork-barrel spending needed to buy votes from reluctant members was politically embarrassing as well as expensive.[27] In the end, Congress delegated even more authority to Treasury than Treasury asked for, allowing Treasury to make crucial choices in later months – including to bail out the auto industry (which Congress had refused to do), and limiting the aid to homeowners (despite congressional pleas to be more generous). Congress enhanced the legitimacy of the crisis response, but it did not make policy; it accepted its marching orders, with a few quibbles, from the executive. Famously, Congress expected Treasury to buy toxic assets; instead, relying on the vague language in the statute, Treasury invested in bank equity. Congress's recognition of its inability to make policy, especially on the fly, explains why it did not impose significant limits on the agencies after the crisis. The FDIC and Treasury were slapped on the wrist, and it remains unclear whether the rule limiting the power of the Fed to make customized loans can have a meaningful effect. The most important reform in the Dodd-Frank Act relating to the lender of last resort was a new provision that gave the FDIC the power to resolve insolvent non-banks in a manner sensitive to crisis conditions. Collectively, the agents were given *more* authority, not less.

A possible counterargument is that agency officials decided that they needed congressional support for the crisis response. In September 2008, Bernanke and Paulson agreed that it was necessary to seek a statute from Congress – even though

[26] Mian and Sufi. *House of Debt: How They (and You) Caused the Great Recession, and How We Can Prevent It from Happening Again.*

[27] Michael Dorsch. "Bailout for Sale? The Vote to Save Wall Street," 155 *Public Choice* 211 (2013).

they apparently believed that the Fed possessed the financial resources and most of the legal authority it needed to resolve the crisis. Their decision may show that executive primacy can operate only with at least some degree of congressional support. That may be so. But the fact remains that Congress was not able to contribute to policy-making, and that the effort to seek congressional support almost threw the rescue into disarray. Whether or not congressional involvement in a crisis response is necessary in order to provide political support to the crisis-response agencies, the primary consideration is to ensure that the agencies are given as much legal authority and financial wherewithal as they need.

In sum, while it is true that the agencies in both crises were influenced by interest groups at least on the margin,[28] and that unhappiness about the agencies' powers and performance motivated reform, the reform was cosmetic rather than real. Congress was unwilling to impose substantial constraints on crisis-responders in either case because agencies with broad powers are needed. While the government is always influenced by interest groups and other actors, the crisis response experience shows that, at least during the crisis itself, agencies act with greater political independence than Congress does. The Madisonian constitution is incompatible with a rational crisis-response process because Congress moves too slowly, and is just as likely to submit to interest group pressure as agencies are, if not more. But the rule-of-law concerns did play a role in public debate and the political reaction. The government's credibility was damaged, and there was an effort, albeit mostly unsuccessful, to curb the power of the lender of last resort.

5. *Reform*

All of this suggests that it is neither politically practicable nor desirable to reform the lender of last resort so as to bring it in conformity with the rule of law, as the critics understand that idea. A lender of last resort is an essential feature of the financial system.

Commentators who supported the crisis response but worry about rule-of-law hazards have proposed modest reforms, mainly focusing on procedural regularity, triggering requirements, and publicity norms.[29] Paul Tucker, a former high-level official in the Bank of England, takes this view, while also advocating a strict prohibition on lending to insolvent institutions. Yet the logic of the delegation dilemma suggests that these reforms can be no more than bandages. Since we don't know what the next crisis will require in terms of rescue, we don't know what limits on executive action are tolerable. If we impose limits that are too strict, we take the risk that we will undermine a rescue or set the stage for illegal action,

[28] The critics' insistence that the agencies were "captured" is a simplification. The agencies were clearly influenced by industry, as was Congress. But the industry did not dictate outcomes; indeed, the industry was riven by conflicts and did not possess a single "preference."

[29] Wallach, *To the Edge: Legality, Legitimacy, and the Responses to the 2008 Financial Crisis.*

with all the attendant problems – complicated circumventions, lack of transparency, and litigation.

For this reason, I have argued in other work that the government must be given more, not less, power to rescue firms.[30] It should be made clear that the lender of last resort can make unsecured as well as secured loans, and that it can buy assets, including equity. To minimize abuse, I advocate an equal treatment principle that would allow affected firms to bring lawsuits after the crisis is over, allowing them damages if they can show that they were treated worse than equally situated firms.

III. CONCLUSION

The rule-of-law controversy over the 2007–08 crisis response is in many ways an old story. In the familiar version of that story, the crisis involves a threat to security, and the executive branch claims discretionary authority to respond. After the 9/11 terrorist attack, the executive branch claimed vast discretionary authority to formulate a response. Congress acquiesced in the early years, but controversies erupted as it became clear that the government conducted surveillance, used interrogation methods, and engaged in other controversial counterterrorism activities, without statutory authority and even in defiance of statutory limits. In response to setbacks at the hands of the courts, and a degree of congressional resistance, the executive branch compromised. But in the end, Congress gave the executive nearly all the authority that it wanted. Security threats pose security-liberty tradeoffs. When a novel security threat materializes, the executive gains additional authority despite the risk to civil liberties. Congress and the courts acquiesce except at the margins because the executive alone can act decisively, secretly, and quickly.

While critics of the 9/11 response also claimed a defeat of the rule of law, the reality is that the system worked as it always has. In the classic Lockean view of liberal democracy, the executive enjoys a prerogative to take such actions that it sees fit to protect the nation from threats to security. Because the executive was a king (or, more accurately, an appointed bureaucracy), he might be tempted to act for the sake of personal aggrandizement, or to help favored supporters, and contrary to the public interest. But the people could hope that conscience and honor would constrain officials, and if not, that those officials would be sensitive to the threat of revolution.

In the modern era, the tension between executive prerogative and liberal democracy are less extreme. The president is an elected official whose every decision is under constant scrutiny. During a crisis, that scrutiny is exercised by an aroused public. Moreover, the president, unlike the king, exercises much of his authority based on delegations from Congress rather than based on inherent or constitutional authority. The delegations are accompanied by procedural requirements, including publicity requirements, and subject to various limits. Congress retains the formal

30 Posner, *Last Resort*.

right to withdraw or narrow the delegations in response to executive misbehavior – a more immediate and credible threat than popular revolution. And the courts have shown a willingness from time to time to back up Congress's claims. Both in theory and in practice, these norms help reconcile the public to executive policymaking authority.

To be sure, the dilemma never goes away completely. If Congress gives an agency too much authority, the agency may abuse it. If Congress gives it too little authority, the agency will either fail to resolve a crisis or, under political pressure, go beyond its statutory limits. In theory, there is an optimum; but there is no way to derive it from first principles. However, if we can draw a lesson from the S&L crisis and the 2007–08 crisis, it is that Congress imposed excessive limits on financial regulators, rather than insufficient limits. In the S&L crisis, those limits prevented the FSLIC from resolving the crisis and then – in response to congressional intransigence – forced it to break the law. In the 2007–08 crisis, the Fed and the other agencies, acting with broader authority, were able to stave off disaster for months. The limits that finally caused the agencies to go to Congress were more political than legal; and those political conditions – involving heightened public awareness – ensured that Congress would act rather than dig in its heels, though it was a near thing.

In the case of the 2007–08 financial crisis, the public seemed to accept the actions of the executive branch – at least during the crisis. The involvement of Congress, even if formulaic, might have helped, and the veneer of legality may have played its role as well.[31] After the crisis, anger toward the agencies gradually dissipated. Congress did not even go through the ritual of abolishing an agency and handing its power to another. The public was more interested in punishing financial executives than agency officials. While the crisis and recession played a role in polarizing American politics, and reducing trust in government, the lender-of-last-resort system survived its biggest test.

The two crises illustrate several themes of this book. During the 2008 financial crisis, constitutional constraints played a limited role, possibly none at all (compare the discussion in Elkins and Ginsburg, this volume; Gulati and Vanberg, this volume; and Kelemen, this volume). The agencies did what they needed to in order to address the crisis, and courts stayed out of the way. In the S&L crisis, legal limits (and hence the constitutional constraints that support them) did play a role. The difference may have to do with the relative magnitudes of the crises. That said, we do not know whether in 2008 the agencies would have gone farther in a counterfactual world in which no constitutional constraints existed (whatever that would mean). Moreover, the agencies faced litigation based on constitutional principles *after* the crisis was over. The importance of this post-crisis litigation is hard to gauge. On the one hand, if the US government is forced to pay damages, the payments will not be made by the agencies themselves, and so the prospect of paying

31 Wallach, *To the Edge: Legality, Legitimacy, and the Responses to the 2008 Financial Crisis*.

damages may not affect the incentives of agencies in the next crisis. On the other hand, strong judicial precedents might deter agencies from violating constitutional norms in the next crisis just because the agency heads or their lawyers normally refuse to openly defy the courts.

The two crises did not result in formal changes to the constitution, but did lead to tinkering with the institutions. In both cases, Congress reallocated authority among different institutions, "punished" (at least symbolically) institutions that acted (in Congress' lights) illegally or wrongly, and both created new legal limits on agency power to prevent a reoccurrence of the perceived bad behavior and enhanced powers so that agencies would be able to respond to the crisis the next time around. Seen from this perspective, neither crisis was in the end understood as a threat to constitutional rules or understandings – and hence appear in a more favorable light than the German and French cases discussed by Ferejohn (this volume), and the financial crisis in the United States during the Great Depression (Cushman, this volume). While the modern crises placed stressed on institutions, those stresses did not call for constitutional change.

4

Balanced Budget Provisions in Constitutions

Tom Ginsburg

In the wake of the financial crises of 2008–09, liberal democracies passed a wave of constitutional amendments to require that revenues be brought in line with spending. Most notably, in 2012 the vast majority of the EU member states adopted the Treaty on Stability, Coordination and Governance in the Economic and Monetary Union (the "EU Fiscal Compact") that introduced the so-called "Golden Rule," also explicitly suggesting (for the first time) that Member states should incorporate the balanced budget rule within their national constitutions (Adams, Fabbrini, and LaRouche 2014).[1] This seemingly pro-cyclical response drew plenty of criticism among scholars, even as others celebrated it as a necessary bit of austerity and discipline.

Meanwhile, in the United States, Congressional Republicans have for many years called for a balanced budget in every year, unless overridden by a supermajority.[2] Most American states already have a version of a balanced budget amendment.[3] At this writing, twenty-nine state legislatures have adopted resolutions demanding a new constitutional convention for the country as a whole, close to the thirty-four needed to call one under Article V of the constitution. Twenty-three of these states

[1] Art. 3(2) of the Treaty on Stability, Coordination and Governance in the Economic and Monetary Union states that: "The rules set out in paragraph 1 shall take effect in the national law of the Contracting Parties at the latest one year after the entry into force of this Treaty through provisions of binding force and permanent character, preferably constitutional, or otherwise guaranteed to be fully respected and adhered to throughout the national budgetary processes." See also Maurice Adams, Federico Fabbrini and Pierre Larouche. "Introduction – The Constitutionalization of European Budgetary Constraints: Effectiveness and Legitimacy in Comparative Perspective." In M. Adams, F. Fabbrini and P. Larouche (eds), *The Constitutionalization of European Budgetary Constraints* (Oxford: Hart Publishing, 2014).

[2] Chye-Ching Huan and Chloe Cho. "Balanced Budget Amendment Extreme by International Standards. Center on Budget and Policy Priorities," May 3, 2016. Available at www.cbpp.org/research/balanced-budget-amendment-proposal-is-extreme-by-international-standards.

[3] Most of these were adopted in the 1840s, following several state defaults. These provisions were then copied in later state constitutions. US state constitutional amendments typically have an exception for payments state borrowing for infrastructural investment. Depending when borrowing occurs, this could be pro-cyclical (states still have to pay the interest payments incurred even in times of plenty, and they may have a bias toward debt finance in good times).

have explicitly linked the call to the need for a balanced budget amendment, while several others have rescinded their calls for a convention. Whether a constitutional convention under Article V can be so limited is itself an interesting question that need not detain us here. And lest it seem like balanced budgets are a partisan issue, then Senator and future Vice-President Joe Biden, a Democrat, explained his support for a balanced budget amendment: "The question for me is not whether the budget must be in perfect balance. The question is whether we can indefinitely sustain deficits of $200 billion and more without permanently and dangerously limiting future options for our children's generation."[4] A balanced budget usually means more to the party *out* of power, than it does to that *in* power.

US calls for balanced budgets tend to come in waves following financial crises: twenty-three state balanced budget amendments were adopted between 1977 and 1979, but then none were passed from 1983 until 2010. Since the recession of 2008, seventeen states have adopted resolutions for a national balanced budget, while nine others have called for fiscal restraints that would limit the overall size of the deficit.

In short, calls for balanced budget amendments are a frequent response to financial crises. Proponents of the amendments argue that constitutionalization will introduce needed fiscal discipline through precommitment.[5] The people, sober, put the bottle away, preventing a binge of drunken spending by their representatives later on. Opponents argue that constitutionalization restricts needed flexibility, and in fact enshrines a policy of austerity that rests on dubious empirical foundations. Constitutionalizing fiscal discipline recalls Oliver Wendell Holmes' classic line, about the Fourteenth Amendment, that it "does not enact Mr. Herbert Spencer's Social Statics."[6] In that Lochner-era quote, Holmes was arguing that the constitution does not embody any particular economic theory, but instead leaves economic policy up to the political process.

Of course, a critical question in such debates is whether balanced budget provisions "work." Does constitutionalization effectively constrain fiscal decision-making? In this chapter, I provide preliminary answers to this question. I begin with a descriptive survey of the prevalence of balanced budget requirements. Such provisions, it turns out, are rare but not unknown, being found in some 6 percent of all national constitutions ever adopted. They are found in a wide range of jurisdictions around the world. I then turn to the question of their efficacy. I show that balanced budget requirements seem to be correlated with modest improvements in the fiscal situation. However, as I also show, there are challenges to a complete estimation of their economic effects, which imply that it is difficult to reach definitive conclusions about the potential impact of constitutionalizing budget balance.

4 Biden, Joe. "Why I Switched." *The New York Times*. 25 February 1995.
5 Stephen Holmes, *Passions and Constraint* (Chicago: University of Chicago Press, 1995).
6 *Lochner* v. *New York*, 198 U.S. 45 (1905) (Holmes, J. dissenting).

I. BALANCED BUDGET REQUIREMENTS: MOTIVE, FREQUENCY, AND USE

We use the term balanced-budget requirement to refer to a range of constitutional phenomena that vary in their rigidity, specificity, and temporal scope. Some constitutions require that in any given year, expenditures must not exceed revenues, absent some emergency. This provides short-term rigidity, though may do nothing about long-term or accumulated deficits. Another version focuses more on long-term deficits but allows short-term flexibility. Poland's 1997 constitution, for example, caps public debt at 60 percent of GDP, but does not limit annual budgets. Other variants explicitly target balance over the course of the business cycle, or apply a so-called structural approach that targets the levels of revenue of expenditure and revenue that would occur at a normal growth rate and full employment. Finally, constitutions vary in whether they require absolute balance or allow some deficit, either in response to current conditions or as a structural matter. The level of detail also varies – some are rather vague, while others quite precise, which might be a form of rigidity.

The EMU Fiscal Compact was a relatively flexible version in that it focused only on the structural deficit, which ignores short-term fluctuations, and permitted governments to run deficits of no more than 0.5 percent of GDP. European requirements tend to focus on annual structural deficit rather than accumulated deficit, which would include cyclical variation.

Balanced budget requirements are not new. Figure 4.1 shows, for all constitutions since 1789, the frequency of their use. They first spread in a few Central American countries in the nineteenth century but were fairly loosely drawn and allowed exceptions. In Portugal's 1822 constitution the government was required to keep taxes and spending "proportional," implying at least a rough balance. This is an example of a vague clause, certainly when compared with modern formulations. Nicaragua's 1848 constitution declares that "the Legislative Power provide the expenses necessary to cover the budget they decree, with a view to the revenues that the Government must present to them at the beginning of the year."[7] On its face, this does not require an absolute balance. In Honduras in 1873, constitution-makers provided that the budget for expenses could not exceed ordinary revenue, providing a firmer limit.[8]

Such requirements were limited to Latin America until the wave of French decolonizations in Africa. The independence constitutions of the Central African Republic (art. 27), Benin (art. 51), Burkina Faso (art 51), Chad (art. 42), Gabon (art. 41), and Mali (art. 33) – all adopted in 1959–60 – contained balanced budget requirements. Burkina Faso's formulation was typical: "The finance bill must provide for the revenues necessary fully to cover expenditures." Chad's was more detailed:

[7] Art. 40.1.

[8] Art. 37.5.

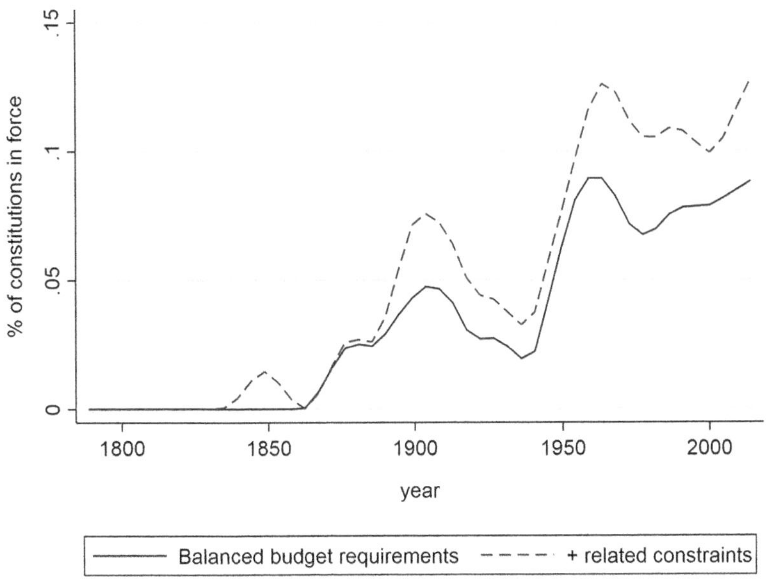

FIGURE 4.1 Constitutional balanced budget requirements over time

> The draft budget bill must provide for the necessary resources to cover integral expenses. If the bill adopted by the Assembly does not provide sufficient revenue to balance spending, the Government must order, in the manner described in the previous paragraph, reduction of credit or the creation of new revenue to the extent necessary to obtain equilibrium.

Many of these provisions, however, were quickly jettisoned by the newly independent countries.

More recently, a new wave of amendments has been adopted in Europe, including in Austria, Germany, Slovenia, Spain, Italy, and the Swiss Federation. Germany's 2009 constitutional amendment requires that, unless there is a disaster or severe economic crisis, the federal government may run a structural deficit of no more than 0.35 percent of GDP, and after 2020 the *länder* can run no structural deficits. Italy's 2012 constitutional amendment also takes a structural approach: it states that "The State shall balance revenue and expenditure in its budget, taking account of the adverse and favorable phases of the economic cycle."[9] Slovenia's provision says that "Revenues and expenditures of the budgets of the state must be balanced in the medium-term without borrowing, or revenues must exceed expenditures. Temporary deviation from this principle is only allowed when exceptional circumstances affect the state."[10] This formulation is rather typical of a flexible clause. Spain's is even

[9] Art. 81.
[10] Art. 148.

more flexible, in that it only requires an organic statute to set the rate of deficit, meaning that no amendment of the constitution would be required to adjust it.

Provisions differ on what happens if the budget cannot be balanced. Some constitutions dictate that if a balanced budget cannot be reached, the previous year's budget allocations carry forward. Other constitutions remove budgetary control from the legislature should the body fail to agree on a budget. For example, Title V, Article 80 of the 2000 Cote d'Ivoire constitution mandates a balanced budget, and further stipulates that "If the National Assembly has not voted the budget by the end of this extraordinary session, the budget is definitively established by ordinance."

The EMU suggestion for constitutional amendment seems to have been ignored entirely in other member states. France had already amended its constitution in 2008 to provide a loose goal, noting that "the multiannual guidelines for public finances shall be established by Programming Acts. They shall contribute to achieving the objective of balanced accounts for public administration."[11] Most of the EU member states have not incorporated the "golden rule" in their constitutions, implementing it instead through provisions of ordinary law. In fact, four contracting parties have adopted fiscal measures at the constitutional level, and seven at a higher hierarchical level than ordinary law (European Commission 2017: 4).[12]

As this account suggests, the provisions are not evenly distributed across regions. Roughly 8 percent of historical Latin American constitutions (n=317) have them, along with close to 14 percent of those in sub-Saharan Africa (n=219). Ukraine's 1996 constitution states that the state aspires to a balanced budget, during a period in which it has averaged 3 percent in deficit spending per year.[13] And Egypt has had such a provision since 2007, which is combined in the most recent constitution with promises to allocate a certain percentage of GDP to certain expenditures: 3 percent of GDP is to go health, 4 percent to education, 1 percent to scientific research, and 2 percent to university education.

Figure 4.1 traces the trends over time. The dashed line includes related provisions that are not strictly speaking balance requirements. Haiti's 1950 constitution, for example, disallows "amendments to the budget increasing spending without a corresponding means of revenue."[14] This is obviously a more limited provision, in that the initial budget may not need to be in balance. In France, a long tradition restricts private bills from diminishing public resources or increasing total spending. Hungary's current constitution states that there is a principle of "balanced,

[11] Art. 34.

[12] Germany, Spain, Italy, and Slovenia have adopted constitutional measures; Estonia, Finland, Lithuania, Latvia, and Portugal have implemented measures at a higher than ordinary level; and Bulgaria, Ireland, Malta, Greece, Cyprus, France, Denmark, the Netherlands, Romania, and Luxemburg at an ordinary level.

[13] Art. 95.

[14] Art 140.

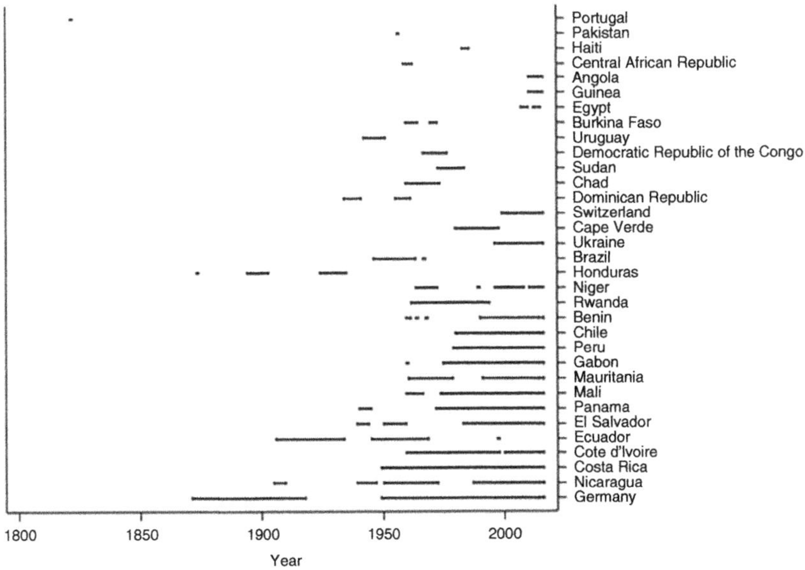

FIGURE 4.2 Periods in which balanced budget provisions have been in force
Sample/Universe: 722 of 854 constitutional systems in force between 1789 and 2015

transparent and sustainable budget management" and goes on to restrict any spending that would lead to state debt exceeding half of GDP, a relatively small number.[15]

Figure 4.2, reproduced from Amick et al. (Forthcoming) provides more detail about the set of countries that have had such provisions.[16]

II. WHY ARE THEY ADOPTED?

As the above discussion makes clear, balanced budget amendments are found in a wide range of countries, suggesting that a general account is difficult to construct. They typically are adopted as *responses* to financial crises (as in US states, or the recent European wave), or in a smaller number of cases, as *precommitments* as a condition of independence from a colonial power (typically the African cases). Both of these conditions seem to suggest that balanced budget requirements are elite or technocratic responses to worsening balance sheets, or devices to avoid them. External pressure seems to be a common theme for many of the cases, including the post-independence African cases and the current wave of European adoptions.

What is interesting about the American, as opposed to European, context is the presence of *popular* demands for fiscal discipline. The Tea Party made the balanced

[15] Art. 36.

[16] Joe Amick, Terrence Chapman and Zachary Elkins. "On Constitutionalizing a Balanced Budget." 2018, manuscript.

budget a central plank of its program, and helped to propel recent calls by seventeen state legislatures for a national constitutional convention. This contrasts with earlier periods in American history when popular movements demanded relief from fiscal austerity, and it also seems to be fairly unique cross-nationally. For most other governments, demands for fiscal discipline come from elites, and very frequently from abroad.

The reasons for this general pattern are easy to understand. Governments, unlike private entities, can manipulate their survival constraints by borrowing money, but this is not true of every government. Most governments rely on external sources to backstop their finances. These creditors may pressure governments into managing their resources better in order to ensure that they are paid back as promised.

But there are a very small number of core states that have the credibility and capacity to borrow virtually without limit, and so the only sources of constraint, if there are to be any, are internal and democratic. One might view the American popular demands for fiscal balance to be an instance in which the primary creditors – the country's own citizens – are concerned about deficit spending eating away the value of their loans. They may also be reflecting a peculiarly American concern with rent-seeking in government, and so seek to limit the scope of spending. This is unusual in historical perspective. Americans also regard debt in moral terms – it is seen as a personal failing, and citizens quite easily analogize the country to the household in this regard.

American exceptionalism aside, we will focus on the more typical pattern as one we would predict for the average nation: balanced budget provisions follow financial crises, and are imposed by outsiders or elites.

III. HOW DO THEY WORK, IF AT ALL?

There is a small literature on the efficacy of balanced budget requirements in US states and it generally finds them to be effective.[17] Poterba, and Alt and Lowry find substantial effects of balanced budget rules on spending levels.[18] Alt and Lowry also find that bond issues by US states that have balanced budget rules enjoy lower interest rates, a finding echoed in a sample of eurozone countries.[19] Von Hagen finds that debt is lower in states with stringent budget requirements.[20] These studies, however, do not focus on the effect of constitutionalization, and are not primarily

[17] Henning Bohn and Robert P. Inman. "Balanced Budget Rules and Public Deficits." *Carnegie-Rochester Conference Series on Public Policy* 45 (1996), 13–76.

[18] James Poterba, "State Responses to Fiscal Crises: The Effects of Budget Institutions and Politics." *Journal of Political Economy* 102 (1994), 799–821. James Alt and Robert Lowry. "Divided Government and Budget Deficits: Evidence from the States." *American Political Science Review* 88 (1994), 811–28.

[19] Mark Hallerberg and Guntram Wolff. "Fiscal Institutions, Fiscal Policy, and Sovereign Risk Premia in EMU." *Public Choice* 136(3-4) (2008), 379–96.

[20] Jurgen Von Hagen. "A Note on the Effectiveness of Formal Fiscal Constraints." *Journal of Public Economics* 44 (1991), 199–210.

focused on national-level restrictions.[21] State constitutions, it has been argued, are of a different type than national level ones.[22]

First, we should consider the mechanism by which constitutional promises might be effective. Kelemen and Teo, in an important contribution, point out that much of the theoretical literature assumes that judicial enforcement is the mechanism by which balanced budgets will be enforced.[23] Yet scholars of judicial politics are skeptical that courts could step in to discipline elected legislators for overspending. Indeed, to the extent that constitutional courts have gotten involved in financial crises, it has been for the opposite reasons: to make sure that internationally imposed cuts do not violate basic rights (as several of the other chapters in this volume explore). For example, in 2005, the Hungarian Constitutional Court found part of the IMF-imposed austerity plan unconstitutional because it required too many cuts to social spending for vulnerable groups.[24] In Latvia, as well as the state of Illinois, courts have stepped in to prevent contractual pension benefits from being cut to help balance the budget.[25] And in 2013, the Portuguese Constitutional Court struck down cuts to public sector salaries and pensions, adopted to help balance the budget, as violating equal protection as between public and private sector workers.[26] In light of these cases, it seems unlikely that courts would ever serve as an effective enforcer of a balanced budget amendment. Kelemen and Teo argue, instead, that the public commitment by the state to limit deficit spending helps serve as a focal point, coordinating decentralized punishment in the bond markets.

One might also consider an alternative account, drawing on the theory of two-level games.[27] This literature highlights the idea that a constraint at the international level can be empowering at the domestic level, and vice versa. This might imply that internal actors voluntarily seek a balanced budget provision, perhaps in alliance with external actors, to provide an excuse to limit rent-seeking, or to resist powerful interest groups. In effect, a balanced budget provision allows such actors to say: "We'd love to help you out by providing interest group benefits, but the IMF, EU Treaty or national constitution will not let us." The political benefit is clear.

21 A notable exception is Ardanaz and Scartascini (2014), who examine how the constitutional allocation of budgetary responsibilities across the executive and legislature affects the common pool resource problem.

22 Tom Ginsburg and Eric Posner. "Subconstitutionalism," *Stanford Law Review* 62 (2010), 1583.

23 R. Daniel Kelemen and Terrence Teo, "Law, Focal Points and Fiscal Discipline in the United States and the European Union" *American Political Science Review* 108(2) (2014), 355–70.

24 Constitutional Court of Hungary, Decision 43/1995 (30 June 1995). See generally Scheppele (2004).

25 Constitutional Court of Latvia, Case no. 2009–43-01 (21 December 2009). See also *Re Pension Reform Litigation*, 2015 IL 118585 (May 2015).

26 Constitutional Court of Portugal, Judgment no. 187/2013 (5 April 2013). See discussion in Violante and Andre, this volume.

27 Robert Putnam, "Diplomacy and Domestic Politics: The Logic of Two-Level Games." *International Organization* 42 (1988), 427–60.

TABLE 4.1 *Average annual budget deficit as percent of GDP 1995–2015 (n)*

Countries	No BBR	BBR
Europe only	−2.75	−2.52
	(55)	(390)
Advanced countries	−2.66	−1.93*
	(140)	(487
All countries	−2.31	−1.92*
	(533)	(346)

* T-test of difference in means significant at 5% level.
Data source: OECD data & Fiscal Rules Database.

The Fiscal Rules Database of the International Monetary Fund (Lledo et al. 2017) provides useful categorizations of various fiscal rules[28] that, when combined with OECD data on government spending, allow us to get some purchase on whether the constitutional constraints are effective. These data cover all balanced budget requirements, not just those involving constitutions. The data are limited to OECD members, so we do not get much insight into their general efficacy, but OECD members can be considered an easy test: given the high levels of institutional quality in the OECD, we ought to expect that if balanced budget rules were to work anywhere, it would be in the OECD.

As an initial cut at the data, we can compare whether countries with a balanced budget requirement (variable BBR in the IMF data) in place tend to have lower annual deficits, as a percentage of GDP, than those that do not. Using the country-year as the unit of analysis, we see that among advanced countries, and the set of all countries, a BBR correlates with lower deficits.

Within this category various possible levels of commitment are identified by the IMF: one can adopt a BBR by political agreement, by formal coalition agreement (a common practice in Scandinavia and Estonia), a statute, a supranational treaty like the EU, or a constitutional commitment. The IMF categorizes these in rank order, with constitutionalization being the highest level. Treaty and constitution categories can overlap but the others are exclusive. Looking at the raw data, it appears that the more informal mechanisms (of mere political commitments or coalition agreements) seem to be associated with countries in good fiscal situations: Finland, Norway, and Luxembourg are the leading countries in this category. Indeed, looking from this angle, there does not appear to be any special benefit from constitutionalization. The marginal difference between constitutionalization and the treaty commitment is not significant.

[28] Victor Lledó et al., "Fiscal Rules at a Glance." *International Monetary Fund* March 2017. Available at www.imf.org/external/datamapper/FiscalRules/Fiscal%20Rules%20at%20a%20Glance%20-%20Background%20Paper.pdf.

TABLE 4.2 *Average budget deficit by highest level of commitment to BBR, 1995–2015*

Countries	Political commitment	Coalition agreements	Statute	Treaty	Constitution
Europe only	−1.03	0.67*	−2.95*	−2.58	−2.01
Advanced countries	6.22*	0.67*	−2.85*	−2.45*	−1.38
All countries	5.42*	0.67*	−2.6*	−2.58*	−1.38

* T-test of difference in means against all other categories of BBR is significant at 5% level.
Source: OECD data & Fiscal Rules Database.

Let us now look at spending levels relative to the time at which the balanced budget requirement is constitutionalized. Here the null hypothesis is that there is no effect across time after adoption. To be sure, there are selection effects at play: perhaps the countries that believe their situation will improve will adopt the balanced budget requirement in order to get some political benefit from having done so. In such a case any subsequent improvement would not be attributed to the balanced budget provision on its own.

Figure 4.3 shows, over a period from 1984 to 2015, the level of deficit spending on average for the five years preceding and following a balanced budget amendment. The vertical axis is the annual budget expenditure as a percentage of GDP, and so is negative when countries run deficits. As one can see, on average, deficit spending is at its nadir *after* the constitutionalization of a BBR, but then improves dramatically to come close to balance at T+5. By two years out, the average country has come within the requirements of the EU 3 percent ceiling for deficit spending; by five years out, the figure is less than 1 percent. From this perspective, any country wishing to tame its spending ought to seriously consider a BBR.

Of course, these data do not control for macroeconomic cycles or the effect of particular years. To provide a rough sense of controls, we look at a particular period within the European Union, many of whose members are bound by a common currency, and share the same business cycle. Figure 4.4 looks at deficit spending for all EU countries (the dashed line) and those that have, for any given year, a constitutional limit in place. (The somewhat ambiguous status of the French constitutional promise leads us to calculate the latter both with and without France, but the basic effect is the same.) Note that, in keeping with the Fiscal Compact, many of the restrictions were adopted in 2012 or thereafter, so the earlier data is noisier and more sensitive to outliers. But the figure demonstrates clearly that post-2012, the countries with constitutionalized BBRs in place do better than EU members on average.

Moving to a regression framework requires specifying a baseline model. Taking the surplus/deficit as a dependent variable, we ran several different models using the IMF data. In all cases, we control for wealth, as wealthier countries tend to run

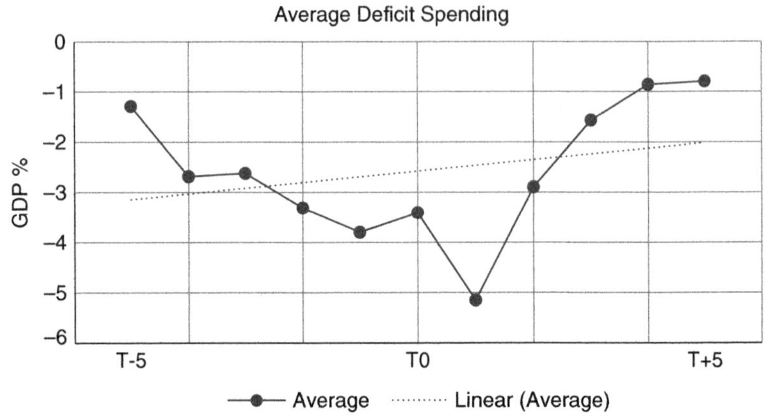

FIGURE 4.3 Spending five years before and after BBR adoption in constitution
Data source: IMF database

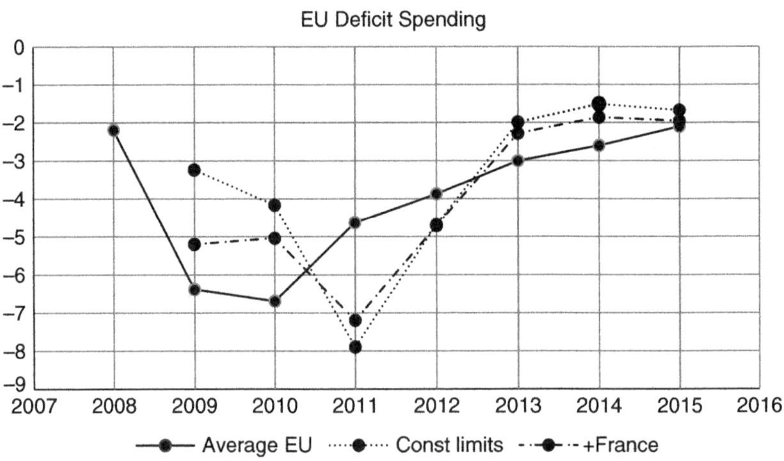

FIGURE 4.4 EU deficit spending from 2008 onward

smaller deficits as a percentage of GDP. I ran two regressions for the whole sample of countries, and two for EU countries only. The unit of analysis is the country-year. The independent variables of interest were two: BBR is a dummy variable, produced in the IMF's Fiscal Rules Dataset, that takes value 1 if there is any balanced budget rule in place. "Stringency of BBR" is another variable from the same dataset that is ordinal: it increases with the highest level at which the BBR is adopted.[29] It takes value 1 for political agreement, value 2 for formal coalition agreement (a common practice in Scandinavia and Estonia), value 3 for a statute, and value 5 for

[29] In our regression data this is labeled Legal_n_BBR.

TABLE 4.3 *Regressions*

VARIABLES	(1) surplus as % GDP	(2) surplus as % GDP	(3) surplus as % GDP	(4) surplus as % GDP
GDP per capita	7.70e-05***	0.000145***	0.000137***	0.000167***
	(1.47e-05)	(2.94e-05)	(1.96e-05)	(4.75e-05)
BBR	−0.262		−1.079	
	(0.362)		(0.966)	
Stringency of BBR		−1.973***		−1.409***
		(0.257)		(0.275)
Constant	−3.713***	0.639	−5.350***	−1.953
	(0.407)	(1.139)	(1.032)	(1.572)
Observations	659	224	297	108
R-squared	0.042	0.273	0.143	0.251
Sample	All countries	All countries	EU only	EU only

Standard errors in parentheses
***$p<0.01$, ** $p<0.05$, * $p<0.1$

a constitutional commitment. (Value 4 is coded for a supranational agreement in the IMF codebook, but in fact appears instead as a separate dummy variable in the data.) One can treat this ordinal independent variable as indicating the legal strength of the BBR.

The results indicate that, on average, wealth has a much greater effect on deficit spending than does the presence of a BBR. Interestingly, the coefficient for the strength of the BBR has a negative sign – stronger protections, such as those associated with a statute or constitutional requirement, are associated with greater deficits than are the softer forms of commitment. This result, however, is likely determined by the specific countries that tend to use coalition agreements or political commitments to enshrine a BBR. And no attempt has been made to deal with potential endogeneity.

IV. DISCUSSION

Constitutionalization of balanced budget limitations is a way of precommitting the polity to fiscal balance, usually imposed by external pressure. One's normative view of this approach depends in large part on whether or not one believes in enforced austerity or a more Keynesian approach in which spending should be counter-cyclical. Even under the latter view, there may be some benefit in having constitutionalized rules so as to allow budget-makers to resist calls from interest groups for pork barrel spending. In almost no case have we seen such restrictions being rigorously enforced, whether by courts or even by national legislators. That is, even requirements of balanced budgets are not observed.

This does not, however, mean they are useless. Constitutionalized BBRs seem to be like speed limits. They raise the costs of deviating even if they may not be observed perfectly in practice. The analysis here suggests that they may be associated with some fiscal restraint, though selection issues bedevil the analysis. In addition, it is probably impossible to measure the effects in terms of interest group demands for spending that are rejected.

A further, deeper complication concerns data. It may be that the chief effect of constitutionalized balance budget restriction is in the realm of accounting. Countries have myriad ways of moving expenditures off-budget, shifting items across years, and otherwise manipulating reported data. Even if we observe, as we do, apparent improvements in the position of states after adoption of balanced budget requirements, we cannot know with confidence that these are genuine, or simply the result of accounting manipulations. This renders even our basic finding somewhat suspect, though also complicates any attempt to figure out the direct effects of these constitutional rules. Even if the effect we observe is an artefact of reporting, however, this still means that the provisions affect behavior – though perhaps not in the way they are intended to.

5

Legislatures and Constitutions in Times of Severe Financial Crisis

Mark D. Rosen[*]

The constitutions of all liberal democracies contain provisions that constrain economic policy. Some provisions grant rights. For example, the United States constitution's contract clause provides that states shall not "pass any Law impairing the Obligation of Contracts."[1] Other provisions are structural rather than rights-conferring, such as balanced budget requirements.

This chapter considers how constitutional provisions designed to constrain economic policy should affect a legislator's decision-making during times of severe financial crisis. The chapter focuses on rights-granting constitutional provisions, though it also briefly considers the implications of the analysis for structural provisions. The chapter explains why unqualified constitutional language, which may appear to absolutely bar the legislature from undertaking a certain course of action, need not always be given literal effect. This means that legislatures have some leeway to infringe constitutional rights. But there is a cost to this degree of freedom: when legislators contemplate infringing a constitutional right, they cannot act as they are permitted to in the course of ordinary politics. In contrast to what might be called the norms of *Hardball Politics* that are usually operative, legislators should undertake their constitutional decision-making pursuant to a set of *Special Norms*.

Special Norms complement, but do not displace, whatever doctrinal test a country's courts use to adjudicate the constitutionality of legislation,[2] such as proportionality analysis or tiered scrutiny. Much of the chapter's analysis carries over to the executive branch.[3] It also may have implications for constitution drafting. To concretize its exposition, the chapter considers a pressing financial challenge presently confronting many state and local governments in the United States:

[*] This essay is dedicated to Daniel Biss, an exemplar of a responsible legislative constitutional decisionmaker.

[1] US Const. Art. I, §10, cl. 1.

[2] See text accompanying nn. 76–90.

[3] See n. 72.

massively unfunded pension liabilities for public workers.[4] This challenge is sufficiently large that it may serve as an example of a financial crisis to which constitutional decision-makers must respond.

I. THE PENSION CRISIS

As has been noted, "Most state and local governments in the United States offer retirement benefits to their employees in the form of guaranteed pensions."[5] These retirement benefits are subject to at least one, and typically two, levels of constitutional protection. Pensions have been deemed to be contracts that fall under the US constitution's contract clause,[6] which provides that "No state shall" pass any law "impairing the obligation of contracts."[7] And most public pensions are also protected by state constitutions. For example, the pension clause of the Illinois constitution provides that membership in a public pension system is "an enforceable contractual relationship, the benefits of which shall not be diminished or impaired."[8]

Over the past several years it has become recognized that a large number of public pension systems have been massively underfunded. The full extent of the problem is not yet known, on account of the great number of local governments, but it appears to be considerable. A recent study of 564 state and local systems found unfunded pension liabilities of nearly 1.2 *trillion* dollars.[9] The state of Illinois holds the unenviable distinction of possessing the country's most underfunded pension system for state employees. In 2013, the state retirement system's unfunded pension liabilities reached approximately $100 billion, and now exceeds $111 billion.[10] To provide some context, the state's entire budget for 2013 was about $64 billion.[11] Pension payments accounted for 24.8 percent of Illinois' general fund budget in 2016.[12] Those

4 I will give particular attention to the problems faced by the state of Illinois. It is appropriate to disclose that I testified before Illinois' legislature, and provided other assistance to individual legislators and to the Attorney General in connection with Illinois' efforts to address its pension crisis.

5 See Joshua D. Rauh, "Hidden Debt, Hidden Deficits: How Pension Promises are Consuming State and Local Budgets," www.scribd.com/document/307464825/Hidden-Debt-Hidden-Deficits-How-Pension-Promises-Are-Consuming-State-and-Local-Budgets-by-Joshua-D-Rauh#download; Eric Pianin, "The Growing Funding Gap for State Pensions Puts Millions at Risk," *The Fiscal Times* (April 21, 2017), www.thefiscaltimes.com/2017/04/21/Growing-Funding-Gap-State-Pensions-Puts-Millions-Risk.

6 See *Allied Structural Steel Co.* v. *Spannaus*, 438 U.S. 234 (1978).

7 See *US Const. Art.* I, §10, cl. 1.

8 *Ill. Const. art.* XIII, § 5. Pension benefits are further protected by the Illinois constitution's contract clause, which largely tracks the language of the United States constitution. See *Ill. Const. art.* I, §16.

9 See Rau, n. 6, at 1 (reporting unfunded liabilities of $1.191 trillion).

10 See John Klingner, "S&P Downgrades Illinois Credit Rating Closer to Junk," *Illinois Policy* (October 4, 2016), www.illinoispolicy.org/sp-downgrades-illinois-credit-rating-closer-to-junk/.

11 See *State of Illinois Budget Summary Fiscal Year* 2014, p. 23, http://cgfa.ilga.gov/upload/fy2014budget summary.pdf.

12 See Klingner, n. 11.

figures do not include the unfunded pension liabilities of Illinois' cities and counties. The City of Chicago alone has unfunded liabilities of approximately $20 billion. These unfunded liabilities have led ratings agencies to substantially downgrade the bond ratings of both Illinois (presently at the near-junk level of BBB) and Chicago (now only three levels above "junk" status[13]), making it more difficult and expensive for these governments to borrow money.

Unsurprisingly, there is substantial finger-pointing to allocate blame for this distressing situation. Without purporting to provide a definitive explanation, it appears safe to say that many factors conspired to create the pension crisis. The accounting standards that governed public pension systems were based on funding calculations that assumed unrealistically aggressive returns and that systematically ignored investment risks,[14] resulting in disastrous outcomes during the recession of 2013. Moreover, because Illinois law did not require the legislature to appropriate money on a yearly basis to pension funds, the legislature did not fully fund its pension system for decades. The public employee unions were aware of this, and along with the legislators seem to have preferred that money be spent on more immediately tangible ends, like salary raises for public employees. In short, although unexpected market events certainly played a role, there is ample blame to spread for the pension crisis, including generations of irresponsibility on the part of the state legislature.

But determining who bears what responsibility for the crisis does not help much, if at all, in crafting a solution. There is broad agreement that the funding shortfalls are simply too large to fix through tax increases and/or reductions in government services alone. After a prolonged period of burying their heads in the sand, state and local legislators in the United States have begun to explore how they might restructure their public pension systems so as to assure both their long-term solvency and the government's ability to discharge its myriad other functions and responsibilities.

II. LEGISLATURES AND CONSTITUTIONAL LIMITATIONS: THREE POSSIBLE APPROACHES

Let us begin by identifying, and rejecting, two often-mentioned approaches that legislatures might take to constitutional restrictions like the pension and contract clauses. The first is that the legislature's role is to legislate, not to interpret the constitution. On this view, determining whether the legislature's actions are constitutional or not is the sole responsibility of courts. But this reflects a profound misconception, and in fact is an abdication of responsibility. Constitutions grant

[13] See Fran Spielman, "Standard and Poor's Predicts Reversal of Rauner Veto," *Chicago Sun Times* (March 28, 2017), http://chicago.suntimes.com/politics/standard-poors-predicts-reversal-of-rauner-pension-veto/.

[14] See Rau, n. 6, at 1–2 (noting that accounting standards assumed contributed assets would achieve returns of 7.5 to 8 percent per year).

powers to, and place limits upon, the legislature. Legislators typically take oaths to uphold the constitution, and this obligation surely encompasses their acting within the constitution's limits. Every action by the legislature necessarily has at least one constitutional ingredient, namely a determination that the legislature has authority under the constitution to undertake the activity it is contemplating.[15] So though legislatures may not have the last word on that subject, they in effect have the first word insofar as legislative action invariably reflects an antecedent determination that the legislature had constitutional authority to act. Further, insofar as judicial doctrines give deference to the legislatures, the doctrines presuppose that the legislature has judged its activity to be constitutional. For if the legislature has not made such a judgment, to what are the courts deferring?

The second approach a legislature might take is to give literal effect to the constitution's language when determining its authority to legislate. So, because the US constitution's contract clause provides that states "shall" not pass "any" law impairing the obligation of contracts, a state legislature simply cannot, under any circumstance, enact a law that impairs contractual obligations. Because public pensions qualify as contracts, pension obligations that overwhelm a state's budgetary capacities, or that threaten to bankrupt the pension system or even the state as a whole, are legally irrelevant to the constitutionality of legislation that reduced pension benefits as part of a wholesale restructuring of the pension system that secured the system's solvency. On account of the constitution's caveat-free language, such pension reform would be beyond the legislature's power because pension benefits simply cannot be impaired. Contract rights are absolute – period, end of story.

The second approach has much more traction than the first. There undoubtedly is strong pull to the proposition that constitutional language means what it says.[16] If legislatures can impair contractual obligations, notwithstanding constitutional language saying they cannot, then the constitutional language might appear to be superfluous.[17] Allowing the legislature to ignore the constitution's language would put contract rights up for grabs, effectively demoting them to mere policy interests. Permitting the legislature to impair contractual obligations might be said to gut the very reason they were constitutionally protected in the first place. Constitutions

15 Whether the legislature has constitutional authority to act comprises at least two components: a determination that it has power to act, and that acting would not run afoul of some constitutional limitation. There sometimes are additional constitutional components to the legislature's decision. Sometimes the determinations as to whether the legislature should act, and if so what it should do, contain constitutional ingredients. See generally Mark D. Rosen, "The Special Norms Thesis," 40 *Cardozo L. Rev.* xx (forthcoming 2019) (hereinafter "Special Norms Thesis").

16 David Strauss, "Does the Constitution Mean What It Says?," *Harv. L. Rev.* 129: 1 (2015). Strauss cogently and persuasively explains why constitutional language frequently does not "mean what it says." See ibid.

17 See Mark D. Rosen, "When Are Constitutional Rights Non-Absolute? McCutcheon, Conflicts, and the Sufficiency Question," *Wm. & Mary L. Rev.* 56: 1535, 1539 (2015) (considering, but then rejecting, this contention).

embody pre-commitments that are designed to limit government precisely when times are most difficult. If constitutional commitments are not absolute, what would be the point of them?

But the second approach reflects a naïve understanding of how constitutions actually work. It is well recognized among constitutional theorists that almost every constitutional right can be "regulated" (or what is interchangeably referred to as "limited" or "infringed") under some circumstances.[18] And this is true even if the constitution grants the right without qualification or caveat. For example, the language of the Privileges and Immunities Clause is literally absolute, providing that "the Citizens of each State *shall* be entitled to *all* Privileges and Immunities of Citizens in the several States."[19] Yet the US Supreme Court has recognized that "like many other constitutional provisions, the privileges and immunities clause is not an absolute."[20] Similarly, "Although the language of the contract clause is facially absolute,"[21] the US Supreme Court has rejected "[l]iteralism in the construction of the contract clause."[22]

Courts in the United States operationalize their judicial review of legislatures' infringement-prerogative[23] with a two-step heightened scrutiny analysis. The first step considers the purpose or "end" that the legislation aims to accomplish. Under the first step, many constitutional rights can be infringed only if there is a "compelling governmental interest."[24] The second step requires a substantial fit between the means the legislature has selected and the constitutionally permissible end. The most demanding judicial test requires legislation to be "narrowly tailored" to accomplishing the constitutionally permissible end.[25] Likewise, the proportionality analysis found in

18 See, e.g., Aharon Barak, *Proportionality: Constitutional Rights and their Limitations*; Rosen, "The Sufficiency Question," n. 18, at 1537–39; *McDonald* v. *City of Chi.*, 561 U.S. 742, 802 (2010) (Scalia, J., concurring) ("No fundamental right – not even the First Amendment – is absolute."); *United States* v. *Alvarez*, 132 S. Ct. 2537, 2547 (2012) ("[I]t is well established that the Government may restrict speech without affronting the First Amendment.").

19 US Const. art. IV, § 2, cl. 1. (emphasis added).

20 *Lunding* v. *N.Y. Tax Appeals Tribunal*, 522 U.S. 287, 297 (1998) (emphasis added) (internal quotation and citation omitted); see also *Supreme Court of N.H.* v. *Piper*, 470 U.S. 274, 284 (1985) (stating that the privileges and immunities clause "does not preclude discrimination against nonresidents where . . . there is a substantial reason for the difference in treatment").

21 US Const. art. I, § 10, cl. 1 I, ("No State shall . . . pass *any* . . . Law impairing the Obligation of Contracts") (emphasis added).

22 *W.B. Worthen Co.* v. *Thomas*, 292 U.S. 426, 433 (1934).

23 Virtually all of what follows applies equally to the executive branch. But it is important to be sensitive to the different institutional contexts, because there are circumstances where constitutional constraints restrict different governmental actors differently. See generally Mark D. Rosen, "The Surprisingly Strong Case for Tailoring Constitutional Principles," U. Pa. L. Rev. 153: 1513 (2005).

24 Constitutional jurisprudence permits some constitutional rights to be regulated for less pressing reasons, for example if there is an "important governmental interest." See, e.g., *Craig* v. *Boren*, 429 U.S. 190, 197 (1976).

25 Constitutional rights that can be regulated for less than compelling reasons likewise call for less strict fit between the regulation's ends and means. See, e.g. *Craig*, 429 U.S. at 197 (regulation must be "substantially related" to achieve an important government interest).

most other liberal democracies directs judges to decide whether legislation infringing constitutional rights aims to accomplish a legitimate and sufficiently important purpose and, if so, to then examine the means used to achieve that end.[26]

To illustrate, during the Great Depression, Minnesota granted homeowners relief by enacting law that extended mortgagees' periods of redemption, thereby postponing foreclosures on account of borrowers' mortgage non-payment.[27] The law was challenged as a violation of the Federal contract clause because it in effect altered the terms of the mortgagees' contracts.[28] Despite the contract clause's absolute language, the US Supreme Court upheld the law. As to the legislative ends, the Court explained, "the legislation was not for the mere advantage of particular individuals but for the protection of a basic interest of society."[29] As to the means, the Court concluded that "The conditions upon which the period of redemption is extended do not appear to be unreasonable."[30]

More generally, constitutional doctrines permit legislatures to infringe constitutional rights so long as there is, we might say, a *sufficiently important* reason, and even then, only if the infringement is undertaken in a *sufficiently careful* manner. Insofar as constitutional rights sometimes may be infringed (or regulated or limited), they are not absolute. And this is so even when the constitutional language establishing the right is literally absolute in that it does not contain any caveats or qualifications.

III. THAT CONSTITUTIONAL RIGHTS DO NOT PROVIDE ABSOLUTE PROTECTION

The bare fact that jurisprudence permits rights-infringements does not mean this allowance is normatively correct. This possibility follows from Hume's Law, which teaches that an "ought" cannot be derived from an "is."[31] After all, a practice may be both widespread and wrongful. But careful thought identifies two powerful reasons to think that the phenomenon of rights-infringements is not per se wrongful.[32]

First consider the circumstance where a constitutional right runs up against a countervailing constitutional right or other constitutional commitment (such as the Illinois constitution's guarantee that the "State shall provide for an efficient

26 See Vicki C. Jackson, "Constitutional Law in an Age of Proportionality," *Yale L. J.* 124: 3094, 3099 (2015).

27 See *Home Bldg. & Loan Ass'n* v. *Blaisdell*, 290 U.S. 398, 445 (1934).

28 Ibid. at 415–16.

29 Ibid. at 445.

30 Ibid.

31 See David Hume, *A Treatise of Human Nature*. London: John Noon, 1739, 335.

32 For a sustained argument as to why this is so, see Rosen, "The Sufficiency Question," n. 18, at 1543–60; Mark D. Rosen, "Two Ways of Conceptualizing the Relationship Between Equality and Religious Freedom," *Journal of Law, Religion and State* 4: 117, 123–26, 139–40 (2016).

system of high quality public educational institutions and services").[33] When this occurs, one constitutional commitment necessarily must give way to the other, and in that sense will be "limited" and non-absolute. This conclusion is avoidable only if constitutional commitments are immune from conflict. Immunity would require that one of two conditions pertained. The first is if all constitutional commitments fit into a harmonious whole such that the commitments, when properly understood, never conflicted. Second, there would be no conflict if it turned out that what we presently perceive as being multiple constitutional commitments actually derive from a single, coherent, and conceptually prior constitutional commitment. On both approaches, any perceptions of conflict among constitutional commitments would reflect a present substantive misperception concerning those commitments.

But neither of these conditions for conflict-immunity is axiomatic. Quite to the contrary. Descriptively, neither condition accurately describes the constitutional practices, past or present, of any modern liberal democracy.[34] For example, a same-sex couple's equality rights appear to be susceptible to conflict with a photographer's freedom to decline to participate in a same-sex wedding celebration on religious grounds. And as a matter of theory, the phenomenon of conflicts between constitutional rights – what we might call *right-right conflicts*[35] – is readily explained. Much as physics has not found a unified field theory that can describe all fundamental forces and elementary particles, there is substantial philosophical consensus that there is not a single value from which all other values are derived.[36] A single set of circumstances can trigger more than one normative commitment, and there is no guarantee that those commitments will always point in the same direction. When they do not, we experience a conflict between (or among) our multiple normative commitments. Insofar as constitutional rights are markers of normative commitments,[37] it is not surprising that rights too can conflict with one another.

Right-right conflicts are not the only circumstance that gives rise to rights-infringements. Neither United States jurisprudence nor the proportionality analysis used in other modern liberal democracies requires that the sufficiently important interest that licenses a right-infringement itself be of constitutional status. This means constitutional rights can be limited to achieve sub-constitutional interests.

33 Ill. Const. Art. X. Many state constitutions guarantee efficient systems of public education. See, e.g., Tex. Const. Art. VII, s. 1.

34 See Rosen, "Two Conceptualizations," n. 33, at 122–30 (identifying the unlikely circumstances that must pertain for constitutional rights to be immune to conflict).

35 I intend the phrase "right-right conflicts" to encompass both conflicts among constitutional rights as well as conflicts between a constitutional right and a non-right constitutional commitment.

36 Isaiah Berlin, *The Crooked Timber of Humanity: Chapters in the History of Ideas* (Henry Hardy, ed.) (2nd edn 2013) 83.

37 For more discussion of this point, see text accompanying nn. 55–62.

And as a descriptive matter, it is this circumstance – what might be called *right-interest conflicts* – that is the most frequent predicate for rights-infringements.

It seems fair to say that rights-infringements on account of right-interest conflicts are more difficult to justify than infringements that owe to right-right conflicts. After all, when rights conflict, one necessarily must give way to the other, and hence will be infringed, and in that sense, will be non-absolute.[38] But it may seem odd that constitutional rights do not automatically and always prevail when they run up against sub-constitutional interests. After all, insofar as *sub*-constitutional interests do not rise to the level of constitutional ones, it may seem to naturally follow that they should always be ordinally inferior to a constitutional commitment. Ronald Dworkin's famed terminology of "rights as trumps" reflects this intuition, and has taken a strong grip on the many people who now think the very point of a constitutional right is to automatically "trump" any and all competing policy interests.[39] If constitutional rights can be infringed to achieve sub-constitutional ends, the thinking goes, rights will cease to serve their constitutional purposes, and instead will be reduced to mere policy interests that are on equal footing with sub-constitutional interests. And treating constitutional matters interchangeably with sub-constitutional interests would be an obvious mistake.

But these critiques of right-infringements for right-interest conflicts are mistaken, insofar as they purport to be definitive. (As will soon be explained, these critiques have contingent validity.)[40] First consider empirics. Insofar as all modern constitutional democracies sometimes allow rights infringements in right-interest conflicts, if the critiques were correct then the universal practices of today's constitutional democracies are all wrong. While this conclusion is not a conceptual impossibility (owing once again to Hume's Law), it seems unlikely. After all, today's constitutional democracies have created the "most robust human and constitutional rights in human history."[41] Although rights do not always trump sub-constitutional interests, it seems mistaken to describe this practice as having resulted in a circumstance in which constitutional rights in today's liberal democracies are indistinguishable from non-constitutional interests.

The critiques not only stand on shaky empirical grounds, but are based on a faulty conceptual premise. The critiques presuppose that rights can perform constitutional work only if they are absolute.[42] But this is mistaken, because rights can perform critical constitutional work without being absolute.[43] Perhaps the most sustained

38 It also is possible that each right will give way to some extent to the other, and hence that both will be non-absolute.

39 See Rosen, "The Sufficiency Question," n. 18, at 1543–45. Though Dworkin retained the terminology of "trumps" throughout his long career, he also recognized that "no political right is absolute." See ibid. at 1553 (discussing Dworkin's approach in his penultimate book, *Justice for Hedgehogs*).

40 See, text accompanying nn. 68–69.

41 Ibid. at 1559.

42 In relation to sub-constitutional interests, at least.

43 See Rosen, "The Sufficiency Question," n. 18, at 1573–96.

demonstration of this point can be found in the work of German constitutional theorist Robert Alexy, who famously argues that constitutional rights are principles that are to be optimized pursuant to the balancing methodology he operationalizes through proportionality analysis.[44] On Alexy's view, principles "represent reasons" that must be taken into account when they are at play, but that may be "displaced by other reasons" in particular circumstances.[45] Alexy does not believe that the "other reasons" that can displace the reasons represented by rights need themselves be represented by another right. Alexy thus accepts the possibility of both right-right and right-interest conflicts.[46]

Other constitutional theorists who also recognize that rights are non-absolute have offered other master metaphors to describe the constitutionally meaningful role rights still can play. In a deliberate contrast to Dworkin's absolutist-sounding rights-as-trumps, American constitutionalist Fred Schauer has argued that rights operate as shields that exclude consideration of non-right interests most of the time.[47] Just as no shield's protection is complete, Schauer's metaphor recognizes that rights have a "susceptibility to override by a sufficient aggregation of mere interests."[48] More recently, Schauer has put forward an alternative conceptualization under which "Rights do not necessarily win against non-rights considerations," nor do they "exclude non-rights consideration."[49] Instead, "rights *devalue non-rights considerations*, such that there need to be more of such considerations in order to prevail than would be the case were rights not part of the picture."[50]

On all three of these approaches – rights-as-principles, rights-as-shields, and rights-as-devaluers of non-right considerations – rights are non-absolute, yet still perform important constitutional work. Thus, these three approaches demonstrate the mistake in presuming that constitutional rights are meaningful only if they are absolute.

IV. THE NEED TO "HARMONIZE" CONSTITUTIONAL RIGHTS WITH OTHER COMPETING COMMITMENTS

Although all three approaches help us understand how constitutional rights operate, each one's explanatory reach has significant limitations. Alexy's rights-as-principles optimization rule overstates the objectivity of the process that determines when

44 See *Robert Alexy, A Theory of Constitutional Rights* (Julian Rivers, trans., Oxford: Oxford University Press, 2002) (1986); Rosen, "The Sufficiency Question," n. 18, at 1579–80.

45 See Alexy, n. 45, at 57; Rosen, "The Sufficiency Question," n. 18, at 1580.

46 See Rosen, "The Sufficiency Question," n. 18, at 1580.

47 See Frederick Schauer, "A Comment on the Structure of Rights," *Ga. L. Rev.* 27: 415, 429 (1993), discussed in Rosen, "The Sufficiency Question," n. 18, at 1573–74.

48 Schauer, n. 48, at 431.

49 Frederick Schauer, "Proportionality and the Question of Weight," in *Proportionality and the Rule of Law* 177 & n. 18 (Grant Huscroft, Bradley W. Miller, and Gregoire Webber, eds.).

50 Ibid. (emphasis supplied).

a rights-infringement is proper.[51] Schauer's rights-as-shields understates the frequency of rights-infringements, mischaracterizes rights' operation in its assumption that rights wholly exclude non-rights considerations in the usual case, and impliedly bemoans rights infringements insofar as a shield's failure is never an occasion for celebration.[52] It also is not clear *why* rights should operate as shields rather than absolute trumps. As to Schauer's second metaphor, it is not evident why the presence of a right should *devalue* a sub-constitutional consideration. And as a descriptive matter, it does not appear that rights have this effect.[53]

I have proposed an alternative master metaphor that holds out the promise of escaping these inadequacies. In providing a superior conceptual framework for understanding why rights are non-absolute, it also helps identify the roles that various societal institutions (including legislatures) should play as each country determines what its constitutional rights entail. And it is this: rights are best understood as markers of the cornerstone constitutive values (or, interchangeably, commitments) that constitute a country's political culture, and that must be accepted as such by members of the political community.[54] This approach – what might be called *rights-as-values* – makes decision-making concerning constitutional rights a part of normative reasoning. Accordingly, philosophy's insights regarding normative reasoning carry over to decision-making concerning constitutional rights.[55] Rights-as-values also treats constitutional decision-making as a component of the production of culture.[56]

Connecting rights decision-making to philosophy and culture yields substantial insights into constitutionalism. To accurately describe a culture, it is not sufficient to simply account for the foundational values to which its members are committed. Among other things, it also is necessary to consider how those values are *harmonized* when they come into conflict.[57] The variable of harmonization provides resources for appreciating why polities whose constitutions embrace the same rights can still be enormously different. For example, though both Germany and the United States identify speech as a constitutional right, US constitutional culture permits speech to be overridden by countervailing interests far less frequently than does Germany.[58] The philosophical literature's

51 See Rosen, "The Sufficiency Question," n. 18, at 1582–87. Because optimization is inextricably interwoven with Alexy's conception of principle, see ibid. at 1579, a critique of optimization amounts to a critique of Alexy's rights-as-principles.

52 See ibid. at 1574.

53 See ibid. at 1575.

54 See ibid. at 1587–92.

55 This is not unique to my approach, for Alexy's and Schauer's accounts likewise connect constitutional decision-making to philosophy.

56 See ibid. at 1588–89.

57 Elsewhere I have provided a more robust model of culture than what I sketch here. See Mark D. Rosen, "Beyond Interpretation: The 'Cultural Approach' to Understanding Extra-Formal Change in Religious and Constitutional Law," 2 *J. Law, Religion & State* 200 (2013).

58 See Rosen, "Two Conceptualizations," n. 33, at 141–42.

analysis of incommensurability deepens our understanding of this phenomenon. Speech and its countervailing interests are incommensurable goods, insofar as no single metric fully captures each good's normative contents such that tradeoffs can be identified that are inter-subjectively binding on all people by virtue of rationality. Instead, just as an individual's choices among her conflicting incommensurable values both reflect (looking backward in time) and determine (looking forward in time) her character,[59] so too a polity's harmonization of its competing incommensurable constitutional commitments simultaneously reflects, and helps to determine, its foundational political character. As even a cursory comparison of German and US constitutionalism demonstrates, different harmonizations of the same constitutional rights reflect, and help constitute, meaningfully different constitutional cultures.

Now consider how rights-as-values stacks up against its three competitor master metaphors. Harmonizing competing incommensurable commitments is a more subjective, identity-determining process than is the objective-sounding process of "optimization" that Alexy describes. There likewise are substantial differences between rights-as-values and Professor Schauer's rights-as-shields and rights-as-devaluers. According to rights-as-values, the presence of a right does not devalue countervailing sub-constitutional interests. Those remain as pressing as ever. Nor do rights somehow exclude sub-constitutional interests for so long as the right is not overridden, as right-as-shields suggests. Although sub-constitutional interests neither disappear nor are devalued, they ordinarily are overridden by the values that are marked out by rights by virtue of their being foundational values. But not always: rights-as-values recognizes that the values marked by rights sometimes will *not* prevail against sub-constitutional interests.

By situating constitutional decision-making in philosophy, rights-as-values has conceptual resources for explaining why rights do not always prevail against sub-constitutional interests. Our normative universe is complex, comprising multiple commitments that are not reducible to a single value. Those multiple distinctive commitments sometimes can come into conflict with one another. And the normative intensity of a given commitment typically is dependent on the particular facts of a given circumstance, such that even modest factual changes may result in dramatic modulations of the value's normative intensity.[60] As result of these characteristics of values, a decisional rubric that resolved conflicts by

59 See Elijah Millgram, "Incommensurability and Practical Reasoning," in R. Chang (ed.), *Incommensurability, Incomparability, and Practical Reason*. Harvard: Harvard University Press, 1997, 151–69 (focusing on individual decision making under circumstances of incommensurability); Joseph Raz, "Incommensurabilty and Agency," in *Incommensurability*, 110–28 (arguing that choice, not rationality, governs the selection among incommensurables); Charles Taylor, "Leading a Life," in *Incommensurability*, 170–83 (arguing that justified choice among incomparables can be made by analyzing how the competing goods fit within the "shape" of a person's life).

60 See Alexy, n. 45, at 50; Rosen, "The Sufficiency Question," n. 18, at 1583 (discussing this).

ordinally ranking multiple commitments could not be relied upon to generate normatively proper outcomes.[61]

These considerations both explain why rights should not always prevail over sub-constitutional interests, and provide additional reasons to resist the metaphor of rights-as-shields. A shield's failure is a misfortune. But if circumstances are such that the values marked by a constitutional right are overwhelmed by sub-constitutional interests, then allowing those sub-constitutional interests to prevail is normatively proper rather than an occasion for regret.[62] Nor does a right-infringement constitute a reason for fortifying the right so the shield does not fail again in the future. So long as the right-infringement was preceded by appropriate due care and consideration, the infringement can be the normatively appropriate outcome in the circumstance at hand.

In connecting constitutionalism to culture, rights-as-values carries other clarificatory benefits. Religious cultures like Catholicism and Islam embrace the value of peace, but they are committed to other values (for instance proselytizing, land acquisition, and theocratic autonomy) that can come into conflict with peace. Catholicism's first-order values did not change from pre-Constantine times to the Crusader and Inquisition eras. Shifts in how its values were harmonized (particularly peace and proselytization) account for meaningful cultural changes between the two eras that allowed increasing amounts of bloodshed. Likewise, although the contract clause remains a constitutional value, twentieth-century US jurisprudence permitted far more countervailing considerations to prevail over it than nineteenth-century jurisprudence did.[63]

As these examples show, shifts in harmonization can result in substantial cultural change.[64] Such shifts are a mechanism for cultural adaptation and development that neither adds to nor subtracts from the values identified by a particular culture's authoritative enumerator of values.[65] Because of this, cultural change from harmonization-shifts can be difficult to spot. Indeed, harmonization-shifting's tendency to cloak cultural adaptation and development likely accounts for the heavy lifting it plays, for cultures typically emphasize continuity with the past and downplay change.[66]

61 See Rosen, "The Sufficiency Question," n. 18, at 1543–53 (demonstrating this through a detailed critique of Dworkin's rights-as-trumps). Ordinally ranking our normative commitments would yield superior results if the ranking reduced decisional and error costs. But that is an ultimately empirical question, and as such it cannot justify an a priori rejection of the practice of all liberal constitutional polities of eschewing ordinal rankings and permitting sub-constitutional interests to sometimes override constitutional ones.

62 This is not inconsistent with recognizing that resolving a dilemma exacts a genuine cost to the superseded commitment. See Rosen, "The Sufficiency Question," n. 18, at 1555–57.

63 See Rosen, "Cultural Approach," n. 57, at 215–16.

64 See ibid. at 222–28.

65 See ibid.

66 See ibid.

V. THE LEGISLATURE'S ROLE IN DETERMINING HOW A POLITY HARMONIZES ITS CONSTITUTIONAL RIGHTS WITH ITS OTHER COMMITMENTS

The previous section's analysis has important implications for legislatures. Politics' usual rules-of-engagement permit a virtually undisciplined, no-holds-barred *Hardball Politics*. Apart from restrictions on bribery, a legislator's decision-making is subject to no constraints beyond her accountability to constituents. A legislator is free to pursue so-called special interest legislation that gives windfall benefits to a subset of the population, and that in the process generates out-and-out political losers. The previous section's analysis provides three grounds for concluding that these norms of Hardball Politics that govern most legislative decision-making should not apply when legislatures make decisions regarding constitutional rights. Instead, a legislature's constitutional decision-making should be taken under some *Special Norms*.[67]

First, Hardball Politics in decision-making concerning constitutional rights risks demoting those rights to mere interests, activating the above-identified contingent critiques of non-absolutism.[68] To be sure, legislative decision-making under Hardball Politics would not automatically vindicate the critiques insofar as other institutions (notably courts) could intervene to rescue imperiled constitutional rights. But exclusive reliance on (say) courts is surely a second-best outcome. Judicial review might not be capable of fully protecting constitutional rights.[69] And the danger that constitutional rights could be mistakenly treated as mere policy interests is best combatted if all governmental actors avoid the error. For these reasons, legislators' decision-making regarding constitutional rights should not be taken under the norms of Hardball Politics, but instead should be made pursuant to some Special Norms.

Second, although the values marked by a constitutional right need not be given absolute effect for rights to perform constitutional work,[70] the decision as to how the fundamental values marked by a right are to be harmonized with

67 See Rosen, "Special Norms Thesis," n. 16, at 20–37.

68 See text accompanying nn. 40–42.

69 There are many readily imagined reasons why this might be so. Jurisdictional limitations might keep some matters from coming to courts. See, e.g., *Baker* v. *Carr*, 369 U.S. 186 (1962) (discussing the political question doctrine). Or judges may be reluctant to strike down legislation due to a concern that that doing so might undermine the judiciary's legitimacy. (This may explain Chief Justice Roberts' surprisingly aggressive savings construction to uphold the Affordable Care Act. See *National Federation of Independent Business* v. *Sibelius*, 132 S. Ct. 2566, 2593–97 (2012).) More generally, legislatures may have unique institutional capacities that play a necessary role in the multi-institutional process by which a polity renders its constitutional judgments. Cf. See generally *Lawrence G. Sager, Justice in Plainclothes*; Mark D. Rosen, "Congress's Primary Role in Determining What Full Faith and Credit Requires: An Additional Argument," *Cal. W. Int'l L. J.*, 41: 7, 8–9 (2010).

70 And indeed, they typically *should not* be given absolute effect, on account of the fact that our normative universe comprises multiple distinct values.

competing considerations must be made with due care and consideration if normatively proper outcomes are to reliably obtain. The norms of Hardball Politics are not conducive to such due care and consideration. To the contrary, Hardball Politics is inimical to that due care and consideration. Accordingly, when legislatures decide how constitutional rights are to be harmonized with competing considerations, those decisions should be rendered pursuant to Special Norms that trigger the due care and consideration that is appropriate for constitutional decision-making.

Third, determining how a political culture's fundamental values are to be harmonized with competing considerations – whether they be of constitutional or subconstitutional dimension – is a crucial step in constructing the political culture's fundamental identity. Decisions that construct a polity's core identity are not properly taken pursuant to Hardball Politics because a democratic polity's core identity should, to the extent possible, come from the people, not be forced upon it by a mere political majority. How the values marked by rights should be harmonized with competing considerations should be made pursuant to Special Norms that are conducive to democratic constitutionalism.[71]

VI. THE SPECIAL NORMS THAT SHOULD DISCIPLINE CONSTITUTIONAL DECISION-MAKING

But just what are those Special Norms? As is true of other behavioral norms, the Special Norms' details are best worked out incrementally, over time, by the parties they govern.[72] Even so, I have tried to provisionally flesh out the Special Norms that should apply to legislators.[73] Although the arguments as to why Special Norms should apply to constitutional decision-making[74] apply to all liberal democracies,

[71] Legislators' constitutional decision-making is not confined to determining how rights should be harmonized with competing considerations. Elsewhere I have provided a comprehensive taxonomy of legislative constitutional decision-making and have explained why Special Norms also appropriately govern those other domains of constitutional decision-making. See Rosen, "Special Norms Thesis," n. 16, at 8–14. The core of that argument is that clarity as to what a legislature's constitutional decision-making consists in, which is a function of what constitutions are and the purposes they serve in a modern constitutional democracy, leads to the conclusion that legislators should be subject to Special Norms when they render decisions that belong to the constitutional domain. See Rosen, "Special Norms Thesis," n. 67, at 21–36.

[72] See ibid. at 16–19; 37. The Special Norms developed in that earlier work and applied below are designed for legislators. Although Special Norms appropriately apply as well to the constitutional decision-making of other governmental institutions, the contents of the Special Norms that apply to executives and courts undoubtedly will vary on account of each's unique institutional characteristics. See, e.g., nn. 79 and 81.

[73] What guides their elucidation is the idea that the existence of Special Norms for constitutional decision-making is implicit in the widely shared understanding of what a constitution is, and the work it performs, in a large, heterogeneous modern democracy. See ibid. at 38–57.

[74] As explained in section V, and at greater length in another work, see Rosen, "Special Norms Thesis," n. 67.

the Special Norms' specific contents may vary across those countries.[75] The details of the Special Norms presented below were developed with the United States in mind, and may not carry over to every other liberal democracy. My claim is more modest: that *some* Special Norms, in contradistinction to the norms of Hardball Politics that govern ordinary politics, appropriately apply to the constitutional decision-making of all liberal democracies.

Some additional clarifications are necessary before showing how the Special Norms should affect a legislator's approach to pension reform. I am playing the role of a norm-entrepreneur who advocates that some norm be recognized and accepted as binding.[76] I do not claim that the Special Norms are presently binding on legislators such that the failure to abide by them is an abdication of a present duty, because the Special Norms have neither been incorporated in positive law, nor have they been generally accepted or complied with. My claim is that the best understanding of constitutional practice in contemporary democracies presupposes that some Special Norms should apply to constitutional decision-making, and that the proposition that constitutional decisions should be taken pursuant to some Special Norms should be accepted for that reason. The three Special Norms identified below are deduced from the very considerations that justify the need for Special Norms in the first place.

Finally, as will become clear from their contents, the three Special Norms apply only to legislators. This means that the Special Norms are fully independent of whatever legal doctrines a country's courts use to adjudicate the constitutionality of their legislature's handiwork.[77] Whereas the legal doctrines used by a court are among the most important determinants of the judiciary's role in determining what a country's constitution allows or demands, the Special Norms are crucial determinants that set the legislature's role in constitutional decision-making. The three Special Norms thus supplement, but do not displace, the courts' legal doctrines. The Special Norms applicable to legislatures, along with the legal doctrines deployed by courts, are components of the full matrix of governmental decisionmakers and decision-making that ultimately determines what a country's constitution allows and demands.[78]

75 This is primarily true because one of the considerations accounting the Special Norms' contents is the nature of the political fraternity that a country aims to establish, and there is a range of possibilities among which a liberal democracy might select. See Rosen, "Special Norms Thesis," n. 67, at 31–33, 37.

76 See Cass R. Sunstein, "Social Norms and Social Roles," 96 *Colum. L. Rev* 903 (1996) (introducing the term "norm entrepreneur").

77 With one caveat. See n. 91.

78 There are other institutional actors, beyond courts and legislatures, that participate in constitutional decision-making in the United States. These include the federal executive branch, states, and the people themselves.

The Special Norms include the norm of *Proactivity*, which imposes a duty for legislatures to act in certain circumstances,[79] and the norm of *Explicitness*, which presumptively requires that legislatures explicitly consider constitutional issues when they arise.[80] These two norms' application to pension reform is straightforward. Where a state's unfunded pension obligations are so massive that they threaten the state's capacities to deliver basic services to its citizens, the norm of Proactivity demands action. And the norm of Explicitness requires the legislature to take account of the constitutional implications of the measures they consider.

The third Special Norm is the most important for present purposes. Legislators' constitutional decision-making should be undertaken pursuant to the norm of *Tempered Politics* instead of Hardball Politics. Tempered Politics comprises a cluster of attitudinal, behavioral, and substantive guidelines that encourage persuasion and compromise in service of finding consensus, in contrast to the brute majoritarianism that Hardball Politics allows.[81] And where consensus is not possible, Tempered Politics imposes substantive restrictions on the majority's decision-making that are designed to generate responsible, constitution-worthy action.

Tempered Politics consists of two sub-norms. The first, *Reciprocity*, is an internal self-disciplining constraint on the substantive constitutional positions each side is permitted to adopt.[82] When engaging in constitutional decision-making, a legislator can only espouse positions she "think[s] it at least reasonable for others to accept, as free and equal citizens, and not as dominated or manipulated, or under the pressure of an inferior political or social position."[83] Reciprocity requires two things. First, she must make two *imaginative leaps*, putting herself into the shoes of her political opponents and then imagining herself on the losing side of her proposal.[84] Second, the constitutional decisionmaker must think *holistically* rather than narrowly.[85] When asking herself whether it is "at least reasonable" to expect her opponent could accept her substantive constitutional position, she must consider her position's implications for related contexts, not just the narrowest possible articulation of the question.[86]

79 In the domain of ordinary politics, legislatures are masters of their agenda. But such unfettered freedom does not carry over to the constitutional domain, where the Norm of Proactivity can impose a duty on a legislature to act. See ibid. at 38–39. The Norm of Proactivity may not apply to courts, which must wait for lawsuits to be filed.

80 The Norm of Explicitness is defeasible where a legislature is incapable of responsibly rendering a particular constitutional decision, or if directly confronting the constitutional question would be inconsistent with a specific institutional need or responsibility. See ibid. at 41–44.

81 Ibid. at 44–53. The Norm of Tempered *Politics* likely would not carry over to courts.

82 See ibid. at 45–49 (discussing Reciprocity's requirements); ibid. at 53–57 (explaining why the Special Norms include Reciprocity).

83 Ibid. at 45–46 (quoting John Rawls, The Law of Peoples, With "The Idea of Public Reason Revisited" 136–37) (1999).

84 See Rosen, "Special Norms Thesis," n. 67, at 47.

85 See ibid. at 48–49.

86 See ibid. at 48.

Reciprocity is a substantial disciplining norm, but on its own cannot satisfy Tempered Politics. This is because even if the majority self-polices by conforming to Reciprocity, a majority's unilateral Reciprocity-compliant decision-making in the constitutional domain is incompatible with what a constitutional democracy requires. Although compliance Reciprocity may guarantee an enlightened constitutional position, unilateral decision-making is a form of political brute force. Tempered Politics' second sub-norm, *Communicative Exchange*, supplements Reciprocity's unilateralism by requiring pre-enactment interaction among the opposing sides that allows a meaningful chance of reaching consensual constitutional decisions by some combination of mutual persuasion and compromise.[87] The sub-norm of Communicative Exchange thus disallows unilateral decision-making in constitutional matters, even if the politically dominant side's position is Reciprocity-compliant.

More specifically, the sub-norm of Communicative Exchange imposes a duty on all disputants to aim to "work out in community what to do" by communicating with each other.[88] Communicative Exchange requires that each side try to influence how the other thinks,[89] while also being open to being influenced. Tempered Politics' sub-norm of Communicative Exchange requires that all sides make a genuine effort to achieve consensus through some combination of persuasion and compromise. Communicative Exchange thereby provides political minorities additional negotiation leverage beyond what they have in the domain of ordinary politics.[90]

The norms of Proactivity, Explicitness, and Tempered Politics respond to the three reasons advanced in section V as to why Hardball Politics should not govern decision-making concerning constitutional rights. First, applying the Special Norms when constitutional rights are at stake ensures that rights are not relegated to the level of mere interests. Second, the Special Norms encourage and facilitate the due care and concern that are necessary to reliably obtain normatively proper harmonizations of a right's fundamental values with competing considerations. Third, the Special Norms help ensure that the harmonization decisions that construct a polity's core identity come from the people themselves to the extent possible, rather than from a mere political majority, as democratic constitutionalism requires.

To put it another way, the Special Norms aim to structure a legislature's constitutional decision-making so as to increase the chances of responsible, constitution-

[87] Cf. Coral Davenport, "A Climate Deal 6 Fateful Years in the Making," *The New York Times* (December 14, 2015) (claiming that an important factor leading to agreement among the 195 nations was that the French convention hosts "made sure that each country, regardless of its size or wealth, felt its voice would be heard").

[88] See Rosen, "Special Norms Thesis," n. 67, at 50 (quoting Allan Gibbard, *Wise Choices, Apt Feelings* 72 (1990)).

[89] By eliciting this information, Communicative Exchange might aid the imaginative leaps that Reciprocity requires. See Rosen, "Special Norms Thesis," n. 67, at 48–52.

[90] See Rosen, "Special Norms Thesis," n. 67, at 50. One side's non-compliance with the Special Norms suspends the norm of Communicative Exchange, but not Reciprocity. See ibid. at 69–70.

worthy action. More than this, the Special Norms – especially Tempered Politics' sub-norm of Communicative Exchange – harness legislatures' special institutional capacities that account for the value they can, and should, add to the multi-institutional process that makes a polity's constitutional judgments. Although the Special Norms typically do not generate a unique solution to constitutional questions, they eliminate many options that otherwise would be fair game under Hardball Politics. And because the Special Norms address the legislature's constitutional decision-making, the norms are independent of the particular doctrinal test a country's courts use to a law's constitutionality.[91]

VII. THE SPECIAL NORMS IN ACTION: THE PENSION CRISIS

We are now in a position to address the question with which this chapter began: how should constitutional constraints such as the pension and contract clauses, which by their literal terms provide absolute constitutional protections against impairing contractual obligations like pensions, affect what a legislator should do during a severe financial crisis? The answer is that legislators cannot ignore constitutional constraints on the view that constitutional interpretation is the sole responsibility of courts. But nor must they always give literal effect to the constitutional language. Although some constitutional language "means what it says," much does not. Constitutional rights fall into the second category, and indeed longstanding US Supreme Court precedent has held that the contract clause's absolute language does not prevent legislatures from impairing contractual obligations in appropriate circumstances. The pension clauses found in many state constitutions (including Illinois') are modeled on the contract clause. This helps explain why state courts have relied on the US Supreme Court's contract clause jurisprudence when construing their constitutions' pension clauses.[92]

That the contract and pension clauses' unqualified language need not be given absolute effect does not grant legislators unfettered license to diminish pension benefits. Pension benefits are constitutionally protected, even if those protections are not absolute. As such, pension benefits can never be treated as a mere policy interest that is subject to the whims and vagaries of ordinary majoritarian politics. For example, while a legislator might oppose public unions as a matter of policy and for that reason aim to undermine them in the domain of ordinary politics,[93] diminishing pension benefits as part of such a plan would be wrongful. The fact that pension benefits are constitutionally protected means that all legislators must

[91] With one important caveat. In many countries, courts review the constitutionality of legislation with doctrinal tests that in effect determine to what extent the court defers to the legislature's judgment. A legislature's compliance with the Special Norms may enhance the deference-worthiness of the legislature's constitutional decision-making, justifiably leading a court to adopt a more deferential doctrinal test.

[92] See, e.g., *Felt* v. *Board of Trustees of Judges Retirement System*, 107 Ill. 2d 158, 165–66 (1985).

[93] Governor Scott Walker of Wisconsin has famously sought to weaken public unions.

accept that protecting pensions against diminution is a foundational commitment that only can be overcome by sufficiently important reasons (the ends), and even then, only if any impairment is made in a sufficiently careful way (the means). In determining what reasons are sufficiently important, and what satisfies sufficient care, legislators must comply with the Special Norms.

To illustrate, think again of a legislator who wanted to dismantle public unions. Might he justify eliminating past pension benefits on the ground that eliminating public unions is a sufficiently important end? No, because such a position is not Reciprocity-compliant. It cannot plausibly be proposed that those who support public unions could reasonably be expected to accept the position that pension benefits should be reduced so as to undermine unions. Though Reciprocity makes no such demands on a legislator in the domain of ordinary politics, Reciprocity limits the grounds that can justify infringing a constitutional right. This illustrates the substantial work constitutional rights can perform despite their not being absolute.

So how would constitutional constraints appropriately inform how a legislator might address a fiscal emergency like the pension crisis? The Special Norms apply to the legislature's consideration of both the ends and means it is considering. As to the former, the constitutional right to undiminished pension rights can be impaired only if there are (a) sufficiently important countervailing interests that are (b) Reciprocity-complaint. These determinations turn both on the legislator's value judgment of how important a competing commitment is, and on the fact-based assessment of to what extent the competing commitment is put at risk by giving full effect to (i.e., not impairing) the constitutional commitment. Reciprocity does not require that the legislator's opponents *in fact* agree with these two assessments; Reciprocity is not a unanimity requirement.[94] But Reciprocity *does* demand that the legislator's position be such that it would be reasonable to propose that her opponent, taken as he is, might accept those assessments.

The pension crisis gives rise to two types of commitments that run up against the pension and contracts clauses. First, the crisis potentially imperils some of the state's other constitutional commitments, such as its responsibilities regarding public education.[95] Second, the pension crisis threatens many non-constitutional interests, for example maintaining the state's financial viability so that it can borrow money and provide adequate health care, human services, and public safety.[96] Tempered Politics requires a legislator to make a good faith judgment as to whether she believes that these countervailing commitments are of sufficient importance to justify a right-infringement, and if so to then decide whether that judgment satisfies Reciprocity. It falls within the legislator's prerogative to render these two judgments, but it seems fair to say that a legislator plausibly could answer "yes" to both.

94 See Rosen, "Special Norms Thesis," n. 67, at 45 and fn. 178.

95 See text accompanying n. 34.

96 See text accompanying nn. 11–14.

The final component to Reciprocity is the fact-based determination of whether giving full effect to the pension and contract clauses would unduly threaten the above-described sufficiently important countervailing commitments. Answering this does not require unanimity among experts. But it does demand genuinely powerful substantiation as to which it would be at least reasonable for her opponents to accept, even if they in fact did not. Reports from respected economists that a state or local government's unfunded pension liabilities are too massive to address solely by raising taxes and cutting governmental services should suffice. There is no such need for experts in the domain of ordinary politics, where legislators are free to move forward with innovative legislation based only on their intuitions and predilections.

Tempered Politics' disciplining role does not end once a legislator decides there are sufficiently important Reciprocity-complaint reasons to infringe pension rights. The legislative specifics of how and to what extent those rights are infringed, and of what other changes are to be made to the pension system, also must be taken pursuant to Tempered Politics. Because the positions a legislator takes on these details must comply with Reciprocity, Tempered Politics disallows legislation that would create wholesale political losers – yet another way that Tempered Politics differs from the Hardball Politics that is permissible during ordinary politics.

More than this, Tempered Politics' sub-norm of Communicative Exchange forecloses unilateralism. It requires that the legislator engage with her opponents when sculpting legislation that would infringe pension rights. The legislator (as well as her opponent) must be open to being influenced, and also must aim to influence the other. Communicative Exchange also requires that they all make a good-faith attempt to arrive at consensus through some combination of persuasion and compromise.[97] If consensus is not possible, Tempered Politics permits the political majority to go forward with legislation that infringes pension rights, but only if the legislation's substantive terms are Reciprocity-compliant.[98]

VIII. STRUCTURAL CONSTITUTIONAL PROVISIONS

Although constitutional rights typically do not "mean what they say" – they are not absolute even when they do not contain any qualifications or caveats – such non-

97 In other work I have explored how the duties under the Special Norms shift if the other side does not comply. As explained there, the other side's non-compliance waives the sub-norm of Communicative Exchange, though not Reciprocity. See Rosen, "Special Norms Thesis," n. 67, at 69–70.

98 Consistent with this, Illinois enacted comprehensive pension reform legislation that widely spreading costs by adopting stricter funding requirements for the state, which affected all taxpayers, and reducing future cost-of-living adjustments for members of the retirement systems, which affected state employees. See Ill. Public Act 98-599, §§1, 15. The Illinois Supreme Court struck down the statute as unconstitutional. See *Re Pension Reform Litigation*, 32 N.E. 3d 1 (2015). The court reaffirmed that "While impairment of a contract may survive scrutiny under the contracts clause if reasonable and necessary to serve an important public purpose," but found that "the State did not select the least drastic means of addressing its financial difficulties." Ibid. at 21–22. This chapter is not the place to explore the propriety of the Illinois Supreme Court's means analysis.

literalism does not carry over to all constitutional language.[99] Consider the "structural" language that specifies the details of the process for generating legislation. The United States constitution provides that vetoed bills become law only if "two third of [each] House shall agree to pass the Bill."[100] It has never been doubted that "two third" literally means two-thirds.

This difference between the constitutional language of structural provisions and rights may have implications in respect of constitution-drafting. Drafters who wished to foreclose legislative action in a certain realm might consider specifying higher-than-usual decision rules for that domain – for instance requiring a supermajority, or even unanimity. To illustrate, instead of protecting the domain by designating a (probably non-absolute) right, drafters might insert constitutional language that permitted infringement of pension rights only if "each member of both Houses shall agree to pass such a Bill." Variegated decisional rules for different sorts of governmental action is not unheard of. Under the US constitution, for example, legislation requires majority rule,[101] treaties require two-thirds of Senators present,[102] and amendments need two-thirds of both houses.[103] In practice, it is much more difficult to ratify treaties and amendments than to enact legislation. This suggests that constitution-drafters may be able to secure greater protections for a given domain by relying on structural language instead of rights-creating language.

Perhaps. But drafters should keep two things in mind. The first is normative: they should think very carefully as to whether they really would want to so super-securely protect a given domain. The very reasons identified earlier that explain why constitutional rights typically are not absolute counsel against giving absolute protection to a select domain by means of artful structural language. The domain may be important indeed, but might there be unforeseen circumstances, or an array of countervailing considerations, that would render absolute protection normatively problematic?

Second, it is unclear to what degree the structural alternative to rights would achieve the drafters' goals. The contract and pension clauses nicely illustrate the point. As written, those clauses do not generate rights, but instead are structural in nature insofar as the constitutional language flatly prohibits legislation that impairs the obligation of contracts or diminishes pension benefits. Yet longstanding judicial precedent treats both clauses as if they were non-absolute.[104]

Would differently drafted constitutional language have brought about a different result? What would have happened, for example, if the constitution had provided

99 See Strauss, n. 17.

100 US Const. Art. I., §7, cl. 2.

101 Though this is not explicitly required. See US Const. Art. I., §7, cl. 2 (specifying only that a bill "pass . . . the House of Representatives and the Senate").

102 See US Const. Art. II., §2, cl. 2.

103 See US Const. Art. V.

104 See text accompanying nn. 21–31 (contract clause); see text accompanying nn. 92 and 98 (pension clause).

a super-majority rule of three quarters or more of legislators in both legislative houses for any law that would impair the obligation of contracts? We cannot be certain, but there is reason to be skeptical. A two-track system that made it more difficult, or practically impossible, to enact certain legislation would put pressure on legislators to game the system so as to avoid the more burdensome track. And this indeed appears to have occurred with treaties and constitutional amendments. On account of the difficulty of obtaining the requisite two-third of senatorial support, the United States formalizes most international obligations today through so-called congressional agreements (i.e., legislation) and executive agreements (commitments made only by the President), not treaties.[105] And because Article V's supermajority requirements for constitutional amendment are so difficult to satisfy, constitutional change in the United States has proceeded almost entirely via an array of "informal" amendments.[106]

No one can deny the descriptive fact that these workarounds have developed. The normative question of whether such workarounds are to be bemoaned or praised is another matter. The arguments this chapter considered as to why constitutional rights are non-absolute are relevant to structural constitutional provisions as well. The implication of those arguments is not that structural language should never be given literal effect, but that not all structural language should be given literal effect.

105 See Bruce Ackerman and David Golove, "Is NAFTA Constitutional?," *Harv. L. Rev.* 108: 799 (1995); Bradford R. Clark, "Domesticating Sole Executive Agreements," *Va. L. Rev* 93: 1573 (2007).

106 See Sanford Levinson, "Our Undemocratic Constitution: Where the Constitution Goes Wrong (And How We the People Can Correct It)," 159–66.

11

Courts and Crises

6

The Place of Economic Crisis in American Constitutional Law

The Great Depression as a Case Study

Barry Cushman

The American constitutional law of political economy underwent significant transformations in the years between the Wall Street Crash of 1929 and the Allied victory in World War II. Both state and federal power to regulate economic activity were enhanced substantially. The reasons for these developments have been explored at length in a voluminous literature.[1] This chapter considers the role that conditions of economic crisis might have played in cases involving judicial review of economic regulation.

From March 1932 to June 1937, the Supreme Court of the United States consisted of nine justices: Chief Justice Charles Evans Hughes, and Associate Justices Willis Van Devanter, James Clark McReynolds, Louis D. Brandeis, George Sutherland, Pierce Butler, Harlan Fiske Stone, Owen J. Roberts, and Benjamin N. Cardozo. Several decisions upholding or invalidating challenged regulatory legislation during this period were unanimous or near-unanimous, but where the Court was closely divided, it was typically the case that Van Devanter, McReynolds, Sutherland, and Butler voted to invalidate, that Brandeis, Stone, and Cardozo voted to uphold, and that Hughes and/or Roberts cast the deciding vote. Before 1937, Hughes and Roberts voted more often to invalidate than they would in 1937 and thereafter, and the literature on the Hughes Court has sought to explain this change.

The change is sometimes explained by reference to the effect of underlying economic conditions on judicial attitudes. For example, as one scholar has put it, "the tragedy of the Great Depression may have affected the attitudes of Hughes Court justices" toward "economically activist federal and state governments."[2] Such explanations appear to suffer from serious difficulties. First, the conditions of the Great Depression were of long standing and abundantly evident by 1935 and 1936, when the Court struck down a good deal of

[1] Barry Cushman, "The Jurisprudence of the Hughes Court: The Recent Literature." *Notre Dame Law Review* 89 (2014), 1929–2028.

[2] William Ross, *The Chief Justiceship of Charles Evans Hughes, 1930–1941* (Columbia: University of South Carolina Press, 2007), 247.

state and federal regulatory legislation. It strains credulity to think that the economic conditions that inspired that legislation and were grasped by the legislators who enacted it, the executives who signed it, and the people who elected these officials, somehow escaped the attention of the justices until nearly eight years into the economic crisis. They certainly were aware of the state of the American economy; and if that was so, and if an appreciation of economic conditions was what animated the behavior of the justices, then it is puzzling that they did not uniformly or at least more frequently uphold regulatory legislation throughout their tenures.

To see the point, consider the difficulties in accounting for the voting behavior of the justices on such a hypothesis. In 1934, a 5–4 Court upheld Minnesota's statute protecting distressed mortgage debtors from foreclosure.[3] In 1935, a unanimous Court invalidated a federal statute providing such protection to farm mortgagors.[4] Congress quickly revised that statute to meet the constitutional objections that had been sustained by the Court,[5] and in 1937, the justices unanimously upheld the revised farm debt relief act.[6] It does not seem likely that a Court majority recognized the need for mortgage moratorium relief in 1934, that all of the justices then failed to appreciate the need for farm debt relief in 1935, but that every one of the justices then suddenly awakened to that need in 1937. Similarly, in 1936, Hughes and Roberts were members of a 6–3 majority that invalidated the Agricultural Adjustment Act of 1933 (AAA), which had endeavored to raise agricultural prices by paying farmers to reduce production of specified commodities.[7] In 1939, however, they voted to uphold a revised AAA grounded in the commerce power.[8] It beggars belief that they could have failed in 1936 to recognize the circumstances of farmers who had been struggling economically for nearly two decades, but then came to grasp them only three years later. Or consider two pairs of decisions involving regulation of the energy sector. In early 1935 every justice except Cardozo joined in the opinion striking down a provision of the National Industrial Recovery Act (NIRA) granting the president broad discretion to prohibit interstate shipments of oil produced in excess of the amount permitted under the law of its state of origin ("hot oil").[9] Here again Congress quickly revised the statute to meet the Court's objections,[10] and in 1939 all of the remaining justices from the earlier case joined the Court's unanimous opinion sustaining the act.[11] Likewise, in 1936 Roberts joined a majority striking

3 *Home Bldg. & Loan Assn.* v. *Blaisdell*, 290 U.S. 398 (1934).

4 *Louisville Joint Stock Land Bank* v. *Radford*, 295 U.S. 555 (1935).

5 Barry Cushman, "The Hughes Court and Constitutional Consultation." *Journal of Supreme Court History* 23-1 (1998a), 81-82.

6 *Wright* v. *Vinton Branch Bank*, 300 U.S. 440 (1937).

7 *United States* v. *Butler*, 297 U.S. 1 (1936).

8 *Mulford* v. *Smith*, 307 U.S. 38 (1939).

9 *Panama Refining Co.* v. *Ryan*, 293 U.S. 388 (1935).

10 Barry Cushman, "The Hughes Court and Constitutional Consultation," 85-86.

11 *United States* v. *Powers*, 307 U.S. 214 (1939). The remaining *Panama Refining* alumni were Hughes, McReynolds, Butler, Stone, and Roberts.

down federal legislation regulating the price of coal.[12] In 1940, he joined a majority upholding such legislation.[13] It seems improbable that these justices were blind to the distressed states of the oil and coal industries in 1935 and 1936, but that by 1939 and 1940 they had come to understand these matters. Indeed, Secretary of the Interior Harold Ickes recorded in his diary that he encountered Roberts at a dinner party shortly after the first Hot Oil decision, and that the justice "assured me that he is entirely sympathetic with what we are trying to do in the oil matter and that he hoped that we would pass a statute that would enable us to carry out our policy."[14] Moreover, if Hughes and Roberts did eventually come to understand the compelling need for more state and federal regulatory legislation, then one must explain why they continued to vote to invalidate so much of it even after 1936.[15] It does not appear that the pattern of their behavior is explicable in terms of an increasing appreciation of contemporary economic conditions.

This is not to say, however, that the existence of an economic crisis played no role in the Hughes Court's jurisprudence. Section I of this chapter conducts a more general examination of the possibility that contemporary economic conditions may

12 *Carter* v. *Carter Coal Co.*, 298 U.S. 238 (1936).

13 *Sunshine Anthracite Coal Co.* v. *Adkins*, 310 U.S. 381 (1940).

14 Harold Ickes, *Secret Diary, Vol. I* (New York: Simon & Schuster 1954), 273.

15 See, *e.g.*, *United States* v. *Willow Power Co*, 324 U.S. 499, 511–15 (1945) (Roberts and Stone dissenting from opinion holding that government action reducing the flow of water available to an electrical power plant did not constitute a taking requiring compensation under the Fifth Amendment); *United States* v. *Commodore Park, Inc.*, 324 U.S. 386, 393 (1945) (Roberts dissenting from opinion holding that the Fifth Amendment did not require compensation of riparian landowner whose property was reduced in market value but not invaded by government dredging operation); *Charleston Fed Savings & Loan Association* v. *Alderson*, 324 U.S. 182, 192–93 (1945) (Roberts dissenting from opinion upholding tax assessments against equal protection challenge); *Bowles* v. *Willingham*, 321 U.S. 503, 529 (1944) (Roberts dissenting on non-delegation grounds from decision upholding Emergency Price Control Act of 1942); *Yakus* v. *United States*, 321 U.S. 414, 448 (1944) (Roberts dissenting on non-delegation grounds from decision upholding Emergency Price Control Act of 1942); *Warren-Bradshaw Drilling Co.* v. *Hall*, 317 U.S. 88, 93–95 (1942) (Roberts dissenting from decision upholding application of Fair Labor Standards Act to local workers on ground that they lay beyond the reach of the commerce power); *Kirschbaum* v. *Walling*, 316 U.S. 517 (1942) (Roberts dissenting from decision upholding application of Fair Labor Standards Act to local workers on ground that they lay beyond the reach of the commerce power); *R.R. Comm'n of Tex* v. *Rowan & Nichols Oil Co*, 310 U.S. 573, 577 (1940) (Roberts and Hughes dissenting from opinion holding that oil proration order of Texas Railroad Commission did not deprive the company of its property without due process); *Madden* v. *Kentucky*, 309 U.S. 83, 93–94 (1940) (Roberts dissenting from opinion upholding state tax against equal protection and privileges or immunities challenges); *United States* v. *Rock-Royal Co-op, Inc.*, 307 U.S. 533, 583–87 (1939) (Roberts and Hughes dissenting from opinion upholding against a due process challenge an order issued by the Secretary of Agriculture pursuant to the Agricultural Marketing Agreement Act of 1937); *H.P. Hood & Sons* v. *United States*, 307 U.S. 588, 603 (1939) (Roberts dissenting on non-delegation grounds from opinion upholding Agricultural Marketing Agreement Act of 1937); *Hartford Steam Boiler Inspection & Ins Co* v. *Harrison*, 301 U.S. 459 (1937) (Hughes joining opinion invalidating Georgia statute imposing differing regulations on stock and mutual insurance companies). See also *Thompson* v. *Consolidated Gas Utilities Corp*, 300 U.S. 55 (1937) (Hughes and Roberts join opinion invalidating gas proration order of Texas Railroad Commission on the ground that it deprived the company of its property without due process).

have operated as an exogenous variable inducing the justices to uphold challenged regulations. Section II explores the extent to which underlying economic conditions might have operated as an endogenous variable that was relevant to analysis of whether particular regulatory measures could be supported by existing constitutional doctrine.

I. ECONOMIC CRISIS AS AN EXOGENOUS VARIABLE

The Great Depression offers a promising setting for reflecting on the relationship between economic crisis and American constitutional development, for several reasons. First, the 1930s witnessed the most profound and prolonged economic crisis in American history. Second, legislative activity designed to address one or more features of the crisis was unusually prolific. Third, much of this legislation elicited constitutional challenges in the courts, at a time when constitutional doctrine still imposed significant restraints on state and federal legislative power to regulate the economy. Fourth, many of these challenges came before the Court during a period of more than five years during which there were no changes in its personnel. Because President Roosevelt had no opportunity to appoint a justice during his first term, this secular Court lasted from Justice Benjamin Cardozo's ascension to the bench on March 14, 1932, until Justice Willis Van Devanter's retirement on June 2, 1937. During this period, personnel changes played no role in the pattern of the Court's performance in cases involving judicial review of economic legislation. Finally, there is for this period a wealth of data concerning various economic indicators. Though most of these data are annual, some are more granular. In either case they illuminate both the state and the direction of the economy at particular points in time.

I have selected from the *U.S. Reports* the forty-seven cases from the period in which legislative or executive action addressing some aspect of the economic crisis was challenged on constitutional grounds before the Supreme Court. This set does not include every case in which the constitutionality of some economic regulation was contested. For example, I have not included cases in which the justices upheld a statute limiting the size and weight of vehicles using state highways,[16] or in which they struck down legislation regulating stock and mutual insurance companies differently.[17] Cases were included only if the regulation involved was in some way designed to ameliorate some condition brought about by the economic crisis. The challenged measures, results, and votes in these cases are summarized in the following chronology.

In 1932, the Court decided three relevant cases. In *Champlin Refining Co. v. Corporation Commission of Oklahoma*,[18] decided on May 16, the Court

16 *Sproles* v. *Binford*, 286 U.S. 374 (1932).

17 *Hartford Steam Boiler Inspection & Ins. Co.* v. *Harrison*, 301 U.S. 459 (1937).

18 286 U.S. 210 (1932).

unanimously sustained an Oklahoma statute prohibiting wasteful petroleum production that was driving down oil prices. In *Stephenson* v. *Binford*,[19] decided on December 5, the Court upheld by a vote of 8–1 a regulation issued by the Texas Railroad Commission that sought to protect the state's railroads from destructive competition with private contract carriers by requiring such carriers to charge certain minimum rates for transport. A week later, on December 12, the justices unanimously held in *Sterling* v. *Constantin*[20] that alleged overproduction of oil in Texas had not created an emergency authorizing the governor to declare martial law, seize control of private oil wells by military force, and discontinue their production of oil.

The lone relevant case handed down in 1933 was the 6–3 decision in *Louis K. Liggett Co.* v. *Lee*.[21] Decided on March 13, *Liggett* invalidated a Florida tax that sought to protect small proprietors from competition with chain stores by imposing a heavier privilege tax per store on owners whose stores were located in more than one county than was imposed on owners whose stores were all located in the same county. By contrast, 1934 produced five relevant decisions, only one of which invalidated the challenged statute. On January 8, the Court upheld the Minnesota Mortgage Moratorium law that sought to protect mortgagors from foreclosure by a vote of 5–4 in *Home Bldg. & Loan Assn.* v. *Blaisdell*.[22] On March 5, a 5–4 majority upheld a regulation that aimed to protect dairy farmers from ruinous competition by imposing minimum prices for retail sales of milk in *Nebbia* v. *New York*.[23] On April 2, in *Magnano Co.* v. *Hamilton*,[24] the justices unanimously sustained a Washington State measure designed to protect struggling dairy interests by imposing a state tax on butter substitutes. On May 28, the Court unanimously invalidated an Arkansas statute retroactively exempting the proceeds of life insurance policies from creditors' claims in *W.B. Worthen Co.* v. *Thomas*.[25] And on November 5, the Court unanimously sustained a New York measure prescribing minimum prices in transactions involving milk producers and milk dealers in *Hegeman Farms Corp.* v. *Baldwin*.[26]

In 1935 the Court decided nine sets of cases relevant to our inquiry. On January 7, in *Panama Refining Co.* v. *Ryan*,[27] an 8–1 majority invalidated a provision of the NIRA that granted the president broad discretion to prohibit interstate shipments of hot oil. On February 18, a 5–4 majority upheld the Administration's program to stabilize the nation's monetary system and to re-inflate the currency in the *Gold*

19 287 U.S. 251 (1932).
20 287 U.S. 378 (1932).
21 288 U.S. 517 (1933).
22 290 U.S. 398 (1934).
23 291 U.S. 502 (1934).
24 292 U.S. 40 (1934).
25 292 U.S. 426 (1934).
26 293 U.S. 163 (1934).
27 293 U.S. 388 (1935).

Clause cases.[28] On March 4, in *Baldwin* v. *G.A.F. Seelig*,[29] the Court unanimously invalidated as an unconstitutional burden on interstate commerce a provision of the New York milk law prohibiting the sale of milk imported from another state unless the price paid to the producer in the state of origin was not lower than the minimum price required to be paid to local producers in the destination state. A week later, on March 11, in *Stewart Dry Goods Co.* v. *Lewis*,[30] a 6–3 majority again invalidated a measure aimed at chain stores, this time in the form of a progressive gross sales tax on retail merchants. The justices decided two cases on April 1. In *Doty* v. *Love*,[31] the Court unanimously upheld a Mississippi law providing for the reorganization rather than the liquidation of insolvent banks. In *W.B. Worthen Co.* v. *Kavanaugh*,[32] by contrast, a unanimous Court invalidated an Arkansas statute retroactively diminishing the rights of mortgagees. On May 6, a 5–4 majority struck down a federal statute establishing a pension system for retired railroad employees in *Railroad Retirement Board* v. *Alton Railroad Co.*[33] Finally, on "Black Monday," May 27, the Court decided two cases of particular interest. First, *Louisville Joint Stock Land Bank* v. *Radford*[34] unanimously struck down the federal Emergency Farm Mortgage Act as a violation of the rights of mortgage creditors. And in *Schechter Poultry Corp.* v. *United States*,[35] a unanimous Court invalidated the Live Poultry Code of the NIRA in a manner that effectively declared the entire program unconstitutional. For the year, the federal and state governments could claim three victories – five if the *Gold Clause* cases are counted as three – with six losses.

The Court rendered no further relevant decisions until early 1936. On January 6, in *United States* v. *Butler*,[36] a 6–3 majority struck down the AAA. On February 3, in *Treigle* v. *Acme Homestead Assn.*,[37] the justices unanimously invalidated a Louisiana statute that retroactively diminished the rights of withdrawing members of building and loan associations. The Court decided two more milk regulation cases on February 10. In *Borden's Farm Products Co., Inc.* v. *Ten Eyck*,[38] a 5–4 majority upheld a provision of the New York Milk Control Act allowing milk dealers without well-advertised trade names to sell milk at a price slightly lower than the minimum

[28] *Perry* v. United States, 294 U.S. 330 (1935); *Nortz* v. *United States*, 294 U.S. 317 (1935); *Norman* v. *Baltimore & Ohio Railroad Co.*, 294 U.S. 240 (1935). In *Perry*, as Mitu Gulati and Georg Vanberg discuss in their contribution to this volume, the Court actually invalidated the abrogation of the gold clause in federal Liberty Bonds, but effectively upheld the program by denying the bondholder a remedy under the circumstances.

[29] 294 U.S. 511 (1935).

[30] 294 U.S. 550 (1935).

[31] 295 U.S. 64 (1935).

[32] 295 U.S. 56 (1935).

[33] 295 U.S. 330 (1935).

[34] 295 U.S. 555 (1935).

[35] 295 U.S. 495 (1935).

[36] 297 U.S. 1 (1936).

[37] 297 U.S. 189 (1936).

[38] 297 U.S. 251 (1936).

price permitted for dealers with well-advertised trade names. In *Mayflower Farms, Inc.* v. *Ten Eyck*,[39] by contrast, a 6–3 majority struck down a price regulation provision of the New York statute that effectively excluded new entrants into the local market for milk dealers. On February 17, in *Ashwander* v. *Tennessee Valley Authority*,[40] an 8–1 Court upheld the constitutional authority of the federal agency to construct the Wilson Dam on the Tennessee River and to distribute the electricity generated there. On March 2, in *Whitfield* v. *Ohio*,[41] the Court unanimously upheld two statutes designed to protect manufacturers and their employees from competition with goods manufactured by prisoners in other states. The federal Hawes-Cooper Act authorized states to regulate the sale of convict-made goods shipped in from other states, while an Ohio statute prohibited the sale of such goods within the state. On May 18, in *Carter* v. *Carter Coal Co.*,[42] a divided Court struck down both the price regulation provisions and the labor regulation provisions of the National Bituminous Coal Conservation Act of 1935 ("Guffey Coal Act"). A week later, on May 25, a 5–4 majority invalidated the federal Municipal Bankruptcy Act in *Ashton* v. *Cameron County Water District*.[43] The following week, on June 1, a 5–4 majority concluded the term by striking down New York's law prescribing minimum wages for women in *Morehead* v. *New York ex rel. Tipaldo*.[44]

The Court decided two more relevant cases when it returned that autumn. Owing to illness, Justice Stone did not participate in either of them. In *Valentine* v. *Great Atlantic & Pacific Tea Co.*,[45] decided November 9, a 6–2 Court invalidated an Iowa chain store tax on the authority of *Stewart Dry Goods*. And on November 23, an equally divided Court affirmed a decision of the New York Court of Appeals upholding that state's unemployment compensation statute in *Chamberlin* v. *Andrews*.[46] The tally for the year was four statutes upheld, and seven struck down.

Before Justice Van Devanter's retirement on June 2, 1937, the Court decided thirteen additional relevant sets of cases. On January 4, in *Kentucky Whip & Collar Co.* v. *Illinois Central Railroad Co.*,[47] the justices unanimously sustained the federal Ashurst-Sumners Act, which made it a federal offense to ship convict-made goods into a state where they were intended to be received, sold, possessed, or used in violation of that state's law. On February 1, in *Thompson* v. *Consolidated Gas Utilities Corp.*,[48] the Court unanimously invalidated a gas proration order of the Texas Railroad Commission that was designed to force companies that had

39 297 U.S. 266 (1936).
40 297 U.S. 288 (1936).
41 297 U.S. 431 (1936).
42 298 U.S. 238 (1936).
43 298 U.S. 513 (1936).
44 298 U.S. 587 (1936).
45 299 U.S. 32 (1936).
46 299 U.S. 515 (1936).
47 299 U.S. 334 (1937).
48 300 U.S. 55 (1937).

constructed their own delivery pipelines to purchase gas from others that had not. On March 29, the justices delivered opinions in four relevant cases. In *West Coast Hotel Co.* v. *Parrish*,[49] a 5–4 majority upheld Washington State's minimum wage law for women. *In Virginian Railway Co.* v. *System Federation No. 40*,[50] the justices unanimously upheld the 1934 amendments to the Railway Labor Act, which required carriers to negotiate exclusively and in good faith with the selected representatives of their employees. In *Wright* v. *Vinton Branch Bank*,[51] the Court unanimously sustained a new Emergency Farm Mortgage Act that had been revised to remedy the constitutional deficiencies that the justices had identified two years earlier in *Radford*. And in *Highland Farms Dairy, Inc.*, v. *Agnew*,[52] a 5–4 Court upheld Virginia's regulation of milk markets against a variety of constitutional challenges.

On April 12, in a set of cases collectively known as the *Labor Board* cases, the Court upheld the application of the National Labor Relations Act to five different enterprises. Courts divided by votes of 5–4 upheld its application to a major steel manufacturer in *NLRB* v. *Jones & Laughlin Steel Corp.*;[53] to a mid-sized manufacturer of trailers in *NLRB* v. *Fruehauf Trailer Corp.*;[54] to a small clothing manufacturer in *NLRB* v. *Friedman-Harry Marks Clothing Co.*;[55] and to a major wire service in *NLRB* v. *Associated Press*.[56] In addition, a unanimous Court sustained the Act's application to an interstate bus company in *Washington, Virginia & Maryland Coach Co.* v. *NLRB*.[57] Finally, on May 24, the justices handed down five relevant cases. In *Senn* v. *Tile Layers Protective Union*,[58] a 5–4 Court upheld a state law authorizing union picketing of an employer's home for the purpose of inducing him to cease working as a tile layer on jobs for which he was the contractor. In *Townsend* v. *Yeomans*,[59] a unanimous Court upheld state regulation of rates charged by tobacco warehousemen. And in a trio of cases commonly known as the *Social Security* cases, the Court upheld features of the new Social Security program. Courts divided by votes of 5–4 upheld the unemployment compensation provisions of the Social Security Act (SSA) in *Steward Machine Co.* v. *Davis*,[60] as well as Alabama's corresponding state unemployment insurance statute in *Carmichael* v. *Southern Coal & Coke Co.*[61] At the same time, the justices upheld the old-age

[49] 300 U.S. 379 (1937).
[50] 300 U.S. 515 (1937).
[51] 300 U.S. 440 (1937).
[52] 300 U.S. 608 (1937).
[53] 301 U.S. 1 (1937).
[54] 301 U.S. 49 (1937).
[55] 301 U.S. 58 (1937).
[56] 301 U.S. 103 (1937).
[57] 301 U.S. 142 (1937).
[58] 301 U.S. 468 (1937).
[59] 301 U.S. 441 (1937).
[60] 301 U.S. 548 (1937).
[61] 301 U.S. 495 (1937).

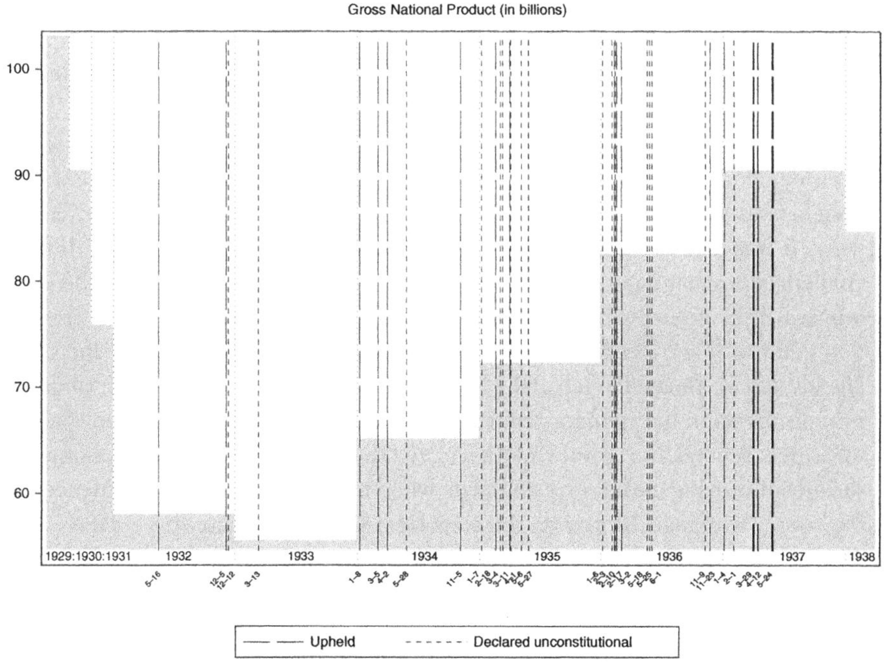

FIGURE 6.1 Gross national product (in billions)
Source: Bicentennial Edition: *Historical Statistics of the United States, Colonial Times to 1970*, Series F 1–5(1975)

pension provisions of the federal statute by a vote of 7–2 in *Helvering* v. *Davis*.[62] If the *Labor Board* cases are counted as five and the *Social Security* cases as three, over the year the Court upheld fifteen statutes while invalidating only one. If those sets of cases are counted as one each, then the ratio becomes nine to one.

In Figure 6.1, these cases are plotted against contemporary annual data for gross national product. Cases in which the challenged legislation was sustained are represented by a line comprised of long dashes; cases in which the challenged legislation was invalidated are represented by a line comprised of short dashes. Some lines are thicker than others because on some dates more than one case was decided. This is particularly the case in 1937, when five cases involving the NLRA were decided on April 12, and three cases involving the SSA were decided on May 24. Data from the years 1929–31 and 1938 are also provided as a frame of reference and to provide the reader with a better sense of the economic contours of the Depression. Those contours and their relationships to the plotted cases are replicated when one consults contemporary data concerning other economic indicators, including gross domestic product, net national product, gross domestic income, gross national

[62] 301 U.S. 619 (1937).

income, personal income, per capita personal income, disposable personal income, per capita disposable personal income, per capita consumption expenditures, gross private domestic investment, industrial production, the Dow Jones Industrial Average, unemployment, and employment compensation.[63]

As one can see, it is difficult to discern any correlation between the Court's decisions and the general state or direction of the economy. The justices both upheld and invalidated challenged statutes when the economy was better and when it was worse, when it was declining and when it was improving. Indeed, challenged legislation enjoyed the greatest rate of success in 1937, when the economy was at its strongest. This should not be attributed to a belated judicial recognition that the "New Deal" was "working," for two reasons. First, because the Court already had invalidated much of the New Deal's recovery program, post-invalidation improvements in the economy could not be attributed directly to such invalidated measures. Second, the Court had invalidated those statutes while the economy was steadily improving during 1935 and 1936, when there was comparable evidence that they were "working." Moreover, the New Deal was not a monolith – such recovery measures as the NIRA and the AAA should be distinguished from the long-term structural reform measures upheld in 1937, such as the NLRA and the SSA. Indeed, the payroll tax of the SSA's old-age pension provisions arguably helped to retard recovery by pulling capital out of the economy through payroll taxes imposed beginning in 1937, while not paying the first benefits until 1940. And as will appear in the next section, the Court repeatedly either explicitly or implicitly rejected claims that regulatory statutes could be sustained as emergency measures. The case for the economic crisis as a salient exogenous variable does not appear to be strong. The pattern of the Court's decisions is better explained by elements internal to the legal system: doctrinal development; statutory draftsmanship; selection, briefing, and argument of test cases; and the learning curve of Congress and Government lawyers, assisted by guidance from the Court.[64]

II. ECONOMIC CRISIS AS AN ENDOGENOUS VARIABLE

Contentions that exercises of federal power might be justified by the existence of an economic crisis were generally unavailing before the Supreme Court. This was particularly the case where the challenged statute raised issues of constitutional

[63] For a complete set of figures illustrating these various data, see https://papers.ssrn.com/sol3/papers.cfm?abstract_id=3253353.

[64] See Barry Cushman, "Inside the 'Constitutional Revolution' of 1937." *Supreme Court Review* 2016, 367–409; Cushman, "The Hughes Court and Constitutional Consultation." Cushman, *Rethinking the New Deal Court* (New York: Oxford University Press, 1998b). For reasons to doubt the causal efficacy of other exogenous factors, such as the 1936 election or the Court-packing plan, see, in addition to these sources, Cushman, "Court-Packing and Compromise." *Constitutional Commentary* 29 (2013a), 1–30; Cushman, "The Court-Packing Plan as Symptom, Casualty, and Cause of Gridlock." *Notre Dame Law Review* 88 (2013b), 2089–06.

federalism.[65] The leading statement of the Court's position came in *Schechter Poultry Corp.* v. *United States*, where the justices unanimously invalidated the NIRA despite both the statute's declaration of emergency[66] and the Government's contention that the regulatory program "must be viewed in the light of the grave national crisis with which Congress was confronted."[67] Importantly, Chief Justice Hughes recognized that "Undoubtedly, the conditions to which power is addressed are always to be considered when the exercise of power is challenged. Extraordinary conditions may call for extraordinary remedies." But he insisted that

> Extraordinary conditions do not create or enlarge constitutional power. The constitution established a national government with powers deemed to be adequate, as they have proved to be both in war and peace, but these powers of the national government are limited by the constitutional grants. Those who act under these grants are not at liberty to transcend the imposed limits because they believe that more or different power is necessary. Such assertions of extraconstitutional authority were anticipated and precluded by the explicit terms of the Tenth Amendment —"The powers not delegated to the United States by the Constitution, nor prohibited by it to the States, are reserved to the States respectively, or to the people."[68]

The justices similarly invalidated the AAA in *United States* v. *Butler*, notwithstanding the statute's declaration of an economic emergency[69] and the Government's defense of the means selected to meet the crisis as appropriate to the circumstances.[70] In *Carter* v. *Carter Coal Co.*, the Court struck down both the price regulation and the labor regulation titles of the Guffey Coal Act, although government counsel contended that "the Fathers, in setting up the Constitution under which we live, were wise enough to see that perpetuation of that Constitution depended on its supplying an instrument of government sufficiently strong to deal with all the crises of the future,"[71] and over Justice Cardozo's dissenting opinion that "Congress was not condemned to inaction in the face of price and wage wars so pregnant with disaster."[72] And in *Ashton* v. *Cameron County Water District* the Court struck down the federal Municipal Bankruptcy Act despite its declaration of an emergency requiring exercise of the congressional bankruptcy power.[73]

65 Michal Belknap, "The New Deal and the Emergency Powers Doctrine." *Texas Law Review* 62 (1983), 67–109.

66 295 at 543 n. 9.

67 Ibid. at 528. See also Brief for the United States at 28, 86–98, 101, 103, 134 (defending the Act as an emergency measure).

68 Ibid. at 528–29.

69 297 U.S. at 53, 55.

70 Brief for the United States at 247–62.

71 298 U.S. at 268. See also Brief of the State of Washington as *Amica Curiae, R. C. Tway Coal Co.* v. *Glenn*, at 12–14 (defending the Act as an emergency measure).

72 298 U.S. at 331 (Cardozo, J., dissenting).

73 298 U.S. at 524.

Rejections of the emergency rationale for federal action were not confined to cases concerning constitutional federalism. They also appeared in cases raising issues of the separation of powers and the Fifth Amendment. The Court struck down the broad delegation to the president of congressional power to prohibit interstate shipment of hot oil in *Panama Refining Co.* v. *Ryan*, notwithstanding the statute's declaration of the existence of an emergency.[74] Similarly, in *Louisville Joint Stock Land Bank* v. *Radford*, the justices invalidated the Emergency Farm Mortgage Act as depriving the creditor of property without due process, even though the government contended that there "had arisen an emergency requiring congressional action."[75]

The Court exhibited comparable reluctance to rely upon an emergency rationale in cases challenging state regulations. In *Nebbia* v. *New York* the statute imposing minimum prices for retail sales of milk declared there to be an emergency in the state's milk markets,[76] and the state's attorneys defended the statute as an emergency measure.[77] Yet the Court declined to base its opinion upholding the statute on that ground, opting instead to revolutionize due process jurisprudence by holding that legislative power to regulate prices would no longer be confined to a narrow class of businesses "affected with a public interest."[78] The Court likewise disdained reliance on the emergency rationale offered in support of Virginia's scheme of milk regulation in *Highland Farms Dairy, Inc.*, v. *Agnew*,[79] instead upholding the statute on the basis of conventional constitutional analysis.[80] In *Stewart Dry Goods Co.* v. *Lewis*, the Court struck down a progressive gross sales tax on retail merchants as a denial of equal protection even though the statute declared "an emergency to exist."[81] The justices unanimously invalidated the natural gas proration order at issue in *Thompson* v. *Consolidated Gas Utilities Corp.* notwithstanding the underlying statute's declaration of emergency.[82] And in three cases involving challenges to state legislation alleged to impair the obligation of contract in violation of the constitution's Article I, Section 10, the justices unanimously refused to sustain the measures as appropriate responses to an emergency. In *W.B. Worthen Co.* v. *Thomas* the Court invalidated the Arkansas statute retroactively exempting the proceeds of life insurance policies from creditors' claims, notwithstanding the legislature's declaration that the measure was justified by an emergency, because the statute was neither limited in its application to the duration of the emergency nor

74 293 at 416–17. See also *Brief for the Respondents*, *Amazon Petroleum Corp.* v. *Ryan*, at 37–39, 125–26, 130, 151 (defending the challenged provision as justified by emergency conditions).

75 295 at 599. See also Brief of Respondent at 30–40 and Supplemental Brief of Respondent at 11 (defending the Act as emergency legislation addressed to crisis conditions).

76 291 U.S. at 518 n.2.

77 Ibid. at 511, Brief for Appellee at 11–13.

78 Ibid. at 525–39.

79 300 U.S. at 609.

80 Ibid. at 611–17.

81 294 U.S. at 553 n.3.

82 Statement as to Jurisdiction at 18.

reasonably tailored to the conditions of the emergency.[83] For similar reasons the Court in *W.B. Worthen Co.* v. *Kavanaugh* invalidated the Arkansas statute retroactively diminishing the rights of mortgagees despite a legislative assertion that it was warranted by "an emergency" endangering "the peace, health, and safety of a multitude of citizens."[84] And in *Treigle* v. *Acme Homestead Assn.*, the appellee attempted to defend a Louisiana statute retroactively diminishing the rights of withdrawing members of building and loan associations on the ground that it "was adopted to meet the existing economic emergency."[85] Yet the justices rejected this contention with the observations that the statute did not "purport to deal with any existing emergency," and that, like the statutes involved in *Thomas* and *Kavanaugh*, the Louisiana statute was "neither temporary nor conditional."[86]

Invocations of crisis conditions did not fall on entirely deaf judicial ears, however. Instead, the Court was receptive to such arguments where they were regarded as relevant to the particular doctrinal analysis for which the question presented called. And indeed, in such cases, the opinions made the doctrinal relevance of such conditions explicit. Perhaps the best-known such instance is *Home Bldg. & Loan Assn.* v. *Blaisdell*. A Minnesota statute enacted in 1933 authorized the state courts to allow defaulting mortgagors in possession to extend the period of redemption for a "just and equitable" period beyond that authorized by prior law, provided the mortgagor paid the reasonable rental value of the mortgaged property during the extended period. The statute declared the existence of an emergency, and provided that it was to remain in effect only during the emergency, and in no case beyond May 1, 1935.[87] The creditor in *Blaisdell* challenged the statute as an impairment of the obligation of contract,[88] while the debtor and the state defended it as a legitimate exercise of the state's police power in an emergency.[89]

In presenting the case to the conference Hughes explicitly stressed the crisis conditions in Minnesota as a justification for the measure,[90] and he would do so again in his opinion for the majority upholding the statute. There, Hughes memorably wrote that:

> Emergency does not create power. Emergency does not increase granted power or remove or diminish the restrictions imposed upon power granted or reserved. The Constitution was adopted in a period of grave emergency. Its grants of power to the Federal Government and its limitations of the power of the States were determined in the light of emergency, and they are not altered by emergency.[91]

83 292 U.S. at 432–44 ("the Act contains no limitations as to time, amount, circumstances, or need").
84 295 U.S. at 59–63.
85 297 U.S. at 195.
86 Ibid.
87 290 U.S. 415–16.
88 Appellant's Brief at 6–7, 23–29.
89 Appellees' Brief at 2–46, 56–60.
90 Cushman, "The Hughes Court Docket Books: The Early Terms, 1929–1933." Journal of Supreme Court History 40 (2015), 111–12.
91 290 U.S. at 425.

Nevertheless, Hughes added, "While emergency does not create power, emergency may furnish the occasion for the exercise of power."[92] For example, "the war power of the Federal Government is not created by the emergency of war, but it is a power given to meet that emergency."[93] Thus, "The constitutional question presented in the light of an emergency is whether the power possessed embraces the particular exercise of it in response to particular conditions."[94]

Hughes surveyed at length numerous instances in which the police power had been exercised in a manner affecting existing contractual rights without impairing the obligation of contract, underscoring the principle that contractual rights and duties were undertaken and held subject to the police power.[95] Most apposite were recent decisions in which the Court had rejected contract clause challenges to rent control laws enacted in response to housing shortages following World War I. Under New York's statute, which declared the existence of a public emergency, tenants whose leases had expired were empowered to remain in possession of the premises provided that they were willing and able to pay a reasonable rent for their use and occupation, and landlords were deprived of ordinary possessory remedies for a period of two years. The Court had held that the law constituted a legitimate exercise of the police power under conditions of emergency,[96] and that such measures could not persist beyond the emergency by which they were justified.[97] Similarly, Hughes reasoned that although the police power could not underwrite the repudiation of debts, Minnesota's "temporary and conditional restraint" on "the immediate and literal enforcement of contractual obligations" where "vital interests would otherwise suffer" was not beyond the protective power of the state.[98] "It cannot be maintained," he insisted,

> that the constitutional prohibition should be so construed as to prevent limited and temporary interpositions with respect to the enforcement of contracts if made necessary by a great public calamity such as fire, flood, or earthquake. The reservation of state power appropriate to such extraordinary conditions may be deemed to be as much a part of all contracts as is the reservation of state power to protect the public interest in the other situations to which we have referred. And if state power exists to give temporary relief from the enforcement of contracts in the

92 Ibid. at 426. Here he relied on the case of *Wilson* v. *New*, 243 U.S. 332 (1917) which had upheld temporary wage regulation in the railroad industry under conditions of emergency. There, Chief Justice White had stated for the majority, "Although an emergency may not call into life a power which has never lived, nevertheless emergency may afford a reason for the exertion of a living power already enjoyed." Ibid. at 348.

93 290 U.S. at 426.

94 Ibid.

95 Ibid. at 434–42; see ibid. at 444 ("The principle of this development is . . . that the reservation of the reasonable exercise of the protective power of the State is read into all contracts").

96 *Marcus Brown Holding Co.* v. *Feldman*, 256 U.S. 170, 198 (1921). See also *Edgar A. Levy Leasing Co.* v. *Siegel*, 258 U.S. 242, 245–49 (1922); *Block* v. *Hirsh*, 256 U.S. 135, 154–58 (1921).

97 *Chastleton Corp.* v. *Sinclair*, 264 U.S. 543, 547–49 (1924).

98 290 U.S. at 439–40.

presence of disasters due to physical causes such as fire, flood or earthquake, that power cannot be said to be nonexistent when the urgent public need demanding such relief is produced by other and economic causes.[99]

In *West Coast Hotel* v. *Parrish*, which upheld a state minimum wage law for women, the Court was confronted with the contrary precedent of *Adkins* v. *Children's Hospital*.[100] There, by a vote of 5–3, the Court had invalidated a similar statute as a violation of both constitutionally protected liberty of contract and of the prohibition on taking the property of A and giving it to B for a private purpose.[101] Chief Justice Taft had written a dissent in which he defended the statute as a legitimate exercise of the police power to protect public health and morals.[102] The *West Coast Hotel* majority concluded that *Adkins* had been decided incorrectly and should be overruled,[103] but Hughes wrote the opinion as if the challenged statute could be upheld even if *Adkins* were left undisturbed. When *West Coast Hotel* came before the conference, Hughes raised the possibility of overruling *Adkins*. He indicated that he "Agreed with Taft's op[inion]" in *Adkins*, adding that Taft's opinion "has more weight now."[104] What Hughes meant by this became clear in his majority opinion, in which he stated that "the close division by which the decision in the *Adkins* case was reached, and the economic conditions which have supervened, and in the light of which the reasonableness of the exercise of the protective power of the State must be considered, make it not only appropriate, but we think imperative, that, in deciding the present case, the subject should receive fresh consideration."[105] In other words, the reasonableness of an exercise of the police power was to be evaluated in light of the conditions to which it was addressed. There were numerous decisions[106] in which the Court had upheld statutes designed to protect employees from what Justice Sutherland described as "unfair" methods of payment,[107] and there was a substantial body of precedent protecting consumers and producers from excessively high or low charges for goods or services under conditions of grossly disproportionate bargaining power.[108] Here, the persistence of alarming levels of unemployment and unparalleled demands for public relief presented a "compelling consideration which recent economic experience has brought into a strong light."[109] It resulted in "The exploitation of a class of workers who are in an unequal position with respect to bargaining power, and are thus relatively

99 Ibid. at 439 (citation omitted).
100 261 U.S. 525 (1923).
101 Ibid. at 546–58.
102 Ibid. at 562–67 (Taft, C.J., dissenting).
103 301 U.S. at 398, 400.
104 Justice Louis D. Brandeis OT 1936 Docket Book, Office of the Curator of the Supreme Court of the United States.
105 300 U.S. at 390.
106 Ibid. at 392–93.
107 *Adkins*, 261 U.S. at 547.
108 300 U.S. at 392 n. 2, citing, inter alia, *Munn* v. *Illinois*, 94 U.S. 113 (1877); *O'Gorman & Young* v. *Hartford Insurance Co.*, 282 U.S. 249 (1931); and *Nebbia* v. *New York*, 291 U.S. 502 (1934).
109 300 U.S. at 399.

defenseless against the denial of a living wage."[110] Hughes concluded that a minimum wage designed to protect the health and morals of women working for "unconscionable employers"[111] could not be considered unreasonable. His claim here was not, as Sutherland suggested in dissent, that the meaning of the constitution changes "with the ebb and flow of economic events."[112] It was instead that changed economic conditions had made appropriate to the question of the minimum wage's constitutionality application of the established principle that gross disparities in bargaining power between buyers and sellers could justify regulation of the price at which a good or service was sold.

These decisions upholding state legislation against contract clause and due process challenges had their analogs at the federal level. In *Wright* v. *Vinton Branch Bank*, the Court upheld as an exercise of the bankruptcy power a revised Emergency Farm Mortgage Act that prescribed a maximum stay of foreclosure proceedings of three years, and authorized the bankruptcy court to shorten the stay in the event that the emergency by which it was justified concluded earlier.[113] In *Norman* v. *Baltimore & Ohio Railroad Co.*, one of the *Gold Clause* cases, the Court upheld the federal abrogation of gold clauses in private contracts. In the *Legal Tender* cases,[114] Congress had enacted legislation during the Civil War making treasury notes legal tender for all debts. Creditors anticipating payment in specie rather than in depreciating paper had contended that the issuance of paper currency exceeded congressional power, but the Court had concluded that it was necessary and proper "for carrying into execution the legitimate powers of the government."[115] It was "not to be denied," Justice William Strong had written for the majority, "that acts may be adapted to the exercise of lawful power, and appropriate to it, in seasons of exigency, which would be inappropriate at other times,"[116] adding that "Every contract for the payment of money, simply, is necessarily subject to the constitutional power of the government over the currency, whatever that power may be, and the obligation of the parties is, therefore, assumed with reference to that power."[117] In *Norman*, Hughes followed Strong in disappointing creditors who had contracted for repayment in gold coin of a specified weight and fineness or in an equivalent amount of paper money as measured by the gold content of the dollar on the date of the contract. Noting that the joint resolution in question had declared that "the existing emergency" had disclosed that gold clauses "obstruct the power of

110 Ibid.
111 Ibid.
112 Ibid. at 400, 402–3 (Sutherland, J., dissenting).
113 300 U.S. at 460–64. See also Brief on Behalf of Robert Page Wright at 32–33, 53 (defending the Act as a proper exercise of the bankruptcy power under conditions of emergency).
114 79 U.S. 457 (1871).
115 Ibid. at 540–44.
116 Ibid. at 540.
117 Ibid. at 549. See also ibid. at 551 ("contracts must be understood as made in reference to the possible exercise of the rightful authority of the government, and no obligation of a contract can extend to the defeat of legitimate government authority").

the Congress to regulate the value of the money of the United States, and are inconsistent with the declared policy of the Congress to maintain at all times the equal power of every dollar, coined or issued by the United States, in the markets and in the payment of debts," the Court could not conclude that "this determination is so destitute of basis that the interdiction of the gold clauses must be deemed to be without any reasonable relation to the monetary policy adopted by the Congress."[118] In other words, under such circumstances the regulation was reasonably related, i.e., necessary and proper, to the exercise of an enumerated federal power.

Something similar may have taken place in the *Labor Board* cases. Some scholars have opined that the sit-down strikes that took place at various manufacturing establishments in early 1937 contributed to the Court's decisions to uphold the National Labor Relations Act, though they have differed concerning the nature of the relationship. Some have suggested that the relationship between the strikes and the decisions was unmediated by legal doctrine. One scholar asserts, for example, that "the Supreme Court plainly and simply bowed to pressure from strikers." "The factory occupations ... forced the Supreme Court to uphold the Wagner Act."[119]

There are reasons to doubt this assessment. First, as Professor Melvyn Dubofsky has observed, the scale of industrial unrest in 1937 was far from historically singular. "[O]nly 7.2 per cent of employed workers were involved in walkouts," he reports, "and their absence from work represented only 0.0043 per cent of all time worked." These percentages were approximately

[118] 294 U.S. at 312–13. See also Brief for the United States, *Perry* v. *United States*, at 5–6 ("The recent emergency has shown that gold clauses constitute a serious obstruction to the effective exercise by the Congress of its monetary and other powers. Their effect, if enforced, is of such serious consequence as substantially to deprive the Congress of the power to regulate the value of the dollar. Gold clauses would, if enforced, interfere with recent monetary measures adopted to protect the gold reserves of the United States, to provide a more effective use of those reserves, and to regulate and protect the interstate and foreign commerce of the United States. These monetary measures were necessary, in the judgment of the Congress, to cope with the disorganized financial and economic conditions which arose out of the World War and reached their crisis in the United States in 1933. Only by declaring that gold clauses should not be enforceable in public as well as private obligations was the Congress able to take the steps required to meet these conditions."). Brief for the United States and the Reconstruction Finance Corporation, *U.S.* v. *Banker's Trust Co.*, at 7–8, is to the same effect. See also ibid. at 28–87 and Respondent's Brief, *Norman* v. *B. & O. R. Co.* at 29–94 (defending abrogation of the gold clause as reasonably related to the exercise of enumerated congressional powers).

[119] See James Gray Pope, "The Thirteenth Amendment Versus the Commerce Clause: Labor and the Shaping of American Constitutional Law, 1921–1957." *Columbia Law Review* 102 (2002), 96, 113. See also Jim Pope, "Worker Lawmaking, Sit-Down Strikes, and the Shaping of American Industrial Relations, 1935–1958." *Law & History Review* 42 (2006), 97 ("the Court was plainly and simply yielding to pressure from the sit-down strikers"). Earlier scholars had suggested a similar role for the sit-down strikes, though they had more circumspectly placed them in the mix with the Court-packing plan and the 1936 election. See, e.g., Peter Irons, *The New Deal Lawyers* (Princeton: Princeton University Press, 1982), 272–73, 289; Richard Cortner, *The Wagner Act Cases* (Knoxville: University of Tennessee Press, 1964), 188; Robert McCloskey, *The American Supreme Court* (Chicago: University of Chicago Press, 1960), 175.

the same as those experienced during the strike wave of 1934, which Commissioner of Labor Statistics Isadore Lubin had concluded "could not match 1919 in intensity, duration, or number of workers involved,"[120]and which appear to have had no effect on the Court's unanimous decision to invalidate the NIRA's labor and other provisions in *Schechter* the following year.[121] Second, it appears that the United Auto Workers, who waged the largest and most serious set of sit-down strikes, did so because they doubted (correctly, it appears) that they had sufficient votes to win recognition elections under the provisions of the NLRA.[122] It therefore is not clear that upholding the Act offered any meaningful prospect of ameliorating those particular labor disturbances. Third, the largest of those strikes – the one at the General Motors plant in Flint, Michigan – was actually settled on February 11, 1937,[123] the day that the *Labor Board* cases were being argued,[124] and more than two weeks before the justices met to deliberate on the cases in their conference of February 27.[125] Fourth, the prospect that state and local authorities might successfully deal with such disputes brightened on February 26, the day before the justices met to vote on the *Labor Board* cases, when police successfully evicted sit-down strikers at the Chicago-area Fansteel Metallurgical plant.[126] The story was front-page news in the morning *Washington Post* on the day of the Court's afternoon conference on February 27.[127]

Nor did the public opinion polls evince a popular desire that the sit-down strikers be propitiated. In early February of 1937, pollster George Gallup asked respondents whether, "In the current General Motors strike," their sympathies were "with the John L. Lewis group of striking employees or with the employers." Some 44 percent of those with an opinion said their sympathies lay with the Lewis group, while 56 percent supported the employers. Sixty-six percent believed that GM was "right in refusing to negotiate with the sit-down strikers until they leave the General Motors

120 Melvyn Dubofsky, "Not So 'Turbulent Years': Another Look at the American 1930's." *Amerikastudien* 24 (1979), 12–13.

121 Nor did the 1935 threat of a nationwide coal strike, which helped to stimulate passage of the Guffey Coal Act that summer, dissuade a majority from invalidating the Act the following year in *Carter Coal*. See Pope, "The Thirteenth Amendment Versus the Commerce Clause: Labor and the Shaping of American Constitutional Law, 1921–1957," 46, 54. Pope, "Worker Lawmaking, Sit-Down Strikes, and the Shaping of American Industrial Relations, 1935–1958," 69.

122 Dubofsky, "Not So 'Turbulent Years': Another Look at the American 1930's," 16; Sidney Fine, *Sit-Down: The General Motors Strike of* 1936–1937 (Ann Arbor: University of Michigan Press, 1969), 111, 118–19, 144, 181–82, 185–88, 255–56; J. Woodford Howard Jr., *Mr. Justice Murphy* (Princeton: Princeton University Press, 1968), 124–26, 137.

123 Fine, *Sit-Down: The General Motors Strike of* 1936-1937, 303–12; Robert Zieger, *The CIO*, 1935–1955 (Chapel Hill: University of North Carolina Press, 1995), 51.

124 The cases were argued February 9, 10, and 11, 1937. 301 U.S. 1, 49, 58, 103, 142.

125 Cushman, "Inside the 'Constitutional Revolution' of 1937," 381.

126 Pope, "Worker Lawmaking, Sit-Down Strikes, and the Shaping of American Industrial Relations, 1935–1958," 88–89.

127 "Sit-Down Strikers Routed," *Wash. Post*, Feb. 27, 1937, 1.

plants," and only 38 percent believed that "John L. Lewis represents a majority of General Motors workers."[128]

In addition, much of the evidence alleged to support the claim of such causal influence pertains to events that transpired after the justices had cast their votes in conference. The fact that there were 170 sit-down strikes initiated in March of 1937 can have had no influence on a decision taken on February 27. Neither can the failure to evict strikers at Detroit's Chrysler plant in mid-March, successful contemporary evictions elsewhere in Detroit and in Chicago, continued agitation and conflict in the Motor City in late March and early April, nor exhortations from congressmen during the same period.[129] These facts, for all of their inherent interest, are simply irrelevant to the question of causation.[130]

An alternative view contends that the sit-down strikes demonstrated to the justices a fact that they had not appreciated previously, namely, that labor disturbances at manufacturing facilities obstructed interstate commerce, and therefore fell within federal regulatory jurisdiction. On this account, "the sit-down strikes educated the Justices about the realities of interstate commerce," making it "undoubtedly clear that interstate commerce was a broader category than the Justices had previously imagined."[131]

It is certainly true that legislators defending what became the NLRA emphasized the "physical and other obstructions to the flow of interstate commerce" caused by strikes, and that NLRB attorneys characterized the relationship between industrial strife and interstate commerce as a matter of "common knowledge" in their briefs and oral arguments before the Court.[132] The problem with this alternative explanation, however, is twofold. First, it underestimates the extent to which the Court previously had recognized the relationship between labor conflict at production facilities and the free flow of commerce. In a series of cases dating back to 1908, the Court had held that strikes and boycotts at such entities fell within the reach of the federal Sherman Antitrust Act if they were undertaken with the intent to restrain interstate commerce.[133] Those decisions were repeatedly cited in the NLRB's

128 George Gallup, *The Gallup Poll: Public Opinion, 1935–1971, Vol. I* (New York: Random House 1972), 48; Barry Cushman, "Mr. Dooley and Mr. Gallup: Public Opinion and Constitutional Change in the 1930s." *Buffalo Law Review* 50 (2002), 26–27 n.96.

129 *See* Pope, "Worker Lawmaking," 89–91, 94–95. It also is asserted that Government victory in all of the *Labor Board* cases was necessary in order to avert the Court-packing threat, though by the time that the justices met in conference there already was significant reason to doubt that the President's proposal could achieve passage. See Pope, "Worker Lawmaking," 97; Cushman, "Inside the 'Constitutional Revolution' of 1937," 381–88.

130 The same can be said of the post-February 27 events related in Hansen (2000: 82–107).

131 Drew Hansen, "The Sit-Down Strikes and the Switch in Time." *Wayne Law Review* 46 (2000), 53–54. See also Jeff Shesol, Supreme Power: Franklin Roosevelt vs. The Supreme Court (2010), 432 (arguing that "'[a]ctual experience' – in the form of the sit-down strikes–may too have had an effect" on the Court's decisions).

132 Drew Hansen, "The Sit-Down Strikes and the Switch in Time," 109–14.

133 See *Local 167* v. *United States*, 291 U.S. 293 (1934); *Bedford Cut Stone Co.* v. *Journeyman Stone Cutters' Ass'n*, 274 U.S. 37 (1927); *Coronado Coal Co.* v. *United Mine Workers*, 268 U.S. 295 (1925); *Duplex Printing Co.* v. *Deering*, 254 U.S. 433 (1921); *Loewe* v. *Lawlor*, 208 U.S. 274 (1908).

brief,[134] and in Chief Justice Hughes's opinion for the majority in *Jones & Laughlin*.[135] The justices did not need the sit-down strikes to educate them about this relationship. It was one that they had long understood.

This brings us to the second problem with this alternative account, namely that it underspecifies the relationship between the strikes and the doctrinal formulations within which Government lawyers were required to operate. They could not simply say to the Court, "You see, strikes affect interstate commerce, so you must uphold the NLRA." The difficulty was that there also was a line of cases holding that, in the absence of a showing of intent to restrain interstate commerce, labor relations in production facilities affected interstate commerce only indirectly and were thus a matter reserved to the states.[136] It would be necessary to explain how the NLRA could be accommodated within established precedents.

The NLRB developed a strategy for doing so long before the sit-down strikes alleged to have affected the decisions were initiated. The plan was to develop cases that could be conceptualized as falling within a line of authority recognizing the power of Congress to regulate local activities – even activities of production – if they were conducted within a "current" or "stream" of interstate commerce. Any activity that threatened to obstruct the flow of that interstate stream fell within federal regulatory jurisdiction. The Labor Board Cases were selected because each of the manufacturing companies involved imported raw or semi-finished materials from other states, and then shipped their finished products out into interstate commerce. The cases were briefed and argued on the theory that labor disturbances in their plants would impede the flow of materials and goods to and from those plants, and thus obstruct a stream of interstate commerce. Congress was empowered to employ reasonable means to prevent such blockages from occurring, and to dislodge them once they had formed.[137]

This is where the sit-down strikes came in. At the conclusion of his oral argument, Government attorney Charles Wyzanski alluded to those strikes immediately before concluding that, "where two colossal forces are standing astride the stream of commerce threatening to disrupt it, it cannot be that this Government is without power to provide for the orderly procedure by which the dispute may be adjusted without interruption to the stream of commerce."[138] Wyzanski thus offered the sit-

134 *Brief for National Labor Relations Board, NLRB* v. *Jones & Laughlin Steel Corp.*, at 13, 14, 27, 40, 41, 42, 43, 47, 48, 78.

135 301 U.S. at 39–40.

136 *Carter* v. *Carter Coal Co.*, 298 U.S. 238 (1936); *Schechter Poultry Corp.* v. *United States*, 295 U.S. 495 (1935); *Levering & Garrigues Co.* v. *Morrin*, 289 U.S. 103 (1933); *United Leather Workers* v. *Herkert & Meisel Trunk Co.*, 265 U.S. 457 (1924); *United Mine Workers* v. *Coronado Coal Co.*, 259 U.S. 344 (1922).

137 Irons, *The New Deal Lawyers*, 240–42, 252–53, 268; Cushman, *Rethinking the New Deal Court*, 164–68. The relevant precedents were *Tagg Bros. & Moorhead* v. *U.S.*, 280 U.S. 420 (1930); *Chicago Board of Trade* v. *Olsen*, 262 U.S. 1 (1923); *Stafford* v. *Wallace*, 258 U.S. 495 (1922); *Swift & Co.* v. *U.S.*, 196 U.S. 375 (1905).

138 *Arguments in Cases Arising Under Labor Acts Before the Supreme Court*, Sen. Doc. 52 (75–1), 173–74.

down strikes as an illustration of the accuracy of the Government's theory of the cases. He did not contend that under such crisis conditions the restraints of the constitution must give way; instead he explained to the Court why an established doctrine could and should be applied to such conditions.

In his opinion upholding application of the statute to the Jones & Laughlin Steel Corporation, Hughes emphasized the far-flung character of its holdings and the integrated, interstate nature of its operations.[139] In summarizing the operations of the company's Pittsburgh and Aliquippa steelworks, Hughes adverted to their characterization by the NLRB as "the heart of a self-contained, highly integrated body. They draw in the raw materials from Michigan, Minnesota, West Virginia, Pennsylvania in part through arteries and by means controlled by the respondent; they transform the materials and then pump them out to all parts of the nation through the vast mechanism which the respondent has elaborated."[140] He then concluded that "the stoppage of those operations by industrial strife would have a most serious effect upon interstate commerce. In view of respondent's far-flung activities, it is idle to say that the effect would be indirect or remote. It is obvious that it would be immediate and might be catastrophic."[141] "Experience" had "abundantly demonstrated that the recognition of the right of employees to self-organization and to have representatives of their own choosing for the purpose of collective bargaining is often an essential condition of industrial peace. Refusal to confer and negotiate has been one of the most prolific causes of strife. This is such an outstanding fact in the history of labor disturbances that it is a proper subject of judicial notice and requires no citation of instances."[142]

Hughes did not explicitly rest his opinion on the stream of commerce theory, treating it instead as one illustration of a broader principle that might be deduced from the Court's commerce clause jurisprudence.[143] But his mode of analysis so closely approximated that theory that the dissenting justices, along with a host of government attorneys, lower federal court judges, members of Congress, and scholarly commentators treated the case as resting on that theory, and thus regarded both *Schechter* and *Carter Coal* as distinguishable and still good law.[144] And writing years later, Justice Roberts suggested that the stream of commerce theory had formed part of the basis of the Court's decisions.[145] It may be that Wyzanski's

[139] 301 U.S. at 26–27.
[140] 301 U.S. 27.
[141] Ibid. at 41.
[142] Ibid. at 42.
[143] Ibid. at 36–37.
[144] Cushman, *Rethinking the New Deal Court*, 174–82; Cushman, "Inside the 'Constitutional Revolution' of 1937," 406–7.
[145] Describing the theory on which the NLRA had been framed and upheld, Roberts wrote: "that act premises its provisions upon the proposition that industrial conflicts interfere with and limit interstate transportation and commerce. Albeit a strike is localized in a given community, the flow of goods to and from that community is interfered with. The interference may be so great as to be a matter of

invocation of the sit-down strikes in the context of his stream of commerce argument helped Roberts (and perhaps others) to appreciate the applicability of that theory.

III. CONCLUSION

In response to the question, "Can the Constitution Protect Private Rights During National Emergencies?" one scholar has replied "The answer is no." With citations to *Blaisdell* and the *Gold Clause* cases, it is argued that the so-called "Crisis Constitution" will always overwhelm the so-called "Normal Constitution."[146] Whatever may be said of other periods in American history, such a claim about the Great Depression oversimplifies. The Hughes Court so resolutely resisted claims to economic emergency powers that the Government simply stopped making them.[147] The Court vindicated three Contract Clause challenges in the two years following *Blaisdell* because the statutes in question were neither temporary nor narrowly tailored to the conditions of emergency. The Court invalidated major New Deal initiatives in cases such as *Panama Refining, Schechter, Radford, Butler, Ashton*, and *Carter Coal*, despite contentions that they were justified by conditions of economic crisis. And in many lesser-known decisions the justices did not shrink from striking down legislation formulated to alleviate those conditions. It was only where the Court regarded such conditions as relevant to doctrinal analysis that assertions of economic crisis resonated.

The economic crisis of the Great Depression did, however, stimulate the enactment of some legislation that could be sustained on the basis of existing doctrines recognizing the relevance of conditions of crisis. The decisions upholding such measures added to the stock of precedents that might have been relied upon by future Courts confronting comparable economic crises, whose justices might in turn have continued the process of doctrinal evolution. Between 1937 and 1943, however, President Roosevelt appointed to the Court a supermajority of justices committed to vastly expanded state and federal regulatory power even in the absence of emergency. The new constitutional doctrine that they fashioned quickly supplanted the crisis jurisprudence of the Hughes Court, leaving its potential legacy unrealized.

national concern ... even though the situations with which the statute deals are in their essence purely local." See Owen Roberts, "American Constitutional Government: The Blueprint and Structure." *Boston University Law Review* 29 (1949), 25.

146 Robert Higgs, "Can the Constitution Protect Private Rights during National Emergencies?" in James D. Gwartney and Richard E. Wagner (eds.), *Public Choice and Constitutional Economics* (Greenwich, CT: JAI Press, 1988), 369, 371–72, 377–78, 380, 381, 383–84.

147 Belknap, "The New Deal and the Emergency Powers Doctrine," 97–98.

7

Financial Crises and Constitutional Compromise

Georg Vanberg and Mitu Gulati[*]

Crises pose challenges for the theory and practice of constitutionalism. A constitution designed for ordinary times may be inadequate to moments of crisis. For this reason, as John Ferejohn argues in his chapter in this volume, it may be prudent to provide mechanisms for the suspension of constitutional procedures in extraordinary circumstances. The Roman Republic had the dictatorship; many modern constitutions feature other "emergency powers." But while there exist reasons to suspend *some* features of constitutions during crisis (most obviously, legislative procedures that may prove problematic when conditions require rapid decision-making), this is not true of *all* aspects of constitutions. The purpose of many constitutional provisions is *precisely* to constrain governmental action in extraordinary times.[1] Consider a common analogy for constitution-making: Ulysses, tying himself to the mast.[2] In calm seas, there is little need for this precaution; Ulysses chose to limit his ability to steer his ship in anticipation of the siren song. Similarly, constitutions are often intended to limit what policymakers can do when circumstances tempt them to engage in actions that the constituent body wants to prevent. The restriction on "paper money" incorporated into Article 1, Section X of the US constitution provides an example. Propelled by the fear that, faced with economic hardship, state governments might bend to pressure to discharge debts through the printing press, the American founders prescribed that "No state shall . . . make any Thing but gold and silver Coin a Tender in Payment of Debts."[3]

* Professors, Department of Political Science and Duke Law School, Duke University. We would like to thank Maggie Lemos, participants in the symposium "Liberal Constitutionalism in Times of Crisis," and participants at a workshop for judges in the Judicial Studies LLM program at Duke.

1 Constraining governments is not the only purpose of constitutions. As Turku Isiksel points out in her chapter, constitutions also "constitute" power by creating a process for collective decision-making. See Charles Hardin, *Constitutional Reform in America: Essays on the Separation of Powers* (Ames: Iowa State University Press, 1989). This desire for a more effective structure for exercising power was a major thrust behind the push for replacing the Articles of Confederation with the current US constitution.

2 Geoffrey Brennan and Hartmut Kliemt, "Logo Logic." *Constitutional Political Economy* 1 (1990), 125–27.

3 Joyce Appleby, "The American Heritage: The Heirs and the Disinherited." *The Journal of American History* 74 (1987), 798–813. "[T]he worries that [Shay's Rebellion] provoked had in fact been growing

More importantly, there are certain kinds of provisions that can only be effective – even in ordinary times – on the assumption that they will bind governments in times of crisis. Consider the so-called "no bailout" clause of the Lisbon Treaty (Article 125), which prohibits the European Union and its institutions from bailing out member state governments. The purpose of this clause is to discipline governments' fiscal behavior through the anticipation that they will not be able to escape the consequences of unsustainable fiscal decisions. But this mechanism only works if governments are convinced that when financial crisis hits, they will not receive bailout funds. In other words, the disciplining effect of the provision *in ordinary times* derives from a credible commitment to enforce the provision *in crisis conditions*. Anticipation that the provision will be suspended in difficult circumstances would immediately render it ineffective.

In this chapter, we are concerned with the enforcement of constitutional provisions that are intended to apply in times of crisis. Such enforcement is problematic because of the dynamic nature of the problem: At the moment of constitution-making, framers may intend a provision to have binding force in future crises. But the decision to adhere to, or to enforce, a provision is not made at the time of its adoption. This decision must be made contemporaneously with the moment of crisis. Thus the challenge: Will a provision "stick" when tested by extraordinary conditions?

The question of how constitutions are enforced is complex, and a number of factors are at play.[4] In this chapter, we focus on one central actor: judges. In most advanced industrial democracies, judicial review constitutes an integral part of constitutional enforcement. Our argument examines two challenges to effective judicial enforcement of constitutional norms that are likely to emerge in times of crisis.

The first is the limited power of judges, which has received considerable attention in the literature. When policymakers are firmly committed to a course of action, they may defy an adverse judicial decision – a possibility that becomes more likely when a crisis raises the perceived necessity of action. Because defiance is institutionally costly, anticipation of non-compliance can lead judges to temper the vigor with which they police constitutional boundaries.[5] Examples of such "judicial self-

stronger since the end of the war . . . Faced with popular demands for paper money with legal tender provisions, for insolvency acts, and for stay laws, legislators in many states adopted policies favorable to their interests and to the interests of their hard-pressed constituents . . . Viewed from the perspective of established leaders, those developments were the stuff of crisis." Ibid. at 799.

4 Stefan Wagstyl, "Weidmann Renews Attack on ECB's Monetary Stimulus." *Financial Times*. February 16, 2016; Daniel Sutter, "Enforcing constitutional constraints." *Constitutional Political Economy* 8, no. 2 (1997), 139–50; Georg Vanberg, *The Politics of Constitutional Review in Germany* (Cambridge: Cambridge University Press, 2005); Georg Vanberg, "Legislative-Judicial Relations: A Game Theoretic Approach to Constitutional Review." *American Journal of Political Science* 45 (2001), 346–61.

5 Vanberg, "Legislative-Judicial Relations: A Game Theoretic Approach to Constitutional Review"; Vanberg, *The Politics of Constitutional Review in Germany*.

censoring"[6] are not difficult to find. In an episode we analyze below, the US Supreme Court, facing likely defiance of an adverse ruling, upheld President Roosevelt's abrogation of the gold clauses in treasury bonds despite significant misgivings.[7] Similarly, the Russian constitutional court became significantly more deferential to presidential authority following a confrontation between the court and President Boris Yeltsin in 1993.[8] In short, because courts are institutions with limited means to enforce their decisions, moments of crisis raise the potential for outright defiance of judicial orders, and may induce strategic withdrawal by judges who are eager to avoid a confrontation.

While scholars have focused on relative judicial weakness (and "judicial self-censoring") as an obstacle to effective constitutional enforcement, we highlight a second challenge. Ironically, this challenge derives from judicial *strength*. Assume, for a moment, that compliance with judicial decisions is guaranteed. In such a setting, judicial decisions can directly impact the direction of a crisis, or at least be seen to do so, including by the media and public. If enforcing strict adherence to constitutional norms risks (or is perceived to risk) disastrous extra-legal consequences (such as exacerbating an economic crisis), judges may be tempted to stretch constitutional boundaries because they do not want to be seen as an obstacle to an effective crisis response. Put differently, few judges are staunch adherents to the maxim "fiat justitia, ruat caelum,"[9] and most are not immune to the practical implications of their decisions. Moments of crisis magnify such considerations. Again, examples are readily available. During World War II, justices of the US Supreme Court were told that a failure to intern Japanese Americans would allow spies to operate with impunity, and the Court's decision to authorize such internment in *Korematsu* v. *United States* resulted in one of the most vilified opinions in US Supreme Court history.[10]

In the next section, we present a simple model that captures both challenges, derives the conditions under which they affect judicial enforcement, and explores the implications for constitutional order. An important implication of the model is that the relationship between judicial strength and effective constitutional enforcement is not monotonic. Existing literature suggests that an increase in judicial power

6 Ibid. at 32.

7 David Glick, "Conditional Strategic Retreat: The Court's Concession in the 1935 Gold Clause Cases." *The Journal of Politics* 71 (2009), 800–16.

8 Lee Epstein, Jack Knight, and Olga Shvetsova, "The Role of Constitutional Courts in the Establishment and Maintenance of Democratic Systems of Government." *Law and Society Review* 35 (2001), 154.

9 "Let justice be done, though the heavens will fall."

10 Over a half century later it was alleged that the Solicitor General arguing the case on behalf of the Roosevelt administration had intentionally withheld information from the Court that would have shown that there was little or no evidence that Japanese American were engaged in, or likely to engage in, spying. See Sandra Lynch, "Constitutional Integrity: Lessons from the Shadows." *New York University Law Review* 92 (2017), 623–35; Richard Primus, "Canon, Anti-Canon, and Judicial Dissent." *Duke Law Journal* 48 (2) (1998), 243–303.

or influence – that is, greater pressure to comply with adverse judicial rulings – reduces judicial self-censoring, and induces more vigorous constitutional enforcement.[11] Our analysis complicates this expectation. It demonstrates that judicial self-censoring can result not only from weakness but also from judicial strength. The knowledge that they may have to live with the consequences of vetoing the crisis response of other branches may temper judges' willingness to insist on strict adherence to constitutional norms. In short, under certain conditions, strong courts may be *less* likely than weak courts to engage in forceful constitutional policing.

The consequences of such judicial self-censoring in moments of crisis are potentially far-reaching. The concrete meaning of constitutional norms often emerges out of the particular ways in which they are interpreted and applied in specific situations.[12] Judicial decisions taken during times of crisis – as well as the reactions to such decisions by other policymakers – affect how particular provisions are understood, and establish precedents. As a result, crises can have consequences for the constitutional order, including protection of individual rights and the relative power of the separate branches. A decision to uphold extraordinary measures today (whether the result of an effort to avoid non-compliance, or the desire not to hamstring a government during a crisis) may affect the ability of future courts to constrain governments when similar issues are at stake. Conversely, insisting on a constitutional principle, and provoking open defiance may damage a court's authority, and limit its ability to police constitutional boundaries in the future. Our argument suggests that ironically, strong courts – which may be tempted to limit the exercise of their power in crisis times – may have more profound negative consequences for the future quality of constitutional enforcement than weaker courts.

We develop this argument in two stages. The next section presents a model of the trade-offs confronting governments and courts in times of crisis. This model encapsulates the logic of strategic retreat induced by judicial weakness, but also exposes why strong courts may engage in strategic retreat when confronting a crisis. After developing the implications of the argument, we turn to two case studies that serve to highlight the different forms of judicial self-censoring.

I. JUDICIAL POWER AS A DOUBLE-EDGED SWORD: A SIMPLE MODEL

In many crises, policymakers perceive "politics as usual" as inadequate to the challenges they face. It is for this reason that crisis often strains constitutional boundaries: Policymakers are tempted to ignore or stretch constitutional limits

[11] For example, in Vanberg (2001), greater pressure for compliance (generated by public support for the court) eliminates judicial self-censoring in equilibrium and leads to more aggressive judicial decisions.

[12] Keith Whittington, "Constitutional interpretation: Textual meaning, original intent, and judicial review" (1999).

when they believe that an extraordinary situation makes "suspension of the rules" necessary. Such situations create challenges for judges whose role is to police executive and legislative action. One challenge is that crisis can bring judges face to face with the limits of their power. As Alexander Hamilton pointed out in the *Federalist*, courts have "neither the purse nor the sword." Judicial influence depends on how costly it is for coordinate branches to ignore or circumvent judicial decisions. By raising the perceived necessity of particular actions, crisis can lower the relative cost of non-compliance. Defiance, in turn, is institutionally costly for judges. Non-compliance reduces a court's authority, exposes its institutional weakness, and establishes a precedent for defying judicial decisions. To avoid these consequences, judges may approach their task strategically, and engage in less rigorous constitutional policing than they might prefer, i.e., "judicial self-censoring."[13]

Governments will not always ignore adverse judicial decisions – the authority of courts may be so substantial that a government feels compelled to comply, even in times of crisis. Ironically, when non-compliance is not a concern, judges face a different challenge: They may not *want* to prevent a government from taking action in a moment of crisis, even if such action stretches constitutional limits. There can be two reasons. First, like other policymakers, judges may be convinced that a particular extra-constitutional measure is required to avert disaster. As Thomas Jefferson expressed it, "to lose our country by a scrupulous adherence to the written law, would be to lose the law itself, with life, liberty, property and all those who are enjoying them with us; thus absurdly sacrificing the ends to the means."[14] Second, even if judges do not regard the government's action as necessary, they may perceive political costs to a veto. Judges may anticipate that following a veto, the court will find itself bearing the blame for worsening or prolonging a crisis. Donald Trump's tweets in response to a federal judge's injunction against his travel ban provide an example of attempting to bring such pressure to bear: "Just cannot believe a judge would put our country in such peril. If something happens blame him and court system. People pouring in. Bad!"[15] Again, the desire to avoid these consequences may induce judges in moments of crisis to be less rigorous in enforcing constitutional limits than they might ordinarily wish.

We employ a stylized model to capture these considerations, to explore the trade-offs confronting judges, and to investigate the implications for constitutional order. The model consists of a two-period, one-dimensional "case space" model involving three players: A court, and two successive governments. The case space orders governmental actions in such a way that they become increasingly extreme with

13 Vanberg, "Legislative-Judicial Relations: A Game Theoretic Approach to Constitutional Review;" Vanberg, *The Politics of Constitutional Review in Germany*; David Glick, "Conditional Strategic Retreat: The Court's Concession in the 1935 Gold Clause Cases."

14 Thomas Jefferson, "Letter to John B. Colvin." In P. Kurland and R. Lerner (eds.), *The Founders' Constitution*, Vol. 4. Indianapolis: Liberty Fund (1810/1987), 127.

15 Aaron Blake, "Trump Is Not-so-subtly Threatening the Judicial System and Even His Supreme Court Nominee is Upset." *Washington Post*. February 8, 2017.

respect to the constitutional principle at stake as we move from left to right. For example, economic regulations might become increasingly stringent, and ultimately include full nationalization. We assume that governments take actions, $a \in \mathbb{R}$, that fall along this continuum. Moreover, somewhere along this continuum there is a threshold, or "constitutional boundary," x_c that separates actions that are constitutionally acceptable ($a \leq x_c$) from those that are constitutionally unacceptable ($a > x_c$). We assume that this boundary is exogenously given (e.g., by a constituent assembly), and that the court's primary interest is in faithfully enforcing it. Thus, for purposes of this chapter, we abstract away from any potential principal–agent problem between the constituent assembly and the judiciary, as well as from issues of interpretive scope. While no doubt relevant to constitutional enforcement, these are secondary for our analysis.[16] Without loss of generality, we assume $x_c = 0$.

Governments may not care *directly* about the constitutional principle at stake. However, we assume that the policies over which governments have preferences implicate the constitutional principle. For example, governments may want to intervene in markets, and such interventions have implications for property rights. To keep things simple, assume that there exists a one-to-one mapping between the (unmodeled) policy space and the case space such that there exists a most preferred action g_i (where $i \in \{1, 2\}$) for each government, and governments prefer actions less the further they are from this ideal action.

The notion of a "crisis" is as follows. Recall our discussion above: a characteristic feature of crisis is that it requires an extraordinary action that may violate a constitutional norm. Thus, we assume that in period 1 (the crisis period), the government believes that it must take a crisis action, $a_1 > 0$. Without loss of generality, we assume $g_1 = a_1 = 1$. The court rules on this crisis action, and the government decides how to respond to the judicial ruling.

After the first period ends, the crisis passes, and a new government is selected. We assume that the preferred action of the second government is drawn from a uniform distribution: $g_2 \sim u[0, t]$, where $t < 1$. This modeling choice captures a number of features: First, by modeling the second-period government's preferences as a random draw, we incorporate the fact that judges face uncertainty over the actions that future governments may want to take. Second, assuming that $g_2 \geq x_c$ ensures that the constitutional boundary imposes a meaningful constraint: It prohibits actions the government would prefer to pursue in its absence. Finally, assuming that $t \leq 1$ ensures that the crisis is a crisis in the sense that future governments have more moderate preferences than crisis governments. Figure 7.1 illustrates this case-space.

[16] Georg Vanberg, "Substance vs. Procedure: Constitutional Enforcement and Constitutional Choice." *Journal of Economic Behavior & Organization* 80(2), 309–18.

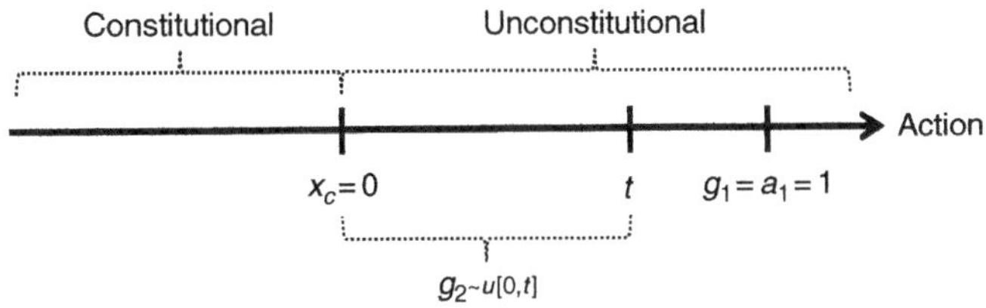

FIGURE 7.1 The case space

Two additional features of the model capture – in a simple fashion – the central factors that characterize the trade-offs confronting judges in times of crisis. One concerns the precedential value of judicial decisions. Suppose the court upholds the government's action a_1 in period 1. A worry for judges is that accommodating crisis action may erode constitutional constraints going forward. Allowing certain policies to pass constitutional muster may make it more difficult to constrain analogous policy choices by governments in the future. We model this aspect through a simple device: We assume that with probability $\gamma \in (0, 1)$, a decision to uphold the crisis action $a_1 = 1$ will be binding in the future, and effectively shift the constitutional boundary to 1. With probability $(1 - \gamma)$, the court will not find itself constrained by its prior decision. In words, as γ approaches 0, the court's crisis decision is increasingly likely to be a "one-off" decision that has little precedential value. On the other hand, as γ approaches 1, the court is more likely to be constrained by the current decision, and will have a difficult time "drawing back" the constitutional boundary once it has been expanded. Substantively, a number of features (some of which will be relevant in our case studies) matter in this respect, including the strength of norms of precedent in the legal system, the specific circumstances of a crisis decision that may make it more or less easy to distinguish future cases, etc.[17]

The second feature concerns the potential implications of defiance for the court's authority. As discussed above, one salient feature of decision-making in times of crisis is that it raises the specter of non-compliance. Governments may ignore judicial decisions that attempt to veto policies that governments are convinced are required to avert a crisis. Open defiance undermines judicial authority, and – by establishing a precedent for ignoring courts – is likely to reduce the pressure policymakers feel to comply with judicial decisions they oppose in the future. This is why judges are typically concerned to avoid defiance.[18]

17 One aspect of this is the ability of judges to issue a decision that is narrowly tailored to confine the "spillover" effects to other situations, and allows judges to make a plausible case that the principles on which a decision rests do not have broad applicability going forward. Note that this implies that γ may be – to some extent – endogenous to judicial decision-making. We ignore this aspect here.

18 Vanberg, *The Politics of Constitutional Review in Germany*.

We capture this feature by assuming that ignoring a judicial ruling imposes a cost of $\alpha > 0$ on a government. This parameter captures a variety of costs, ranging from the potential for a public backlash for ignoring judicial rulings,[19] to loss of market value if investors get jittery, or a reduced willingness of foreign governments to enter into agreements in the future. In other words, α represents the authority of the court, in the sense that it comprises the pressure that governments feel to comply with judicial rulings: The greater α, the more willing governments are to comply with rulings they oppose. We model the implications of defiance for judicial authority by assuming that if the first-period government ignores the court's decision, the authority of the court in the second period is given by $\tau\alpha$, where $\tau \in [0, 1]$. That is, as τ approaches 0, the implications of defiance for the court's authority are severe: An act of defiance by the first-period government largely eliminates pressure to comply in the future. In contrast, as τ approaches 1, the court's authority is not undermined in a meaningful sense by an act of defiance in the first-period. Thus, in the latter case, judges must be much less concerned about the strategic implications of confronting the crisis government than in the former.

We embed these features in a game played between a court and two successive governments. In the initial period, the first government confronts a crisis, and the court must rule on the government's policy choice. In the second period, a newly elected government chooses a policy in light of the outcomes of the crisis period. Specifically, the sequence of play is as follows:

1) In period 1, the government takes action $a_1 = 1$ in response to a crisis. The court reviews this action and can choose to uphold or to veto it, demanding that action conform to the constitutional boundary x_c, i.e. $S_c = \{\text{Uphold, Veto}\}$.
2) If the court vetoes, the crisis government chooses whether to accept the court's decision (which implies adopting x_c), or to ignore the court's ruling, i.e., $S_{g_1} = \{\text{Comply, Defy}\}$. Ignoring the court's ruling imposes a cost of $\alpha > 0$ on the government. The first period ends.
3) At the beginning of period 2, nature determines whether the court's first-period decision is binding. The decision is binding with probability $\gamma \in (0, 1)$. Nature also chooses a new government for the second period. The ideal action of this government is uniformly distributed on the interval $[0, t]$, where $t < 1$. Finally, if the government in period 1 complied with the court's ruling, the court's authority in period 2 is given by α. If the government defied the court, the court's authority in period 2 is given by $\tau\alpha$, where $\tau \in [0, 1]$.
4) The second-period government chooses an action, $a_2 \in \mathbb{R}$. The court reviews this action and either upholds it or vetoes it. If the court vetoes, the government chooses whether to comply with the decision or to ignore it.

19 Ibid.

The final feature of the model is the payoffs of the players. We assume that governments care about two aspects: First, they are concerned with the actions they take: They want to take an action as close as possible to their ideal. We capture this aspect with a standard quadratic loss function. Second, governments care about the potential costs of defying a judicial decision. For example, if the first-period government takes action $a_1 = 1$, the court vetoes this action, and the government defies, the government's payoff is given by:

$$U_{g_1}(a_1 = 1, Defy) = -\alpha$$

In contrast, if the government complies with the court's veto, it's payoff is given by:

$$U_{g_1}(a_1 = 1, Comply) = -(1 - x_c)^2$$

The payoffs for the second-period government are constructed analogously. For example, suppose the second-period government takes action a_2, which is vetoed, and the government complies. Its payoff is then given by:

$$U_{g_2}(a_2, Comply) = -(g_2 - x_c)^2$$

We assume that judges care about two aspects. One is the consistency of prevailing actions with the constitutional regime. To capture this, we assume that actions that violate the constitutional boundary yield a quadratic loss for judges. Thus, $U_c(a_i > x_c) = -(x_c - a_i)^2$. The more severe a constitutional violation, the lower the court's payoff. In contrast, actions that are consistent with the constitutional boundary provide a payoff of 0, i.e., $U_c(a \leq x_c) = 0$. In addition, we allow for the possibility that during the crisis period, the court is concerned with the practical consequences of not allowing the government to address the crisis. We capture this feature by assuming that if the court effectively vetoes the government's action, and prevents a crisis response, it pays a cost of $t_c \geq 0$. Thus, when $t_c = 0$, judges are unconcerned with the practical consequences of the decision for the crisis at hand, and only care about the consistency of policy with the constitutional boundary. As t_c increases, judges are increasingly concerned not to stymie the government's crisis response. The court's payoff equals the sum of the payoffs from each of the two periods (for simplicity, we ignore discounting). For example, suppose the court effectively vetoes the crisis response in period 1, but upholds action a_2 by the second-period government. The court's payoff is then given by:

$$U_C(Veto, Uphold) = -t_C - (x_c - a_2)^2$$

Importantly, note the court does not care about its authority *directly* – although this will matter *indirectly* because it affects the governments' policy choices.

II. EQUILIBRIUM

The appropriate solution concept for this model is subgame-perfection. Loosely speaking, subgame perfection ensures that players do not employ "non-credible threats," that is, that they respond optimally to the strategic situation confronting them over time. We reserve a formal statement of the unique pure-strategy equilibrium to the appendix, which also contains all proofs. Instead, we focus here on providing the intuition behind the equilibrium, and exploring the implications of the model through a series of observations.

Two implications of the model that we are particularly interested in are the exercise of constitutional review by the court in the crisis period, and the long-term implications of the crisis and the court's response for the constitutional order. In the context of the model, we can think of these long-term consequences as represented by the policy choice that prevails in the second (non-crisis) period: How closely does this policy conform to the constitutional boundary ($x_c = 0$)?

Before we focus on these issues, however, we begin with the intuition underlying the model's equilibrium. To do so, consider the choice confronting the two governments. The trade-off they face is simple: They can comply with the boundary imposed by the court in its decision and live with the policy consequences of doing so, or they can ignore the court in order to pursue their preferred policy while paying the price for defiance (α or $\tau\alpha$). The details of the governments' equilibrium strategies are stated in the appendix, but the logic is straightforward. Governments are more likely to comply with an unwelcome decision as the court's authority increases, i.e., the greater the cost of non-compliance.

For the second-period government, the choice between these alternatives also depends critically on the outcome of the crisis period: If the first-period government ignored the court's decision during the crisis, the court's authority has been reduced to $\tau\alpha$, thus making second-period governments more willing to defy judicial decisions. And if the court upheld the crisis government's action, the decision to do so may have significant precedential effects, shifting (with probability γ) the effective constitutional boundary to 1, allowing the second-period government free rein.

Finally, consider the court's decision. On the one hand, its decision in the crisis period has potential long-term consequences for its ability to constrain the second-period government. On the other hand, its decision may also have ramifications for the crisis government's ability to confront the crisis. In particular, if the court's authority is sufficiently high, the crisis government will comply with a judicial veto. As a result, if the court prefers not to constrain the government in its response to the crisis (i.e., $t_c > 0$), it must weigh the long-run consequences of its decision against the short-term implications for the government's ability to manage the crisis.

Figure 7.2 summarizes how the court resolves this trade-off, and illustrates the model's equilibrium implications for the court's exercise of constitutional review in the crisis period. We summarize the intuition behind the equilibrium, and then

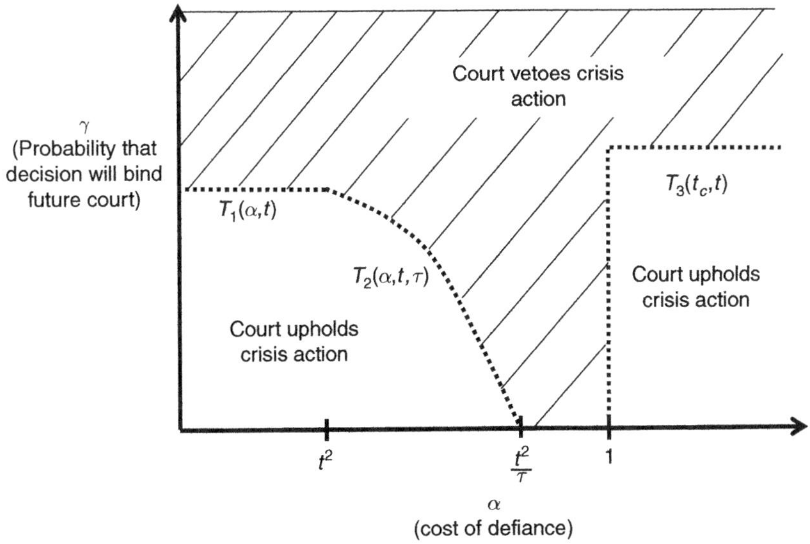

FIGURE 7.2 The court's equilibrium crisis-period decision

explore the implications of this equilibrium through several observations. The figure graphs the court's authority (α) along the x-axis, and the probability that a decision to uphold the crisis action will be binding in the future (γ) along the y-axis. The figure displays the court's decision for various combinations of these parameters, conditional on the potential damage to the court's authority of defiance (τ), and the extent to which the court is concerned about the crisis (t_c).

On the right-hand side of the figure, where $\alpha \geq 1$, the court's authority is so substantial that the crisis government will comply with a judicial veto. This means that the court now confronts the following trade-off: Striking down $a_1 = 1$ prevents the government from effectively confronting the crisis, but it ensures that the constitutional boundary for the second period remains at $x_c = 0$. In contrast, upholding a_1 allows the government to deal with the current crisis, but does so at the risk that the constitutional boundary will erode, and the court will not be able to rein in the second-period government. How the court views this trade-off depends critically on two aspects: First, how concerned is the court about the current crisis, i.e., how large is t_c? As t_c increases, the boundary $T_3(t_c, t)$ shifts up, enlarging the parameter space in which the court chooses to uphold the crisis action. Second, how detrimental is a decision to uphold the crisis action for the constitutional order in the second period? Thus, if a decision to uphold the crisis action is sufficiently likely to be binding in the future (γ is large enough, in the northeastern part of the figure), the court chooses to veto the crisis action despite the fact that doing so prevents effective crisis management because the implications of acquiescence for the integrity of the constitutional order in the second period are more significant. Similarly, as t becomes larger, and second-period governments are expected to have more extreme preferences, the boundary $T_3(t_c, t)$ shifts down, enlarging the parameter space in which the court will choose to veto rather than uphold the crisis action. Once again, the intuition is clear: As second-period governments are more likely to have extreme preferences, the costs of eroding the constitutional boundary for the future loom larger in the judicial calculus.

Now consider the left side of Figure 7.2. When $\alpha < 1$, the court's authority is insufficient to induce the crisis government to comply with a judicial veto. If the court tries to enforce the constitutional boundary, the crisis government will defy its decision. As a result, the scenario confronting the court changes significantly. How the court feels about the current crisis (t_c) becomes immaterial: The current government will deal with the crisis no matter what the court decides. Instead, the only question confronting the court now is how the outcome of the crisis will affect the second period. The central trade-off is simple: The court could choose to "mask" its inability to force compliance by upholding the crisis action. The advantage of forestalling a conflict in this way is that it preserves the court's authority. The downside is that a decision to approve the crisis action may erode the constitutional boundary in the future. Alternatively, the court could strike down the crisis response. Doing so will preserve the court's ability to insist on the constitutional boundary in the future. But it will also result in defiance and a loss of authority.

The left-hand side of Figure 7.2 illustrates how these trade-offs play out. One aspect of this dynamic is already familiar: As γ increases, and a decision to uphold the crisis action is more likely to be binding, the costs of endorsing the government's action increase. At some point, these costs are too high, and the court vetos, despite the fact that its decision will be ignored. It does so to protect its ability to insist on the constitutional boundary in the future. A second aspect concerns the impact of the court's authority, α. In the south-western part of the figure, the court's authority is limited, and a decision to uphold the crisis action is unlikely to be binding. As a result, the court chooses to mask its weakness by upholding. But as the court's authority grows, the court will eventually choose to veto the crisis action. The logic is the following: As the court's authority grows, for a given τ, the court's authority in the second period – even after being defied – is more formidable, and it can generate greater pressure to comply with the constitutional boundary. As a result, the court is more willing to veto and suffer defiance during the crisis in order to protect the constitutional boundary for the future. Moreover, as τ increases, and the court's authority is less vulnerable to defiance, the thresholds $T_1(\alpha, \tau)$ and $T_2(\alpha, t, \tau)$ shift down – the court becomes more aggressive in its exercise of judicial review since the costs of defiance have decreased.

III. IMPLICATIONS OF THE MODEL FOR CONSTITUTIONALISM AND CRISIS

What are the implications of this model for constitutional review in times of crisis, and the long-term implications of crisis for the constitutional order? We begin with the implications for the court's exercise of constitutional review.

Observation 1: Strategic judicial retreat can result from both judicial weakness *and* from judicial strength. Weak courts may engage in strategic retreat in order to avoid non-compliance, while strong courts may engage in strategic retreat in order to avoid the costs of constraining a government from responding to a crisis.

Existing scholarship has highlighted that moments of crisis – in which governments may be so committed to particular courses of action that they are likely to resist or defy judicial attempts at enforcing constitutional constraints – can lead to "judicial self-censoring." In an attempt to mask the limits of their power, and protect against the damaging effects of open defiance for their authority, judges may choose to uphold policies they would prefer to strike down. This dynamic is clearly evident in our model – the left-hand side of Figure 7.2 illustrates that as the court's authority declines (α decreases), the court is more likely to uphold the crisis action. Moreover, as the damage of defiance becomes more pronounced (i.e., as τ decreases), the court engages in judicial self-censoring for a larger portion of the parameter space ($T_1(\alpha, \tau)$ and $T_2(\alpha, t, \tau)$ shift up).

Importantly, however, the figure also reveals that judicial self-censoring is not *only* a means to avoid defiance. On the right-hand side of Figure 7.2, the court also engages in judicial self-censoring, provided that γ is not too high. Here, judges approve the crisis action because they know that the government will comply with a judicial veto – and judges are concerned about curbing the ability of governments effectively to deal with the crisis. In short, in times of crisis, judicial self-censoring can result not only from judicial weakness, but also from judicial strength. This implies that for some values of γ, the court's exercise of its veto powers is not monotonic in the court's authority: When the court is weak, it upholds the crisis action to avoid defiance. As its authority grows, it begins to issue vetoes in an effort to protect its ability to enforce the constitutional boundary in the future. But as the court's authority continues to increase, it once again begins to uphold the crisis action: Recognizing its strength, the court engages in self-restraint in order to avoid hamstringing the government from being able to confront a crisis.

Of course, a principal reason for being interested in the manner in which the court confronts the crisis government is that this interaction has consequences for the future: If the court's authority is challenged, it may be weakened. If the court chooses to tolerate the crisis government's actions, the future constitutional boundary may expand significantly. In either case, the crisis period may weaken enforcement of the constitutional boundary in the second period. We can explore the extent

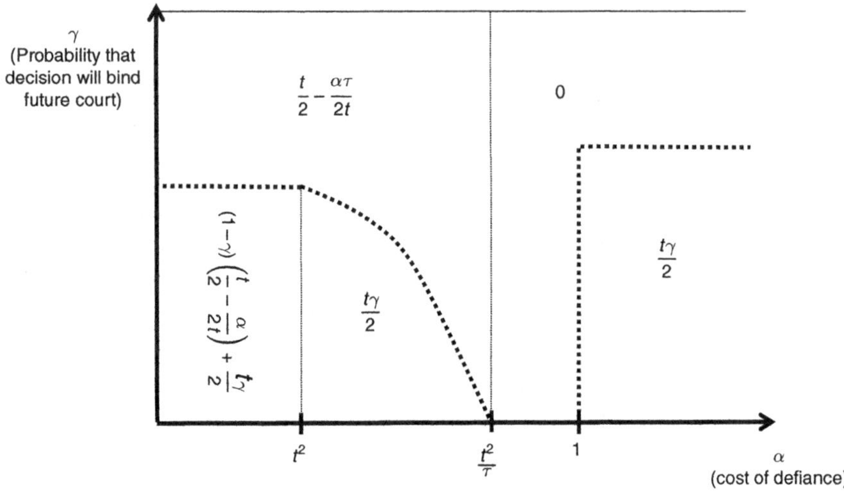

FIGURE 7.3 Expected second-period policy outcome

to which the constitutional order is reshaped by the crisis moment by considering the expected governmental action in the second period.

In Figure 7.3, we graph the action that is expected to prevail in the second period. Once again, the figure plots the court's authority (on the x-axis) against the likelihood that a judicial decision will be binding in the second period (the y-axis). Note several features. In the upper right-hand part of the parameter space, the court successfully enforces the constitutional boundary in the second period. In this area, the court issues a veto, and its authority is so high that the second-period government complies with the court's decision. In the southeastern part of the figure, the court upholds the crisis action, a decision that will be binding and shift the constitutional boundary to 1 with probability γ. As a result, the second-period government may be able to implement its ideal point. In the northwestern part of the space, the second-period action depends on the court's authority and the damage of defiance: Recall that in this area, the court strikes down the crisis action despite the expectation that it will be defied. The court's authority suffers as a result. Some second-period governments – those sufficiently close to the constitutional boundary – will comply with the court's demands, but those with more extreme preferences will ignore them. The extent to which this happens depends, obviously, on the court's authority – the greater the court's authority, and the more limited the damage of defiance, the greater the set of governments that will comply with the court's demands. Finally, in the southwestern part of the figure, the expected policy outcome depends on the court's authority and the stickiness of judicial decisions. In this part of the parameter space, the court chooses to engage in self-censoring, and upholds the crisis action. As a result, the constitutional boundary may shift to 1 if the court's decision is binding. Once again, second-

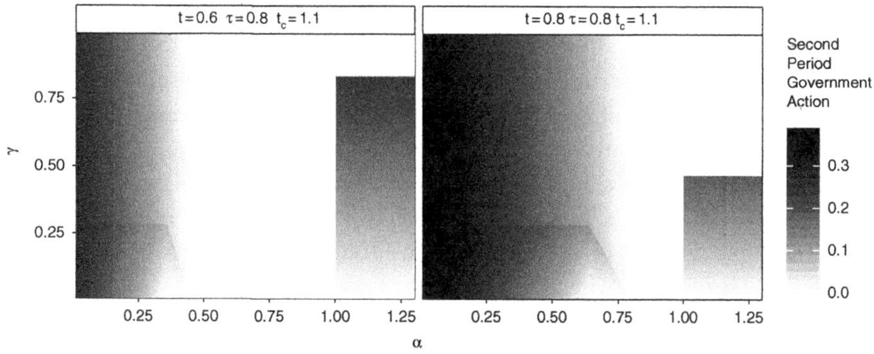

FIGURE 7.4 Expected second-period policy outcome

period governments may be able to implement their ideal point. These results lead to a second observation:

Observation 2: Under certain conditions, *moderately* powerful courts may be more effective in preserving the integrity of the constitutional order in the long run than either weak or powerful courts.

We illustrate this observation in a more intuitive way by transforming Figure 7.3 into a contour graph that directly maps the expected second-period policy in the parameter space. Darker regions correspond to second-period policies that deviate further from the constitutional boundary $x_c = 0$, while lighter regions indicate second-period policies that more closely conform to the boundary. Moving across the two panels of Figure 7.4, t increases from 0.6 to 0.8, i.e., the second-period government is likely to have more extreme preferences in the right panel. Figure 7.4 reveals that the second-period policy does not respond monotonically to the key parameters of the model. Most importantly, in the lower part of the figure, increases in judicial authority do not lead to consistent decreases in the second-period action as we might naively expect. As the court becomes more powerful, constitutional enforcement does not steadily improve. Instead, the relationship between the second-period policy and the court's authority is non-monotonic. It is moderately strong courts that are best able to preserve the constitutional order in the long run. The intuition behind this result is that moderately strong courts are freed from the quandary that can lead very powerful courts to sanction unconstitutional policies in times of crisis for fear of hamstringing the government – a decision that can have detrimental consequences for the constitutional order if such a decision limits the court's ability to enforce the constitutional boundary going forward.

IV. ILLUSTRATION: FINANCIAL CRISIS, THE GOLD CLAUSES, AND GREECE

The lessons that emerge from our model are that crises can have profound implications for the manner in which courts exercise their powers and for the long-term nature of the constitutional order. Crisis can induce judicial self-censoring for two starkly different reasons: In one case, it is a defensive mechanism to avoid defiance, in the other, a response to judicial strength, as judges seek to avoid hemming in governments in times of crisis. As a consequence, the aggressiveness with which courts exercise judicial oversight in times of crisis is not monotonic. Weak as well as strong courts may choose not to police constitutional boundaries as vigorously as moderately strong courts. Moreover, the long-run nature of the constitutional order may be more faithful to the original constitutional boundary when courts are moderately strong than when they are either weak or very strong.

In this section, we turn to two case studies to illustrate these insights. These illustrations do not provide rigorous evidence for our argument. Rather, they are intended to demonstrate that the model provides a plausible lens for understanding salient judicial decisions rendered in crisis conditions.

V. ABROGATING THE GOLD CLAUSES

We begin with a case that illustrates the paradigm of a weak court capitulating in the face of government pressure.[20] In 1933, the United States was mired in the Great Depression, and Franklin Roosevelt had been elected in part on a promise to move the country out of crisis. One pressing issue concerned the fact that the combination of adherence to the gold standard, persistent deflation, and a drop in GDP had dramatically increased government debt obligations (and those of private debtors). Reducing these debt levels was a part of the Roosevelt administration's planned set of economic reforms.[21] One strategy to do so was to inflate the currency.[22] However, such a policy faced a contractual barrier in the form of "gold clauses," which gave bondholders the option of asking for repayment in either the existing currency or a pre-specified amount of gold.[23] These clauses, which had been added to bond issues explicitly as an inflation hedge, were widespread, affecting roughly $100 billion of the $168 billion federal debt.[24]

[20] In his essay in this volume, Barry Cushman offers an account of the Supreme Court's New Deal jurisprudence, including the *Gold Clause* cases, that argues that the Court felt less constrained by the general political climate than is often supposed. Cushman's interpretation is not necessarily at odds with ours; we focus on the stakes confronting the Court in a specific case with significant implications for the FDR administration rather than a broad assessment of the Court's jurisprudence during this era.

[21] Sebastian Edwards, "Gold, the Brains Trust, and Roosevelt." *History of Political Economy* 49 (2017), 1–30.

[22] Kenneth Dam, "From the Gold Clause Cases to Constitutional Necessity: A Half Century of American Monetary Law" *University of Chicago Law Review* 50 (1983), 504–32, 520.

[23] Gerard Magliocca, "The Gold Clause Cases and Constitutional Necessity." *Florida State Law Review* 64 (2012), 1243–78.

[24] See Government Brief in Perry, at 13. See also Randal Kroszner, "Is It Better to Forgive than to Receive? Repudiation of the Gold Indexation Clause in Long-term Debt During the Great Depression." CRSP Working Paper 481, University of Chicago (1999).

By including the gold clauses in its bond issues, the federal government had, in effect, promised its creditors that it would not try to inflate its way out of its debt obligations – which is just what the Roosevelt administration wanted to do. In June 1933, the administration decided to push ahead. Congress passed a joint resolution declaring gold clauses as "against public policy" and, therefore, illegal.[25] Creditors faced a haircut of roughly 30 cents on the dollar.[26] Not surprisingly, bondholders sued, and four cases made their way to the Supreme Court, involving both private and government bonds. We focus on the most high-profile of these cases, *Perry* v. *United States* (294 U.S. 330), which involved a Liberty Bond, and thus the debt obligations of the federal government.[27] In a 5–4 decision that provoked a blistering dissent, a majority of justices argued that the abrogation had imposed no injury on bondholders, in effect upholding the Roosevelt administration's action. They did so despite the fact that even the justices in the majority had significant legal reservations about the constitutionality of abrogation.[28] As others have argued (see Glick 2009), one way to understand this episode is as an instance of "strategic retreat" by a weak court confronted by a determined executive. Put in the language of our model, the *Perry* Court found itself in the southwestern part of Figure 7.2. On this interpretation, the Court chose to uphold the government's crisis action to mask its institutional weakness, and forestall a confrontation with the Roosevelt administration that could damage the Court's authority. To make a plausible case for such an interpretation, we need to show that:

1. The justices' sincere preferences were to strike down the government's action.
2. There was no compelling legal case that would have pointed to a decision favorable to the government.
3. The Court was weak in the sense of our model, i.e., it faced the likely prospect that a decision to nullify the abrogation of the gold clauses would be met with defiance.
4. As a result, the Court chose not to enforce the gold clauses.

We begin with the political context of the *Perry* case, which speaks directly to the justices' likely expectations about how a decision to strike down the abrogation might be met. The *Gold Clause* cases, and in particular *Perry*, were salient politically, and "dominated the news throughout the period."[29] Given the enormous

25 Joint Resolution, 48 Stat. 112, 6/5/33.

26 What must have been particularly galling to some of these creditors is that many of the bonds involved were so-called "Liberty Bonds," issued with a patriotic appeal to support the government's war effort.

27 Our discussion draws heavily on Glick (2009). Glick argues that the Court engaged in "strategic retreat" in refusing to enforce the gold clauses in federal government bonds in *Perry*.

28 Paul Moreno, *The American State from the Civil War to the New Deal* (New York: Cambridge University Press, 2013), 251.

29 As Glick (2009: 805) notes, "The phrase 'gold clause' appeared in more [New York] *Times* articles (49) on the day after the decisions than did 'poultry,' (10) 'minimum wage,' (19) and 'abortion' (15) combined, on the days after *Schecter*, *West Coast Hotel*, and *Roe*." See Glick, "Conditional Strategic Retreat: The Court's Concession in the 1935 Gold Clause Cases," 805.

financial impact of abrogation on the federal government, there was little doubt that the Roosevelt administration had an interest in not seeing its policy subverted. It took clear steps to impress this fact upon the justices. The focus of the government's brief was economic rather than legal, emphasizing the potential costs of reversing Congressional action. As Glick argues, the brief also "made [the government's] willingness to directly challenge the Court very clear" and "planted the idea that it would not comply with a ruling requiring it to pay gold clause value."[30] The government's strong interest in the outcome was underscored when Attorney General Cummings personally argued the case before the Supreme Court – the first time he had done so. To veto abrogation, he claimed, would cause the national debt to skyrocket, resulting in a "stupendous catastrophe" and a "[return to] chaos" for the nation.[31]

The very real potential for defiance was further illustrated by FDR's decision to draft, and then leak to the media, a speech explaining that in his view, upholding the gold clauses would result in an undeserved windfall for bondholders while imposing higher taxes, higher unemployment, and economic hardship on the general public. As a result, FDR announced, he would refuse to honor such a decision.[32] In the weeks following oral arguments, The *Los Angeles Times*, *Washington Post*, and *New York Times* all ran stories indicating that the President stood ready to disregard an unfavorable Supreme Court decision.[33] With respect to federal bonds – the instrument at issue in *Perry* – he was unquestionably in a position to do so: Because honoring the gold clauses would have required the Treasury to pay the value of gold clauses, refusing to do so was directly within the executive's power. In short, the political landscape surrounding the *Perry* decision likely left little doubt in the justices' minds that any attempt to interfere with abrogation for federal government bonds would provoke a confrontation, and resistance.

When the Court issued its decision in *Perry*, a majority of justices in effect refused to enforce the gold clauses for federal government bonds, thus handing the FDR administration the victory it had sought. But was this decision a response to the political climate confronting the court? To make this argument persuasive, two alternative explanations must be eliminated. The first is a purely legal explanation, i.e., that legal doctrine and precedent compelled the result, no matter what the justices' personal attitudes or the political situation might have been. As Glick has

30 Id. at 806.

31 Magliocca, "The Gold Clause Cases and Constitutional Necessity," 1257; Glick, "Conditional Strategic Retreat: The Court's Concession in the 1935 Gold Clause Cases," 806.

32 Magliocca, "The Gold Clause Cases and Constitutional Necessity," 1263–65.

33 The *Los Angeles Times* report on FDR's draft speech threatening defiance appeared *after* the Supreme Court's conference vote on *Perry*. Thus, the decision not to enforce the gold clauses could not have been a direct response to this specific threat. However, from our perspective, the general atmosphere surrounding the *Perry* decision made clear that defiance was "in the air," and FDR's draft speech is one indicator of this mood. See also Magliocca, "The Gold Clause Cases and Constitutional Necessity," 1260–61; Glick, "Conditional Strategic Retreat: The Court's Concession in the 1935 Gold Clause Cases," 806.

shown, however, "the legal landscape was not controlling in the *Gold Clause cases*."[34] The issues presented were either novel, or there existed conflicting precedents that pointed in opposite directions. Of course, the fact that the justices had legal maneuver room raises the other potential explanation that must be ruled out: Did the majority sincerely favor the government's position?

It is impossible to establish the justices' sincere views conclusively. But there are strong indications that a majority of justices profoundly disagreed with what they were being pushed to do. During oral argument, a majority of justices displayed open hostility to the government's actions. Four justices, of course, dissented. The dissent, written by Justice McReynolds, charged that *Perry* amounted "to a declaration that the Government may give with one hand and take away with the other. Default is thus made both easy and safe!" He predicted that the long-term consequences for the United States were going to be significant: "Loss of reputation for honorable dealing will bring us unending humiliation; the impending legal and moral chaos is appalling." From the bench, McReynolds pronounced that "This is Nero in his worst form"[35] and that "the Constitution as many of us have understood it has gone."[36] More importantly, there is evidence that the justices in the *majority* were convinced of the illegality of the government's actions. Informally, Justice Brandeis made clear that he was unhappy with what had been done.[37] Similarly, Justices Stone and Hughes expressed grave concerns.[38]

Perhaps the best evidence that the justices in the majority decided to uphold abrogation despite their reservations comes from the majority opinion itself. The argument laid out in the Court's opinion is, in many ways, strange – an apparent tension that can be readily explained if the majority felt compelled to act against its better judgment, and tried to limit the potential impact of "judicial self-censoring." The first part of the opinion presented a powerful attack on the Roosevelt administration's policy, and ruled the abrogation of the gold clauses in federal bonds unconstitutional. The Court argued that while the government could use its authority over monetary matters to abrogate the clauses in debt contracts in the broader market, it was an altogether different matter to abrogate provisions in the government's own debt contracts. And yet, at the last moment, the Court snatched victory from the plaintiffs in an illogical if not bizarre fashion. The Court argued that while the government's actions were illegal, the plaintiffs had no remedy: Since the gold market had been shut down, plaintiffs could not receive payment in gold. Even if payment were made in gold tender (that is, gold as currency or legal tender), gold as currency had a fixed price set by the government.[39] At bottom then, Chief Justice

34 Id. at 811.

35 Magliocca, "The Gold Clause Cases and Constitutional Necessity," 1272.

36 Glick, "Conditional Strategic Retreat: The Court's Concession in the 1935 Gold Clause Cases," 812.

37 Melvin Urofsky, *Louis D. Brandeis* (New York: Schocken Books, 2009), 698.

38 Glick, "Conditional Strategic Retreat: The Court's Concession in the 1935 Gold Clause Cases," 811.

39 Kenneth Dam, "From the Gold Clause Cases to Constitutional Necessity: A Half Century of American Monetary Law," 516.

Hughes' opinion argued, there was no loss suffered by the plaintiffs.[40] This logic was strange: It was well recognized that the plaintiffs had purchased an inflation hedge.[41] So long as they were paid the value of their hedge (and the price of gold was readily available on the international market), the plaintiffs would be happy. Put differently, the court seemed to assert that plaintiffs could not be helped because the tort measure of damages could not be satisfied. But the plaintiffs had a contract claim, and the contract measure of damages (the difference between what was promised and what was received) could indeed be satisfied.[42]

How could the Court, with luminaries like Brandeis and Cardozo, have issued a decision that strains logic and common sense in this way? The answer, we conjecture, is that confronted with a determined Roosevelt administration and the specter of defiance, the justices in the majority felt forced to accept the abrogation of the gold clauses in federal bonds. Compelled to consent to the government's actions, they sought to do so in a fashion that would stay as close as possible to the rule that contract terms must be respected, and make it difficult for future governments to use as precedent. In other words, the justices consciously attempted to construct a decision that would have limited impact on the future development of the law – in the language of the model presented above, the justices wanted to write an opinion that would reduce γ as much as possible.[43] An illogical decision might fit that bill. Feeling forced to abandon their preferred constitutional rule, the justices wrote the kind of narrow, fact specific, and badly reasoned opinion that they hoped would never be applied again. History suggests that they were right. At the time, the *Gold Clause* cases were among the most famous that the Court had ever tackled. Yet today, they are not part of the constitutional canon. They are rarely, if ever, applied and have largely been forgotten by constitutional scholars.

40 Ibid. This logic perhaps made more sense in the *Nortz* case where plaintiffs had gold certificates, entitling them to payment in gold. But there, the logic the court used was that that gold was required to be turned in to the Treasury at a fixed price.

41 The Court had itself taken this view in the *Norman* case (involving private debt contracts): *Norman* v. *Baltimore & O.R.R.*, 294 U.S. at 302, 314. The view had also been recognized by the Permanent Court of International Justice and the House of Lords. *See Concerning the Payment of Various Serbian Loans Issued in France (Fr.* v. *Serbia)*, 1929 P.C.I.J., ser. A, No. 20, at 48 (Judgment of July 12); *Concerning the Payment in Gold of the Brazilian Federal Loans Issued in France (Fr.* v. *Braz.)*, 1929 P.C.I.J., ser. A, No. 21, at 110 (Judgment of July 12); *Feist* v. *Société Intercommunale Belge d'Electricité*, 1934 A.C. 161, 175 (H.L. 1933). See ibid. at 518–19.

42 Henry Hart wrote that "[few] more baffling pronouncements, it is fair to say, have ever issued from the United States Supreme Court" (Hart 1935). On the damages point, see Glick (2009: 814). The court also seemed to say that the plaintiffs would be unjustly enriched since their hedges were to protect them from inflation, but not to reward them for deflation. The theory somehow being that plaintiffs had inadvertently agreed to contract terms that gave them more value than they paid for (294 U.S. at 357–58). Once again, from a contract perspective, the logic is strange – courts rarely make determinations of substantive value in contract, and particularly not when there was no evidence that the party being penalized had misbehaved in any way in drafting the contract (indeed, they are not supposed to).

43 This observation points to a potential extension of the model presented here, which would recognize that γ may, within constraints, be under the control of judges, and thus partially endogenous.

VI. "WHATEVER IT TAKES"

While the US Supreme Court's decision in *Perry* arguably illustrates strategic retreat by a weak court in the face of likely defiance, our second case study is designed to showcase the other end of the spectrum: Judicial "self-censoring" by a strong court concerned about the potential consequences of limiting a government's ability to respond to crisis. This case study revolves around two decisions issued by the German Federal Constitutional Court (FCC) in a dispute surrounding the European Central Bank's (ECB) response to the economic crisis enveloping Europe in 2012. By the summer of that year, it appeared that threats to the viability of the common currency were becoming real for the countries of the eurozone: Borrowing costs were skyrocketing for a number of European countries, putting them in an increasingly dire financial situation.

In the face of this threat, ECB governor Mario Draghi promised in August 2012 to do "whatever it takes" to calm financial markets, and to protect the financial stability of eurozone governments.[44] The policy he announced in order to accomplish this was the Outright Monetary Transactions policy (OMT). Under the OMT program, the ECB promised to buy the short-term bonds of euro area member countries in unlimited amounts should circumstances call for it (lending credence to the promise to do "whatever it takes"). Moreover, the ECB promised that should a restructuring of a euro member nation's bonds occur, the ECB would not claim priority status (as it had some months prior with Greece).[45]

The hope of the ECB, shared by other European policymakers, was that the OMT program would lower the cost of financing for distressed countries. Knowing that the ECB was standing ready to buy bonds in the secondary market in "unlimited" amounts, purchasers in the primary market for bonds would feel safer, leading to a lowering of interest rates. The ultimate goal of the policy was thus to avert the risk of "redenomination" – that is, the need for a member nation to exit the euro. Greece, of course, was the primary candidate for such a development. By all appearances, the combination of Draghi's statement and the announcement of the OMT program worked to calm the markets.[46] Interest rates fell dramatically, including for the bonds of countries in distress.

Despite its apparent success, the ECB's OMT policy was not met with applause in all corners of the eurozone, particularly in Germany. In Germany, European Union efforts to "prop up" Southern European countries, including through OMT, were

44 Draghi's specific words were: "Within our mandate, the ECB is ready to do whatever it takes to preserve the euro. And believe me, it will be enough." See Carsten Gerner-Beuerle, Esin Küçük and Edmund Schuster, "Law Meets Economics in the German Federal Constitutional Court: Outright Monetary Transactions on Trial." *German Law Journal* 15 (2014), 282; Mehreen Khan, "Happy Mario Draghi Day: Four Charts After 'Whatever it Takes.'" *Financial Times*, July 26, 2016.

45 Benoit Coeure, "Outright Monetary Transactions: One Year On", Speech at Conference on the ECB and OMT, Sept 2, 2013. Available at www.ecb.europa.eu/press/key/date/2013/html/sp130902.en.html.

46 Claire Jones, "German High Court Backs ECB on Crisis-fighting Tool." *Financial Times*, June 21, 2015, 63.

unpopular. At its core, the ECB is a collection of central banks. Thus, the guarantee to do "whatever it takes" was, in effect, a guarantee by the stronger central banks to purchase bonds issued by financially distressed governments. The strongest of these central banks was the Bundesbank – and the potential that German taxpayers might be liable for what would amount to significant transfer payments to Southern European countries raised significant, and politically salient, concerns in Germany.

Moreover, to many German observers, OMT represented a violation of the terms under which Germany had entered the euro, and submitted to the authority of the ECB.[47] Under the Maastricht Treaty, the ECB has a circumscribed mandate to engage in monetary policy to keep prices stable, but not to engage in monetary financing of individual euro area countries (Art. 123 TFEU). A promise to buy unlimited quantities of a member country's debt in order to prop it up when it did not enjoy the confidence of the markets seemed inconsistent with the ECB's mandate.[48] It also appeared in tension with the so-called "no bail-out clause" of the Lisbon Treaty (Art. 125), which prohibits the European Union from "bailing out" member state governments in financial distress. From the perspective of the critics in Germany, OMT constituted not only a violation of European law, but also a violation of German law.[49] Significantly, these concerns were shared by the Bundesbank itself: Jens Weidemann, the head of the Bundesbank, was staunchly opposed to OMT.[50] Led by a German legislator, Peter Gauweiler, a number of prominent politicians and academics lodged constitutional complaints in front of the German Constitutional Court to challenge the legality of the ECB's OMT program, arguing that the policy violated both European law and the budgetary autonomy of the German parliament.

Potentially, these challenges posed a significant threat to the OMT policy.[51] There were two reasons. One was the authority of the constitutional court. The FCC enjoys tremendous confidence among German citizens – exceeding trust in other political institutions, including parliament and the federal government by significant margins.[52] Opposing a negative ruling on OMT by the court – especially given the general public skepticism towards German financial obligations

47 The title of a Bloomberg article reporting on the case is telling: "ECB Bond Program Dubbed 'Financial Dictatorship' in German Court" (Matussek and Speciale 2016).

48 The fact that the ECB seemed to have announced a willingness to take haircuts on the same terms as ordinary investors made things worse: It further increased the risk that countries like Germany faced in the event that another member nation of the euro area acted irresponsibly in accumulating too much debt. *See* Ashoka Mody, "The German Court Does Europe a Favor." Bruegel (2014). Available at http://bruegel.org/2014/10/the-german-court-does-europe-a-favour/; David Art, "The German Rescue of the Eurozone: How Germany is Getting the Europe it Always Wanted." *Political Science Quarterly* 130 (2015), 181–212.

49 Michael Wilkinson, "The Euro Is Irreversible! ... Or Is It?: On OMT, Austerity, and the Threat of Grexit." *German Law Journal* 16 (2015), 1050.

50 Wagstyl, "Weidmann Renews Attack on ECB's Monetary Stimulus."

51 Hans Werner Sinn, "Germany's Constitutional Court Prepares to Make Crunch Decision." *The Guardian*, June 26, 2013.

52 See Vanberg, *The Politics of Constitutional Review in Germany*; Hans Vorlaender and Andre Brodocz, "Das Vertrauen in das Bundesverfassungsgericht." In H. Vorlaender (ed.), *Die Deutungsmacht der Verfassungsgerichtsbarkeit* (Heidelberg: Springer, 2013).

towards Southern European countries – would likely incur significant political costs on the part of the German government. Second, the German institution most directly involved in the OMT program – and therefore most immediately affected by a potential FCC veto – was the Bundesbank. And the Bundesbank had already taken the position that participating in the OMT was improper, including in materials submitted to the FCC.[53] Put differently, given that implementation of an order from the FCC finding the OMT to be ultra vires would have been in the hands of the Bundesbank (in its role as Germany's representative at the ECB), compliance with a veto of OMT seemed assured. Moreover, even though the German government led by Mrs. Merkel had indicated its support of Mr. Draghi's program,[54] it gave no indication of being willing to cross the combination of two of the most respected institutions in Germany should the FCC rule against OMT.

In short, it is probable that the German court found itself on the right edge of Figure 7.2: the judges of the FCC likely knew that they were in a position – via a veto – to undercut the ECB's crisis response, and to cripple the OMT policy. When the court issued its final decision in June 2016, it refused to veto OMT, and largely upheld the ECB's policy. To make a case that this decision can be interpreted as an instance of "strategic retreat" by a powerful court concerned to avoid the consequences of a veto, we need to show that it is plausible that:

1. The judges of the FCC believed that OMT constituted a violation of German and/or European law.
2. That they chose to uphold OMT because they were concerned about the consequences of hamstringing the ECB's crisis response.

Of course, as in the case of *Perry*, it is not possible to establish the views of the judges conclusively. However, strong evidence regarding the judges' sincere views of the legality of OMT emerge out of a curious feature of the OMT dispute. The FCC's decision in June 2016 was its *second* decision on the constitutional complaints. The court had issued an earlier, initial decision in January 2014 – a decision in which the court announced its view of the OMT program, but sent the case to the European Court of Justice (ECJ) for a ruling on the compatibility of the program with EU law.[55] This initial opinion left little doubt that the six-member majority (two judges dissented) viewed the OMT program as inconsistent with European law. Moreover, the court explicitly laid out the narrow conditions under which, in the opinion of the judges, the OMT policy would be legal. Specifically, the FCC posited that there could not be a commitment to buying bonds in unlimited quantities, and that a meaningful time-gap between the issuance of debt by a distressed sovereign and

53 For a report on the amicus brief filed by the Bundesbank, see Jan Hildebrand, "Weidmann rechnet mit der EZB ab," *Handelsblatt*, April 4, 2013.

54 Mody, "The German Court Does Europe a Favor."

55 Bundesverfassungsgericht [BVerfG] [Federal Constitutional Court], Jan. 14, 2014, Case No. 2 BvR 2728/13.

its purchase by the ECB would be required. Moreover, the FCC insisted that the purpose of the ECB's actions must be price stability (not economic resuscitation), and that the ECB's bonds would not face the risk of being restructured. In effect, the conditions laid out by the German court in its initial decision would gut the OMT.[56] "Whatever it takes" would no longer be the policy promise.

However – despite clearly articulating its view that the program was illegal – the court refrained from striking it down. Instead, the judges forwarded the case to the European Court of Justice (ECJ) under the preliminary reference procedure – the first time the Second Senate of the FCC had done so. The decision to do so was widely seen as unusual and historic,[57] in part because the judges had the option of ruling on the case as a matter of domestic German law by focusing on the question whether the OMT program was in violation of Germany's accession to the monetary union – a position that had been taken by the petitioners. One interpretation of this move fits well within the framework of our model: By sending the case to the ECJ, the judges of the FCC – knowing that a decision to strike down the OMT would place tremendous pressure to comply on the German government, putting the risk of a return to economic upheaval on the table – stepped back from a line they were reluctant to cross. As an editorial in one of the major German newspapers put it at the time, "First, the judges ruled that the conduct of the ECB was illegal. Afraid of their own courage, they then turned to the ECJ for help."[58]

Given its forceful language, and the explicit conditions demanded, the initial German decision seemed to indicate that if the ECJ failed to impose the specified restrictions on the OMT program, the FCC might strike down the program in a subsequent decision. Of course, should the ECJ follow the FCC's demands and rule OMT illegal (or subject to conditions that would make it unworkable), there loomed the risk of returning the euro area to crisis. In the end, the judges of the ECJ – generally much more favorable to the program of European integration – called the FCC's bluff. The ECJ ruled OMT legal as a matter of European law, without the need to respect the conditions that the FCC had demanded.[59] The case now returned to the FCC for final decision.

The situation confronting the judges of the FCC at this juncture was both similar, and significantly different than it had been in 2014. It was similar in the sense that given the authority of the FCC, the support the Court enjoyed from the Bundesbank, and the significant public opposition in Germany to continued German financial support for distressed euro area governments, supporting OMT in the face of a negative FCC decision would have been difficult if not impossible for the German

56 Fritz Mayer, "Rebels Without a Cause." *German Law Journal* 15 (2014), 111–46.

57 Mattias Wendel, "Exceeding Judicial Competence in the Name of Democracy: The German Federal Constitutional Court's OMT Reference." *European Constitutional Law Review* 10 (2014), 263–64; Gerner-Beuerle, Küçük and Schuster, "Law Meets Economics in the German Federal Constitutional Court: Outright Monetary Transactions on Trial," 282.

58 See Holger Steltzner "Die Angst der Verfassungsrichter" ("The fear of the constitutional court judges"), *Frankfurter Allgemeine Zeitung*, February 7, 2014.

59 Wilkinson, "The Euro Is Irreversible! . . . Or Is It?: On OMT, Austerity, and the Threat of Grexit."

government.[60] A negative decision would almost certainly undermine the OMT policy in a significant way. The situation was different in the sense that, unlike in 2014, the court no longer had the option of "passing the buck," at least for a time, to the ECJ. By 2016, the judges of the FCC understood that they would now have to make a decision, and that that decision would be implemented by the relevant German institutions. Moreover, the apparent effectiveness of the OMT program was clear: Four years had passed since the crisis. A decision to rule the OMT program illegal raised the specter of a return to chaos and the most significant crisis the EU had faced in its existence. The blame for such an outcome would fall on the FCC.

Despite the forceful argument in its original decision that OMT could not pass muster without significant limitations, in June 2016, the FCC caved in: In its second decision, the court accepted the ECJ's judgment, and upheld the OMT program despite the fact that the ECJ had not imposed any of the conditions demanded by the FCC.[61] Importantly, *all* of the six judges who had comprised the majority in the 2014 decision remained on the court: The switch in the court's position cannot be explained as the result of turnover on the bench. In our view, a plausible interpretation of the court's "about face" is as an instance of strategic retreat by a strong court: Knowing that a veto carried the real risk of plunging the eurozone back into financial crisis, the judges of the FCC chose to uphold the ECB's policy despite their legal reservations.[62] Thus, this episode illustrates that – as suggested by our model, and contrary to the traditional view of courts – judicial self-censoring may not only result from judicial weakness, but also from judicial strength.

VII. CONCLUSION

Moments of crisis can test the effectiveness of a constitutional order, and they can also shape constitutional meanings in significant ways. These two features are intimately connected. Although constitutions typically include "emergency powers" that allow suspension of some provisions, many constitutional constraints are designed precisely with the intention of binding the hands of policymakers in extraordinary circumstances. Framers often wish to constrain the exercise of power in those situations in which policymakers will be tempted to take actions that violate underlying normative commitments. But can such constraints be enforced when crisis strikes? Or do crisis times lead to "constitutional stretching" as policymakers

60 Case C-62/14, *Peter Gauweiler and Others* v. *Deutscher Bundestag* (June 16, 2015), http://curia.europa.eu/.

61 Perhaps to save face, the FCC noted that it reserved the right to revisit the matter if OMT were to be used to assist countries without "market access." But this was an empty threat given that the ECB's promises were going to ensure market access in the first place. See Ambrose Evans-Pritchard, "German Court Capitulates to Imperial ECJ in Landmark Ruling." *Daily Telegraph*, June 2, 2016; Claire Jones, "German High Court Backs ECB on Crisis-fighting Tool."

62 A second, and not inconsistent, aspect of this episode is that a veto of OMT following the ECJ's decision would have created a direct confrontation between the ECJ and the FCC.

successfully avoid the restraints a constitution is supposed to impose? If so, do such moments of crisis have a long-term impact on the nature of a constitutional order?

In exploring these questions, existing scholarship has focused primarily on the possibility that the institutional weakness of courts – which play a key role in constitutional enforcement – may prevent effective judicial policing of constitutional boundaries in moments of crisis. As a result, the long-term consequences of crisis – and particularly, the possibility of constitutional erosion – have been linked primarily to *weak* courts that retreat strategically in the face of an executive determined to deal with a crisis. The central argument of our chapter is that strategic judicial retreat may also, and paradoxically, result from judicial strength. In times of crisis, courts that command significant authority, and are likely to garner compliance with their rulings, confront a quandary that weaker courts can escape: The rigorous enforcement of constitutional boundaries may prevent an effective governmental response to a crisis. If judges are sufficiently concerned about the practical consequences of hamstringing a government, they may engage in judicial self-censoring not because they are weak, *but because they are strong*.

Ironically, the consequence of this is that – confronted with the challenges of crisis – weak *and* strong courts may be less able to protect the long-run integrity of a constitutional order as effectively as moderately strong courts. The intuition behind this counterintuitive finding is the following: Weak courts are unable to enforce constitutional norms in crisis or normal times. Courts that are so strong that their decisions garner respect even in times of crisis must – if they want to allow governments the flexibility to address a crisis – stretch constitutional meanings in order to accommodate crisis actions. Such stretching establishes precedents and alters constitutional meanings in ways that are potentially detrimental to the long-term nature of constitutional order. Moderately strong courts do not face this predicament. Unable to garner compliance with adverse judicial decisions in crisis times, they are free to condemn constitutional violations and insist on constitutional values in ways that do not undermine the long-term meaning of constitutional provisions.

Of course, our analysis raises deeper questions that offer fruitful avenues for future work. Perhaps most importantly, as we already indicated, the degree to which crisis decisions are likely to shape future constitutional meanings is, in part, under the control of judges. How, and under what circumstances, can judges minimize (or exacerbate) the impact of crisis decisions on the future development of law and the constitutional order? In the *Perry* decision, the justices of the Supreme Court may have consciously attempted to limit the precedential value of upholding the abrogation of the gold clauses in federal bonds, and they largely succeeded in doing so. On the other hand, the expansive interpretation of the ECB's mandate and the "no-bailout" clause in the ECJ's and FCC's decisions on the OMT policy may be more difficult to contain. These decisions may have long-lasting implications that will undermine the ability of EU member states to enforce a constitutional framework that imposes fiscal discipline on member governments.

APPENDIX

This appendix provides formal proofs of the unique, pure-strategy subgame perfect equilibrium of the model. We assume that players do not play weakly dominated strategies.

Lemma: In period 2, the court will strike down any action $a_2 > x_c$, and uphold all other actions. The second-period government will always propose its ideal point a_2.

Proof: Consider the court's strategy first. If it upholds a_2, it receives payoff $-(x_c - a_2)^2$. If it vetoes, it receives either this same payoff (if the government defies the veto) or a payoff of 0 (when the government complies with the veto). Thus, for any $a_2 > x_c$, vetoing is weakly dominant. Now consider the government. Given that the court will veto any $a_2 > x_c$, for any such proposal, the government receives payoff $-(g_2 - x_c)^2$ if it complies with the veto, and payoff $-(g_2 - a_2)^2 - \tau\alpha$ if it defies the veto (assuming the first-period government also defied. If not, the cost to the second-period government of defiance is α.) The only payoff that depends on a_2 is the payoff for defiance, and this payoff is maximized for $a_2 = g_2$. Thus, the government has a weakly dominant strategy to propose its ideal point.

Lemma: In period 1, the government will comply with a judicial veto if $\alpha \geq 1$ and defy a judicial veto otherwise.

Proof: Given the government's ideal point of $a_1 = 1$, the payoff of complying with a judicial veto is given by -1. The payoff of defying the court and implementing its ideal point is given by $-\alpha$. Thus, compliance is a best response for $\alpha \geq 1$.

Lemma: In period 2, if the crisis government complied with court's decision, the second-period government will comply with a judicial veto if $\sqrt{\alpha} \geq g_2$ and defy a judicial veto otherwise. If the crisis government defied court's decision, the second-period government will comply with a judicial veto if $\sqrt{\tau\alpha \geq g_2}$ and defy a judicial veto otherwise.

Proof: Suppose the first-period government complied. Given the second government's ideal point of g_2, the payoff of complying with a judicial veto is given by $-(g_2)^2$. The payoff of defying the court and implementing its ideal point is given by $-\alpha$. Thus, compliance is a best response for $\sqrt{\alpha} \geq g_2$. Analogous reasoning applies if the first-period government defied the court's decision and the court's authority has decreased to $\tau\alpha$.

With these lemmas in hand, we can now consider a series of cases to derive the equilibrium.

Case 1: $\alpha \geq 1$

For this case, the governments in both periods will comply with a judicial veto. Thus, in the first period, the court must choose whether to strike down the government's action $a_1 = 1$, or to uphold it. The payoff of a judicial veto (which prevents the crisis response) is given by

$$U_c(Veto) = -t_c$$

If the court chooses to uphold, the constitutional boundary in the second period shifts to $a_1 = 1$ with probability γ. The payoff of upholding is therefore given by

$$U_c(Uphold) = -1 + \gamma \int_0^t -g_2^2 \frac{1}{t} dg = -1 - \frac{t^2 \gamma}{3}.$$

This implies that the court will (weakly) prefer to uphold the government's action in period 1 whenever $\gamma \leq \frac{3(t_c - 1)}{t^2}$. Label this cutoff $T_3(t_c, t)$.

Case 2: $\alpha < 1$

If the court vetoes the first-period action, the first-period government always defies the court. The constitutional boundary for the second period remains at 0, but the court's authority shrinks to $\tau\alpha$. If the court upholds the crisis action, its authority is unaffected, but with probability γ, its decision is binding, and the constitutional boundary shifts to $a_1 = 1$ in the second period. The court's and government's second-period behavior are described in Lemmas 1 and 2.

This implies that there are three subcases to consider:

Subcase I: $\alpha < t^2 < \frac{t^2}{\tau}$

In this case, the expected utility of a judicial veto in period 1 is given by:

$$U_c(Veto) = -1 + \int_{\sqrt{\tau\alpha}}^{t} -g_2^2 \frac{1}{t} dg = -1 - \frac{t^2}{3} + \frac{\tau\alpha\sqrt{\tau\alpha}}{3t}$$

The expected utility of upholding the crisis action is given by:

$$U_c(Uphold) = -1 + \gamma \int_0^t -g_2^2 \tfrac{1}{t} dg + (1-\gamma) \int_{\sqrt{\alpha}}^{t} -g_2^2 \tfrac{1}{t} dg = -1 - (1-\gamma) \tfrac{t^3 - \alpha^{\frac{3}{2}}}{3t} - \gamma \tfrac{t^2}{3}$$

Given these expected utilities, the court prefers to veto if the following condition is met:

$$\gamma \geq 1 - \tau\sqrt{\tau}$$

Label this cutoff $T_1(\tau)$.

Subcase II: $t^2 \leq \alpha < \frac{t^2}{\tau}$

In this case, the expected utility of a judicial veto is given by:

$$U_c(Veto) = -1 + \int_{\sqrt{\tau\alpha}}^{t} -g_2^2 \frac{1}{t} dg = -1 - \frac{t^2}{3} + \frac{\tau\alpha\sqrt{\tau\alpha}}{3t}$$

The expected utility of upholding the crisis action is given by:

$$U_c(Uphold) = -1 + \gamma \int_0^t - g_2^2 \tfrac{1}{t} dg = -1 - \tfrac{t^2 \gamma}{3}$$

Given these expected utilities, the court prefers to veto if the following condition is met:

$$\gamma \geq 1 - \tfrac{\alpha\tau\sqrt{\alpha\tau}}{t^3}$$

Label this cutoff $T_2(\alpha, t, \tau)$.

Subcase III: $\frac{t^2}{\tau} \leq \alpha < 1$

In this case, the second-period government always complies with a veto, and the expected utility of a judicial veto in period 1 is given by:

$$U_c(Veto) = -1$$

The expected utility of upholding the crisis action is given by:

$$U_c(Uphold) = -1 + \gamma \int_0^t - g_2^2 \tfrac{1}{t} dg = -1 - \tfrac{t^2 \gamma}{3}$$

The utility of a veto always exceeds the utility of upholding the crisis action.

The full statement of the equilibrium strategies follows from Lemmas 1 and 2, and the subcases above that derive the conditions under which the court will uphold or veto the crisis action. These conditions and corresponding actions in period 1 are summarized in Figure 7.2.

8

Commitment for Cowards

Why the Judicialization of Austerity Is Bad Policy and Even Worse Politics

R. Daniel Kelemen

In response to the eurozone crisis, EU leaders turned to the courts for help. At an intense moment in the crisis in 2012, they abandoned the eurozone governance rules that had been established when the common currency, the euro, was created. Among other things, the original Maastricht Treaty rules had required eurozone states to maintain fiscal discipline and had prohibited EU institutions or other member governments from providing bailouts to member states that might become insolvent. But when push came to shove, EU leaders largely threw those rules out of the window and provided bailouts to the states that needed them, beginning with Greece. With the Maastricht regime in tatters, leaders designed a new governance regime that sought to judicialize austerity, calling on national courts to enforce the fiscal rules in a way that the politicians themselves had refused to do.

The judicialization of austerity was a commitment device used by political leaders who sought to evade responsibility for fiscal policy choices and their consequences. Jean Claude Juncker, today the President of the Commission and earlier Luxembourg's prime minister, famously once said of economic reform, "We all know what to do, we just don't know how to get re-elected after we've done it."[1] Facing this conundrum in the context of the eurozone crisis, European leaders sought to commit themselves to fiscal prudence, while deflecting blame for the pain austerity would cause, by entrenching balanced budget rules in national law and asking courts to enforce these rules.

This chapter argues that European leaders' effort to judicialize austerity has and will continue to fail in both policy terms and political terms. This is true notwithstanding the fact that the eurozone crisis has abated, at least for the time being. In policy terms, attempting to judicialize austerity is misguided for two reasons. First, it is based on a misunderstanding of how balanced budget rules are actually enforced. Second, it ignores the fact that background structural conditions in the EU make it impossible for member states to credibly commit to maintaining balanced budgets. In political terms, committing to balanced budget rules and attempting to

[1] "The Quest for Prosperity," *The Economist*, 15 March 2007, www.economist.com/node/8808044.

shift fiscal policy decisions out of the political realm and into the courts is misguided, because it will likely add to the growing sense among many voters that their elected leaders do not control key policies. In other words, the effort to judicialize austerity in reaction to the eurozone financial crisis feeds into the TINA (There Is No Alternative) politics narrative that has disillusioned so many voters with mainstream politicians and encouraged them to turn to populists who promise to "take back control" and make their countries great again in one way or another.[2] As Sheri Berman (2017: 37) has put it, "the more the people view democratically elected governments as being overruled by unelected bureaucrats, unaccountable regional or international institutions, and global economic forces, the more attractive populism's call to regain national sovereignty – to 'Put America First' or 'Choose France' – becomes."[3] Yascha Mounk has made the link to judicial power explicit, arguing that as more and more policy controversies are removed from the political arena and settled by courts, "voters are flocking to populists who . . . promise to cast aside the institutional roadblocks – from critical media and *independent courts to international institutions like the EU* [emphasis added] or the World Trade Organization – that stand in the way of the collective will."[4] Thus, the notion that leaders can escape the political costs of austerity policies by judicializing them is a chimera: this strategy is unlikely to fool voters in the short term and is very likely to alienate them in the long term.

The remainder of this chapter is divided into four sections. Section I explains how congenital defects in the design of eurozone governance helped give rise to the eurozone crisis. Section II explains why European leaders turned to the courts when reforming the system in reaction to the crisis. Section III explains why this judicialization strategy is misguided and destined to fail in terms of both policy and politics. Section IV concludes.

I. THE EUROZONE'S DESIGN FLAWS

Any federal-type system in which state governments retain substantial control over their fiscal policies faces a moral hazard problem. If a state government in such a system defaults on its debt, this may generate negative spillovers for other states in the system or for the federal government itself. If the negative spillovers of a default would be highly costly, the federal government may be tempted to step in with a bailout to avoid these destructive repercussions. The moral hazard dilemma,

[2] Müller, Jan-Werner, "Populists and Technocrats in Europe's Fragmented Democracies," *World Politics Review*, 31 March 2016, http://worldpoliticsreview.com/authors/1426/jan-werner-muller.

[3] Berman, Sheri, "The Pipe Dream of Undemocratic Liberalism," *Journal of Democracy*, 28(3): 37 (2017).

[4] Mounk, Yascha, "Illiberal Democracy or Undemocratic Liberalism?," *Project Syndicate* 9 June 2016, www.project-syndicate.org/commentary/trump-european-populism-technocracy-by-yascha-mounk-1–2016-06; see also Mounk, Yascha, *The People vs. Democracy*. New Haven CT: Harvard University Press, 2018.

therefore, stems from the fact that state governments may foresee that the federation will treat them as "too big to fail" in the event of a fiscal crisis, and, knowing this, some states may be tempted to build up unsustainable deficits. The moral hazard problem may extend beyond the direct ambit of fiscal policy to other fields where the state may act as an implicit guarantor for the debt of private sector actors. For instance, states may be tempted to regulate banks in a lax manner, believing that if lax regulation leads to a financial crisis that ends up threatening the solvency of the state,[5] the federal government would bail out the state.

In light of this moral hazard problem, any such federal or quasi-federal governance system must find a credible way to discourage member states from taking on unsustainable deficits.[6] There are essentially two strategies to achieve this – tough love and rules – and the two can be combined in various ways. The tough love strategy involves establishing a credible commitment not to bail out insolvent states. A federal pledge that there will be no bailouts is insufficient to establish such a credible commitment. Tough love requires more than words: to establish a credible commitment, the federation would actually have to allow one or more states to default, regardless of the costly spillover effects a default may have. This was the approach pursued by the US federal government in the early 1840s when a number of American state governments experienced financial crises.[7] Having built up unsustainable debts (largely through borrowing to finance infrastructure projects), the states turned to the federal government for a bailout. However, Congress resisted their entreaties and practiced tough love, allowing eight states and the (then) territory of Florida to default. In the wake of these defaults, the states temporarily lost access to international credit markets. To restore investors'

5 This could happen, for instance, in the event of a banking crisis, if a state intervened to save its banking system by socializing banks' debts. Given the pressures generated by the bank–sovereign nexus, banking crises can very rapidly transform into sovereign debt crises in countries, such as Ireland, that previously had low levels of public sector debt. See Kelemen, R. Daniel, "Law, Fiscal Federalism and Austerity," *Indiana Journal of Global Legal Studies* 22(2): 379–400, (2015) at 383.

6 Likewise, in light of the comments above about how the moral hazard problem may extend to areas where the state acts as an implicit guarantor, any quasi-federal governance system with a common currency must also establish a banking union. Discussion of the need for banking union in the EU is beyond the scope of this chapter, but for a thorough analysis see Erik Jones, "The Forgotten Financial Union." In Matthias Matthijs and Mark Blyth, eds., *The Future of the Euro*. Oxford: Oxford University Press, 2015, 44–69.

7 See English, William B., "Understanding the Costs of Sovereign Default: American State Debts in the 1840's," *American Economic Review*, 86: 259 (1996); Grinath, Arthur, John J. Wallis and Joseph Sylla, "Debt, Default and Revenue Structure: The American State Debt Crisis in the Early 1840s," 1 *National Bureau of Economic Research Working Paper Series on Hist. Factors in Long Run Growth*, Paper No. 97 (1997); Wallis, John Joseph and Barry Weingast. "Dysfunctional or Optimal Institutions: State Debt Limitations, the Structure of State and Local Governments, and the Finance of American Infrastructure." In Elizabeth Garrett, Elizabeth Graddy and Howell Jackson, eds., *Fiscal Challenges: An Interdisciplinary Approach to Budget Policy*. Cambridge: Cambridge University Press, 2008; Henning, C. Randall and Martin Kessler, "Fiscal Federalism: US History of Architects of Europe's Fiscal Union." WP 12-1, *Peterson Institute for International Economics Working Paper Series*, January 2012.

confidence that they would not build up unsustainable debts, states began to impose on themselves balanced budget rules – often entrenching these in their state constitutions. This self-binding practice spread, and eventually such rules were adopted by forty-nine of the fifty US states. Thus, the US model as it developed in the nineteenth century represents one possible combination of tough love and rules: the federal level practices tough love to establish a credible commitment not to bail out states, and states impose clear fiscal rules on themselves to gain the confidence of markets.[8]

The architects of eurozone governance established a system designed to rely on a different combination of rules and tough love, with elements of each imposed from the center. First, the Maastricht Treaty that established the euro as the common currency put in place a set of fiscal rules. These rules required that euro area member states' annual deficits should not exceed 3 percent of gross domestic product (GDP) and that their total debt should not exceed 60 percent of GDP, and they were backed up by an enforcement process, called the Excessive Deficit Procedure (EDP).[9] If a state failed to rectify its excessive deficit, the Council of Ministers (meeting as the Economic and Financial Affairs Council) could impose fines on it or force it to post a substantial non-interest-bearing bond until the deficit was brought back into line. Member governments even strengthened these fiscal supervision and enforcement rules in 1997 by adopting the Stability and Growth Pact (SGP).[10] Second, the Maastricht Treaty promised tough love in the form of a "no bailout" clause, which stipulated that neither the EU nor any Member State could bailout (i.e., assume the debts of) another Member State.[11]

There were some obvious design flaws in this governance system, and in the end the entire edifice came crumbling down. The greatest problem with the fiscal rules in the EDP and SGP was that the system for enforcing them was highly politicized.[12]

8 To be clear, this system is not without its flaws. An abundant literature demonstrates how state governments use creative accounting to evade balanced budget requirements (see for instance Briffault, Richard, *Balancing Acts: The Reality Behind State Balanced Budget Requirements*. New York: The Twentieth Century Fund Press, 1996). Also, it remains to be seen whether the federal government would still today stand by its historic commitment not to bail out state governments that face insolvency. In today's deeply integrated national financial system, a default by a state government would have far greater spillover effects on other states and on the national financial system than such defaults did in the mid-nineteenth century.

9 Treaty on European Union (hereinafter TEU), art. 104c (later relabeled as art. 126 of the Treaty on the Functioning of the European Union (hereinafter TFEU)), and Protocol (No. 12) on the Excessive Deficit Procedure.

10 The SGP took the form of two Council Regulations: Council Regulation 1466/97, on the Strengthening of the Surveillance of Budgetary Positions and the Surveillance and Coordination of Economic Policies, 2d recital, 1997 O.J. (L 209) 1 (EC); and, Council Regulation 1467/97, on Speeding Up and Clarifying the Implementation of the Excessive Deficit Procedure, 3d recital, 1997 O.J. (L 209) 6 (EC).

11 TEU, art. 104b (later relabeled as art. 125, TFEU).

12 See the procedure elaborated in TEU, Protocol (No. 12) on the Excessive Deficit Procedure, Feb. 7, 1992. The politicized enforcement system was the chief problem, but by no means the only one. Other

If the European Commission recommended action against a state for excessive deficits, enforcement could only move ahead with the support of a majority in the EU's Council of Ministers. In 2003, the Commission concluded that Germany and France had violated the deficit rules of the SGP and called for enforcement action against the two countries under the Excessive Deficit Procedure. However, these two powerful member states argued that the rules should not be applied to them in this case. This was more than a bit ironic in Germany's case, since Germany in particular had demanded that strict fiscal rules be put in place when the euro was created. Ultimately, in a meeting of the EU's Economic and Financial Affairs Council on November 25, 2003, a majority of member states voted to block enforcement against France and Germany, and instead simply encouraged them to do more to improve their public finances. Two years later, the Council adopted two regulations formally loosening the requirements of the SGP and EDP, reforms that essentially eviscerated both sets of rules.[13]

While the deficit rules had been loosened, the promise of tough love in the form of the Maastricht Treaty's no-bailout rule remained in place. However, when that commitment was put to the test in the context of the Greek debt crisis, it too was cast aside. In 2010, after the Greek government had issued a series of restatements revealing the true scale of its deficit and debt, Greek sovereign debt yields soared and the government faced insolvency.[14] Had other EU leaders stuck to the Maastricht rules, they would have let Greece default – much as the US government let several states default in the early 1840s. As discussed below, some prominent analysts of the eurozone crisis argue that this is in fact what European leaders should have done in 2010.[15] Instead, they chose to violate the Maastricht rules, and, working in cooperation with the IMF, they provided Greece with a bailout. The bailout of Greece set the stage for subsequent bailouts of Ireland and Portugal, and eventually the establishment of a permanent EU bailout fund (the European Stability Mechanism)[16] and a new set of rules governing fiscal policy in the EU. Before analyzing the new system of fiscal governance they created, it is important to understand why EU leaders chose to abandon the no bailout rule.

First, EU leaders feared that a disorderly Greek default – possibly leading to its exit from the euro – could lead to a massive financial meltdown across the eurozone. German Finance Minister Wolfgang Schäuble summed up the dilemma

problems included the fact that the rules, while clear on the surface, allowed for significant exceptions that rendered them highly ambiguous. See for instance art. 104c of the TEU Protocol on the EDP.

13 See Council Regulation 1055/2005, 2005 O.J. (L 174) 1 (EC) (strengthening surveillance of budgets and surveillance and coordination of economic policies); and, Council Regulation 1056/2005, 2005 O.J. (L 174) 5 (EC) (speeding up the implementation of the excessive deficit procedure).

14 For a description of this episode, see Sandbu, Martin, *The Future of the Euro and the Politics of Debt*. Princeton NJ: Princeton University Press, 2015: 48–79.

15 Ibid.: 166–68.

16 Eurozone governments signed the Treaty Establishing the European Stability Mechanism (ESM) on February 2, 2012, and the Treaty came into force in September 2012. The ESM replace the temporary European Financial Stability Facility (EFSF), which had been established in 2010.

in April 2010: "We cannot allow the bankruptcy of a Euro member state like Greece to turn into a second Lehman Brothers. Greece's debts are all in Euros, and it isn't clear who holds how much of those debts. The consequences of a national bankruptcy would be incalculable."[17] In the context of the EU's integrated financial markets and banking system, a Greek default might have sparked a disastrous series of sovereign debt crises and bank runs. If Greece had defaulted, then bondholders would have questioned the solvency of governments across the eurozone periphery. Bond yields on sovereign debt of Portugal, Spain, Ireland, and even Italy would have soared, potentially creating a self-fulfilling prophecy where higher borrowing costs drove several states into default. The debt crisis could have also sparked a systemic banking crisis. In the event of a Greek default, depositors across peripheral eurozone countries would have worried about the security of their savings and many would have taken advantage of the free movement of capital in the eurozone to transfer their deposits to accounts in safer havens such as Germany – quickly leading to bank failures across the periphery. But the banking crisis would not have been confined to the periphery: because banks in core eurozone countries such as France, Germany, and the Netherlands held massive amounts of the sovereign debt of peripheral eurozone governments, a series of defaults would have put the stability of the banking systems in the core at risk as well.[18] In short, EU governments decided that the uncertainties and potential costs associated with a Greek default were simply too high to bear.

But it was not only economic considerations that led European leaders to bail out Greece; political considerations also made a bailout more attractive than allowing a "tough-love" default. As noted above, because banks in the core held huge portfolios of sovereign debt and other loans from peripheral eurozone economies, a series of defaults and financial crises across the eurozone periphery would have posed a threat to the survival of banks in the core. If their own banking systems faced collapse, core governments would have been compelled to step in with bank bailouts. And that is where politics came in: the real choice for Germany, France, and other governments in the core was never between a bailout and no bailout. Rather, it was a choice between bailing out peripheral governments, or letting them default but then having to bail out banks at home. The first option was more attractive politically for national politicians in the core, even if it damaged the EU's image.[19] Consider the political optics, had core governments allowed the so-called

[17] Dorsch, Gary, "Could Greek Debt Tragedy Morph into a Lehman Meltdown Market Crash?," *Market Oracle*, Apr. 28, 2010, marketoracle.co.uk/Article18997.html. Also see Sandbu, n. 14 at p. 58 noting that ECB President Jean-Claude Trichet expressed similar fears.

[18] See Jones (2015), n. 3; see also Blyth, Mark, "A Pain in the Athens," *Foreign Affairs*, 7 July 2015, www.foreignaffairs.com/articles/greece/2015-07-07/pain-athens.

[19] As Mark Blyth puts it, the eurozone bailouts enabled governments in the core to rebrand a systemic banking crisis – where much of the fault would lie with lax regulation by governments in the core – as a sovereign debt crisis that could be blamed on the supposed profligacy of governments in the periphery. See Mark Blyth *Austerity: The History of a Dangerous Idea*. Oxford: Oxford University Press, 2012.

PIGS (Portugal, Ireland, Greece, and Spain) to default and then stepped in to save banks in the core: voters would have attacked their governments for bailing out wealthy, reckless bankers – and for their own irresponsibility in having allowed for such shoddy banking supervision in the first place. On top of that, they would have been blamed for their heartlessness as the PIGS descended into financial meltdown while banks in the core received billions in aid. Moreover, to finance these bank bailouts, governments in the core would have had to borrow heavily, ballooning their own deficits and increasing pressure for unpopular austerity measures at home. As the acclaimed historian of accounting Jacob Soll points out, where borrowing to finance bank bailouts would have added to the deficit numbers for core governments, when these countries made loans to the PIGS at below market rates, these loss-making loans were not treated for accounting purposes as adding to the core countries' deficits.[20] Thus, accounting rules added to the political advantages of bailing out peripheral governments, rather than directly bailing out banks in the core.

For Merkel, Sarkozy, and other leaders in the core countries, the political optics of bailing out peripheral countries were – at least in the short term – considerably better than those of bailing out their own banks. The bailouts functioned as a kind of money laundering – or political blame laundering – operation: Core governments provided bailouts to peripheral governments, who then used substantial portions of the money to pay back their debts to banks in the core. While the money still ended up with the banks in the core, the political blame and the deficit numbers were apportioned differently than they would have been had the banks been bailed out directly. Massive, taxpayer-funded bailouts for banks in the core would have been politically unpopular with voters in those countries, and any borrowing by core governments to finance bank bailouts would have added to their deficits. But by channeling the bailouts via countries on the periphery, this money was politically sanitized: voters in the core pinned much of the blame for the sorry situation on profligate southern European states and on the poorly designed structures of the eurozone rather than on their own leaders. Merkel and other leaders in the core were instead cast as responsible saviors of the eurozone who had little choice but to help their feckless European partners. Throughout the crisis German tabloids laid blame for the crisis at Greece's door, castigating the Greeks as lazy while German leaders escaped most blame. Of course, Merkel was attacked in the Greek press – where she was sometimes depicted in a Nazi uniform – but since Greeks could not vote in German elections such attacks were unthreatening.[21]

20 Soll, Jacob, "Greece's Accounting Problem," *N.Y. Times*, Jan. 20, 2015, www.nytimes.com/2015/01/21/opinion/greeces-accounting-problem.html?_r=0.

21 Adler-Niessen, Rebecca, "Are We 'Lazy Greeks' or 'Nazi Germans'? Negotiating International Hierarchies in the Euro Crisis." In Ayse Zarakol (ed.), *Hierarchies in World Politics*. Cambridge: Cambridge University Press, 2017: 198–218.

II. THE EU TURNS TO THE COURTS

Casting aside the original Maastricht regime and its no bailout clause forced EU leaders to come up with a new set of rules for governing the eurozone. It was at this point that they turned to a judicialization strategy. Because EU leaders had agreed to provide bailouts to eurozone states at risk of insolvency, they faced an overwhelming moral hazard problem. Clearly, if there were going to be bailouts, there had to be conditions attached to them. EU leaders passed a new set of far stricter fiscal rules designed to tighten budget discipline. But stricter rules alone were inadequate if governments could block their enforcement. The experience of the mid-2000s, when Germany and France had led other states in blocking the Commission's enforcement of EU fiscal rules, showed that the enforcement process had to be depoliticized.

To achieve this, member governments sought to establish a new arrangement that would insulate the EU's fiscal rules from politics, so they turned to the courts. Initially, the fiscal surveillance and enforcement mechanisms of the Stability and Growth Pact were strengthened by a raft of EU legislation passed in 2011.[22] But German Chancellor Angela Merkel led a drive to see such rules entrenched in a Treaty that would require states enshrine balanced budget rules in national law. The result was the Fiscal Compact, an intergovernmental Treaty that states had to ratify to be eligible for bailouts from the ESM.[23] The Fiscal Compact established a "structurally balanced" budget rule and an automatic debt brake. Crucially, the Treaty required states to entrench the balanced budget rules in national law, "through provisions of binding force and permanent character, preferably constitutional, or otherwise guaranteed to be fully respected and adhered to throughout the national budgetary processes."[24] In other words, the Treaty demanded that the fiscal rules be entrenched in national law where they could be enforced by national courts without political leaders being able to interfere. Moreover, the Treaty established a secondary tier of judicial oversight, providing that governments could face legal action before the European Court of Justice if they failed to put in place the balanced budget rules and enforcement mechanisms required by the Fiscal Compact.[25]

22 To this end, six pieces of legislation – collectively known as the "six-pack" – were adopted in November 2011. These were supplemented in May 2013 with two additional regulations – the so-called "two-pack" – that further enhanced EU supervision of Member state budgets. See Kelemen (2015: 390).

23 The full formal name of the Fiscal Compact was the Treaty on Stability, Coordination and Governance in the Economic and Monetary Union (TSCG). The Treaty was signed at the EU summit on March 2, 2012, and took effect on January 1, 2013. See Quentin Peel et al. "Eurozone States Sign up to Fiscal Pact," *Financial Times*, March 2, 2012, www.ft.com/intl/cms/s/0/18ca1e80-6455-11e1-b50e-00144feabdc0.html#axzz3TB8TBZqQ .

24 TSCG, art. 3(2).

25 TSCG, art. 3(2).

Certainly, some European leaders may have sincerely believed that these binding legal commitments would make their (and future governments') commitments to fiscal discipline more credible. But, as discussed below, a close examination of the Fiscal Compact's rules suggests that they were crafted with exceptions and procedures designed to preserve the possibility of political interference in enforcement. Viewed as a whole, the approach European leaders took in crafting a new governance regime for the eurozone seems to have been more about political optics than truly credible commitments: their approach reflects what we can call "commitment for cowards." Lacking the political courage to face their electorates, and to take responsibility for their fiscal policy choices, they established a system that would enable them to claim that they had no choice when imposing austerity. Henceforth, they could claim that they were forced to impose painful cuts by EU legal requirements and by the national and European courts that enforced these. They hoped this approach would deflect blame for the pain of austerity measures away from governments, and redirect it at the EU and the courts.

III. WHY THE JUDICIALIZATION OF AUSTERITY IS BAD POLICY AND BAD POLITICS

Has the EU's strategy of judicializing austerity worked thus far as a matter of policy or politics? Are there reasons to believe it will work going forward? In policy terms, is the threat of judicial enforcement of balanced budget rules improving fiscal discipline? Have the new arrangements yielded political benefits for national politicians, relieving them of some of the blame for austerity? With the new system only in place a few years, it remains rather early to reach a definitive judgment. To date, however, the EU's new approach appears to be a failure in terms of both policy and politics, and there is reason to believe it will continue to fail in both respects.

1. *Judicialization of Austerity as a Failed Policy*

The EU's effort to judicialize austerity is failing in policy terms because it is based on a misunderstanding of how and under what conditions balanced budget rules can work to restrain government borrowing. First, existing research demonstrates that in practice, bond markets rather than courts discipline governments that violate fiscal rules. To the extent that state governments respect balanced budget rules, it is because they fear "punishment" by bond markets (in the form of a sudden spike in yields) not because they fear any judicial enforcement.[26] Strikingly, in the US case,

[26] See for instance Bayoumi, Tamim, Morris Goldstein, and Geoffrey Woglom, "Do Credit Markets Discipline Sovereign Borrowers," *Journal of Money, Credit and Banking* 27 (4): 1046–59 (1995); Poterba, James, "State Responses to Fiscal Crises," *Journal of Political Economy* 102 (4): 799–821 (1994); Lowry, Robert, and James Alt, "A Visible Hand? Bond Markets, Political Parties, Balanced Budget Laws, and State Government Debt," *Economics and Politics* 13 (1): 49–72 (2001).

in the more than 170 years that state balanced budget rules have existed, a state court has only acted to enforce such a rule once.[27] Second, as Terence Teo and I have shown, balanced budget rules are only effective where they are sufficiently clear to coordinate decentralized punishment by bond market investors.[28] In essence, such rules can only work when they present, "an unambiguous 'red line,' the crossing of which would be evident to all investors" and which would establish, "a shared understanding of the point at which other bond buyers are likely to withhold further financing."[29] Under such conditions, states may avoid crossing that red line for fear of sparking a coordinated market punishment. However, as discussed below, the "structurally balanced" budget rules imposed by the EU's Fiscal Compact were highly vague and subject to interpretation, and thus there is no hope they could serve this focal point function.

Third and finally, EU policy-makers' efforts to judicialize austerity did not fail simply because the rules were poorly designed, but because of more basic structural reasons rooted in the design of the eurozone. In the EU context, leaders could not impose clear, nominal balanced budget rules of the sort US states imposed on themselves in the nineteenth century. US states can only maintain such rules because the federal government engages in substantial fiscal transfers and can run deficits. Thus, when their balanced budget rules lead US states to impose pro-cyclical policies in periods of recession, this is compensated for by the fact that the federal government can borrow and engage in countercyclical policies. Likewise, in periods of national emergency that absolutely require deficit spending – such as wars – state governments can only maintain balanced budgets because the federal government can borrow. Given the EU's small budget (amounting to approximately 1 percent of the EU's collective GDP) and the absence of significant EU-level countercyclical policies, it would be untenable to impose strict nominal balanced balanced budget rules on eurozone members. To do so would put them in a true fiscal straightjacket, which would forever prohibit Keynesian policies and would be politically unsustainable. Likewise, so long as it is national governments, rather than the EU, that finance security and defense, it is impossible to require them to balance their budgets in periods of emergency. Finally, bond markets will not act to enforce balanced budget rules, however clearly they are drafted, so long as they believe EU authorities will bail out insolvent states. Until and unless the EU demonstrates that it is willing to allow a state that violates EU fiscal rules to default, bond markets are unlikely to view these rules as credible.

27 Richard Briffault, "The Disfavored Constitution: State Fiscal Limits and State Constitutional Law," *Rutgers Law Journal* 34: 907, 939–40 (2003).

28 R. Daniel Kelemen and Terence Teo, "Law, Focal Points and Fiscal Discipline in the United States and the European Union," *American Political Science Review* 108: 355 (2014).

29 Ibid, p. 356.

To date, the EU's experience with the fiscal rules imposed in the Fiscal Compact Treaty and related measures (such as the six-pack and two-pack) supports the foregoing theoretical and comparative conclusions. Overall, the new fiscal governance arrangements established in the wake of the eurozone crisis appear to have had little effect. An early assessment by Daniel Gros and Cinzia Alcidi of the Center for European Policy Studies in Brussels still holds true today; as they put it in 2014, "All this legal apparatus seems to have had little impact on actual fiscal policy-making."[30]

There are several reasons why the new regime has proved so ineffective. First, reforms that were supposedly intended to depoliticize enforcement of EU fiscal requirements have in practice done little of the sort. Initial depictions of the Fiscal Compact by policy-makers and media analysts generally suggested that it imposed strict balanced budget rules on eurozone states. In reality, the rules are vague and riddled with exceptions and the procedures for enforcing them still allow for political interference. Consider the balanced budget rule itself. The headline rule seems strict, with the Fiscal Compact stating, "The budgetary position of the general government ... shall be balanced or in surplus."[31] But beneath that clear headline comes the fuzzy fine print. Careful readers will note that national budgets do not need to be balanced every year but only across a multi- year business cycle. As the Treaty explains:

> [T]he [balanced budget] rule under point (a) shall be deemed to be respected if the annual structural balance of the general government is at its country-specific medium-term objective, as defined in the revised Stability and Growth Pact, with a lower limit of a structural deficit of 0,5 percent of the gross domestic product at market prices. The Contracting Parties shall ensure rapid convergence towards their respective medium-term objective. The time-frame for such convergence will be proposed by the European Commission taking into consideration country-specific sustainability risks. Progress towards, and respect of, the medium-term objective shall be evaluated on the basis of an overall assessment with the structural balance as a reference, including an analysis of expenditure net of discretionary revenue measures, in line with the revised Stability and Growth Pact.[32]

Any reader at a loss to understand precisely what this means would not be alone. Exactly what might constitute such a "structurally balanced budget" on these terms is subject to interpretation, and policy-makers and economists would have great difficulty agreeing on it. Moreover, if this vagueness were not problematic enough, the Fiscal Compact provides for exceptions to this already ambiguous balanced budget rule. States may "temporarily deviate" from the budget rules in "exceptional circumstances," which the Treaty defines as "the case of an unusual event outside the control of the Contracting Party concerned which has a major impact on the

[30] Daniel Gros and Cinzia Alcidi, "The Case of the Disappearing Fiscal Compact," in *CEPS Commentary* 1 (Ctr. for European Policy Studies, Nov. 5, 2014).

[31] TSCG, n. 3, art. 3(1)(a).

[32] Ibid. art. 3(1)(b).

financial position of the general government or to periods of severe economic downturn."[33]

With all of this ambiguity, it is no wonder that policy-makers in the Commission and member governments have interpreted the rules of the SGP and the Fiscal Compact loosely. In 2014, most analysts agreed that the deficits of Belgium, Italy, and France violated the stability and growth pact's deficit rules, but the Commission nevertheless chose not to impose disciplinary measures on them.[34] Again in 2016, the Commission chose not to fine Spain and Portugal after ruling earlier that they had violated EU deficit rules.[35] Even Wolfgang Schäuble, the German finance minister viewed by many observers as the arch fiscal hawk in the eurozone, was reported to have pressed the Commission not to fine Spain or Portugal for their fiscal breaches.[36]

National courts too have been loath to strictly enforce of EU fiscal rules. Rather than strictly applying these fiscal rules, courts have tended to balance them against other constitutional values and more generally to grant policy-makers considerable discretion. In a study of the application of EU fiscal rules by the Italian, Spanish, and Portuguese constitutional courts, Fasone finds that the new fiscal rules have had a very limited impact.[37] Likewise, Fabbrini[38] notes that national courts have so far taken a deferential posture vis-à-vis governments when asked to enforce the Fiscal Compact's balanced budget rules. Prior to the eurozone crisis, national constitutional courts already had years of experience balancing the enforcement of various fiscal rules against the protection of other constitutionally guaranteed values. Fasone finds that the introduction of new fiscal rules to comply with the Fiscal Compact and other EU fiscal requirements has had little discernable impact on these courts' jurisprudence.[39] They continue to adjudicate conflicts between fiscal rules and other norms much as they have in the past. In many instances, courts continue to safeguard various social rights (such as rights to healthcare) or general legal principles (such as legitimate expectations) where they would be threatened by an uncompromising application of austerity measures taken in the name of balanced budget rules. In other words, the introduction of a raft of supposedly strict new EU requirements has made these courts no more willing to privilege fiscal rules above other constitutional values than they were previously. In fact, Fasone suggests in the case of the Portuguese Constitutional Court, "Its deferential approach towards the

33 Ibid. art. 3(1)(c), and art. 3(3)(b).

34 Kanter, James, "E.U. Gives 3 Nations More Time on Budgets," *New York Times*, Nov. 29, 2014, at B2.

35 Khan, Mehreen and Jim Brunsden, "Brussels Drops Fines Against Spain and Portugal for Fiscal Breaches," *Financial Times*, July 27, 2016.

36 Ibid.

37 Fasone, Cristina, "Constitutional Courts Facing the Euro Crisis: Italy, Portugal and Spain in a Comparative Perspective." *EUI Working Paper* MWP 2014/25. European University Institute, Fiesole (2014).

38 Fabbrini, Federico,"The Fiscal Compact, the 'Golden Rule,' and the Paradox of European Federalism," *Boston College International and Comparative Law Review* 36 (1): 22 (2013).

39 Fasone (2014: 3–4, 50).

legislator usually shown in this field has been partially abandoned,"[40] in favor of stricter scrutiny of austerity measures for compliance with other constitutional norms.

2. *Judicialization of Austerity as a Political Catastrophe*

The effort to judicialize austerity has failed not only as a matter of policy; it has been a spectacular failure in political terms as well. Member governments may have believed that framing austerity as an EU legal requirement would help them to shift the blame to "Brussels" for unpopular cuts to social spending programs, but this was short-sighted. While some of the blame may have been deflected to the EU, the strategy has proved self-defeating. Trying to frame fiscal policy choices as a matter of EU legal rules that would be enforced by courts fed a sense amongst many voters that major aspects of public policy, such as taxation and social spending, had been removed from the realm of democratic decision-making. As many scholars have pointed out, this situation has sparked a crisis of democratic legitimacy across Europe, exacerbating longstanding concerns about the EU's supposed "democratic deficit."[41] Frustration with this type of TINA (There Is No Alternative) politics was one of the major forces that has led many voters in a number of European countries increasingly to turn away from mainstream parties and toward populists on the extreme left and right who promised to "take back control" from elite technocrats and give power back to "the people." As political theorist and scholar of populism Jan-Werner Müller has explained, "Populism is more likely to arise when leaders present their policies as having no alternative, as Ms. Merkel did during the Eurozone crisis. The tragedy of European politics today is a polarisation between technocracy – to use a shorthand for 'there is no alternative' rhetoric – and populism."[42]

A pair of widely cited – and derided – quotes capture the essence of the problem. In late 2014, reacting to Syriza leader Alexis Tsipras' promise that if elected he would end austerity, German finance minister Wolfgang Schäuble said, "New elections change nothing about the agreements that the Greek government has entered

40 Ibid. at 24.

41 Scharpf, Fritz W. "Monetary Union, Fiscal Crisis and the Disabling of Democratic Accountability," in Armin Schäfer and Wolfgang Streeck, eds., *Politics in the Age of Austerity*. Cambridge: Polity Press, 2014:108–42; Schmidt, Vivien A., "The Forgotten Problem of Democratic Legitimacy: 'Governing by the Rules' and 'Ruling by the Numbers'," in Matthias Matthijs and Mark Blyth, eds., *The Future of the Euro*. Oxford: Oxford University Press, 2015:90–114; Crum, Ben, "Saving the Euro at the Cost of Democracy?," *Journal of Common Market Studies*, 51(4): 614–30 (2013); Streeck, Wolfgang, *Buying Time: The Delayed Crisis of Democratic Capitalism*. Brooklyn NJ: Verso, 2014.

42 Müller Jan-Werner, "Genuine Political Choice Serves as the Best Antidote to Populism," *Financial Times*, October 4, 2016, www.ft.com/content/54240580-75db-11e6-bf48-b372cdb1043a; see also Müller, "Populists and Technocrats," n. 1.

into."[43] Shortly after Syriza had won the election, European Commission President Jean Claude Juncker commented, "there can be no democratic choice against the European treaties."[44] There was of course an element of truth in both statements: new governments are expected to respect the legal commitments made by and the debts incurred by their predecessors. But, as many scholars have pointed out, the message behind such quotes was one that robbed voters of any sense of meaningful choice, undermining national democracies and pushing voters to embrace populists.

The promotion of such TINA politics by European leaders has had severely damaging effects on constitutional democracy across Europe. The damage has been most pronounced in southern Europe. Southern European countries hit hardest by the crisis – Greece, Spain, Portugal, and Italy – have experienced a noticeable weakening in their democratic institutions.[45] In 2008, all of these countries were ranked as "full democracies" on the Economist Intelligence Unit's "Democracy Index." By 2011, three of them (Greece, Portugal, and Italy) had been downgraded to "flawed democracies," while Spain barely retained its "full democracy" ranking, sinking to just above the cut-off. As Matthias Matthijs notes, "Between 2006 and 2015, Greece's overall ranking on the EIU's Democracy Index plummeted from twenty-second to fortieth worldwide (behind Lithuania and South Africa) and Portugal's from nineteenth to thirty-third (behind Chile and Cape Verde)."[46] Not only did such expert rankings of democracy drop, citizens' satisfaction with and trust in their own democracies also deteriorated across all Southern European countries. Most dramatically, satisfaction with national democracy in Spain dropped from 79 percent to 26 percent between 2007 and 2013, while dropping from 63 percent to 12 percent in Greece.[47] This dissatisfaction resulted in a dramatic decline in support for traditional, centrist parties and a surge in support for populists on the political extremes. In Spain, the collective vote share of the dominant center right (PP) and center left (PSOE) parties fell from 83.8 percent in 2008 to 50.7 percent in 2015. Meanwhile, the far-left Podemos party emerged as a major new electoral force, with over 20 percent of the vote. Centrist parties experienced similar declines in Italy, and the populist Five Star Movement (M5S) – which promised to take Italy out of the euro – captured more than 25 percent of the vote in the 2013 elections. In Greece, which has suffered most from the crisis, there was a collapse of the traditional party system, as voters propelled the far-left Syriza party into office in 2015 on its promises of ending EU-imposed austerity.

43 "Greece Crisis: Germany's Schäuble Warns over Reform," BBC News, December 30, 2014, www.bbc.com/news/world-europe-30629269.

44 Hewitt, Gavin, "Greece: The Dangerous Game," BBC News, February 1, 2014, www.bbc.com/news/world-europe-31082656.

45 Matthijs, Matthias, "Integration at What Price? The Erosion of National Democracy in the Euro Periphery," *Government and Opposition* 52 (2): 266–94 (2017).

46 Ibid.: 269–70.

47 Ibid.: 271.

While the effects of the eurozone crisis on democratic institutions may have been most intense in the South, they have been felt across Europe. By 2013, in the aftermath of the peak of the eurozone crisis, public trust in and support for the European Union hit record lows.[48] In 2007, before the onset of the crisis, only 32 percent of Europeans surveyed said that they did not trust the EU; by 2013 the share who did not trust the EU had risen to 60 percent.[49] An early indicator of the impact of shifting attitudes came in the 2014 European Parliament elections. While centrist parties retained the majority, far-right, anti-EU parties achieved their best results ever, gaining fifty-two members of the European Parliament (MEPs) in all. In France and Denmark, far-right parties (the National Front and the Danish People's Party) were the top vote-getters in their countries' European Parliament elections. National elections since then have seen far-right politicians make historic gains in Austria, the Netherlands, and France. Most recently, in Germany the far-right AfD (*Alternative für Deutschland*) party achieved a stunning success in the 2017 Bundestag elections, capturing 12.6 percent of the vote, making it the third largest party in the Parliament and the first far-right party represented there in half a century. On aggregate, across the twenty-eight member states which were members of the EU at the time the euro was launched or have joined since, support for populist, anti-EU parties on the far right and far left has risen from a total of roughly 13 percent of the vote in national parliamentary elections in 2002 to approximately 23 percent today.[50] To be sure, a host of other issues – above all immigration and the refugee crisis – have been central to the recent successes of many of these parties, but opposition to the EU and the euro was a key theme for many of them, including the National Front in France and the AfD in Germany. Even in the UK, which is not a member of the eurozone and was not a signatory to the Fiscal Compact Treaty, the EU's combination of bailouts and imposed austerity fed the anti-EU sentiment that culminated in the vote for Brexit. During the Brexit referendum campaign, many on the left who favored Brexit (so-called Lexiters) argued that the EU was undermining national democracies by imposing austerity on eurozone member states.[51] Meanwhile, Leavers on the right alternated between claiming (falsely) that "UK taxpayers will keep paying for the huge bills caused by the Euro crisis" and that

48 See "Trust in European Union Hits Record Low," *Deutsche Welle*, April 26, 2013, www.dw.com/en/trust-in-european-union-hits-record-low/a-16775428; Traynor, Ian,"Crisis for Europe as trust hits record low," *The Guardian*, April 24, 2013, www.theguardian.com/world/2013/apr/24/trust-eu-falls-record-low.

49 European Commission, "Public Opinion in the European Union," Standard Eurobarometer 81/ Spring 2014–TNS Opinion & Social (2013), 9 European Commission, Eurobarometer, http://ec.europa.eu/public_opinion/archives/eb/eb79/eb79_first_en.pdf.

50 Hix, Simon and Giacomo Benedetto, *Dataset: The Rise and Fall of Social Democrats, 1918–2017*, LSE/Royal Holloway College, 2017.

51 See for instance, John Hilary, "It's Time the Left Saw the EU for What It Really Is," politics.co.uk, January 8, 2016, www.politics.co.uk/comment-analysis/2016/01/08/comment-it-s-time-the-left-saw-the-eu-for-what-it-really-is.

"these bills will only increase,"[52] and castigating the EU for usurping Greek democracy and governing the country by fiat.

Clearly, these developments have been politically disastrous for many of the centrist parties that have dominated post-war European politics, particularly those on the center-left whose voters saw their embrace of neoliberal economic reform and austerity policies as a betrayal of their core values.[53] Even more worryingly, declining support for mainstream parties and increasing support for populists seems to be linked to a broader decrease in support for democracy itself and an increased openness to authoritarian alternatives.[54] As Foa and Mounk explain, democracy has "lost the trust of many citizens who no longer believe that democracy can deliver on their most pressing needs and preferences."[55] While a host of factors having nothing to do with eurozone governance help explain these worrying trends, EU leaders' attempts to judicialize austerity – and thereby to escape responsibility by establishing a kind of "There-Is-No-Alternative" fiscal policy – have clearly contributed to the hollowing-out of support for mainstream democratic politics and parties across Europe.

IV. CONCLUSION

The eurozone crisis confronted European leaders with a stark reality: the system of eurozone governance they had constructed was woefully incomplete, unstable, and unsustainable without major reform. They had launched the euro without a series of institutions necessary to underpin a monetary union. Among its many deficiencies (including its lack of a banking union, any macroecononomic adjustment mechanisms, a system of fiscal transfers or a common debt instrument), the eurozone lacked a credible mechanism to limit national deficits. When the Greek crisis hit, in 2009 and 2010, EU leaders could have stuck with their Maastricht Treaty commitment not to bail out insolvent states. Though many observers and leaders at the time feared this could lead to a catastrophic financial meltdown across the eurozone, other leading analysts have argued that eurozone leaders could have stuck by the no-bailout rule, avoiding a disorderly default by organizing a major restructuring of public and private debt in Greece and other countries where this was deemed necessary.[56] Had they taken this approach, EU leaders could have established a credible commitment not to bail out states. This in turn would have prompted eurozone member governments to find their own ways to make credible

52 "Reality Check: Will the UK pay for future euro bailouts?" BBC News June 5, 2016, www.bbc.com/news/uk-politics-eu-referendum-36456277.

53 "European Social Democracy: Rose Thou Art Sick," *The Economist*, April 2, 2016, www.economist.com/news/briefing/21695887-centre-left-sharp-decline-across-europe-rose-thou-art-sick.

54 Foa, Roberto and Yascha Mounk, "The Danger of Deconsolidation," *Journal of Democracy*, 27(3): 5–17 (2016).

55 Ibid.: 16.

56 Sandbu (2015: 268).

commitments to fiscal prudence in order to regain the trust of bond markets. Instead, EU leaders made the fateful choice to rescue states facing financial crises and to involve themselves in micromanaging their fiscal policy and structural reform programs. This may have seemed politically expedient in the short term, but it has proved politically disastrous in the long term. As Federico Fabbrini has emphasized, the outcome of this reform was that the EU ended up with a system with far greater central control over state fiscal policy than exists in the United States.[57] The US federal government refuses to bailout struggling states, but imposes no restrictions on their fiscal policies. The EU meanwhile offers the promise of bailouts through the ESM and further support through the European Central Bank's Outright Monetary Transactions (OMT) program, but in exchange it imposes fiscal rules from the center.

This situation yields perhaps the worst of all possible worlds: for a series of reasons discussed above, the judicialized fiscal rules do not actually work in constraining member state borrowing. Importantly, courts in a number of countries have demonstrated that they will not blindly prioritize fiscal rules over other constitutional values – including social rights. Nevertheless, many citizens believe the EU has saddled them with strictly enforceable rules and that national politicians have no real say over fiscal policy. Frustrated with the impotence of establishment politicians who claim "There is no alternative" to EU-imposed austerity, many voters have turned against mainstream parties and against the EU itself, and embraced populists on the far right and far left. The hopes of politicians who believed they might escape the responsibility – and the blame – for difficult fiscal choices by calling on courts to enforce austerity have been sorely disappointed.

57 Fabbrini, n. 13, at p. 28; Fabbrini, Federico, "The Euro-crisis and the Courts: Judicial Review and the Political Process in Comparative Perspective," *Berkeley Journal of International Law* 32(1): 113–14 (2014).

9

Protecting Fundamental Rights During Financial Crisis

Supranational Adjudication in the Council of Europe

Eva Brems

I. INTRODUCTION: FINANCIAL CRISIS AND FUNDAMENTAL RIGHTS

The financial crisis throughout Europe has led many countries to adopt austerity measures, some of which have imposed harsh costs on citizens. Fundamental rights provide one framework for assessing the impact of both the economic crisis and the austerity measures. Several studies have documented the effects of the crisis and austerity measures on fundamental rights, in particular economic and social rights such as the right to work, to social security, to housing, health and education, but also civil and political rights including the right of access to justice, and the freedom of assembly and expression.[1]

In Europe, the ultimate guarantors of fundamental rights are situated at the supranational level. In addition to the EU bodies (in particular the European Court of Justice) – which are not addressed in this chapter – it is mainly the monitoring bodies within the Council of Europe system that are responsible for overseeing fundamental rights. Individuals and legal persons who have failed to obtain a remedy at the domestic level can address a complaint to the European Court of Human Rights (ECtHR) concerning violations of the European Convention on Human Rights (ECHR) and its additional protocols. This Convention and its additional protocols protect mainly civil and political rights. However, of particular relevance in the present context is the inclusion of the right to property in Article 1 of the First Additional Protocol. Cuts in social allowances for example, may be addressed under this provision. If, however, the alleged human rights violation concerns social rights, the remedy is a collective

[1] Dalila Ghailani, 'Violations of fundamental rights: collateral damage of the Eurozone crisis?' Research paper Observatoire social Européen, 2016; Council of Europe Commissioner for Human Rights, 'Safeguarding human rights in times of economic crisis', 2013; European Parliament, 'The impact of the crisis on fundamental rights across Member States of the EU', Study for the LIBE committee, 2015; UN Office of the High Commissioner on Human Rights, 'Report on austerity measures and economic and social rights', 2012.

complaint[2] before the European Committee of Social Rights (ECSR) based on the European Social Charter (ESC). Both the ECHR and the ECSR have addressed several cases concerning austerity measures that have been adopted during the recent financial crisis in Europe. The present chapter will analyse this case law,[3] and assess the role that these supranational human rights monitoring bodies are playing, or may play, in the context of financial crisis.

The chapter will analyse the case law of each body in turn (sections II and III). As will become clear, the approach of the ECtHR to this type of cases is very different from that of the ECSR, resulting in strikingly different outcomes. Institutional differences between the ECtHR and the ECSR largely explain these differences (IV.1). Yet from a holistic perspective of human rights law, that explanation does not necessarily suffice as a justification of such differences. The final sections of the chapter (IV.2 and IV.3) will examine the question of the justifiability of this kind of pluriformity within the supranational human rights protection system through the lens of the concept of 'smart integration'.

II. EUROPEAN COMMITTEE OF SOCIAL RIGHTS: A PRINCIPLED STANCE LEADS TO FINDINGS OF VIOLATIONS

The financial crisis case law of the ECSR consists of seven decisions against Greece, two of which were adopted on 23 May 2012[4] and the remaining five on 7 December 2012.[5] In each of these decisions, measures that were adopted by the Greek government in 2010 and 2011 in response to the financial crisis were found to violate the European Social Charter.

1. *Labour Law Cases*

The first set of two complaints were brought by the same two trade unions, acting together. In both decisions, the Committee starts its analysis of the merits with the

2 Under a 1995 additional protocol to the ESC, a collective complaints mechanism was installed, that allows for complaints by non-governmental organisations and social partners.

3 In addition to the complaint mechanism, the ECSR also comments on regular state reports. Its output under the reporting mechanism, however, is not included in this chapter, with the exception of a reference in n. 6.

4 *General Federation of Employees of the National Electric Power Corporation (GENOP-DEI) /Confederation of Greek Civil Servants' Trade Unions (ADEDY)* v. *Greece*, Complaint No. 65/2011, 23 May 2012; *General Federation of Employees of the National Electric Power Corporation (GENOP-DEI)/Confederation of Greek Civil Servants' Trade Unions (ADEDY)* v. *Greece*, Complaint No. 66/2011, 23 May 2012.

5 *Federation of Employed Pensioners of Greece (IKA-ETAM)* v. *Greece*, Complaint No. 76, 7 December 2012; *Panhellenic Federation of Public Service Pensioners (POPS)* v. *Greece*, Complaint No. 77, 7 December 2012; *Pensioners' Union of the Athens-Piraeus Electric Railways (ISAP)* v. *Greece*, Complaint No. 78, 7 December 2012; *Panhellenic Federation of Pensioners of the Public Electricity Corporation (POS-DEI)* v. *Greece*, Complaint No. 79, 7 December 2012; *Pensioners' Union of the Agricultural Bank of Greece (ATE)* v. *Greece*, Complaint No. 80, 7 December 2012.

same 'preliminary remarks', in which it refers to the government's arguments about the economic crisis. These are interesting because they frame the analysis of the case at hand in a general principled approach of the Committee to measures taken in a context of economic crisis. Repeating a statement it had made earlier,[6] the Committee stated[7] that

> While the increasing level of unemployment is presenting a challenge to social security and social assistance systems as the number of beneficiaries increase while tax and social security contribution revenues decline, by acceding to the 1961 Charter, the Parties have accepted to pursue by all appropriate means, the attainment of conditions in which inter alia the right to health, the right to social security, the right to social and medical assistance and the right to benefit from social welfare services may be effectively realised. Accordingly, . . . the economic crisis should not have as a consequence the reduction of the rights recognised by the Charter. Hence, the governments are bound to take all necessary steps to be sure that the rights of the Charter are effectively guaranteed at a period of time when beneficiaries need the protection most.

The Committee added that this applies to labour law, and that

> greater employment flexibility in order to combat unemployment and encourage employers to take on staff, should not result in depriving broad categories of employees, particularly those who have not had a stable job for long, of their fundamental rights in the field of labour law, protecting them from arbitrary decisions by their employers or from economic fluctuations.

It stated moreover that

> doing away with such guarantees would not only force employees to shoulder an excessively large share of the consequences of the crisis but also accept pro-cyclical effects liable to make the crisis worse and to increase the burden on welfare systems, particularly social assistance, unless it was decided at the same time to stop fulfilling the obligations of the Charter in the area of social protection.

In the first case (Complaint No. 65/2011), the Committee ruled on a legal provision that declared that the first year of employment on a permanent contract is to be considered a trial period during which employment may be terminated without notice and with no severance pay.[8] The Greek government had argued that this was

[6] General Introduction to Conclusions XIX-2 (2009).

[7] Complaint No. 65/2011, para. 16.

[8] A second complaint concerned the introduction of the possibility for a collective agreement at enterprise level to derogate from the provisions set out in a collective agreement concluded at sectoral level, which according to the complainant organisations led to a deterioration in working conditions for the employees concerned, and the rule that if there is no trade union in the enterprise, sectoral unions or the relevant federation can conclude enterprise-level collective agreements directly. However, the Committee ruled that it could not address these issues, as they fall under

reasonable, 'given the current economic crisis and the unstable nature of Greek enterprises' business activities'. Article 4, Part II of the ESC, however, recognises 'the right of all workers to a reasonable period of notice for termination of employment'. The Committee ruled that this provision applies 'to all categories of employees, independently of their status/grade, including those employed on non-standard basis,' including during the probationary period. Without dwelling further on the crisis context, the Committee concluded that the Greek law was in violation of this ESC provision.

The second case (Complaint No. 66/2011) concerned the introduction by law of 'special apprenticeships contracts' for individuals aged fifteen to eighteen that were intended to fall outside of the scope of the labour law, as well as a measure that provided lower wages for new entrants to the labour market aged under twenty-five. Regarding the special apprenticeships contract, the Committee found violations of Article 7 § 7 (right to holiday with pay),[9] Article 10 § 2 (right to vocational training)[10] and Article 12 § 3 (right to social security). The most interesting reasoning is found under the last-mentioned right. For 'special apprenticeships contracts', the Greek law limited social security coverage to sickness benefits in kind, while excluding sickness allowances and the reimbursement of prescription charges, and limiting occupational accident coverage to a rate of 1 per cent. In the eyes of the Committee, the law thus established 'a distinct category of workers with qualified entitlement to social security'.[11] The Committee then concluded that[12]

> Article 12 § 3 requires state parties to 'endeavour to raise progressively the system of social security to a higher level'. In this respect, the Committee recognises that it may be necessary to introduce measures to consolidate public finances in times of economic crisis, in order to ensure the maintenance and sustainability of the existing social security system. However, any such measures should not undermine the core framework of a national social security system or deny individuals the opportunity to enjoy the protection it offers against serious social and economic risk. Therefore, any changes to a social security system must maintain in place

Arts 5 and 6 of the Charter, which have not been accepted by Greece (Complaint No. 65/2011, para. 40).

9 Art. 7 § 7 ESC explicitly states that 'employed persons of under 18 years of age shall be entitled to not less than three weeks' annual holiday with pay'. As the provisions of labour law did not apply to the 'special apprenticeships contracts', this right was not guaranteed.

10 This is because the Committee defines apprenticeship in the context of Art. 10 § 2 as involving training based on a contract between the young person and the employer, which is regulated by a body of rules which govern the length of the apprenticeship, the division of time between practical and theoretical learning, the manner in which apprentices are selected, the selection and qualifications of trainers, the remuneration of apprentices, and termination of the apprenticeship contract. It is essential that an apprenticeship should combine theoretical and practical training. However, the relevant legislation does not comply with most of these requirements (Complaint No. 66/2011, paras 36–8).

11 Complaint No. 66/2011, para. 45.

12 Complaint 66/2011, para. 47.

a sufficiently extensive system of compulsory social security and refrain from excluding entire categories of workers from the social protection offered by this system . . .[13] The Committee considers that financial consolidation measures which fail to respect these limits constitute retrogressive steps which cannot be deemed to be in conformity with Article 12 § 3.

Regarding the measures affecting employees under twenty-five, the Committee found a violation of Article 4 § 1 (the right to a fair remuneration) insofar as the Greek provisions authorised a minimum wage below the poverty level, as well as discrimination on the ground of age. As to the latter, the Committee thought the measure pursued a legitimate aim, 'namely to integrate younger workers into the labour market in a time of serious economic crisis', but nevertheless concluded that the measure violated the ESC because it was disproportionate.

2. *Pension Rights Cases*

The five cases decided on 7 December 2012 concerned drastic cuts in pensions.[14] The Committee found these cuts to be in violation of the right to social security, and more specifically the obligation under Article 12 § 3 'to endeavour to raise progressively the system of social security to a higher level'. The reasoning on the merits in these cases is identical. Again, the decisions contain interesting 'introductory remarks',[15] this time regarding the Greek government's general defence that it was obliged to take the measures at issue under the loan arrangement with the EU institutions and the International Monetary Fund. The Committee pointed out that 'the fact that the contested provisions of domestic law seek to fulfil the requirements of other legal obligations does not remove them from the ambit of the Charter',[16] and stated that states should take full account of their Charter commitments when they agree on binding measures that relate to matters within the remit of the Charter.[17]

The Committee concluded that the cumulative effects of the measures violated the Charter, as they 'appear to have the effect of depriving one segment of the population of a very substantial portion of their means of subsistence.'

[13] The Committee refers here to an earlier statement it made: Conclusions XVI-1, Interpretative statement of Art. 12, p. 11.

[14] An overview is given at the outset of each decision, e.g. Complaint No. 76/2012, paras 17–29. By way of example, any primary and auxiliary pensions of pensioners having taken early retirement have been reduced by approximately 50 per cent. With regard to pensioners under the age of fifty-five years, any share of a primary pension exceeding 1000 EUR has been reduced by 40 per cent. With regard to pensioners aged fifty-five years or over, any share of a primary pension exceeding 1200 EUR has been reduced by 20 per cent.

[15] E.g. Complaint 76/2012, paras 50–1.

[16] Ibid., para. 50.

[17] Ibid., para. 51.

The Committee also stated that the measures 'have been introduced in a manner that does not respect the legitimate expectation of pensioners that adjustments to their social security entitlements will be implemented in a manner that takes due account of their vulnerability, settled financial expectations and ultimately their right to enjoy effective access to social protection and social security.'[18] In addition to its concerns with the measures' substance, the Committee expressed concern with the process by which the measures were adopted. The Committee 'considers that the Government has not conducted the minimum level of research and analysis into the effects of such far reaching measures that is necessary to assess in a meaningful manner their full impact on vulnerable groups in society. Neither has it discussed the available studies with the organisations concerned, despite the fact that they represent the interests of many of the groups most affected by the measures at issue'.[19] The Committee thus combined two procedural concerns: evidence-based governance and participation/representation. The Committee then linked these procedural concerns to the substantive concern of minimising rights interference, noting that 'as a result' of the procedural inadequacies 'it has not been discovered whether other measures could have been put in place, which may have limited the cumulative effects of the contested restrictions upon pensioners'.[20]

3. *Follow-up*

In the two follow-up procedures[21] of the ECSR decisions, the Greek government argued on complaints 65/2011 and 66/2011 that the measures were of a provisional nature and would be revoked as soon as the economic situation of the country allowed this. It could however not envisage a set timeframe. The Committee of Ministers, on 5 February 2013, called on Greece to revoke the measures as soon as possible.[22] On 4 December 2015, the ECSR found that none of the issues had been brought in conformity with the Charter.[23] Regarding Complaints 76–80/2012, the Greek government cited a long list of measures adopted as 'product of a long social dialogue' to reform the social security system. The Committee stated on 2 July 2014 that it 'looks forward to

[18] Complaint No. 76/2012, para. 82.

[19] Ibid., para. 79.

[20] Ibid., para. 80.

[21] The follow-up of the decisions of the ECSR is done by the Council of Ministers of the Council of Europe. In the event of violation of the Charter, the state is asked to notify the Committee of Ministers of the Council of Europe of the measures taken or planned to bring the situation into conformity. The Committee of Ministers may adopt a resolution that takes account of the respondent state's declared intention to take appropriate measures to bring the situation into conformity. If the state in question does not indicate its intention to bring the situation into conformity, the Committee of Ministers may also adopt a recommendation to the state.

[22] Resolution CM/ResChS(2013)2 and Resolution CM/ResChS(2013)3.

[23] ECSR, follow-up assessment decisions in Complaints Nos 65 and 66/2011.

Greece reporting, at the time of the submission of the next report ... that the situation has been brought into conformity'.[24] On 4 December 2015, the ECSR found that the violations at issue in the decisions persisted.[25]

III. EUROPEAN COURT OF HUMAN RIGHTS: A WIDE MARGIN UNDER ARTICLE 1 OF PROTOCOL 1

In comparison with the ECSR, the 'financial crisis' case law of the European Court of Human Rights (ECtHR) is much more extensive, and at the same time more heterogeneous. For these reasons, it is more challenging to determine which cases appropriately belong to the category of 'financial crisis case law'. A 'fact sheet' on 'austerity measures' prepared by the Press Unit of the ECtHR mentions eleven cases, yet an analysis of scholarly literature on the topic harvests over thirty cases. Much depends on one's definition of 'crisis' or 'austerity',[26] as well as on the types of rights one is interested in.[27] The main focus in this section will be on cases concerning cuts in social allowances and financial assets, which were brought under the right to property (Article 1 of Protocol 1). These are set against the backgrounds of other types of cases in which resource constraints were invoked – in vain – by governments as a defence to alleged shortcomings in human rights protection that required the large investment of resources, in particular concerning prison conditions and fair trial. In principle, cuts in social allowances could under some circumstances constitute inhuman or degrading treatment under Article 3 ECHR,[28] or could violate the right to privacy under Article 8 ECHR.[29] However, this chapter does not include the case law that makes reference to these possibilities because the ECtHR to date has not yet had to examine any clear 'financial crisis' cases under these headings.

1. *Civil and Political Rights*

Although it has been argued that the economic/financial crisis has had a strong negative impact on the enjoyment of several civil and political rights, such as

24 Resolution CM/ResChS(2014)7–11.

25 ECSR, follow-up assessment decisions in Complaints Nos 76, 77, 78, 79 and 80/2012.

26 Cf. Aoife Nannery's presentation of a 'spectrum', with the 'bailout' euro-crisis cases from Greece and Portugal on one end, 'tapering towards cases where the links with the crisis are more oblique, in the Hungarian, Latvian and Romanian cases' (Nannery 2015).

27 For this chapter, the corpus of ECtHR case law that was examined, was composed mainly on the basis of the aforementioned fact sheet and the literature that is mentioned in the footnotes. The most recent case law was detected through a systematic review of ECtHR case law in the bi-weekly meetings of the 'Strasbourg Club' at the Human Rights Centre of Ghent University.

28 The Court considered that a 'wholly insufficient' pension might raise an issue under Art. 3 (*Larioshina* v. *Russia* (dec.), 23 April 2002, and *Budina* v. *Russia* (dec.), 18 June 2009).

29 Cf. *McDonald* v. *UK* (20 May 2014) which the Court included in its fact sheet on austerity measures.

with regard to prison conditions and access to justice,[30] the ECtHR does not take a crisis context into account in its reasoning in such cases. Indeed in such cases, the Court as a rule rejects economic and budgetary arguments as justifications for rights restrictions.[31] For example, the Court has held that 'lack of resources cannot in principle justify prison conditions which are so poor as to reach the threshold of treatment contrary to Article 3 of the Convention'.[32] Similarly, the Court systematically rejects resource constraints as potential justifications for infringements of the right to a fair trial under Article 6 ECHR. This includes the obligation for the government to honour judgment debts,[33] and the obligation to avoid excessive delays in the administration of justice. The Court has not hesitated to apply this categorical approach to Greece in a number of pilot judgments in 2010 and 2012 regarding violations of the reasonable time requirement.[34] The implicit reasoning by the Court appears to be, that under all circumstances, budgetary priority should be given to measures that are required to respect human rights.

2. *Cuts in Salaries and Social Benefits Under Article 1P1*

However, when it comes to challenges under the right to property (Article 1 Protocol 1) of cuts in salaries and social benefits as a result of austerity measures, the Court gives a lot more leeway to the crisis argument. It does so indirectly, by holding that national governments have a wide margin of appreciation to determine the economic and social policies that are required in the specific contexts of their societies. Yet when it comes to budget cuts in the prison system or the judiciary that result in infringements of Articles 3 or 6 ECHR (cf. above), no such wide margin is granted. Gerards has remarked that from the viewpoint of effective and equal protection of Convention rights, as well as the indivisible nature of human rights, 'there are hardly any intrinsic reasons of principle' to

30 See ECtHR 2013: 14; CECHR 2013: 21 and EP 2015: 95; COE Steering Committee for Human Rights, 'The impact of the economic crisis and austerity measures on human rights in Europe. Feasibility study', CDDH (2015) 584, Addendum IV: 10 and 13

31 Janneke Gerards, 'The ECtHR's response to fundamental rights issues related to financial and economic difficulties. The problem of compartmentalisation'. *Netherlands Quarterly of Human Rights* 33(3): 275-76 (2015); European Court of Human Rights, Dialogue between Judges 2013: 'Implementing the European Convention on Human Rights in times of economic crisis', p. 9; Françoise Tulkens, 'The contribution of the European Convention on Human Rights to the poverty issue in times of crisis', European Court of Human Rights – European Judicial Training Network Seminar on Human Rights for European Judicial Trainers, 8 July 2014, p. 4.

32 E.g. ECtHR, *Poltoratskiy* v. *Ukraine*, 29 April 2003, para. 148. The Court added in this case: 'Moreover, the economic problems faced by Ukraine cannot in any event explain or excuse the particular conditions of detention.'

33 E.g. ECtHR, *Nosov a.o.* v. *Russia*, 20 February 2014, para. 41: 'it is not open to a State authority to cite the lack of funds or other resources (such as housing) as an excuse for not honouring a judgment debt'.

34 ECtHR, *Vassiliou Athanasiou* v. *Greece*, 21 December 2010; ECtHR, *Michelioudakis* v. *Greece*, 3 April 2012; ECtHR, *Glykantzi* v. *Greece*, 30 October 2012.

explain this difference.[35] In her words, 'the degree of compartmentalisation is too absolute', and 'may hamper the effectiveness of the Court's contribution to protection of individual fundamental rights in times of crisis.'[36] (I discuss my views on this question at the end of this chapter.)

The large majority of Article 1P1 challenges to austerity cuts in salaries and social benefits have not only failed, but have even been declared inadmissible for being 'manifestly ill-founded'. Nevertheless, a small number of applicants have been successful in such cases.[37]

To facilitate comparison with the ECSR approach, let's zoom in on a Greek case in this category, which is representative of the Court's approach. The case of *Koufaki and ADEDY* v. *Greece*[38] concerned reductions in the remuneration, benefits, bonuses and retirement pensions of public servants. The applicants – an individual public servant and a public service trade union confederation – argued that the cuts amounted to 'deprivation of possessions' under Article 1P1. The Court requalified the matter as one of 'interference with the peaceful enjoyment of possessions'.[39] This interference did not violate the provision in the eyes of the Court because it had a legal basis, pursued a public interest, and remained within the state's margin of appreciation. Noteworthy in the Court's reasoning is its emphasis on the impact of the measures on the individual applicant. The Court stated that the applicant was not made to bear an excessive burden because the reduction of her salary 'was not such as to place her at risk of having insufficient means to live on'.[40] Remarkably,[41] the Court also briefly assessed the impact of the measures on the members of the trade union applicant. Referring simply to the memorandum of understanding between Greece and the European Union, the Court held that there were sufficient measures in place to protect those in the lowest income segments.[42] This suggests that protection against deprivation of property, in this context at least, does not extend beyond protection against poverty.[43]

35 Gerards, 'The ECtHR's response to fundamental rights issues related to financial and economic difficulties. The problem of compartmentalisation', p. 289.

36 Ibid. at 290.

37 Under the ECtHR system, a case can be declared inadmissible, and hence will not formally be examined on the merits, if the bench considers that it is manifest that no Convention rights are violated in the case: see Art. 35(3) ECHR. The fact that, depending on the facts of the case, some austerity cases can be successful, makes one wonder how the Court can reasonably consider other cases of the same type to be 'manifestly' ill-founded. Consistency would appear to suggest that those other cases also should be examined on the merits.

38 ECtHR (dec.), *Koufaki and ADEDY* v. *Greece*, 7 May 2013.

39 Ibid., para. 34.

40 Ibid., para. 46. Her net salary was reduced from EUR 2,435.83 to EUR 1,885.79.

41 The Court left open the question whether the trade union applicant could be considered a 'victim' within the meaning of Art. 34 of the Convention. See para. 30. Under the Convention system, an applicant has to show an individual interest in the case. This means that a trade union can apply to the Court to defend its own interests, but that it cannot act on behalf of its members.

42 Para. 47.

43 Similar reasoning is found for example in ECtHR, *Valkov a.o.* v. *Bulgaria*, 25 October 2011, para. 97; *Panfile* v. *Romania* (dec.), 20 March 2012, para. 23; *Savickas a.o.* v. *Lithuania* (dec.), 15 October 2013, para. 94; *Markovics a.o.* v. *Hungary* (dec.), 24 June 2014, para. 42.

Another noteworthy feature of the ruling in *Koufaki* is the Court's crisis rhetoric. First, introducing its argument about the 'public interest' aim of the measures, the Court states that 'the adoption of the impugned measures was justified by the existence of an exceptional crisis without precedent in recent Greek history'.[44] Additionally, the Court refers to 'the particular context of crisis' in justifying its finding that the measures do not impose an excessive burden on the applicant.[45] While the temporary nature of an austerity measure appears to have played a role in the Court's proportionality analysis in some other cases,[46] the non-temporary nature of the measures did not appear to disturb the Court in this case.[47] Finally, it is noteworthy that the wide margin of appreciation entailed the dismissal of any argument that less restrictive measures should have been adopted, or that there should be evidence that the government had at least considered less restrictive measures. The Court ruled:[48]

> As regards alternative solutions, their possible existence does not in itself render the contested legislation unjustified. Provided that the legislature remains within the bounds of its margin of appreciation, it is not for the Court to say whether the legislation represented the best solution for dealing with the problem or whether the legislature's discretion should have been exercised in another way.

All in all, in this line of case law, its willingness to dismiss cases at the threshold admissibility stage on grounds of manifest ill-foundedness, in conjunction with its granting of a (very) wide margin of appreciation, has led the Court to accept, with only a brief examination of the merits and very light scrutiny, far-reaching measures such as an overall salary cut of 25 per cent for all civil servants for a period of six months,[49] a 16 per cent pension reduction,[50] or a 50 per cent reduction of parental benefits.[51]

Nevertheless, the Court has found violations of Article 1P1 in a number of other cases of this type. Most notable are two cases against Hungary.[52] These cases deal

44 *Koufaki & ADEDY*, para. 37. Similarly: *Panfile* v. *Romania* (dec.), 20 March 2012, para. 20; *Da Conceição Mateus and Santos Januário* v. *Portugal* (dec.), 8 October 2013, para. 25–6; *Savickas a.o.* v. *Lithuania* (dec.), 15 October 2013, para. 92; *Da Silva Carvalho Rico* v. *Portugal* (dec.), 1 September 2015, para. 40.

45 Para. 46. Similarly: *Da Conceição Mateus and Santos Januário* v. *Portugal*, para. 29; *Savickas a.o.* v. *Lithuania*, para. 93; *Da Silva Carvalho Rico* v. *Portugal*, para. 44.

46 E.g. ECtHR (dec.), *Da Conceição Mateus and Santos Januário* v. *Portugal* (dec.), 8 October 2013, para. 26 and 29; ECtHR (dec.), *Savickas a.o.* v. *Lithuania*, para. 94; ECtHR (dec.), *Da Silva Carvalho Rico* v. *Portugal* (dec.), 1 September 2015, paras 44 and 46.

47 *Koufaki & ADEDY*, para. 44.

48 Para. 48.

49 ECtHR (dec.), *Mihăieş and Senteş* v. *Romania*, 6 December 2011.

50 ECtHR (dec.), *Markovics a.o.* v. *Hungary*, 24 June 2014.

51 ECtHR (dec.), *Sulcs* v. *Latvia and 22 other cases*, 6 December 2011.

52 Several commentators have hypothesised that the fact that the Hungarian Constitutional Court had viewed the austerity measures as unconstitutional, may have played a role in the background (Palmstorfer 2014: 132; Nannery 2015: 34).

with the introduction of a 98 per cent tax on severance payments above a certain level for public sector employees. For the applicant in the first case, this led to a 52 per cent tax on the severance payment overall, while the general personal income tax rate was 16 per cent.[53] Despite its affirmation of a wide margin of appreciation, the Court found a violation in these cases. Interesting features of the Court's reasoning include its emphases on honouring the legitimate expectations of public servants as a matter of public interest,[54] and on the social function of severance payments.[55] Yet the factors that appear decisive for the finding of a violation seem to be the following. First, there is the impression that a category of people has been singled out to bear a much heavier burden than others:[56]

> The Court finds that the applicant, who was entitled to statutory severance on the basis of the law in force and whose acting in good faith has never been called into question, was subjected to a tax whose rate exceeded about three times the general personal income tax rate of 16% ... and this notwithstanding the fact that the severance served the specific and recognised social goal of labour reintegration. It does not appear that any other revenue originating from the public purse was subjected to similarly high tax

A second factor is the impact on the personal situation of the applicant, which – interestingly, in light of the inadmissibility case law discussed above – while significant, remained short of pushing her into poverty:[57]

> For the Court, it is quite plausible that the element that she was subjected to the impugned measure while unemployed, together with the unexpected and swift nature of the change of the tax regime which made any preparation virtually impossible for those concerned, exposed the applicant to substantial personal hardships.

Finally, some procedural elements are mentioned: the absence of a transitional period,[58] the lack of an individualised assessment of the applicant's situation,[59] and a retroactive application.[60]

Crisis rhetoric is almost wholly absent from these judgments.[61]

The two main criteria mentioned above can be traced back to the 2004 case of *Asmundsson v Iceland*,[62] in which the Court found a violation of Article 1P1 on

53 ECtHR (dec.), *NKM* v. *Hungary*, 14 May 2013, paras 66 and 68.
54 Ibid., para. 37.
55 Ibid., para.38.
56 Ibid., para. 68. More references to this aspect in paras 71 and 72. *RSz* v. *Hungary* (dec.), 2 July 2013, para. 58.
57 *NKM*, para. 70; *RSz*, para. 59.
58 *NKM*, para. 71; *RSz*, para. 59
59 *NKM*, para. 73.
60 *NKM*, para. 74.
61 *NKM*, para. 72: 'Assuming that the impugned measure served the interest of the State budget at a time of economic hardship'. Idem in *RsZ*, para. 60.
62 ECtHR, *Asmundsson* v. *Iceland*, 12 October 2004.

account of the applicant's loss of entitlement to a disability pension as a result of legislative change. Compared to the Icelandic case, however, the Hungarian cases have allowed the Court to extend the range of scenarios that might constitute a violation. After all, the category that was singled out to bear an excessive burden was particularly narrow in *Asmundsson*,[63] and the impact on the applicant's economic situation was also harsher, in that it deprived him of an allowance that constituted a third of his income and that he had been receiving for nearly twenty years.[64]

In a recent Grand Chamber judgment, the Court set out the general principles of its proportionality analysis under Article 1P1 in regard to social benefits (regardless of a crisis context):[65]

> In considering whether the interference imposed an excessive individual burden the Court will have regard to the particular context in which the issue arises, namely that of a social-security scheme. Such schemes are an expression of a society's solidarity with its vulnerable members ... The Court reiterates that the deprivation of the entirety of a pension is likely to breach the provisions of Article 1 of Protocol No. 1 and that, conversely, reasonable reductions to a pension or related benefits are likely not to do so. However, the fair balance test cannot be based solely on the amount or percentage of the reduction suffered, in the abstract. In a number of cases the Court has endeavoured to assess all the relevant elements against the specific background ... In so doing, the Court has attached importance to such factors as the discriminatory nature of the loss of entitlement ... ; the absence of transitional measures ... ; the arbitrariness of the condition ... as well as the applicant's good faith ... An important consideration is whether the applicant's right to derive benefits from the social-insurance scheme in question has been infringed in a manner resulting in the impairment of the essence of his or her pension rights.[66]

This list contains several very concrete criteria that are useful to assess the chances of future litigation. However, the central criterion of 'impairment of the essence' of one's rights is fairly vague, and hence uncertain. Further, it seems that the Court may not be applying this vague standard consistently. The impact of the measure on the applicant's personal situation seems to have been assessed under a more lenient standard in the successful cases ('substantial personal hardship') than in the cases found to be inadmissible ('risk of having insufficient means to live on').

63 *Asmundsson*, para. 43: 'the Court is struck by the fact that the applicant belonged to a small group of 54 disability pensioners ... whose pensions, unlike those of any other group, were discontinued altogether on 1 July 1997'.

64 *Asmundsson*, para. 44.

65 ECtHR (GC), *Béláné Nagy* v. *Hungary*, 13 December 2016, paras 116–18. In this case the reduction of the applicant's social benefits did not arise out of a crisis context.

66 Applying this criterion, the Court held in *Baczúr* v. *Hungary* ruled on the same day (13 December 2016), that a two-thirds reduction of a disability benefit 'undoubtedly' falls within the category of impairment of the essence of the right (para. 29).

3. *Cuts in Financial Assets*

Another situation in which Article 1P1 has been invoked is when anti-crisis measures affect individuals' or legal entities' financial assets in the banks. In 2012, the Court ruled on a case about lack of compensation for shareholders at the time of the nationalisation by the United Kingdom of the Northern Rock bank in 2008.[67] Applying an irrationality test[68] under a very wide margin of appreciation, the Court found no violation, ruling that the case was inadmissible for being manifestly ill-founded. This is linked to strong crisis rhetoric.[69]

More recently, the Court ruled on the obligation of private individuals holding Greek state bonds in 2012 to exchange their bonds for other debt instruments worth 53.5 per cent less in nominal value. This case was examined on the merits, and the Court likewise found that the national authorities had remained within their margin of appreciation. More than in previous cases, the Court emphasised the relevance of a wide margin of appreciation in the field of socio-economic policies, and in particular in the context of the financial crisis.[70] Also, more than in previous cases, the Court expanded on the crisis context in examining the public interest aim of the measure.[71] In addition, the good faith of applicants plays a role in the negative sense, with the Court – referring to the ECJ's dismissal of a claim by Italian holders of Greek bonds – suggesting that many held Greek bonds for speculative reasons, and any others should at least have been aware of the risks they were taking.[72] Despite the wide margin of appreciation, the Court dwelt briefly on the possibility of less restrictive alternatives, which it dismissed on the basis of arguments of political and economic realism.[73]

A third case of this type was examined only under Article 6 ECHR. When the Dutch government nationalised the banking and insurance conglomerate SNS Reaal in 2008, the law provided only a ten-day window in which to challenge the lawfulness of the expropriation of bondholders' assets. The Court held that the application was manifestly ill-founded. It found that the right to a fair trial was not affected because the applicants had in fact been able to launch an effective appeal. The Court put its assessment of the matter in the context of an acute financial crisis.[74]

67 ECtHR (dec.), *Grainger a.o.* v. *UK*, 10 July 2012.

68 *Grainger* para. 39: 'the Court must respect the decisions of the national authorities unless it finds them to be "manifestly without reasonable foundation"'.

69 *Grainger*, para. 39.

70 *Mamatas & Others* v. *Greece* (Application nos. 63066/14, 64297/14 and 66106/14) [2016] ECHR 694, para. 80.

71 *Mamatas*, paras 101–3.

72 *Mamatas*, para. 118.

73 *Mamatas*, para. 115.

74 ECtHR, *Adorisio a.o.* v. *the Netherlands* (dec.), 17 March 2015, para. 92.

IV. CRITICAL REFLECTIONS: EUROPEAN HUMAN RIGHTS MONITORING IN TIMES OF FINANCIAL CRISIS

The European Committee of Social Rights has addressed seven cases concerning austerity measures and has found human rights violations in all seven. The Committee adopts the stance that social rights have to be upheld regardless of the crisis context. In the labour law cases, the Committee found clear-cut violations of explicit Charter rules. In those cases, not finding a violation would have been possible only by straying from the interpretation of Charter provisions that the Committee had endorsed in previous case law. In the pension cases, the Committee had more room for manoeuvre. It chose to look at the cumulative effect of a series of measures on an entire social group, finding fault with the fact of depriving people of 'a substantive portion of their means of subsistence'. It also chose to take into account the process that lead to the adoption of the measures, which in the Committee's eyes was defective. It has linked this to a procedural control of the consideration of less restrictive measures.

The European Court of Human Rights in some contexts uses a similar rhetoric, to the effect that resource constraints cannot justify violations of fundamental rights. This is the case in particular when the Court addresses 'traditional' civil and political rights issues, such as prison conditions or fair trial issues. However, when assessing cuts in social benefits, salaries and financial assets in the light of Article 1P1, it has mobilised the crisis argument as a ground for judicial restraint. This affects both its acceptance of the public interest aim of the austerity measures, and its proportionality assessment. The latter is characterised by a very wide margin of appreciation for the national authorities, which the Court justifies both by the crisis context and by the nature of the (socio-economic) policy field. As a result, the threshold for the finding of a violation is very high for this type of case. Less restrictive means reasoning has been explicitly rejected. In its attitude of restraint, the Court has even gone so far as to hold most such complaints inadmissible for being 'manifestly ill-founded'.

Nevertheless, violations have been found in a few cases. Important criteria in this respect appear to be the singling out of a category of people who bear a disproportionate burden compared to others, and the impairment of the 'essence' of a person's rights. The latter has been operationalised in the successful cases as the plausibility that applicants have been exposed to 'substantial personal hardships', even though in some inadmissibility cases, a stricter criterion ('insufficient means to live on') seems to have been applied. In the successful cases, the Court also briefly refers to procedural inadequacies regarding the adoption or operationalisation of the measures, in particular retroactive application, the absence of transitory measures, and the lack of an individual assessment.

1. Roles and Mandates

It is clear that there are significant differences between the approaches of the two Council of Europe bodies to the protection of fundamental rights in times of financial crisis. To some extent these can be explained by the differences between the respective monitoring mechanisms and their mandates.[75] The European Court, ruling on an individual complaint, has to assess the situation of the applicant(s), while the Committee, ruling on a collective complaint concerning the impact of laws and policies on broad categories of people, can take a more structural approach to the matter. Also, in the European Court system, the idea of social protection is only indirectly involved, through the far-from-ideal vehicle of the right to property, whereas for the ECSR, social protection is its core business. That alone might explain stronger rhetoric and a firmer stance on behalf of the ECSR. In addition, the different approaches may be due to the monitoring bodies' divergent views of their role vis-à-vis the states parties. After all, the Court's judgments are binding upon the defendant states, and have a strong legal authority across all states parties, whereas the Committee's views are not binding as such. A body that issues non-binding views may experience less pressure toward restraint. The views of the Committee are an authoritative human rights analysis of a situation. They will be picked up by national actors (in the defending state or other states) that are willing to pursue or promote a human rights approach to the matter. These may include the defendant government, a subsequent government, local authorities, opposition actors, a national human rights institution, or civil society actors. Thus, the function of the Committee's views is arguably more inspirational than decisional. They can best perform this role if the Committee conducts a thorough human rights analysis of all aspects of the case. Should the Committee wish to leave certain matters unaddressed out of respect for the discretion of the national authorities, that would reduce the inspirational value of the views. The Court, on the other hand, issues decisive judgments and is under constant pressure from states parties to respect its subsidiary role. Increasingly, its legitimacy is seen as tied up with subsidiarity. And the granting of a wide domestic margin of appreciation is a prime tool to operationalise subsidiarity.

These factors may explain the divergent approaches of the two Council of Europe bodies to similar issues. In what follows, the existence of this divergence will be critically assessed.

2. An Integrated Perspective

Is there a legitimate expectation that different supranational human rights bodies adopt similar approaches to similar problems, leading to similar outcomes? Can

[75] Lorenza Mola, 'The margin of appreciation accorded to states in times of economic crisis. An analysis of the decisions by the European Committee of Social Rights and by the European Court of Human Rights on national austerity measures', *Lex Social* (2015), 189–90.

rights-holders and states parties in the Council of Europe expect that the human rights guidance they receive from the ECtHR is aligned with that of the ECSR, and vice versa? In a holistic view of human rights law, the question of alignment between the ECtHR and the ECSR is very salient. It is submitted that a holistic view is relevant from the perspective of states as well as rights-holders, as 'users' of human rights.[76] Forty-three out of the forty-seven Council of Europe member states (all except Liechtenstein, Monaco, San Marino and Switzerland) adhere to both the European Convention on Human Rights and the European Social Charter.[77] The vast majority of the Council of Europe member states thus are simultaneously bound by both treaties, and individuals and legal persons under their jurisdiction simultaneously enjoy the rights of both treaties. Moreover, it should be clear that many situations that are experienced as injustice can be usefully analysed under both treaties, either because they involve multiple violations of different rights, or because the same situation can be brought both under an ECHR right and under an ESC right. These considerations naturally raise the question of to what extent alignment between the two systems can be expected. My overall approach to that question is to promote what I have termed 'smart integration' based on a global human rights conversation.[78] That is to say, that I consider it desirable for a human rights monitoring body to be aware of its being part of a global network of human rights protection, and for it to reflect upon its specific role as a node within that system, as well as its connections with other nodes. Under this view, an integrated perspective of human rights is quite different from the idea of unifying or uniformising human rights. It is accepted that pluriformity in human rights standards and mechanisms has numerous benefits.[79] But smart integration does consider 'silo mentality' a bad thing for human rights protection overall. This is because issues such as indivisibility[80] and intersectionality[81] are not just theoretical constructs, they correspond to real, lived realities that may not easily fit into any of the many boxes of

[76] Ellen Desmet, 'Analysing users' trajectories in human rights: a conceptual exploration and research agenda'. *Human Rights & International Legal Discourse* (2014) 121–41.

[77] These four states have not ratified the European Social Charter (neither the 1961 version nor the revised 1996 version).

[78] Eva Brems, 'Smart human rights integration', in Eva Brems and Saïla Ouald Chaib (eds.), *Fragmentation and Integration in Human Rights Law: Users' Perspective* (Cheltenham: Edward Elgar Publishers, 2018, 165–193).

[79] Ibid.

[80] The principle of indivisibility is one of the dogmas of international human rights law. It refers to the idea that human rights are one, a package deal, that it is not possible to pick and choose some of them while ignoring others. It also refers to the claim that in real life, a violation of one right is often connected to a violation of or more other rights. The term 'indivisibility' is mobilised in particular to emphasise the connections between civil and political rights on the one hand and economic, social and cultural rights on the other.

[81] The term 'intersectionality', when used in the context of human rights law, refers to the fact that an individual may simultaneously belong to several categories that are singled out for special protection (e.g. in a special treaty: women, children, persons with disabilities), or that are considered particularly vulnerable for human rights violations.

human rights law. The shapes in which injustice manifests itself does not necessarily naturally fit into the predetermined categories of civil and political rights/economic and social rights, or 'women's rights/children's rights/disability rights' and the like. Also, innovations and solutions developed in one of these silos may never reach some of the other silos, without good grounds. For these reasons, a silo mentality can lead to a loss of efficiency, and may create needless obstacles to optimal human rights protection. The proposed global human rights conversation is a matter of mind-set, process and discourse at the level of human rights monitoring bodies. The idea is not so much that one human rights monitoring body ought to act in the same way or come to the same conclusion as another body on the same issue, but rather that it should be informed about what others do/have done, and engage with it. This may include an awareness of the strengths and limits of a monitoring body's institutional expertise.

What does 'smart integration' imply in respect of the ECSR and the ECtHR? First, the fact that both are bodies within the same regional supranational organisation, namely the Council of Europe, constitutes a strong ground on its own for each to show awareness of the other's work. Moreover, regional human rights monitoring bodies generally aim to tailor human rights protection to the needs and context of the region in which they operate. In this case, the relevant regional context is that of the impact of the financial crisis on European economies. That both bodies have had to address similar cases about austerity measures in the crisis context, and that they are talking to the same set of states about how to protect human rights in this crisis context, are additional reasons for the conclusion that both bodies should be seen as being in dialogue with the other.[82] In practice, this occasionally occurs. For example, the ECSR views in the pension cases include a section on the ECtHR case law in the chapter on 'relevant domestic and international law' that makes reference to the *Ásmundsson* criteria (among others). No ECtHR reference is found in the reasoning on the merits though. On the other hand, the ECtHR has not returned the favour in its crisis case law. This stands out in particular in the case of *Koufaki & ADEDY*, which addresses issues quite similar to those under the Greek ECSR cases.[83] The absence of any cross-reference is remarkable because in other contexts, the Court regularly refers to human rights standards and decisions from outside the Convention system, occasionally even in the reasoning on the merits.[84]

Second, there is the issue of the respective specialisations of these two bodies, which could be seen as each other's complement. This is highly relevant in a context

[82] There is informal exchange between the members of the two bodies, which is a good thing. However, when the awareness of each other's work is not visible in the bodies' output, there is little added value for either the rights-holders or the states.

[83] Luis Jimena Quesada, 'Adoption and rejection of austerity measures: current controversies under European law (focus on the role of the European Committee of Social Rights)' *Revista catalana de dret public* 49: 41 (2014).

[84] Dorothea Staes, 'When the European Court of Human Rights refers to external instruments Mapping and justifications', PhD thesis ULB and USL-B (2017).

of financial crisis, when resource constraints threaten the enjoyment of all human rights. Arguably, the enjoyment of economic and social rights is even more dependent on state resources than that of civil and political rights. In principle, the issue of resource constraints is accounted for in the concept of 'progressive realisation' of economic and social rights,[85] whereas this concept does not exist as such for civil and political rights. Yet surprisingly, in the Council of Europe context, it is the economic and social rights body – the ECSR – that has taken a stance against giving states more leeway to restrict rights in times of crisis. The civil and political rights body – the ECtHR – has abandoned this stance when dealing with its cuckoo's egg – the right to property, an economic right. Standing in contrast to its attitude under other Convention articles, under Article 1P1 the Court has given states very broad leeway to address the crisis with rights-restrictive measures, primarily by means of its use of the margin of appreciation. The respective specialisations of the two bodies thus cannot fully explain their divergent approaches. Whereas the ECSR has adopted a principled stance towards the crisis context that is strongly inspired by a civil and political rights logic under which resource constraints cannot excuse rights violations, the ECtHR has not seen fit to stand that ground when addressing an economic right. The Court however has not explained this divergence, nor even shown awareness of the split in its approach. As explained above, the Court strictly upholds some human rights in the face of arguments of resource constraints caused by financial crisis, whereas under the right to property, it accepts the crisis argument as a justification for far-reaching restrictions. In addition to the question about an integrated human rights view across the different Council of Europe bodies, there is thus the question about internal integration within the case law of a single body. Seeming inconsistencies concerning matters of principle within the case law of a single body do not serve legal certainty. They should either be explained or solved.[86]

A third issue of relevance in the relation between the ECtHR and the ECSR is the difference in legal value of their output. Given the binding nature of ECtHR judgments and the non-binding nature of ECSR views, it is arguably more important for the ECSR to refer to the ECtHR than the other way around. Indeed, states parties to the ECSR are at the same time parties to the ECHR and will be obliged to respect the ECHR as interpreted by the ECtHR. ECtHR judgments are a relevant part of

85 While the principle of progressive realisation is not mentioned in the European Social Charter, the ECSR has applied it in practice in its case law.

86 One ECtHR judge has given an explanation for this phenomenon in a lecture, but it is not clear to what extent his position is shared by other judges. According to Judge Sicilianos, the Court is 'both prudent and firm' in the face of the economic crisis. On the one hand 'it invokes the principle of subsidiarity to avoid intervening in large-scale decisions reflecting major political choices in economic matters – choices which ultimately fall within the sovereign power of the State'. On the other, 'the Court is careful to preserve the core Convention rights and refuses to enter into economic considerations when it is necessary to protect non-derogable rights, principles related to the concept and values of the rule of law, or the principle of non-discrimination' (Sicilianos 2015: 5).

the legal environment in which ESCR views will land, hence in order to facilitate optimal reception of ECSR views, it is best to take the ECtHR judgments into account. The same incentives do not exist in the other direction.

It is submitted that both the legitimacy and the efficiency of supranational human rights law would benefit from a coherent narrative, both within a single system (e.g. within the case law of the ECtHR) and across different systems (e.g. between the ECHR and ESC systems). This is even more relevant when it concerns coherence between systems that are created by the same international organisation (as in this case, the Council of Europe). A coherent narrative does not require similar outcomes, though. Different emphases and even opposite approaches to similar issues are not problematic if they are explained in a convincing manner by the monitoring bodies themselves. Yet it is submitted that in the absence of such explanation, opposite approaches to a matter of great importance[87] (such as whether or not states should have more leeway to restrict human rights in the context of a financial crisis) weaken the coherence, strength and ultimately the credibility of the human rights project.

It seems highly unlikely that the ECtHR would not be aware of the inconsistency in its own case law in this respect.[88] It is theoretically possible that the Court was not aware of the 2012 ECSR case law on the Greek crisis when it issued its rulings on the Greek and Portuguese crisis measures in 2013, 2015 and 2016. Whether or not the Strasbourg Court was unaware of what the other Strasbourg-based body had been doing, smart integration suggests it should have been aware. And it would have been proper to either take the same principled stance on supranational human rights scrutiny in times of crisis, or to forthrightly acknowledge that the Court was adopting a different stance, and to explain why it was doing so. The analysis above suggests that a persuasive explanation may be perfectly possible. For example, the 'smart human rights integration' framework can accommodate an explanation that links differences in approach to the different roles that each body plays within the global human rights protection system (cf. above). When it comes to other differences in the two bodies' approaches that are not related to cross-cutting matters of principle, explicit justification is not necessary. Differences are to be expected given the fact that both bodies, even when they examine similar measures, rule on the basis of different rights. Nevertheless, smart integration suggests that it may be useful, even if it not strictly necessary, if supranational human rights monitoring bodies would also recognise relevant case law of other bodies even when the bodies analyse similar governmental measures on the basis of different rights. Both rights-holders and states

87 See also Engström's suggestion that what is at stake is a 'hegemonic struggle' between human rights and global economy frameworks (Engström 2016).

88 E.g. In the 'Dialogue between Judges' in 2013 on 'Implementing the European Convention on Human Rights in times of economic crisis', the analysis of ECtHR Judge Julia Laffranque, starts with noting 'the well-established principle in the Court's case-law to the effect that a lack of resources cannot justify non-compliance with the Convention' (ECtHR 2013: 7).

would benefit for example from clear language as to how a property rights analysis of cuts in social benefits (the ECtHR ruling under Article 1P1) differs from a social rights analysis of such cuts (the ECSR ruling under the ESC).

3. *Supranational Human Rights Guidance in Times of Crisis*

The multi-layered nature of law in twenty-first-century Europe is at the centre of the legal challenges resulting from the financial crisis. Indeed, austerity measures are in some cases not only a matter of domestic law, but also of EU law. The responsibility of the EU remains out of reach of both the ECtHR and the ECSR, as the EU is not a party to either the ECHR or the ESC.[89] Given the transboundary nature of the financial crisis, and the role of international actors in the adoption of some austerity measures, an argument for restraint of supranational human rights monitoring bodies that is based on national sovereignty is far from self-evident. Concretely, the argument for restraint as it is reflected in the ECtHR judgments, is of a more practical nature. The idea that states should have leeway to deal with crisis situations, is largely based on considerations of proximity: national authorities are better informed of all aspects of the domestic economic and social context, and hence better placed to assess the needs and possibilities than a supranational monitoring body. This is a common-sense argument that, however, does not address the need for strong human rights protection in times of crisis. There can be little doubt that the many crises that simultaneously afflict Europe today – the financial crisis, but also the security crisis and the refugee crisis – are also human rights crises. That is to say, that part of what makes the crisis a crisis, consists of human rights violations. In addition, many of the measures that are taken to address each of these crises in turn violate human rights. These are uncontested facts that emphasise the supreme relevance of human rights protection in times of crisis – whether financial or other. Crisis times are indeed – as stated by the ECSR – the times when people need human rights protection most. It is submitted that a human rights protection system that brackets human rights when they are needed most, undermines the legitimacy of human rights.[90] This means that it is problematic for a supranational human rights monitoring body to grant a wide domestic margin of appreciation on account of a crisis context, unless that supranational body has verified that a serious human rights control has taken place at the domestic level. Indeed, it is submitted that a wide margin of appreciation does not indicate that human rights scrutiny as such can be absent or very light. Instead, it indicates a division of labour with regard to

89 The need to hold international institutions/organisations accountable for the human rights impact of austerity measures is voiced by several authors, most notably Margot E. Salomon (2015). For a view on why and how the ECSR could/should involve the EU and IMF, see Wouter Vandenhole (2017).

90 See in that context, the criticism of the ECtHR austerity measures case law by former ECtHR Judge Françoise Tulkens (2014: 4–6).

human rights scrutiny between the supranational and national levels, in which the supranational level exercises only light control. For the national level, this implies a heavier responsibility in terms of domestic human rights scrutiny. As a result, the wide margin of appreciation between the supranational and national levels cannot be copied within the national level – in the sense that the domestic courts would abstain from thorough human rights scrutiny of a measure adopted by the legislative or executive power. It is to be feared that in practice, the ECtHR's margin of appreciation is often misunderstood in this manner. That becomes extremely problematic in times of crisis. It is therefore submitted that a wide domestic margin of appreciation should be conditional upon evidence that a thorough human rights scrutiny of the measures has taken place at the domestic level.[91] The ECtHR should in addition provide some guidance as to the vital components of qualitative human rights scrutiny of austerity measures.[92] Under this position, light substantive supranational human rights scrutiny can be justifiable, if thorough procedural scrutiny has taken place and resulted in a satisfactory outcome. At the same time, more thorough supranational human rights scrutiny remains the preferred option. What is essential, is that the supranational human rights monitoring bodies offer significant guidance to domestic authorities on how to guarantee the protection of human rights in times of financial crisis. In the global human rights protection system, domestic authorities have first line responsibility for human rights scrutiny. Probably the most important task of supranational human rights monitoring bodies is therefore to steer or nudge domestic authorities toward adopting processes and procedures that optimise human rights scrutiny and human rights protection.

91 As shown in the pension rights case law of the ECSR, serious procedural shortcomings are a real risk in the context of austerity measures, given the manifold pressures under which authorities operate. It has been argued that the national legislation at stake in *Koufaki & ADEDY* 'was enacted by the government under the emergency procedure, with almost no parliamentary debate, due to the state's obligation to satisfy its lenders' fiscal claims', and the Greek Supreme Administrative Court in its review 'significantly lowered the threshold of the constitutionality test' and 'incorporated political factors in its decision' (Pervou 2016: 113–38).

92 This type of procedural review, that gives clear guidelines to domestic authorities as to how to conduct their human rights assessment, has been called 'substance-flavoured procedural review'. It can be found in some lines of the ECtHR case law, most notably in defamation cases (Brems 2017: 35).

III

Supranational Governance and Crisis

10

Constitutionalism as Limitation and License

Crisis Governance in the European Union

Turkuler Isiksel[*]

In the Anglo-American tradition, but certainly also beyond, constitutionalism is often associated with safeguarding a broad sphere of individual liberty against encroachment by public power. In his seventeenth-century manifesto against tyranny, John Locke famously depicted the sovereign as a fearsome lion, far more powerful than the petty varmints it was meant to control, and therefore ever-ready to devour them.[1] Liberals have since prized resilient institutional structures that conquer the authoritarian odds. Being constantly on guard against "the encroaching spirit of power,"[2] they rejoice whenever sovereign power is "effectually restrained from passing the limits assigned to it."[3] In this sense, the purest function of a liberal constitution is thought to be bridling the sovereign's prerogatives, firmly delineating the sphere of individual liberty in respect of which the state and its organs "shall make no law."

This limited government paradigm of constitutionalism has been challenged not only by those who highlight constitutionalism's republican pedigree in the Roman and Florentine traditions,[4] but also from a rival *liberal* perspective that highlights constitutionalism's role in building power.[5] Stephen Holmes has argued that many

* Parts of this chapter draw on the material first presented in Turkuler Isiksel, *Europe's Functional Constitution. A Theory of Constitutionalism beyond the State* (Oxford: Oxford University Press, 2016), esp. Ch. 2 and Conclusion. I am thankful to Sam Issacharoff for several discussions that helped me develop the arguments presented here.

1 John Locke, *Second Treatise of Government*, ch.7, para.93.

2 James Madison, "Federalist No. 48" in Alexander Hamilton, James Madison, and John Jay, *The Federalist Papers* (Ian Shapiro ed., New Haven CT: Yale University Press, 2009).

3 Madison, "Federalist No. 48."

4 J. G. A. Pocock, *The Machiavellian Moment. Florentine Political Thought and the Atlantic Republican Tradition* (Princeton NJ: Princeton University Press, 1975); Philip Pettit, *Republicanism: A Theory of Freedom and Government* (Oxford: Oxford University Press, 1999).

5 Douglass C. North, "Institutions and Credible Commitment" (1993) 149 *Journal of Institutional and Theoretical Economics* 11; Douglass C. North and Barry R. Weingast, "Constitutions and Commitment: The Evolution of Institutions Governing Public Choice in Seventeenth-century England" (1989) 49 *Journal of Economic History* 803; Hilton Root, "Tying the King's Hands" (1989) 1 *Rationality and Society* 240; Francis Sejersted, "Democracy and the rule of law: some historical experiences of contradictions in the striving for good government," in J. Elster and R. Slagstad (eds),

of the earliest instances of legal limits on sovereign power can be understood as "enabling devices."[6] For instance, the *leges imperii* of early modern monarchies bound absolutist rulers to respect the right of succession, barred them from appointing their successors, charged them with safeguarding the territorial integrity of the realm, and ruled out arbitrary transfers of territory.[7] When observed, such "laws of rule" helped to ensure the permanence of monarchical power even where they seemingly limited its scope. Although different institutional mechanisms may have the same effect, the fixity of constitutional rules can lend stability to a political system, enable credible commitment, provide a coordination device,[8] and discourage political actors and institutions from tampering with rules for short-term advantage.

In all of these respects, the logic of constitutional rule is not purely Lockean. It is also Hobbesian, even if Hobbes's authoritarian reputation makes this an odd proposition at first blush. Indeed, nobody relishes laying bare the aporias of legally constraining the sovereign quite as much as the Beast of Malmesbury. To take one emblematic passage: "The sovereign of a commonwealth, be it an assembly, or one man, is not subject to the civil laws. For having power to make and repeal laws, he may, when he pleases, free himself from that subjection by repealing those laws that trouble him, and making of new, and consequently he was free before." And the coup de grâce: "he that can bind can release; and therefore, he that is bounded to himself only, is not bound."[9]

Clearly, this view is incompatible with constitutional rule as the establishment of legal constraints on sovereign power. But constraining power is not the constitution's only role. In fact, its eponymous role is *constituting* power.[10] Before you can tame your Leviathan, Hobbes would remind us, you must call it into being. In what we might term their licensing role, constitutions establish judicial, legislative, and executive powers; allocate competences between different levels and units of government; provide for the common defense against domestic and foreign threats, the administration of public order, the encouragement and regulation of economic activity, and the collection of revenue for the public purse. In other words, as the basic law of the

Constitutionalism and Democracy (Cambridge: Cambridge University Press, 1988); Stephen Holmes, *Passions and Constraint* (Chicago, IL: University of Chicago Press, 1995); Samuel Issacharoff, "The enabling role of democratic constitutionalism: fixed rules and some implications for contested presidential elections" (2002) 81 *Texas Law Review* 1985–2012.

6 Holmes, *Passions and Constraint* 7.

7 Holmes, *Passions and Constraint* 106–7.

8 Russell Hardin, "Why a Constitution?" in Bernard Grofman and Donald Wittman (eds), *The Federalist Papers and the New Institutionalism* (New York: Agathon Press, 1989).

9 Thomas Hobbes, *Leviathan* (first published 1651, Richard Tuck ed., Cambridge: Cambridge University Press, 1996), Ch. XXVI, 184.

10 Although I focus on constitutionalism in this essay, scholars of democracy have also noted the importance of state capacity as a necessary (though not sufficient) prerequisite for democratic rule. See Charles Tilly, *Democracy* (Cambridge: Cambridge University Press, 2007), 15–21, 58.

land, the constitution guides the complex system of institutions, offices, and procedures that deliver the public goods for the sake of which civil association exists. Hence, constitutions are as often valued or criticized with reference to their conduciveness to expeditious decision-making, competent administration, and the efficient provision of public goods, as they are on the basis of such principles as individual liberty, collective self-rule, equality, or justice. Like the proverbial fish that asks "what the hell is water?", we may frequently forget to account for the licensing function of the constitution because it is so ubiquitous.

As Ferejohn and Posner observe in their respective contributions to this volume, Locke himself acknowledged that a system of limited government must allow sufficient leeway for public power to address existential threats to that system. But the point I wish to underscore is that even constitutional rules that act as immediate fetters on public power can nonetheless perform the Hobbesian function of empowering the sovereign in the long run.[11] More importantly for our purposes, the limiting and licensing logics of constitutional rule tend to dovetail when it comes to provisions governing private property, monetary policy, public revenue, expenditure or debt. For instance, in their well-known study of the Glorious Revolution, North and Weingast argue that institutional reforms that curbed the monarch's ability to expropriate the wealth of his subjects (including the transfer of power over taxation to a permanent parliament and the reinforcement of the independence of common law courts) served to augment rather than diminish the fiscal capacity of the sovereign.[12] Similarly, Hilton Root's study of eighteenth-century France suggests that monarchs "expanded the privileges and protected the property belonging to ... constituted bodies" such as village communities, guilds, and provincial estates, which were among its major creditors.[13] These indirectly limited the sovereign's ability to repudiate its debts, as a consequence of which the state secured access to bigger loans at lower interest. These early or proto-constitutional mechanisms address the paradox of commitment whereby "the ability to commit often ... expands one's opportunity set, whereas the capacity to exercise discretion ... reduces it."[14] The absence of limits on the sovereign's authority poses an obstacle to the effective exercise of its power. Conversely, once credibly established, such limits can enhance sovereign power in the long term, such as by improving the sovereign's creditworthiness. In other words, if all goes well, the Hobbesian and Lockean logics of constitutional rule can run together.

11 Holmes, *Passions and Constraint*

12 North and Weingast, "Constitutions and Commitment" 816–17.

13 Root, "Tying the king's hands" 251. Also, North, "Institutions and Credible Commitment" 14–15.

14 Kenneth A. Shepsle, "Discretion, Institutions and the Problem of Government Commitment," in Pierre Bordieu and James Coleman (eds), *Social Theory for a Changing Society* (New York: Russell Sage, 1991), 246.

I. THE EU'S SYSTEM OF FUNCTIONAL CONSTITUTIONALISM

While the Lockean project of constraining sovereign power is often successfully realized in the domestic realm, sovereignty as it is exercised in the international realm is subject to few such constraints. In this respect the EU represents a notable exception. In the endlessly chanted incantation of *Van Gend en Loos*, supranational institutions represent "a new legal order of international law for the benefit of which the states have *limited* their sovereign rights, albeit within limited fields, and the subjects of which comprise not only the member states but also their nationals."[15] The EU applies the constitutional idea of "*garantisme*" to relations among states, ensuring that they adhere to a "fundamental law, or a fundamental set of principles, and a correlative institutional arrangement, which would restrict arbitrary power and ensure a 'limited government.'"[16] According to many observers, the EU complements domestic constitutionalism by constraining the arbitrary exercise of power among states, expanding the scope of moral concern beyond the national group,[17] and establishing a deliberative community among its member states.[18] Jürgen Habermas has characterized the EU's success in bringing its member states under a supranational legal system as a "further stage in civilizing state power."[19]

But European integration is not simply, or even primarily, about limiting power. In fact, it should be understood first and foremost as a power-building exercise. Although there has always been heated debate over the factors that explain the course of European integration, competing research programs tend to agree that integration responds to policy challenges that member states cannot, or can no longer, effectively tackle on their own.[20] Member states have delegated power to

15 Case 26/62 *Van Gend en Loos v Nederlandse Administratie der Belastingen* [1963] ECR 1, emphasis added.

16 Giovanni Sartori, "Constitutionalism: A Preliminary Discussion" (1962) 56 *American Political Science Review* 853, 855.

17 E.g. Miguel Poiares Maduro, "Sovereignty in Europe: The European Court of Justice and the Creation of a European Political Community" in Mary L. Volcansek and John F. Stack Jr. (eds), *Courts Crossing Borders: Blurring the Lines of Sovereignty* (Carolina Academic Press, 2005).

18 Christian Joerges and Jurgen Neyer, "From Intergovernmental Bargaining to Deliberative Political Processes: The Constitutionalisation of Comitology" (1997) 3 *European Law Journal* 273, 294.

19 Jürgen Habermas, *The Crisis of the European Union: A Response* (Cambridge: Polity Press, 2012) 45.

20 The empirical literature is conventionally grouped along two major camps, neofunctionalism and intergovernmentalism, with a number of conciliatory approaches in between, most notably that of multilevel governance. Although the common ground between these approaches can often be quite extensive, the most important point of divergence regards the agents that each theory privileges as the motor of integration. While intergovernmentalists explain the success of integration with reference to the preferences of member states, their relative bargaining power, and their willingness to accept limitations on their sovereignty, neofunctionalist theories tend to highlight the cooperative interaction between sub- and supranational agents and norms, including national courts, litigants, interest groups, and supranational actors such as the Commission, Central Bank, and the Court of Justice in extending the initial concessions made by states in directions neither foreseen nor approved by them. Under both accounts, however, the *capacity to govern* increases as a result of integration: either accruing to the states themselves (under the intergovernmentalist account) or strengthening sub- and supranational authorities at the expense of states (under the neofunctionalist account). See especially,

supranational institutions to enhance "legitimacy in functional, political and administrative terms."[21] To be sure, the fact that states would benefit from cooperation says very little about whether they will be able to do so. As Jeremy Bentham quipped, "hunger is not bread."[22] Problems of collective action or social cooperation do not automatically generate their own solutions. In particular, interstate cooperation is conditional on, among other things, resolving the problem of credible commitment. In the absence of coercive enforcement, states are motivated to avoid the steps they must take to satisfy the terms of international cooperation.[23] The European integration process has required member states to take costly actions such as lifting barriers to the cross-border movement of factors of production, and dismantling measures that advantage domestic producers or otherwise burden commercial mobility.

In other words, international cooperation is beset by the same "paradox of omnipotence" that bedeviled absolutist monarchs in the fiscal domain: the lack of constraints on sovereign power can get in the way of exercising that power effectively.[24] The EU responds to this problem – at least in part – by providing a commitment device.[25] The story of Ulysses tying himself to the mast of his ship to avoid future temptation by the sirens, invoked by Jon Elster as an allegory for

Stanley Hoffman, "Obstinate or Obsolete: The Fate of the Nation State and the Case of Western Europe" (1966) 95 *Daedalus* 862; Alan Milward, *European Rescue of the Nation-State* (Abingdon: Routledge, 1992); Geoffrey Garrett and Barry R. Weingast, *Ideas, Interests and Institutions: Constructing the EC's Internal Market* (University of California Center for German and European Studies, 1991); Andrew Moravcsik, "Preferences and Power in the European Community: A Liberal Intergovernmentalist Approach" (1993) 31 *JCMS* 473; Geoffrey Garrett, "The Politics of Legal Integration in the European Union" (1995) 49 *International Organization* 171; Andrew Moravcsik, *The Choice for Europe. Social Purpose and State Power from Messina to Maastricht* (Ithaca, NY: Cornell University Press, 1998). Mainstays of the neofunctionalist camp include Ernest B. Haas, *The Uniting of Europe* (University of Notre Dame Press, 2004 [1968]); Philippe C. Schmitter "Three Neo-Functional Hypotheses about International Integration" (1969) 23 *International Organization* 161; Anne-Marie Burley and Walter Mattli, "Europe Before the Court" (1993) 47 *International Organization* 41; Wayne Sandholtz and Alec Stone Sweet (eds), *European Integration and Supranational Governance* (Oxford: Oxford University Press, 1998); Alec Stone Sweet, Wayne Sandholtz, and Neil Fligstein (eds), *The Institutionalization of Europe* (Oxford: Oxford University Press, 2001); A. Stone Sweet, *The Judicial Construction of Europe* (Oxford: Oxford University Press, 2004). On multilevel governance, see especially: Gary Marks, Liesbet Hooghe, and Kermit Blank, "European Integration from the 1980s: State-Centric v. Multi-level Governance" (1996) 34 *JCMS* 341; Liesbet Hooghe and Gary Marks, *Multi-level Governance and European Integration* (Rowman & Littlefield, 2001).

21 Anand Menon and Stephen Weatherill, "Transnational Legitimacy in a Globalising World: How the European Union Rescues its States" (2008) 31 *West European Politics* 397, 398.

22 Jeremy Bentham, "Anarchical Fallacies; being an examination of the *Declaration of Rights* issued during the French Revolution" [c. 1791].

23 Robert Axelrod, *The Evolution of Cooperation* (New York: Basic Books, 1984), 11. For a classic account of this problem in the international security context, see Robert Jervis, "Cooperation Under the Security Dilemma" (1978) 30 *World Politics* 167.

24 David S. Law, "The Paradox of Omnipotence: Courts, Constitutions, and Commitments" (2003) 40 *Georgia Law Review* 407.

25 Moravcsik, *The Choice for Europe* 73.

constitutional constraint, is also an apposite metaphor for supranational governance.[26] Since the collective "self" of a sovereign state is polycephalous and multigenerational, it faces many more temptations to renege on commitments.[27] Delegating competence over the making, monitoring, and enforcement of policies to an authority beyond their immediate control enables member states not only to make their commitments credible to one another and to third parties, but also to follow through on them in practice.[28] Furthermore, it helps to "insulate policy-making from partisanship and short-term electioneering."[29] In fact, the European Commission and the European Court of Justice habitually invoke this functionalist rationale when their decisions contradict the expressed preferences of the member states.[30]

Elsewhere, I have developed the term "functional constitutionalism" to characterize the European Union's legal system.[31] In using this phrase, I do not mean that the EU is the functional *equivalent* of a constitutional system in the sense of resolving the kinds of problems traditionally addressed by constitutional mechanisms. I claim both more and less than this. On the one hand, the EU is not merely *analogous to* a constitutional regime; it *is* a particular kind of constitutional regime, insofar as it constitutes an autonomous node of authority at the supranational level and is equipped with the institutional trappings of constitutional rule. On the other hand, I wish to systematically highlight three features that distinguish the EU's system of constitutionalism from conventional paradigms tailored to the domestic context. First, the EU's scope of authority is functionally delimited rather than comprehensive. It lacks the pervasive claim of validity associated with a traditional constitutional order, which leaves "no space for proprietors of public power outside the constitution."[32] While typical federal systems also allocate competences between constituent units and the central authority, the federal constitution is usually the

26 Jon Elster, *Ulysses and the Sirens. Studies in Rationality and Irrationality* (Cambridge: Cambridge University Press, 1984). Elster himself later observed the limitations of the self-binding analogy with respect to constitutional constraints, in *Ulysses Unbound: Studies in Rationality, Precommitment, and Constraint* (Cambridge: Cambridge University Press, 2000), 91–5.

27 Jervis, "Cooperation Under the Security Dilemma" 168.

28 Robert Axelrod and Robert O. Keohane, "Achieving Cooperation Under Anarchy: Strategies and Institutions" (1985) 38 *World Politics* 226, 250. The distinction between credible or persuasive and effective commitments draws on Law, "The Paradox of Omnipotence."

29 Christopher J. Bickerton, *European Integration: From Nation-States to Member States* (Oxford: Oxford University Press, 2012), 14.

30 For an analysis of pragmatic appeals to the effectiveness and uniformity of Community law at the Court of Justice, see Mitchel Lasser, *Judicial Deliberations: A Comparative Analysis of Transparency and Legitimacy* (Oxford: Oxford University Press, 2004), ch. 4.

31 See especially, Isiksel, *Europe's Functional Constitution*, ch.2

32 Dieter Grimm, "Treaty or Constitution? The Legal Basis of the European Union after Maastricht" in Erik Oddvar Eriksen, John Erik Fossum, and Augustin Jose Menendez (eds), *Developing a Constitution for Europe* (Abingdon: Routledge, 2004), 72; Frank I. Michelman, "What do Constitutions Do that Statutes Don't (Legally Speaking)?" in Richard W. Bauman and Tzvi Kahana (eds), *The Least Examined Branch: The Role of Legislatures in the Constitutional State* (Cambridge: Cambridge University Press, 2006).

authoritative basis for this allocation. By contrast, the EU's constitutional norms enjoy no such primacy vis-à-vis the constitutional norms of member states. Or, more accurately, such claims to primacy (periodically raised by member states and by the EU's judiciary) are fundamentally contested. Broadly speaking, while "neither [EU] Member States nor its institutions can avoid review of the conformity of their acts with the basic constitutional charter" consisting of the founding treaties,[33] the EU's authority binds member states and their citizens only within a functionally delineated domain (whose contours are undoubtedly fuzzy). Such a constitutional system is distinctive because it eschews any conventional sovereignty claim, acknowledges its place within a composite constitutional context, and concedes the primacy of other legal systems in matters that fall outside of its scope of authority (though not always graciously!).[34] Second, whereas constitutional norms are usually expected to be open-ended,[35] EU law is substantively elaborate in the way of ordinary legislation, but entrenched in the manner of constitutional norms.[36] Third, as I argued above, the EU's authority rests primarily on a claim to govern effectively, meaning that its mode of legitimacy is functionalist rather than democratic or rights-based.[37] Taken together, these features distinguish the EU's constitutional system from the conventional models (most notably the democratic and rights-based ones) that constitutional theory makes available with reference to the domestic context.[38]

To be sure, all political systems rely to some extent on a functionalist claim of justification (though the EU does so disproportionately). As Alfred Stepan points out, the effective governance justification is particularly prominent in "coming-together federations" in which "previously sovereign polities agree to give up part of their sovereignty in order to pool their resources to increase their collective security and to achieve other goals, including economic ones."[39] In his emblematic defense of the proposed US constitution, Alexander Hamilton emphasizes "The utility of the Union to your political prosperity," "the insufficiency of the present confederation to preserve that Union," and "the necessity of a government at least equally energetic

[33] Joined Cases C-402/05 P and C-415/05 P *Yassin Abdullah Kadi and Al Barakaat International Foundation* v. *Council of the European Union and Commission of the European Communities* [2008] ECR I-6351 para. 281.

[34] Seminally, see Neil MacCormick, *Questioning Sovereignty: Law, State, and Nation in the European Commonwealth* (Oxford: Oxford University Press, 1999).

[35] See, for instance, Geoffrey Brennan and James M. Buchanan, *The Reason of Rules. Constitutional Political Economy* (Cambridge: Cambridge University Press, 1985), 20; Dennis C. Mueller, *Constitutional Democracy* (Oxford: Oxford University Press, 1996), 62.

[36] Dieter Grimm, "The Democratic Costs of Constitutionalisation: The European Case" (2015) 21 *European Law Journal* 460.

[37] This quality is often termed "output legitimacy," following Fritz Scharpf's coinage. Fritz W. Scharpf, *Governing in Europe. Effective or Democratic?* (Oxford: Oxford University Press, 1999).

[38] For a more detailed defense of what I identify as the distinctive features of the EU's system of functional constitutionalism, see Isiksel (2016: 72–92).

[39] Alfred Stepan, "Federalism and Democracy: Beyond the US Model" (1999) 10 *Journal of Democracy* 19, 21.

with the one proposed."[40] This parallel was noted by none other than Altiero Spinelli, one of the seminal figures of the European integration process: "when it comes to the supranational unification of certain aspects of political life," Spinelli observed in 1957, "one cannot fail to take into account the American model, because the logic of the American system is the very logic of political power building."[41]

As these examples suggest, functionalist justifications make reference to specific *teloi* to be achieved, such as internal and external security, public order, large markets, or territorial expansion. In the EU's case, the telos is economic union, understood in the broad sense of a single market complemented by a supranational monetary and regulatory apparatus. The 1957 Treaty of Rome aimed to create a shared economic space capable of generating prosperity and, ultimately, peaceful order among European nation-states.[42] Guided by "the principle of an open market economy with free competition, favoring an efficient allocation of resources,"[43] the EU has been tasked with, inter alia, "establishing [and] ensuring the functioning of the internal market," understood as "an area without internal frontiers in which the free movement of goods, persons, services and capital is ensured,"[44] coordinating member states' economic policies,[45] and defining and implementing a monetary policy with the cardinal aim of price stability.[46] Although the EU has amassed a formidable portfolio of policy competences over time, "The enhanced effectiveness generated by the supranational regulation of transnational economic exchange," not to mention the benefits of a competitive, integrated, and expanding market in goods, services, capital, and labor, "represents an important legitimizing function of supranationalism."[47] Member states have delegated extensive powers to the EU in order to reap the efficiency gains of an integrated and competitive market, respond to the pressures of global economic interdependence, project their collective clout abroad, and coordinate labor, consumer, and other regulatory standards. Where this institutional framework lends itself to cooperation in areas such as

40 Alexander Hamilton, "Federalist No. 1" in Alexander Hamilton, James Madison, and John Jay, *The Federalist Papers* (Ian Shapiro ed., New Haven CT: Yale University Press, 2009). On this rationale, see David C. Hendrickson, *Peace Pact: The Lost World of the American Founding* (University of Kansas Press, 2003).

41 Altiero Spinelli, "The American Constitutional Model and Attempts at European Unification" (first published 1957) (2005) 47 *The Federalist* 115, www.thefederalist.eu/site/files/PDF/EN/2000/2005–2-EN.pdf.

42 On the economic focus of EU law, see, among others, Miguel Poiares Maduro, *We the Court: The European Court of Justice and the European Economic Constitution* (Oxford: Hart Publishing, 1998); Christian Joerges and Michelle Everson, "Law, Economics and Politics in the Constitutionalization of Europe" in Erik Oddvar Eriksen, John Erik Fossum, and Augustin Jose Menendez (eds), *Developing a Constitution for Europe* (Abingdon: Routledge, 2004).

43 Art. 120 TFEU.

44 Art. 26(1–2) TFEU.

45 Art. 119(1) TFEU.

46 Art. 127(1) TFEU.

47 Menon and Weatherill, "Transnational Legitimacy in a Globalising World" 402.

security or environmental protection, these issues have been added to the EU's portfolio. However, the EU derives its normative claim to authority "not from any strong popular backing, but primarily from the economic credibility it claims to generate."[48] The term "functional constitutionalism" captures the EU's character as a political system that is justified overwhelmingly with reference to producing shared benefits that states acting alone cannot guarantee, as distinct from one that is guided by ideals such as democratic self-rule, individual liberty, national destiny, and religious salvation.

To be sure, democratic embellishments to its façade have softened the functionalist mainstays of the EU's constitutional structure over time. For instance, the Treaty on European Union proclaims that the Union is "founded on the values of respect for human dignity, freedom, democracy, equality, the rule of law and respect for human rights, including the rights of persons belonging to minorities."[49] However, the EU lacks the institutional structure required to realize these lofty aspirations. To appreciate this point, compare the EU's extensive powers of oversight over member states in the fiscal domain with the weakness of the remedies available to redress grave violations of Article 2 principles.[50] When member states run unacceptable budget deficits and levels of public debt, they are subjected to the rigors of the excessive deficit procedure (EDP), which allows, inter alia, for the Council to prescribe measures for reducing it within a given period.[51] Where a member state fails to follow the Council's recommendations, the Council can take drastic measures, including urging the European Investment Bank to restrict lending to the member state in question, requiring the state to make a deposit with the Union for a period of time, and fining the member state.[52] Since 2004, the EDP has been invoked against all but two EU member states, and has more often than not been faithfully implemented by the states concerned.[53]

In stark contrast, the Council does not exercise a similar supervisory role over violations of liberal and democratic principles by a member state. The most serious institutional mechanism available to the EU for addressing threats to domestic constitutional democracy, namely the Article 7 procedure that allows the Council to suspend the voting rights of a member state in the event of a "serious and persistent breach" of the standards enumerated in Article 2, has never been invoked. In fact, it is

48 Michael A. Wilkinson, "The Specter of Authoritarian Liberalism: Reflections on the Constitutional Crisis of the European Union" (2013) 14 *German Law Journal* 527, 548.

49 Art. 2 TEU.

50 Ulrich Sedelmeier, "Anchoring Democracy from Above? The European Union and Democratic Backsliding in Hungary and Romania after Accession" (2014) 52 (1) *Journal of Common Market Studies* 105–21.

51 Art. 126(6) and (7) TFEU.

52 Art. 126(11) TFEU.

53 An up-to-date tabulation of EDP procedures applied against each member state along with the relevant legal documents is available at http://ec.europa.eu/economy_finance/economic_governance/sgp/corrective_arm/index_en.htm.

widely regarded as unusable.[54] The "pre-Article 7" procedure, which requires a four-fifths majority in the Council to establish a "clear risk" of a serious breach of democratic principles on the part of a member state, has also never been invoked, and not for lack of such risks. Finally, the Council recently rejected a rule of law monitoring mechanism proposed by the Commission, and instead adopted a much looser, intergovernmental dialogue framework.[55]

As the EDP procedure shows, the EU is highly effective in exerting pressure on member states in what both sides consider to be the EU's central areas of competence, namely that of enforcing discipline in the economic and fiscal realm. The EU's lack of comparable clout in safeguarding Article 2 principles underlines that neither side considers these to be among the EU's actionable priorities. In other words, the contrast between strong enforcement in the fiscal domain and weak enforcement of the constitutional principles enumerated in Article 2 exposes what I characterize as the functionalist basis of the EU's authority, which undermines the EU's credibility in exercising any kind of political and constitutional (as opposed to fiscal and technical) oversight over member states. Having configured the EU as a framework of economic prosperity, member states do not expect normative back-talk – let alone disciplinary action – concerning the health of their political systems (even though they are willing to go along when such prescriptions pertain to their economic health). In fact, matters of domestic constitutional integrity are deliberately *excluded* from the EU's scope of competence by Article 4(2) of TEU, which provides that "The Union shall respect the equality of Member States before the Treaties as well as their national identities, inherent in their fundamental structures, political and constitutional, inclusive of regional and local self-government." What the treaty giveth with Article 2, it taketh away with Article 4(2).

II. IT'S ONLY PARCHMENT

I have so far argued that the EU's competence in the fiscal domain illustrates the ways in which constitutionalism can be understood not merely as a device for limiting public power, but also for amplifying it. However, financial crises can strain the accord between the Hobbesian and Lockean logics of constitutional rule. We might understand a crisis as a severe shock that disrupts the exercise of public authority in an essential domain such as finance, public health, national security, or domestic order, and which has reverberations across society as a whole.[56] As Posner

[54] Sedelmeier, "Anchoring Democracy from Above?" 108.

[55] Council of the European Union (2014) General Affairs Council Press Release 16936/14 EN, 16/12/2014, www.consilium.europa.eu/uedocs/cms_data/docs/pressdata/EN/genaff/146348.pdf.

[56] In order to talk coherently about financial crises and liberal constitutions, one needs a crisis theory and a theory of constitutionalism. Although I concentrate on the latter theme, more rigorous study would give equal attention to the concept of crisis. In such a study, a key question to consider would be whether the crisis is endogenous or exogenous to the constitutional framework. For Marxists, who usually get first dibs on crisis theory, any such correlation is spurious: liberal constitutions have no

and Rosen argue in this volume, crises demand the mobilization of such resources as only the sovereign can command, but constitutional rules may put those resources out of reach at critical times. If the Lockean logic prevails, the restraints that ordinarily keep the fearsome lion from preying on lesser varmints may prevent it from mounting an effective response to the challenge at hand. If the Hobbesian logic prevails and the fetters are loosed, the discretionary exercise of power may do greater harm to the basic framework of constitutional rule in the long run than the crisis would.[57]

The financial and sovereign debt crisis that cast its pall on the EU from 2009 onwards illustrates this dilemma. Since its inception, the lopsided design of Europe's Economic and Monetary Union (EMU) has meant that while monetary policy was a supranational matter, fiscal policy rested with member states, who pledged to observe the targets enumerated in the Stability and Growth Pact in lieu of endowing the EU with the fiscal capacity to match.[58] The escalation of the global financial crisis into a sovereign debt crisis in many euro area states was attributed partly to the incomplete architecture of the EMU.[59] To make up for what was lacking from the original constitutional design, member states scrambled to establish new financial assistance and oversight facilities. The Treaty on Stability, Coordination, and Governance (TSCG), together with a series of secondary legislation known as the "six-pack" and the "two-pack," was intended to consolidate fiscal coordination and monitoring and further tighten existing constraints on domestic budgets and macroeconomic policy. Supervisory measures such as the EDP and participation in the European Semester have corralled member states into a tight zone of budgetary discipline, forcing them to pare down public spending, and with

causal force of their own, but merely reflect the capitalist mode of production that sustains them. Crises are endemic to the structural features of capitalism; elements of the superstructure such as constitutional rules have little explanatory power. Institutionalists, on the other hand, would tell a more nuanced story, even if "in the very long run almost everything is endogenous" (Duncan Snidal, "Endogeneous Actors, Heterogeneity, and Institutions," in Robert O. Keohane and Elinor Ostrom (eds.), *Local Commons and Global Interdependence* (Sage, 1995), 55). In the shorter run, a crisis may be the result of an extraneous shock (the Lehman Brothers collapse sending the Eurozone into a tailspin), or it may result from, or get exacerbated by, features of the constitutional order, such as the design flaws of the EMU. Broadly speaking, constitutional systems that codify global economic interdependence by delegating powers to supranational entities, facilitating capital mobility across borders, or curtailing the scope of national regulation may create additional vulnerabilities.

57 This is the logic behind proposals for creating time-limited constitutional procedures for emergency rule. Locke himself believed that "prerogative power" was compatible with limited government. Locke, *Second Treatise*, chap. XIV. Also see Clinton Rossiter, *Constitutional Dictatorship: Crisis Government in the Modern Democracies* (Transaction Publishers, 2002 [1948]); Bruce Ackerman, *Before the Next Attack: Preserving Civil Liberties in an Age of Terrorism* (New Haven, CT: Yale University Press, 2006).

58 Barry Eichengreen, "European Monetary Integration with Benefit of Hindsight" (2012) 50 (1) *Journal of Common Market Studies* 123–36.

59 Fritz W. Scharpf, "No Exit from the Euro-Rescuing Trap?" MPIfG Discussion Paper No. 14/4 (Max-Planck-Institut für Gesellschaftsforschung, 2014), 5; Martin Feldstein, "EMU and International Conflict" (1997) 76 *Foreign Affairs* 60.

it, the social protections they afford their citizens.[60] In an audacious flouting of national constitutional autonomy, the TSCG obligates member states to implement balanced budget rules "through provisions of binding force and permanent character, *preferably constitutional*,"[61] demanding not only tighter fiscal discipline but its constitutional entrenchment.[62] Although each of these measures can be understood as instantiating the principle of limited government in the fiscal domain, the expected payoff in the name of which they are adopted is not greater individual liberty (as it would be in a Lockean scheme) but more effective exercise of public power in the economic realm. (Of course, whether or not they successfully generate that payoff is a different question.)

The fact that some of the pragmatic fixes adopted by member states in response to the euro crisis circumvent the EU's own legislative and constitutional procedures lends further credence to my proposition that the logic of *licensing* power has prevailed over that of *limiting* it. For instance, the TSCG was framed as an international agreement rather than as an EU legislation in part because this was "a less contestable route" by which to mandate the adoption of balanced budget rules in domestic law that "would at the very least run counter to the very discretion which directives are supposed to afford Member States."[63] In another creative move, euro area member states chose to route emergency funds destined for Ireland, Greece, and Portugal through a private corporation created for the purpose, the European Financial Stability Facility (EFSF). This ad hoc remedy has since been subsumed under the European Stability Mechanism (ESM), which has greater capacity to provide financial assistance to states but took the form of a separate international treaty, since "the EU itself was not empowered to establish such a stability mechanism."[64] When called upon to rule on the compatibility of these measures with the EU treaties, including constitutional limits on the powers of EU institutions, the Court of Justice bent the knee before the pragmatic imperatives motivating the crisis response.[65]

60 Dorte Sindbjerg Martinsen and Hans Vollaard, "Implementing Social Europe in Times of Crises: Re-established Boundaries of Welfare?" (2014) 37 *West European Politics* 677; Caroline de la Porte and David Natali, "Altered Europeanisation of Pension Reform in the Context of the Great Recession: Denmark and Italy Compared" (2014) 37 *West European Politics* 732; OECD Directorate for Employment, Labour, and Social Affairs, "Social Expenditure Update" (November 2014), www.oecd.org/els/soc/OECD2014-Social-Expenditure-Update-Nov2014-8pages.pdf.

61 Treaty on Stability, Coordination, and Governance, Art. 3(2).

62 Kenneth Armstrong, "The New Governance of EU Fiscal Discipline" (2013) 38 *European Law Review* 601.

63 Kenneth A. Armstrong, "Differentiated Economic Governance and the Reshaping of Dominium Law," in *The Constitutionalization of European Budgetary Constraints* 70.

64 Paul Craig, "Economic Governance and the Euro Crisis: Constitutional Architecture and Constitutional Implications," in Maurice Adams, Federico Fabbrini, and Pierre Larouche (eds.), *The Constitutionalization of European Budgetary Constraints* (Oxford: Hart Publishing, 2014), 25.

65 Case C-370/12 *Thomas Pringle* v. *the Government of Ireland, Ireland, and the Attorney General* [2012] ECLI:EU:C:2012:756. For an analysis of the predictable outcome of this decision, see Paul Craig, "*Pringle*: Legal Reasoning, Text, Purpose, and Teleology" (2013) 20 *Maastricht Journal of European and Comparative Law* 3.

Meanwhile, new configurations of bureaucrats, government ministers, and international institutions took charge of a slate of decisions that concern domestic revenue and expenditure, emergency funding, and banking regulation, in some instances marginalizing the EU's constitutionally mandated decision-making structure. ECOFIN and the Eurogroup emerged from the crisis with a remarkable degree of autonomy, acting in the manner of an *imperium-in-imperio* within the Council. Under the ominous epithet of "the Troika," the ECB, International Monetary Fund, and the European Commission are in charge of administering memorandums of understanding that codify, down to minute detail, structural reforms that cash-strapped member states must adopt in exchange for much-needed financial assistance. Since these fiscal roadmaps are adopted pursuant to the ESM, which formally exists outside the EU's constitutional framework,[66] they are not subject to all of the procedural constraints and accountability mechanisms afforded by the latter.[67] These new configurations of power tend also to sideline the European Parliament in its hard-won status as co-legislator and undermine its effectiveness as an institutional actor.[68]

As Ferejohn and Posner note in their respective chapters, crises generate two types of systemic danger: first, the immediate danger that the crisis might overwhelm the political system; and second, the indirect danger that the crisis *response* might undermine the liberal constitutional order. The eurozone crisis was no exception, insofar as it forced the EU to choose between the survival of the EMU on the one hand (the immediate risk), and the constitutional principles that the EU and its member states affirm (the indirect risk), on the other. Accordingly, while some critics have challenged the EU's crisis response for failing to meet the first challenge, others have condemned it for "disregard[ing] Europe's commitments to democracy and the rule of law."[69] In Müller's view, the EU's dramatic intervention in member states' social and political systems (such as by forcing Greece to "renegotiate [its] basic social contract") represents not just a quantitative but a "qualitative" break from the EU's limited constitutional role of "constraining democracy" within member states and securing their "liberal-democratic arrangements."[70] Others have gone further, glimpsing the specter of authoritarian thinkers such as Carl

66 Although as Fabbrini notes, disputes arising under the ESM Treaty are subject to the CJEU's jurisdiction. Federico Fabbrini, *Economic Governance in Europe: Comparative Paradoxes and Constitutional Challenges* (Oxford: Oxford University Press, 2016), 7.

67 Craig, "Economic Governance and the Euro Crisis" 26.

68 Sergio Fabbrini, "Executive Power in the European Union: The Implications of the Euro Crisis," Paper presented at the EU Studies Association 14th Biennial Conference, Boston, March 5–7, 2015, 12.

69 Christian Joerges, "Law and Politics in Europe's Crisis: On the History of the Impact of an Unfortunate Configuration" (2014) 21 *Constellations* 249, 255. Also see Edoardo Chiti, Agustín José Menéndez, and Pedro Gustavo Teixeira, "The European Rescue of the European Union" in Edoardo Chiti, Agustín José Menéndez, and Pedro Gustavo Teixeira (eds.), *The European Rescue of the European Union? The Existential Crisis of the European Political Project* (ARENA Report No. 3/12; RECON Report No. 19, 2012) 392.

70 Jan-Werner Müller, "Beyond Militant Democracy?" (2012) *New Left Review* 39, 44.

Schmitt in the EU's crisis response,[71] and describing the outcome as a form of "post-democratic executive federalism,"[72] "authoritarian liberalism,"[73] or "executive emergency constitutionalism" designed to "minimize public debate and to avoid the ordinary filters of the democratic constitutional state."[74] On each of these accounts, the crisis response prioritized functional imperatives at the expense of legal limitations, tipping the balance of economic union away from a Lockean system of constitutional checks in favor of a Hobbesian one of arbitrary power.

Although these observers are right to be critical, I maintain that the EU's crisis response mechanisms do not represent a radical break with its constitutional system as much as they throw into high relief the profound functionalist reflex already built into it. Whereas democratic legitimacy demands that citizens be able to recognize their political institutions as representative of their values and interests, the primary source of legitimation for a functionalist polity is its ability to consistently realize the objectives it has been established to pursue. As I observed at the start of this essay, the legitimacy of *all* constitutional regimes hinges to some extent on their ability to effectively provide certain essential public goods. What distinguishes a system of functional constitutionalism (and marks its key weakness) is its relatively rigid orientation towards a specific goal (such as economic and monetary union). Of course, the pursuit of this goal need not become pathological as long as it does not come into serious conflict with other important values and ends. While democratic and rights-based constitutional regimes possess mechanisms for adjudicating these conflicts and recalibrating existing trade-offs between values and ends, functional constitutionalism behaves as a one-way ratchet.

The EU's response to the euro crisis, which generated a serious conflict between competing constitutional values, illustrates this ratchet effect. The fact that the EU has so far managed to save the euro at the cost of other principles such as the rule of law, democracy, and solidarity between member states simply reflects its configuration as a system of functional constitutionalism. In a stark acknowledgment of this ordering of values, a 2012 report on the Future of Europe, signed by foreign ministers of eleven eurozone countries, held that "Strengthening the Economic and Monetary Union has absolute priority"[75] and called for a dramatically strengthened framework of economic union among member states, including supranational oversight of member states' budgets, banking supervision, and the mutualization of sovereign risk. The declaration also proclaimed that "The Euro has profound

71 For an overview of recent commentary summoning Schmitt's ghost, see Joerges, "Law and Politics in Europe's Crisis" 253–5.

72 Jürgen Habermas, *The Crisis of the European Union: A Response*, trans. Ciaran Cronin (Cambridge: Polity, 2012) 12.

73 Wilkinson, "The Specter of Authoritarian Liberalism."

74 Chiti, Menendez, and Teixeira, "The European Rescue of the European Union" 417.

75 Future of Europe Group comprising the Foreign Ministers of Austria, Belgium, Denmark, France, Italy, Germany, Luxembourg, the Netherlands, Poland, Portugal, and Spain, *Final Report of the Future of Europe Group* (September 17, 2012) 1.

economic advantages and is *the most powerful symbol* of European integration,"[76] confirming not only the pragmatic importance of the single currency but giving it pride of place among the EU's constitutional values.

From its inception, EMU ratcheted up the functionalist logic of the market integration project, not only by ensconcing member states in a system of fiscal discipline, but also by intensifying their interdependence. Up to that point, even persistent failures by member states to observe the rules of the single market would not seriously endanger the stability of the errant member state, much less threaten the viability of the Union as a whole. By contrast, delegating control over monetary policy has made the health and stability of the euro an existential matter for all. In other words, EMU created an extensive community of fate, without, however, establishing the fiscal, social, and political infrastructure necessary for fairly allocating its risks, burdens, and benefits. Under intense strain, singular regard for the survival of economic and monetary union has led the EU and its member states to abandon some of the constitutional means by which they have pursued that aim.

During one of the frantic moments of the crisis, ECB President Mario Draghi encapsulated this contradiction in a single, now famous sentence: "Within our mandate, the ECB is ready to do whatever it takes to preserve the euro." With Machiavellian bravado, he added, "And believe me, it will be enough."[77] Could the ECB stay within its constitutional mandate *and* do whatever was necessary? Or would the adage – *necessitas non habet legem* – prevail? Shortly after Draghi's statement, the ECB unveiled the controversial Outright Monetary Transactions (OMT) program, which would enable it to purchase sovereign bonds issued by eurozone states on the secondary market.[78] The program was meant primarily to reassure lenders. However, critics, among them the German Federal Constitutional Court, have charged that the program exceeds the ECB's mandate by enabling it to act as a de facto lender of last resort.[79] Guided once more by its solicitude for the successful realization of the EU's *telos*, the CJEU affirmed the legality of OMT.[80] However, the CJEU's own status as an institutional guardian of purposive integration serves only to heighten the tension between respect for constitutional constraints on public power and the EU's single-minded fealty to the substantive goals entrusted to it.

76 Future of Europe Group, *Final Report*, emphasis added.

77 Mario Draghi, speech at the Global Investment Conference in London, July 26, 2012, www.ecb.europa.eu/press/key/date/2012/html/sp120726.en.html.

78 Samuel Dahan, Olivier Fuchs, and Marie-Laure Layus, "*Whatever It Takes?* Regarding the *OMT* Ruling of the German Federal Constitutional Court" (2015) 18 *Journal of International Economic Law* 137.

79 Bundesverfassungsgericht Case No. 2 BvR 2728/13 *OMT* Judgment 14 January 2014.

80 Case C-62/14 *Gauweiler and Others v Deutscher Bundestag* ECLI:EU:C:2015:400.

In sum, the euro crisis has exacerbated the tension endemic to functional constitutionalism, bringing purpose into conflict with the finite conditions of legal validity that constitutional rule demands. In Neil MacCormick's astute formulation, "Constitutionalism as a *minimal* virtue involves duly respecting the conditional quality of powers conferred … and involves observing faithfully the (interpreted) conditions of the respective agencies' empowerment."[81] The functional imperative of keeping the euro afloat has been pursued at the cost of circumventing the grant of powers in the EU's constitutional settlement and disregarding their conditional quality. Just as the profligate is wont to exclaim, "money is only paper!", fiscal crises expose the vulnerability of parchment barriers.[82]

Still, these irregularities have to some extent been camouflaged by the pliability of the EU's constitutional settlement. In the end, the dynamism inherent in the project of ever-closer union defies constitutional limitation, indicating that the polity (and not just the legal order that undergirds it) is fundamentally incomplete. One may bemoan the EU's lack of a *finalité politique*[83] or celebrate it as a utopian commitment to perfectibility,[84] but either way the unfinished quality of the European "project" makes for an uneasy setting for constitutional rule. Perhaps the provisional nature of its institutional architecture better equips the EU to absorb the pressure of crises. Attributed to Winston Churchill (though probably apocryphally), "never let a good crisis go to waste" might as well be the EU's credo.

Finally, insofar as the EU's response to the financial crisis pushed European integration further along its particular path, it serves as a reminder that not all crises lead to revolutionary rupture. Circumstances impelled member states to take steps that were politically unfeasible when the EMU was negotiated, including the transformation of the ECB into a de facto lender of last resort, the inauguration of a €700 billion bailout fund to underwrite member state finances, and the establishment of the Single Supervisory and Resolution Mechanisms that effectuate a banking union.[85] One may lament that although the EU acquired a significant new fiscal capacity as a result of the crisis (most notably in the form of the ESM), it used that capacity to double down on a disciplinary mode of economic governance, ensnaring member states in a protracted austerity zone. The ambitious new fiscal facilities could have been used to reinforce threadbare

81 MacCormick, *Questioning Sovereignty* 103.

82 Madison, Federalist No. 48.

83 Joschka Fischer, "From Confederacy to Federation: Thoughts on the Finality of European Integration." Speech delivered at Humboldt University in Berlin, May 12, 2000.

84 Zenon Bańkowski and Emilios Christodoulidis, "The European Union as an Essentially Contested Project" (1998)4(4) *European Law Journal* 341–54.

85 Damian Chalmers, Markus Jachtenfuchs, and Christian Joerges, "The Retransformation of Europe," in Damian Chalmers, Markus Jachtenfuchs, and Christian Joerges (eds.), *The End of the Eurocrats' Dream: Adjusting to European Diversity* (Cambridge: Cambridge University Press, 2016), 3.

social welfare provisions in troubled member states and to compensate those who have lost out as a result of economic competition instead of being dispensed as loans to service public debt obligations. In other words, the impetus towards greater fiscal centralization could have helped to fulfill the original promise the founders of European integration made to citizens, namely "the constant improvement of the living and working conditions of their peoples."[86] Perhaps that will take a bigger crisis – if it doesn't bring down the EU first.

86 Preamble, *Treaty of Rome* [1957]; Preamble, *Treaty on the Functioning of the European Union* [2007].

11

The Institutional Origins of Europe's Constitutional Crises

Grexit, Brexit, and the EU Form of Government

Federico Fabbrini[*]

I. INTRODUCTION

In the last decade, the European Union has faced a plurality of crises. Since 2008, the economic and financial crisis, generally known as the euro-crisis, has challenged the functioning of Europe's Economic and Monetary Union (EMU), to the point of threatening the unity of the single currency. In the last few years, the EU has also faced a dramatic migration crisis, triggered by the mass migration of people from North Africa and the Middle East. Moreover, the EU has encountered internal and external pressures, with national security and foreign affairs calling into question the cohesion of the EU member states, and their common resolve against international threats. Last but not least, in June 2016 the United Kingdom voted to leave the EU, exposing more explicitly than ever the disintegrative forces at play in the EU. While these crises are diverse, they have all revealed the inability of the EU to deal with unforeseen events, highlighting the executive deficit that currently characterizes Europe's system of governance. The purpose of this chapter is to investigate the structural reasons for the EU's institutional weaknesses, and to consider appropriate proposals for constitutional reform that would allow the European integration project to move forward. As such this chapter advances three interconnected claims.[1]

First, this chapter asserts that the EU has failed to successfully address the recent challenges facing it because of its current institutional power-structure, which is deeply unsatisfactory. The architecture of governance in the fields of economic affairs, home affairs, and foreign affairs is premised on a continuing intergovernmental negotiation between member states. Intergovernmentalism has expanded in the EU following the

[*] Full Professor of EU Law, School of Law & Government, Dublin City University and Director of the DCU Brexit Institute.

[1] See further Federico Fabbrini, "Constitutional Crises and Institutional Reform: the European Union at the Cross-Road." *Conn. J. Int'l L.* 32: 285 (2017) from which this chapter draws. Please notice that this chapter is updated as to the state of the law in January 2018. Subsequent legal and political developments are not included.

euro-crisis and migration crisis, as evidenced by the rise of the European Council as the center of decision-making in almost all EU policies, including trade. The European Council is composed of heads of state and governments of the EU member states: national leaders are democratically elected in their home states, and they have a mandate to represent and protect the national interests. But experience has shown that a Union of national democracies is bound to place states against each other, as the electoral mandate each national leader has may conflict with the mandates of other presidents or prime ministers. In this context, as the Greek crisis has made patently clear, tensions between member states are certain to emerge – and ultimately dynamics of domination by larger, more powerful states over smaller, less powerful ones are bound to entrench.

Second, as a result of the problematic nature of the current EU system of governance, this chapter claims that broad institutional reforms are needed to endow the EU with an effective and legitimate form of government. While the concept of legitimacy is complex and multi-faceted,[2] this chapter interprets it as essentially referring to "input legitimacy" – the capacity of citizens to influence decision-makers – and explains that the EU lacks a decision-making authority which can claim to speak in the name of the EU as a whole. In particular, the main weakness of the EU institutional architecture relates to executive power: while each of the EU member states is led by democratically elected executives, the EU itself currently lacks an executive power with the vigor and the electoral mandate to act in the interest of the Union as a whole. But a Union of national democracies is unable to integrate the interests of several state electoral processes running in parallel. Therefore, I posit that the EU should develop into a European democratic Union, featuring an institutional authority which is popularly chosen by the peoples of Europe and directly responsible to them. In this context, I suggest that the creation of a President of the EU, to be elected by the EU citizens in the EU member states, would offer a way to channel popular preferences from across the EU toward the same electoral office and simultaneously create a forum for the contestation of EU policies.

Third, this chapter maintains that the United Kingdom's decision to withdraw from the EU affords an opportunity to change the EU form of government. While the institutional reforms spelled out above are far-reaching, Brexit increases the urge – and at the same time creates the possibility – to structurally improve the form of government of the EU so as to enhance its efficacy and legitimacy. Brexit represents a wake-up call for the EU, as it challenges the integration paradigm that has dominated the process of European unification since March 1957. Signaling the potential unraveling of the EU, the United Kingdom's March 2017 activation of the EU Treaty withdrawal clause should be used as an opportunity to engage in a

[2] See Joseph H.H. Weiler, "The Political and Legal Culture of European Integration." *Int'l J. Const. L* 9: 678 (2011) (distinguishing the notions of input legitimacy and output legitimacy, and suggesting that the EU has traditionally relied also on the idea of messianic legitimacy – namely the idea of pursuing ever-closer integration among the member states as a way to preserve peace).

thorough soul-searching within the EU, and to prepare those constitutional changes that will be necessary to adapt Europe to a Union of twenty-seven member states. Treaty amendments necessitated by Brexit should address the legitimacy gap exposed by Europe's crises through appropriate institutional reforms. Dynamics of disintegration inevitably arise in a Union that is incapable of properly governing itself. For this reason, no chance should be wasted to redefine the nature of the cooperation between EU member states and their citizens through a constitutional pact that better compounds their interests.

The chapter is structured as follows. Section II discusses the problems of intergovernmentalism, underlining how a system of executive decision-making premised on the continuing negotiations between heads of state and government of the EU member states is unable to deliver effective decisions, and is poised to produce outcomes that are perceived as illegitimate by some of the players. Section III provides evidence of this by discussing the Greek drama that unfolded in the context of the euro-crisis, in particular the events in the summer of 2015 that led to a potential Grexit (Greece expulsion from the eurozone). Section IV then advances a proposal for overhauling executive authority in the EU through the establishment of a new office – the President of the EU. Here, I explain how this office could be elected, and how it would function within a reformed system of separation of powers in the EU. Fully aware that creating such a new institution would represent a relevant break with the current regime, section V then discusses the possibility, if any, of reforming the EU constitutional system along these lines, and suggests that Brexit represents an opportunity to achieve this result. With the United Kingdom leaving the EU, the remaining EU member states will need to revise the EU treaties to adapt to the reality of a Union of twenty-seven nations. Section VI concludes by suggesting that the EU institutional architecture can be fixed through reflection and choice.[3]

II. THE PROBLEM OF INTERGOVERNMENTALISM

Recent crises – notably the euro-crisis and the migration crisis – have brought about and accelerated a major shift in the form of governance of the EU: the rise of intergovernmentalism.[4] Traditionally, EU scholarship distinguishes between supranational and intergovernmental authorities, defining as intergovernmental those institutions that represent states and reflect national interests, and as supranational those bodies which are instead designed to promote the common EU interest.[5] Admittedly, the distinction is questionable, since it reflects a sui generis approach to

[3] See *The Federalist* No. 1 (Alexander Hamilton).

[4] See also Federico Fabbrini et al. (eds.), *What Form of Government for the European Union and the Eurozone?* (2015).

[5] See generally Ben Rosamond, *Theories of European Integration* (2000).

EU institutions,[6] and has only limited heuristic value.[7] Yet, it is a point acknowledged by most observers that during the last decade, intergovernmental institutions like the European Council – which groups heads of state and government of the EU member states together with the President of the European Commission, under the leadership of a semi-permanent European Council president[8] – have come to acquire a leading function in the EU decision-making structure, often at the expense of other EU institutions, like the European Commission.[9] According to Uwe Puetter, the centrality of the European Council in EU governance generally, and in EMU specifically, is not a haphazard development.[10] Rather, it is the result of a deliberate institutional choice made at the time of the Maastricht Treaty of 1992. When the EU member states decided to transfer to the EU level a number of competences, including in the field of economic policy and migration, they resisted delegating powers to the European Commission and other supranational bodies, and instead created an intergovernmental framework in which they could remain in control of decision-making.[11]

Be that as it may, since the beginning of the euro-crisis the European Council has become "ever mightier."[12] Meeting with great frequency,[13] the European Council has emerged as the institution regularly involved in deciding the agenda of the EU and its member states across the board.[14] In the field of economic governance in particular, the European Council has turned into the leading EU institution, and "economic governance occupies 50–65 % of the total time the heads [of states and governments] spend debating within the European Council."[15] The role of the European Council has emerged as crucial also in other areas of EU law – from

6 See Robert Schutze, *From Dual to Cooperative Federalism* (2009) (criticizing sui generis approaches to the studies of the EU and claiming that the EU should be examined in comparative perspective with other federal systems of government).

7 See e.g. Hussein Kassim et al., *The European Commission of the Twenty First Century* (2013) (emphasizing supranational nature of the European Commission) but see also European Council decision concerning the number of members of the European Commission, EUCO 176/12 (Oct 2, 2012) (maintaining the rule that each member states shall have the right to appoint a European commissioner – hence increasing the intergovernmental nature of the European Commission).

8 See Consolidated Version of the Treaty on European Union Art. 15, 2012 O.J. (C 326) 23 (hereinafter TEU).

9 See Christopher Bickerton et al. (eds.), *The New Intergovernmentalism: States and Supranational Actors in the Post-Maastricht Era* (2015).

10 See Uwe Puetter, *The European Council and the Council: New Intergovernmentalism and Institutional Change* 68 (2014).

11 Ibid. at 17.

12 Editorial Comments, "An Ever Mighty European Council – Some Recent Institutional Developments." *Common Mkt. L. Rev.* 46: 1383 (2009).

13 See Dieter Smeets & Marco Zimmerman, "Did the EU Summits Succeed in Convincing the Markets during the Recent Crisis?" *J. Common Mkt. Stud.* 51: 1158, 1160 (2013).

14 See Frederic Eggermont, *The Changing Role of the European Council in the Institutional Framework of the European Union* (2012).

15 Uwe Puetter, "The European Council – the New Center of EU Politics." Swedish Institute for European Policy Studies, European Policy Analysis 16/2016.

migration[16] to foreign affairs,[17] from internal security[18] to trade.[19] In fact, the European Council has increasingly sidelined and overtaken other EU institutions, including the European Commission and the Council. Hence, while the EU treaties grant to the European Commission exclusive authority to conduct EU commercial policy,[20] the European Council has acquired a crucial role in endorsing and shaping EU international trade agreements.[21] And while the EU treaties grant legislative power to the Council[22] (as opposed to the European Council, which should instead exercise executive powers[23]), it has come to be the rule for the Council to shift high-level legislative files to the European Council for consideration and negotiation.[24] Since the European Council is composed mostly of national

16 See EU-Turkey Statement (Mar. 7, 2016), www.consilium.europa.eu/en/press/press-releases/2016/03/07-eu-turkey-meeting-statement/ (setting out a deal with Turkey to stem migration flows across the East Mediterranean Sea); European Council Conclusions EUCO 12/16 (March 18, 2016), http://data.consilium.europa.eu/doc/document/ST-12–2016-INIT/en/pdf (outlining implementation of the EU–Turkey deal); Malta Declaration by the Members of the European Council on the External Aspects of Migration PRESS 43/17 (Feb. 3, 2017), www.consilium.europa.eu/press-releases-pdf/2017/2/47244654402_en.pdf (addressing the problems posed by migration through the central Mediterranean route and developing a strategy to address that).

17 See generally Statement by the Heads of State and Government on Ukraine (Mar. 6, 2014), www.consilium.europa.eu/en/press/press-releases/2014/03/pdf/Statement-of-the-Heads-of-State-or-Government-on-Ukraine,-Brussels,-6-March-2014/ (calling for a ceasefire in Ukraine); European Council Conclusions EUCO 7/1/14 (Mar. 21, 2014), www.consilium.europa.eu/uedocs/cms_Data/docs/pressdata/en/ec/141749.pdf; European Council Conclusions EUCO 147/14 (July 16, 2014), http://data.consilium.europa.eu/doc/document/ST-147–2014-INIT/en/pdf; European Council Conclusions EUCO 237/14 (Dec. 18, 2014), www.consilium.europa.eu/uedocs/cms_data/docs/pressdata/en/ec/146411.pdf; European Council Conclusions EUCO 11/15 (March 20, 2015), www.eesc.europa.eu/resources/docs/european-council-conclusions-19–20-march-2015-en.pdf.

18 See Statement by the Members of the European Council (Feb. 12, 2015), www.consilium.europa.eu/en/press/press-releases/2015/02/150212-european-council-statement-fight-against-terrorism/ (reacting to terrorist attacks in Paris and outlining a list of policy measures to be adopted of the EU Passenger Name Record Directive).

19 See European Council Conclusions EUCO 31/16 (Oct. 21, 2016), www.consilium.europa.eu/en/meetings/european-council/2016/10/21-euco-conclusions_pdf (reaffirming the importance of concluding the Comprehensive Economic Trade Agreement between the EU and Canada following the vote by the Belgian devolved legislature of Wallonia in September 2016 to veto the agreement, and calling to a solution to the outstanding issues); European Council Conclusions, annex I EUCO 34/16 (Dec. 15, 2016), https://eeas.europa.eu/sites/eeas/files/euco-conclusions-final_0.pdf (reporting a decision of the heads of state and government of the 28 member states on the Association agreement between the EU and Ukraine to allay concerns that emerged in the Netherlands where a consultative referendum had rejected the terms of the agreement in March 2016, and to pave the way toward a provisional entry into force of the agreement).

20 See Consolidated Version of the Treaty on the Functioning of the European Union Art. 207, 2012 O.J. (C 326) 140 (hereinafter TFEU).

21 See Charles de Marcilly, "La politique commerciale de l'UE au risqué des defies internes," Fondation Robert Schuman Policy Paper 407, October 17, 2016.

22 TEU, above n. 8, Art. 16.

23 TEU, above n. 8, Art. 15.

24 See Federico Fabbrini, "The Relation between the European Council and the Council." *Eur. Pub. L.* 22: 489 (2016).

leaders, this institution claims to be the authority endowed with the greater legitimacy to act – if need be, by displacing the other EU institutions.[25]

The rise of the European Council as the power-house of the EU institutional structure has been noticed by many – and criticized by most. According to Jürgen Habermas, the EU decision-making regime, centered on the EU heads of state and government in the European Council, represents a system of "post-democratic executive federalism."[26] As Sergio Fabbrini underlined, decision-making within the European Council has delivered too little too late, since heads of state and government faced challenges in reaching agreement on the measures to be taken, and then met selective non-compliance by some member states in the implementation of the agreed measures.[27] Moreover, as Deirdre Curtin has pointed out, the strengthening of the European Council has created problems of transparency and accountability, since this body operates behind closed doors and with limited oversight by other institutions.[28] Hauke Brunkhorst has defined the exercise of power by the European Council as "collective Bonapartism," and accused this body of trumping European democracy.[29] In fact, the European Council is a democratic institution, since each of its members is elected (either directly by the people, or indirectly by parliament) in every EU member state.[30] Yet, from an EU constitutional law perspective, the European Council has proved highly problematic as the institution governing the EU, for two main reasons.

First, the European Council has deepened pre-existing cleavages between member states, fueling the resurgence of a clash between conflicting national interests. Yet this was, and is, an inevitable consequence of the structural composition of the European Council and the electoral incentives underpinning it. Although a number of scholars had sought to mythologize the European Council as a bucolic institution in which member states can reconcile their interests and find consensus through deliberation,[31] the reality is that the European Council is made up of national leaders whose job it is to represent and promote the national interest.[32] But because EU member states often have conflicting national interests – from economic policy to trade, and from security

[25] See notably Nicolas Sarkozy, President of France, Speech, Toulon, (Dec. 1, 2011) (stating that "La crise a poussé les Chefs d'Etats et du gouvernments à assumer des responsabilités croissantes parce qu'au fond eux seuls disposaient de la légitimité démocratique qui leu permettai de décider.").

[26] Jürgen Habermas, *The Crisis of the European Union* 12 (2012).

[27] See Sergio Fabbrini, "Intergovernmentalism and Its Limits: Assessing the European Union's Answer to the Euro Crisis." *Comp. Pol. Stud.* 46: 1003, 1022 (2013).

[28] See Deirdre Curtin, "Challenging Executive Dominance in European Democracy." *Mod. L. Rev.* 77: 1, 18 (2014).

[29] See Hauke Brunkhorst, "Collective Bonapartism – Democracy in the European Crisis." *Ger. L.J.* 15: 1177, 1179 (2014).

[30] TEU, above n. 8, Art. 15.

[31] See Luuk van Middelaar, *The Passage to Europe: How a Continent Became a Union* (Liz Waters trans., 2013).

[32] See Petya Alexandrova & Arco Timmermans, "National Interest Versus the Common Good: The Presidency in European Council Agenda Setting." *Eur. J. of Pol. Res.* 52: 316 (2012).

policy to foreign affairs – it is not surprising that disagreement has emerged in the functioning of the European Council. With each head of state and governments going to the European Council with the aim of winning the best deal for *its* home country, clashes between national leaders representing conflicting national interests have become a regular feature of European Council life, with negative repercussions in the European public debate.[33]

Second, in an institution that structurally favors a clash between conflicting national interests, it has become inevitable that the leaders representing the larger and more powerful member states have gained the upper hand. Although formally speaking all heads of state and government sitting at the European Council table are equal, in reality state power matters – and some member states are more powerful than others.[34] As Jonas Tallberg has explained, bargaining within intergovernmental institutions is the result of several sources of power, and "differences between large and small Member States" shape inter-state relations within the European Council.[35] States' economic and political sources of power play the most fundamental role in explaining negotiation in the European Council, with the result that larger member states can dominate the decision-making process.[36] In this context, it is not surprising that Germany has emerged as the hegemonic player in defining the agenda of the EU,[37] from economic policy[38] to migration.[39] As I have argued elsewhere, the euro-crisis has produced a dynamic of domination.[40] Yet, this has raised a major challenge to the anti-hegemonic nature of the EU project.[41] It is in fact evident that a system of governance that structurally disfavors the interests of

33 See Ingolf Pernice et al., *A Democratic Solution to the Crisis: Reform Steps towards a Democratically Based Economic and Financial Constitution for Europe* 83 (2012).

34 See Mark Dawson & Floris de Witte, "Constitutional Balance in the EU after the Euro-Crisis." *Mod. L. Rev.* 76: 817 (2013).

35 Jonas Tallberg, "Bargaining Power in the European Council." *J. Common Mkt. Stud.* 46: 685, 687 (2008).

36 In another, specular intergovernmental context, that of the Eurogroup – which brings together the finance ministers of the eurozone member states, under the chairmanship of a semi-permanent presidency – the former President of the Eurogroup, Jean-Claude Juncker, famously decided to step down from the job, complaining that it was impossible for him to make decision because of the way Germany and France were running the show. See Brian Parkin, "Juncker Says Ceding Euro Job Due to Franco-German Interference." *Bloomberg News*, April 30, 2012 (reporting Mr Juncker as stating that Germany and France acted in the Eurogroup "as if they are the only members of the group").

37 See William Paterson, "The Reluctant Hegemon? Germany Moves Center Stage in the European Union." *J. Common Mkt. Stud.* 49: 57 (2011).

38 See Georgios Maris & Pantelis Sklias, "Intergovernmentalism and the New Framework of EMU Governance." In Federico Fabbrini et al. (eds), *What Form of Government for the European Union and the Eurozone?* 57 (2015).

39 See Filippo Scuto, "Le difficoltà dell'Europa di fronte alla sfida dell'immigrazione: superare il 'sistema Dublino'." Centro Studi sul Federalismo Research Paper 2017.

40 See Federico Fabbrini, "States' Equality v States' Power: The Euro-crisis, Inter-state Relations and the Paradox of Domination." *Cambridge Y.B. Eur. Legal Stud.* 17: 1 (2015).

41 See Simone Bunse and Kalypso Nicolaïdis, "Large versus Small States: Anti-Hegemony and the Politics of Shared Leadership", in Erik Jones et al. (eds), *The Oxford Handbook of the European Union* 249 (2012) (explaining that the European project was established as an anti-hegemonic enterprise, in

smaller/weaker member units vis-à-vis larger/mightier sister states deeply undermines the fabric of the EU and its promise of continental pacification.[42]

In conclusion, the consolidation of intergovernmentalism as the leading mode of European governance has increased conflict and decreased legitimacy in the EU. The structural incentive for each member of the European Council is to focus on the interests of the state where he/she is elected – not the interest of the EU as a whole. Due to its composition, the European Council has fueled interstate conflicts, rather than taming them. And while conflict is part of politics,[43] domination by larger/mightier states has become the mechanism for solving interstate disagreement. This institutional state of affairs has undermined the legitimacy of the measures decided by the European Council. Citizens of smaller or weaker countries do not have a way to influence the position of elected leaders of other member states, because they cannot vote in the national elections of other EU countries. This naturally raises the legitimacy question as to why they should accept decisions taken by the European Council that they perceive as simply reflecting the diktat of the larger/stronger nations. In this context, opposition to the EU – which has increased in every election in Europe since 2009[44] – has become a proxy for opposition to a system that is unresponsive to the interests of all citizens affected by decision-making. In fact, when voice is limited, exit becomes an attractive option.[45] The current form of government of the EU has therefore called into question the EU itself.

III. GREXIT?

If there were any remaining doubt as to the unsustainability of the existing architecture of European governance, this was dispelled by the events occurring in the eurozone, and specifically in Greece, after 2015.[46] After a new anti-austerity government was elected in Greece in January 2015, there were more than five months of tough talks within the framework of the EU intergovernmental institutions between Greece and its European and international creditors to renegotiate the conditions attached to the Greek program of financial assistance.[47] Based on a clear electoral

marked contrast with the previous history of Europe which had been constantly characterized by the attempts of larger states to impose their dominion over smaller neighboring countries).

42 See also Andrew Glencross & Alex Trechsel (eds.), *EU Federalism and Constitutionalism: the Legacy of Altiero Spinelli* (2010) (emphasizing the influence of Spinelli's idea of a united and free Europe in the creation of the EU).

43 See Damian Chalmers, "The European Redistributive State and a European Law of Struggle." *Eur. L.J.* 18: 667, 686–92 (2012).

44 See also Donatella Viola (ed.), *The Routledge Handbook of European Elections* (2016).

45 See Albert O. Hirschman, *Exit, Voice, Loyalty: Responses to Decline in Firms, Organizations and States* (1970).

46 See also Federico Fabbrini, *Economic Governance in Europe* (2016).

47 See Derek Scally & Suzanne Lynch, "Greek and German Ministers Can't Even 'Agree to Disagree'," *The Irish Times*, Feb. 5, 2015 (reporting tense meeting between German Finance Minister Wolfgang Schäuble and Greek Finance Minister Yanis Varoufakis).

mandate from the people, the new Greek government sought to renegotiate the policy measures agreed upon by the previous Greek governments in the two memoranda of understanding,[48] which were blamed for a dramatic humanitarian crisis with 25 percent unemployment and a 25 percent fall in GDP since the start of the crisis. Moreover, the new government also demanded measures that would relieve Greece from its skyrocketing domestic public debt.[49] However, the requests were dismissed by most other EU member states and supranational institutions as a breach of previously agreed commitments.[50] Unable to come to a compromise solution, and with its financial conditions quickly deteriorating due to the expiration of the second bailout, Greece failed to repay on-time a tranche of the loans received by the International Monetary Fund (IMF) on June 30, 2015, technically making a selective default on its debt.[51]

Moreover, in a maverick attempt to alter the course of the intergovernmental negotiations, the Greek government called for a national referendum that asked the electorate to reject or approve the conditions for a new, third program of European financial assistance that had been proposed by the European Commission to replace the expired second program[52] and was still only in draft form. Remarkably, the Greek government actively campaigned for the 'no' vote. On July 5, 2015, the Greek people by a wide margin rejected the proposed bailout,[53] opening de facto the prospect for a Greek exit from the eurozone. Contrary to the expectations of the Greek government, the referendum did not strengthen the position of the Greek government vis-à-vis its eurozone partners. With Greek banks closed for weeks, and capital controls introduced to prevent the melt-down of the financial systems,[54] the Greek government had no other option. After a cabinet shake-up, it advanced on July 8, 2015, a request for new financial assistance to the European Stability Mechanism (ESM),

48 See Economic Adjustment Programme for Greece, May 2, 2010; Memorandum of Understanding on Specific Economic Policy Conditionality, Aug. 6, 2010 www.imf.org/external/np/loi/2010/grc/080610.pdf; Second Economic Adjustment Program for Greece, March 1, 2012; Memorandum of Understanding between the European Commission and the Hellenic Republic, March 1, 2012 http://ec.europa.eu/economy_finance/eu_borrower/mou/2012-03-01-greece-mou_en.pdf.

49 See Lina Papadopoulou, "Can Constitutional Rules, Even if 'Golden', Tame Greek Public Debt?" In Federico Fabbrini et al. (eds), *The Constitutionalization of European Budgetary Constraints* 223 (2014).

50 A most explicit statement of this position was offered by Vice-President of the European Commission, Jyrki Katainen, statement, Brussels, Jan. 28, 2015, proclaiming that "we don't change our policy according to elections." See Liz Alderman, "Tsipras's Debt Plan Sends Athens Stock Mark Sliding," N.Y. *Times*, Jan. 28, 2015.

51 See IMF, Statement Press release 15/310, June 30, 2015, (reporting failure by Greece to repay loan).

52 See above n. 48.

53 Ευρωεκλογές [Euroelections], http://ekloges.ypes.gr/current/e/public/index.html#{%22cls%22:%22main%22,%22params%22:{}}.

54 Nomos (2015:4350) Official Gazette [ΦΕΚ] 2015, A:65 (Greece) (Act of legislative content introducing capital controls and a mandatory bank holidays).

indicating its willingness to accept the previous creditors' requests for tough measures of economic adjustment.[55]

With trust between the member states at an all-time low, the Greek government's policy-turn was met with half-hearted feelings. Despite meeting in almost permanent session between July 7 and 11, 2015, the Eurogroup of finance ministers could not muster a compromise between its members, some of which openly called to force Greece out of the eurozone.[56] With time running out quickly and the financial markets showing increasing unease, heads of state and government of the eurozone countries met on July 7, 2015, and again on July 11, 2015, for emergency meetings in the Euro Summit. After seventeen hours of negotiation, on July 12, 2015, the President of the Euro Summit announced an agreement[57] that secured Greece's position within the eurozone on the condition that the Greek government propose, and the national parliament approve in record time, sweeping legislation on a wide set of policies (including pension reform, tax reform, labor market reform, the drafting of a new code of civil procedure, and the launching of a new program of privatization).[58] But by explicitly rejecting the Greek request to consider debt relief, the Euro Summit left unanswered the question whether Greece would be able to follow-up effectively on these austerity measures and restore its economic condition.

In fact, the IMF refused to join the new program of financial assistance to Greece because it believed that without a debt haircut, Greece would not be able to return to finance itself on the financial markets.[59] Alas, the practical implementation of the new third bailout agreement mostly failed to achieve the expected results, due to the actions of both international creditors and the Greek government.[60] International creditors dug their heels in and required that Greece continue to carry forward austerity measures, including the running of ambitious budget surpluses, as a condition for receiving several tranches of financial assistance.[61] And Greece mostly dragged its feet in the execution of the agreed-upon plan, unilaterally deciding among other things in December 2016 to redistribute the yearly budget surplus as a 13th monthly salary to overtaxed public

[55] See Letter from the Greek Minister of Finance to the Managing Director of the ESM (July 8, 2015).

[56] See Leaked Document from the German Ministry of Finance to Other Eurozone Countries and Institutions, Comments on the latest Greek proposal (July 10, 2015) (proposing that Greece should be offered a five-year time-out from the eurozone).

[57] Remarks by President Donald Tusk after the Euro Summit of 12 July 2015 on Greece, PRESS 579/15 (July 13, 2015).

[58] Euro Summit Statement SN 4070/15, (July 12, 2015).

[59] See Heather Stuart, "IMF Will Refuse to Join Greece Bailout Until Debt Relief Demands are Met." *The Guardian*, July 30, 2015.

[60] See Memorandum of Understanding between the European Commission and the Hellenic Republic and the Bank of Greece, Aug. 19, 2015 https://ec.europa.eu/info/files/memorandum-understanding-greece-august-2015_en.

[61] See also Joschka Fischer, "The Return of the Ugly German." *Project Syndacate*, July 23, 2015, (criticizing creditors' obsession for the imposition of austerity in Greece).

employees and pensioners.[62] As a result the possibility of Greece repaying its loans was once more under question at the beginning of 2017. With electoral pressures in a number of northern EU member states pushing against any relief for Greece, the Eurogroup failed in February 2017 to reach agreement on the payment of a next installment of financial aid,[63] and the IMF warned that Greece might again be effectively on the brink of exiting the eurozone.[64]

Although the Greek drama lends itself to different readings, and none of the actors appear blameless, one feature of the story looks increasingly undeniable: the unsustainability of the current institutional architecture of the EMU. As the ten meetings of Eurogroup ministers in the month between June 18 and July 18, 2015, make clear, a Union that is dependent on the continuing negotiation between its member states is a house divided, bound to implode. In fact, notwithstanding the attempt by the Greek government to inject national democratic input into a highly diplomatic and technocratic process, through the calling of a popular referendum (a step which had already been considered, but aborted in October 2011), the exercise of electoral democracy in one eurozone member state clashed with the reality of democratic processes being in place also in each and every one of the other eurozone countries. But as the Greek drama made clear, these national democratic processes can be irreconcilable, pushing in opposite directions. The current system of EU governance has created a constant collision of the respective electoral mandates of the member states, ensuring the continuing instability – if not outright failure – of the European integration project, in EMU and beyond.[65]

IV. THE PROMISE OF PRESIDENTIALISM

As the previous sections have pointed out, intergovernmentalism has produced more problems than it has solved in the EU system of governance – and the Greek crisis testifies to that. With decision-making in Europe centered in an institution such as the European Council that is largely unresponsive to the interests of all EU citizens, the pull toward disintegration in the EU started to grow stronger. In my view, this is a threatening development, as the achievements of sixty years of European integration ought to be safeguarded. Moreover, it is a development that can be reversed. The dissatisfaction of European citizens and states should not be interpreted as an opposition to European integration as such. Rather, discontent vis-à-vis the EU should be

62 See "Greece Pensioners Receive Controversial Bonus Payment." *Euronews* Dec. 22, 2016.

63 See Statement by Eurogroup President Jeroen Dijsselbloem after the Eurogroup meeting (Feb. 20, 2017).

64 See IMF, Greece 2016 Article IV Consultation, at 14, 48, IMF Country Report No. 17/40 (Feb. 7, 2017), www.imf.org/en/Publications/CR/Issues/2017/02/07/Greece-2017-Article-IV-Consultation-Press-Release-Staff-Report-and-Statement-by-the-44630.

65 See also Miguel Poiares Maduro, "A New Governance for the European Union and the Euro: Democracy & Justice," report commissioned by the European Parliament Constitutional Affairs Committee, September 2012, PE 462.484.

seen as the product of an unsatisfactory settlement in the EU constitutional architecture.[66] Intergovernmentalism is a source of the growing popular discontent against the EU. Hence, reforming the European architecture of governance in a way that addresses its structural flaws is not a passing fancy: it is a necessity to ensure the survival of the EU.[67] In other words, the EU needs institutional reforms to enhance its form of government if it wants to weather the challenges it is currently facing.

Based on the analysis of the weaknesses of the EU system of governance, I submit that the EU needs an executive institution that can speak in the name of the Union, channeling citizens' preferences from across the EU member states, and offering a venue in which all of them can feel they have a stake. At a time of increasing disunity in the EU, this chapter makes the case for an institution that can promote unity – an integrative force taming disintegrative pressures. Specifically, my suggestion is to establish a new authority: the President of the EU. The President of the EU should be vested with the executive power of the EU, should be elected by the citizens of the EU member states through a process that combines majoritarian with federalism concerns, and should be checked and balanced by the EU legislature – along a logic of separation of powers.[68] An EU president would fare comparatively better than the European Council as the locus of executive authority in the EU for two main reasons.[69] First, a monocratic office would enjoy greater vigor than a collective body, and accordingly would be able to act more effectively. Second, a single officeholder chosen by the citizens of the EU member states through a collective electoral exercise would enjoy greater legitimacy – and could plausibly claim to represent the interests of all EU member states and citizens, rather than just a fraction thereof.

The proposal to reform the EU institutional system through the creation of a new elected office of President of the EU joins an expanding debate about the need for greater executive capacity in the EU.[70] In the context of the euro-crisis, in particular, a number of top EU policy-makers have made calls in this direction. In its June 2012 inaugural report "Towards a Genuine EMU," the President of the European Council, jointly with the Presidents of the European Commission, Eurogroup, and European Central Bank (ECB), acknowledged the need to "strengthen … democratic legitimacy and accountability" in the EMU,[71] and in its December

66 See also Jürgen Habermas, "Democracy in Europe: Why the Development of the EU into a Transnational Democracy Is Necessary and How Is It Possible." *Eur. L.J.* 21: 546 (2015).

67 See Joseph H. H. Weiler, "Europa: 'Nous Coalisons des Etats, Nous n'Unissons pas des Hommes'" in Marta Cartabia & Andrea Simoncini (eds.), *La Sostenibilità della Democrazia nel XXI Secolo* 51, 62 (2009).

68 See also Sergio Fabbrini, *Which European Union? Europe after the Euro Crisis* (2015).

69 See Paul Craig & Adam Tomkins (eds.), *The Executive and Public Law: Power and Accountability in Comparative Perspective* 315–45 (2006).

70 This debate had already taken place in the context of the constitutional convention that drafted the then aborted Treaty establishing a constitution for Europe. See also Deirdre Curtain, *Executive Power of the European Union* 69 (2009).

71 Report of President of the European Council SN 25/12 (June 25, 2012), 6 www.consilium.europa.eu/en/workarea/downloadasset.aspx?id=17220.

2012 final report, it claimed that "the crisis has shown the need to strengthen not only the EMU's surveillance framework but also its ability to take rapid executive decisions to improve crisis management in bad times and economic policymaking in good times … Reinforcing the capacity of the European level to take executive economic policy decisions for the EMU is essential."[72] In the June 2015 report, "Completing Europe's EMU" the President of the European Commission, jointly with the Presidents of the European Council, the Eurogroup, the ECB, and the European Parliament (EP), indicated the need for an institutional strengthening of EMU, including through better steering of EMU affairs.[73] Moreover, countries such as France,[74] Italy,[75] and Spain[76] have spoken in favor of strengthening the government of the EU or the eurozone.[77]

Certainly, the proposal advanced in this chapter goes beyond those articulated in the above-mentioned position papers by national governments and EU institutions. Those proposals, unlike mine, do not explicitly endorse the establishment of a presidential system of government in the EU.[78] And I certainly recognize that presidentialism has its own perils, which scholars have examined extensively.[79] Particularly in light of the troubled experience of South American and Asian regimes, it has been recognized that presidential systems can result in permanent conflict between the executive and the legislature, and run the risk of degenerating

72 Report of the President of the European Council, in close coordination with the Presidents of the European Commission, of the Eurogroup and the ECB, "Towards a Genuine Economic and Monetary Union" 17 (Dec. 5, 2012) www.consilium.europa.eu/uedocs/cms_Data/docs/pressdata/en/ec/134069.pdf.

73 Report of the President of the European Commission, in close coordination with the Presidents of the Euro Summit, of the Eurogroup, of the ECB and the European Parliament, "Completing Europe's Economic and Monetary Union" 18 (June 22, 2015).

74 See Francois Hollande, President of France, "Intervention liminaire de lors de la conférence de presse," (May 16, 2013) (speaking of "un gouvernement économique qui se réunirait, tous les mois, autour d'un véritable Président nommé pour une durée longue et qui serait affecté à cette seule tâche.").

75 See Matteo Renzi, Italian Prime Minister, Speech at the European Parliament (July 2, 2014). See also "Europa: Un nuovo inizio. Programma della Presidenza Italiana del Consiglio dell'Unione Europea," at 30 (July 11, 2014) www.governo.it/governoinforma/documenti/programma_semestre_europ_ita.pdf. See also Sandro Gozi, Italian Secretary for EU Affairs, Op-Ed, "Europa, quegli scossini che facilitano il rilancio di una nuova governance." *Il Sole 24 Ore*, May 28, 2015 (stating that Europe needs "un Presidente della zona euro a tempo pieno").

76 See Government of Spain, "Better Economic Governance in the Euro area: Spanish Contribution," May 2015, 7 (expressing support in favor of "an authority responsible for economic policy in the Eurozone").

77 See also Emmanuel Macron, French Minister of the Economy, and Sigmar Gabriel, German Minister of the Economy, Op-Ed, "Europe Cannot Wait Any Longer," *The Guardian*, June 3, 2015 (stating that "to make its institutions work … Europe will need to address its democratic deficit as well as its executive one.").

78 But see also Mario Monti and Sylvie Goulard, *De la démocratie en Europe* (2012) (suggesting that the presidential system of government, together with parliamentarianism, is an option for the future of the EU).

79 See Juan Linz, "The Perils of Presidentialism." *Journal of Democracy* 1: 51 (1990).

into a dictatorial government.[80] Indeed, the dominant view in the field of comparative constitutional studies seems to regard parliamentarism as a preferable system of government over presidentialism,[81] and Bruce Ackerman has even famously suggested that the United States should abandon its centuries-old system of separation of powers to embrace a German-style parliamentary regime.[82] This chapter does not minimize the well-known risks that are associated with presidential regimes. But it still suggests that the EU should consider this institutional model, for the following reasons.

First, for almost forty years – at least since the first direct election of the EP in 1979 – the proposals to strengthen the EU executive power have been associated with efforts to enhance the role of the European Commission as the government of the EU along a parliamentary logic.[83] Yet these efforts have empirically failed to achieve the objective of transforming the European Commission into the government of the EU. In fact, even the recent attempts to connect the selection of the European Commission president to the elections of the EP, fostered by the decision of the main EU political parties to nominate *Spitzenkandidaten* (lead candidates) for the position of Commission President, have not delivered the expected results.[84] Because the EP is elected by proportional representation, and on the basis of state constituency, no party has a clear majority in the house, and thus the appointment of the College of European Commissioners and its internal composition is much more the result of inter-state negotiations than of party politics.[85] As Joseph Weiler has acknowledged, the selection of the Commission President in light of the result of the election of the EP "compromises the ability in a political sense for this or that candidate to say with authority 'I was elected by the peoples of Europe'."[86]

Second, as I have argued elsewhere,[87] even if the EU could be transformed into a full-fledged parliamentary regime, it is normatively questionable whether this would cure the institutional weaknesses described in section II. Because seats in the EP are

80 See Gabriel Negretto, "Choosing How to Choose Presidents." *Journal of Politics* 68: 421 (2006) and Francis Fukuyama, "Challenge and Change in East Asia: Facing the Perils of Presidentialism." *Journal of Democracy* 16: 102 (2005).

81 But see also Richard Alberts, "Presidential Values in Parliamentary Democracies." *Int'l J. Con. L.* 8: 207 (2010) (suggesting that parliamentary systems may often incorporate features of presidential systems).

82 See Bruce Ackerman, "The New Separation of Powers." *Harvard L.Rev.* 113: 633 (2000).

83 See Julian Priestley & Nereo Peñalver Garcia, *The Making of a European President* (2015).

84 See Editorial Comments, "After the European Elections: Parliamentary Games and Gambles." *Common Mkt. L. Rev.* 51: 1047, 1048 (2014) (discussing the political origin of the process of the leading candidates and arguing that "Somewhat tellingly, and indicating a certain unwillingness to embrace the concept in other Member States, the candidates have become known under their German name *Spitzenkandidaten* throughout the EU.").

85 See Andrea Gratteri, "Parlamento e Commissione: Il difficile equilibrio fra rappresentanza e governabilità nell'Unione Europea." *Comunità Internazionale* 2: 237, 241 (2014).

86 See Joseph H. H. Weiler, Editorial, "Fateful Elections? Investing in the Future of Europe." *Eur. J. Int'l L.* 25: 361, 365 (2014).

87 See Fabbrini, above n. 40.

allotted between the member states based on population, albeit along a criteria of "degressive proportionality,"[88] larger member states have a much greater sway than smaller ones in influencing executive appointments.[89] Just as the rise of the European Council produced a dynamic of inter-state domination because in an intergovernmental setting larger states have been able to exploit their relative power to the detriment of smaller states, a transition to a parliamentary system likewise would risk entrenching the domination of larger over smaller states, albeit for different reasons.[90] Given the profound asymmetries that characterize the Member States, the EU cannot afford to be governed by a single institution – be it a congress of heads of state or government, or a parliamentary assembly giving its confidence to the executive. A union of states and citizens such as the EU can only prosper in an institutional regime in which separated institutions, each reflecting different logics of representation, share the power.[91] From this point of view, the creation of a President of the EU that were separate from the other EU institutions, and controlled by them, would better fit the compound nature of the EU.[92]

Third, if it is true that political culture is central to the functioning of a constitutional regime,[93] it is suggested here that the EU is a mature enough democratic polity to manage the dangers of presidentialism that have been revealed elsewhere. Let me be clear: this argument should not be interpreted to mean that Europe is some kind of democratic paradise. Far from it: Populism and nationalism are resurging, and forms of authoritarian and illiberal governance have recently taken hold – particularly in Central and Eastern Europe.[94] Nevertheless, in Europe the judiciary and civil society are strong, the army is weak, and now decades of experience of open political competition and ordinary transition of power have educated the citizenry to accept the results of the democratic process. And while it is true that presidential systems function pursuant to a winner-take-all logic insofar as there can be only one president at a time, such regimes simultaneously constrain the executive power through mechanisms of checks and balances. Hence much depends also on the specific design of the presidency, its competences and its mode of legitimation.[95]

88 TEU, above n. 8, Art. 14.

89 See Federico Fabbrini, "Representation in the European Parliament: of False Problems and Real Challenges." *Zeitschrift für ausslandisches öffentliches Recht und Völkerrecht* 75: 823 (2015).

90 See European Parliament press release, "Members Elect Chairs and Vice-Chairs of Parliamentary Committee," July 8, 2014 (reporting that the chairmanship of 19 of 22 committees of the EP had been assigned to MEPs elected from the six largest member states of the EU).

91 See, ceteris paribus, Richard Neustadt, *Presidential Power and the Modern President* 42 (1964).

92 See Sergio Fabbrini, *Compound Democracies* (2012) (defending the logic of separation of powers in the EU).

93 See Seymour Martin Lipset, "The Centrality of Political Culture" (1990) 1: 80 *Journal of Democracy*.

94 See Jan-Werner Müller, *What Is Populism?* (2016) and Armin von Bogdandy and Pal Sonnevend (eds.), *Constitutional Crisis in the European Constitutional Area* (2015)

95 See Giovanni Sartori, *Comparative Constitutional Engineering* (1994).

Elsewhere I have discussed more extensively what the powers of the new President should be – and how he or she should be elected.[96] In my view, the President of the EU should execute EU laws, head the EU administration – including the highly competent services of the European Commission – and he or she should be empowered to veto EU legislation.[97] At the same time, I have suggested that the President should be elected through a system that tempers majoritarianism with federalism concerns: hence EU citizens would vote directly for the EU President but via state constituencies – each of which gets a number of "electoral votes" which equals the number of seats that state has in the EP plus the number of votes that state had in the Council.[98] Since smaller member states are over-represented in the EP and the Council compared to their population – despite having fewer seats and votes than the larger member states – this solution allows them to have a voice in the selection of the chief executive – just as it is the case in the US thanks to the Electoral College mechanism.[99] If no presidential candidate reached the majority of electoral votes in a first round, the two most voted candidates would face each other in a runoff fourteen days after the first election.[100] Needless to say, these technical proposals can be criticized, and better crafted solutions can be brought forward.

Yet, the bottom-line remains the following: in my view the EU needs an executive institution which is able to ensure centripetal force, against centrifugal pressures. A monocratic executive office, elected through a pan-European process and endowed with defined powers would represent a promising development in this direction. In fact, an EU President would outperform the European Council (and a European Commission acting as the government responding to the EP) in smoothing inter-state conflicts and cleavages. Since EU citizens would have a direct voice in choosing who governs the EU, it would be more acceptable for them to abide by the decisions taken, even if they do not agree with them. Put otherwise, while the national leaders in the European Council only represent their member states, the EU President would represent the EU as a whole, and its actions would enjoy the greater legitimacy that follows from its popular election across the EU. In conclusion, at a time when EU citizens appear increasingly disillusioned vis-à-vis the EU, the institution of a President of the EU would offer the way through which citizens in the member states could channel their preferences and feel they have a stake in what the EU is and does.

[96] See Federico Fabbrini, "Austerity, the European Council and the Institutional Future of the European Union: A Proposal to Strengthen the Presidency of the European Council." *Ind. J. of Global Leg. Stud.* 22: 269, 274 (2015).

[97] Ibid. at 310–13.

[98] TEU, above n. 8, Art. 3, Protocol No. 36 on Transitional Provisions.

[99] See Norman R. Williams, "Reforming the Electoral College: Federalism, Majoritarianism and the Perils of Subconstitutional Change." *Georgetown L.J* 100: 173 (2011).

[100] Fabbrini, above n. 96, at 317–20.

V. BREXIT

Implementing the institutional reforms outlined in the previous section would require constitutional change in the EU.[101] As the rules governing the functioning of the EU are codified in the EU treaties, amending them would be necessary to establish a President of the EU. This is of course not an easy option. Nevertheless, it is submitted here that Brexit – the decision of the United Kingdom to leave the EU – creates a window of opportunity to this end.[102] On the one hand, from an ideological perspective, Brexit challenges the optimistic reading of the process of European integration as an inevitable progress forward, exposing the rifts in the current EU and increasing the urge for reforms aimed at preventing the break-up of the Union. On the other hand, from a pragmatic perspective, Brexit creates the need for the remaining member states and EU institutions to adapt the EU to the new reality of a Union of twenty-seven member states. Institutional engineering and treaty changes will be necessary among others to reallocate seats between member states in the EP and to define the new rules on the financing of the EU. Because formal institutional changes already must be made, proposals to overhaul the EU architecture of executive power might conceivably emerge as elements of a package deal that can win the endorsement of the member states committed to the European cause.

The decision of the United Kingdom to leave the EU was rooted in the United Kingdom's idiosyncratic approach to the project of European integration.[103] Since joining the EU in 1973, the United Kingdom remained a wary member of the EU, resisting most steps forward in European integration and securing for itself a number of opt-outs from measures endorsed by almost all other member states.[104] Opposition to the EU became entrenched within UK politics, particularly within the Conservative Party, reaching its apex during the governments led by David Cameron. To tame the Eurosceptic fringe, the UK Parliament in 2011 adopted the EU Act,[105] which committed the government to calling a referendum to authorize any further expansion of EU powers. And a year later the UK government launched a balance of competence review that was designed to assess areas where competences ought to be repatriated from the EU to the national sphere.[106] When running for parliamentary elections in 2015, the Conservative Party committed to calling a referendum on membership in the EU. Winning an unexpected majority in Westminster, Prime Minister Cameron thereafter spelled-out his demands for a new deal between the United Kingdom and the EU (in the fields of migration, sovereignty and

[101] See TEU, above n. 8, Art. 48.

[102] See Federico Fabbrini (ed.), *The Law & Politics of Brexit* (2017).

[103] See Paul Craig, "Brexit: A Drama in Six Acts." *Eur. L. Rev.* 41: 447 (2016).

[104] See Sarah Hobolt, *Europe in Question* (2009).

[105] European Union Act 2011, c. 12 (UK), See also Paul Craig, "The European Union Act 2011: Locks, Limits and Legality." *Common. Mkt. L. Rev.* 48: 1915 (2011).

[106] Foreign & Commonwealth Office, Review of the Balance of Competencies (Dec. 12, 2012), www.gov.uk/guidance/review-of-the-balance-of-competences.

competitiveness), while Parliament approved the 2015 EU Referendum Act.[107] Negotiations between the United Kingdom and its European partners concluded in February 2016, when the European Council reached a legally binding agreement which, among others, exempted the United Kingdom from participating to the process of achieving an "ever closer union."[108] Based on this deal, Prime Minister Cameron called a referendum in June 2016 and campaigned to remain in the EU.

As is well known, on June 23, 2016, the British people voted, with 52 percent in favor of leaving the EU and 48 percent in favor of remaining in the EU.[109] This precipitated one of the most dramatic constitutional crises the United Kingdom has ever faced. Following David Cameron's resignation, and the formation of a government led by Theresa May, the new Prime Minister committed to implement the will of the British people, triggering Article 50 EU Treaty (TEU). Yet, litigation also began on the question of whether the notification of withdrawal decision required parliamentary approval. In January 2017, in the *Miller* case, the UK Supreme Court ruled 8 to 3 that the government could not trigger Article 50 TEU without parliamentary legislation, but it unanimously held that consent by the devolved legislatures in Scotland, Wales and Northern Ireland was not needed.[110] Emphasizing that "Parliamentary sovereignty is a fundamental principle of the UK constitution,"[111] the UK Supreme Court noted that "The Royal prerogative encompasses the residue of powers which remain vested in the Crown, and they are exercisable by ministers, provided that the exercise is consistent with Parliamentary legislation."[112] The Court stressed that while the UK government enjoyed prerogative powers in foreign affairs,[113] only Parliament could give domestic effect to treaties within the United Kingdom.[114] As the Court explained, the European Communities Act (ECA) 1972 represented an act of "constitutional character"[115] since it served as the "conduit pipe"[116] to incorporate within UK law all EU law – a body of norms with direct effect and supremacy over other sources of UK law.[117] The Supreme Court thus concluded that an act of the executive could not displace the rights and privileges accorded to UK citizens that Parliament had created by means of the ECA.[118]

107 European Union Referendum Act 2015, c. 36 (UK).

108 See European Council Conclusions, EUCO 1/16 annex I "A New Settlement for the United Kingdom within the EU" (Feb. 19, 2016).

109 See The Electoral Commission, EU referendum results (June 23, 2016), www.electoralcommission.org.uk/find-information-by-subject/elections-and-referendums/past-elections-and-referendums/eu-referendum/electorate-and-count-information.

110 *R.* v. *Secretary of State for Exiting the European Union, ex parte Miller* [2017] UKSC 5.

111 Ibid. at 43.

112 Ibid. at 47.

113 Ibid. at 54.

114 Ibid. at 57.

115 Ibid. at 67.

116 Ibid. at 65.

117 Ibid. at 60.

118 Ibid. at 69.

The judgment of the UK Supreme Court in *Miller* slightly complicated the UK government plan to start the official withdrawal from the EU. While the House of Commons had agreed already in December 2016 to a resolution calling on the executive to activate Article 50 TEU before March 31, 2017,[119] the Supreme Court was crystal-clear that if "ministers cannot give Notice [of withdrawal] by the exercise of prerogative powers, only legislation which is embodied in a statute will do. A resolution of the House of Commons is not legislation."[120] Nevertheless, Brexit was never put in question by the UK Supreme Court. In fact, just days ahead of the UK Supreme Court ruling, Prime Minister May had outlined her strategy for withdrawal in a major speech, where she had expressed her intention to also pull the United Kingdom out of the EU single market and customs union.[121] Two days after *Miller*, the UK government introduced a lightly worded bill in Parliament.[122] The bill was quickly approved by the House of Commons and the House of Lords, and received royal assent on March 16, 2017[123] – and on March 29, 2017 the UK Prime Minister formally notified the President of the European Council of the United Kingdom's decision to leave the EU.[124] The notification started the two-year process of withdrawal,[125] and – following snap parliamentary elections in the United Kingdom on June 8, 2017[126] – negotiations have now started to settle the terms of the divorce, as well as the possible new relation between the United Kingdom and the EU.[127]

With the United Kingdom on a course out of the EU, the EU's remaining member states will have to amend the EU treaties to adapt the EU to the reality of a Union of twenty-seven. As I have argued elsewhere, there are a number of constitutional and quasi-constitutional provisions of EU law that must be changed following Brexit.[128] First, changes will need to be made to Article 52 TEU, which currently lists all the member states of the EU, including the United Kingdom. Although this is a fairly formal amendment, an *ordinary* treaty revision is needed to remove the name of the United Kingdom from the list of Article 52 TEU: neither the withdrawal agreement between the United Kingdom and the EU,[129] nor a *simplified*

119 7 Dec 2016, Parl Deb HC (2016) col. 336 (UK).
120 *Miller* at 123.
121 See Theresa May, UK Prime Minister, "The Government's Negotiating Objectives for Exiting the EU: PM Speech" (Jan. 17, 2017).
122 See European Union (Notification of Withdrawal) Bill 2017, HL Bill [108] cl. 1.
123 See European Union (Notification of Withdrawal) Act 2017, c. 9.
124 See Theresa May, UK Prime Minister, Letter to the President of the European Council (Mar. 20, 2017).
125 TEU, above n. 8, Art. 50(2).
126 See The Electoral Commission, UK general elections 2017 (June 8, 2017), www.electoralcommission.org.uk/find-information-by-subject/elections-and-referendums/upcoming-elections-and-referendums/uk-general-election-2017.
127 See European Council Conclusions EUCO XT 20004/17 (Apr. 29, 2017) (outlining the guidelines for the negotiations).
128 See Federico Fabbrini, "How Brexit Creates a Window of Opportunity for Treaty Change in the EU." Bertelsmann Stiftung Spotlight Europe 1/2016.
129 TEU, above n. 8, Art. 50.

treaty revision,[130] can modify Article 52 TEU. According to Article 48(3) TEU, the ordinary treaty revision requires the European Council to "convene a Convention composed of representatives of the national Parliaments, of the Heads of State or Government of the Member States, of the European Parliament and of the Commission" and charged to "adopt by consensus a recommendation [to amend the treaties] to a conference of representatives of the governments of the Member States." The European Council may decide by a simple majority "not to convene a Convention should this not be justified by the extent of the proposed amendments,"[131] but it must obtain the consent of the EP to do so. This means that the EP can insist on calling a Convention to examine proposals for revisions to the EU treaties.[132] Finally, amendments to the treaties have to be agreed by common accord by a conference of representatives of the member states and "shall enter into force after being ratified by all the Member States in accordance with their respective constitutional requirements."[133]

Moreover, following Brexit, the other EU member states also will have to modify EU quasi-constitutional provisions on the allocation of seats in the EP, and the financing of the EU. As to seat allocation, Article 14(2) TEU provides that the EP shall be composed of 751 members of the EP (MEPs), and the specific allocation of EP seats in the various member states is determined in a European Council decision, "adopted by unanimity, on the initiative of the European Parliament and with its consent." Currently, the composition of the EP is set in a European Council decision adopted in June 2013,[134] which assigns to the United Kingdom seventy-three seats in the EP – the third largest delegation (after Germany and France, and on a par with Italy).[135] As to financing, Article 311 TFEU provides that the Council, acting unanimously and after consulting the EP, shall adopt a decision laying down the system of own resources of the Union. This decision, which "shall not enter into force until it is approved by the Member States in accordance with their respective constitutional requirements," defines the revenue side of EU financing. National contributions to the EU budget are today set in a Council decision adopted in May 2014.[136] Although the United Kingdom enjoys a famous rebate (obtained in 1984, and preserved ever since) which allows it to pay less than it should, it nevertheless remains one of the major contributors to the EU budget

130 TEU, above n. 8, Art. 48(6).

131 TEU, above n. 8, Art. 48(3).

132 See Jean-Claude Piris, *The Lisbon Treaty: A Legal and Political Analysis* 104 (2010).

133 TEU, above n. 8, Art. 48(4).

134 See Council Decision 2013/312/EU of 28 June 2013 establishing the composition of the European Parliament, 2013 O.J. (L181) 57.

135 See ibid. Art. 3.

136 See Council Decision 2014/335/EU of 26 May 2014 on the system of own resources of the European Union, 2014 O.J. (L 168) 105.

– the fourth largest net payer into the EU coffers (after Germany, France and Italy), according to the figures of the European Commission for 2014.[137]

Historically negotiations on the European Council decision allocating seats to the EP, as well as the Council decision on the EU's own resources, have been extremely contentious: states have an interest in maximizing their seats in the EP, and in minimizing their contributions to the EU budget, which is today mostly made up of states' transfers.[138] After Brexit, both these measures will need to be renegotiated, through a process that is akin to treaty change on account of the requirements of unanimity and national ratification. But more is up-for-grabs than usual: since the United Kingdom is one of the most populous and richest member states of the EU, its withdrawal will significantly change the stakes of the renegotiation of the decision on the EP composition and the rules on EU financing. It seems clear, therefore, that without the United Kingdom, the other member states and the EU institutions will need to engage in a much more significant grand bargain, both to reapportion seats and to re-think the revenues and expenditures of the EU for a post-Brexit era.[139] In this context, a broader overhaul of the EU constitutional architecture, tackling deep structural flaws in its system of government, seems more possible than usual, and could become part of the package deal of reforms and compromises that the EU member states may be willing and able to accept, to move the EU forward.[140]

In conclusion, Brexit both catalyzes the urge for reform and provides the opportunity to do so by forcing the member states to engage in some significant revisions of the EU treaties and related constitutional acts. While many uncertainties still surround the United Kingdom withdrawal from the EU, particularly following the June 2017 UK parliamentary elections, which deprived the Conservative Party of their overall majority in the House of Commons, and forced Prime Minister May to enter into a confidence and supply agreement with the Democratic Unionist Party of Northern Ireland[141], the negotiations between the United Kingdom and the EU are subject to unforessen developments, the United Kingdom will leave the EU.[142] Although Brexit occurred due to the miscalculations of Prime Minister Cameron,

137 See European Commission, "EU Expenditure and Revenue 2014–2020," http://ec.europa.eu/budget/figures/interactive/index_en.cfm.

138 See Jonathan Rodden, "Strengths in Numbers? Representation and Redistribution in the European Union." *Eur. Union Pol.* 3: 151 (2002).

139 See also Rep. of High-Level Group on Own Resources, "Future Financing of the EU" (Dec. 2016).

140 See Michael Klarman, *The Framers' Coup. The Making of the United States Constitution* (2016) (explaining grand bargain at the Philadelphia Constitutional Convention).

141 See Confidence and Supply Agreement between the Conservative and Unionist Party and the Democratic Unionist Party (June 26, 2017), www.gov.uk/government/publications/conservative-and-dup-agreement-and-uk-government-financial-support-for-northern-ireland/agreement-between-the-conservative-and-unionist-party-and-the-democratic-unionist-party-on-support-for-the-government-in-parliament.

142 See now Joint Report from the negotiators of the European Union and the United Kingdom Government on the progress during phase 1 of the negotiations under Article 50 TEU on the United Kingdom's orderly withdrawal from the European Union, TF50 (2017) 19 (Dec. 8, 2017).

and moved forward in ways that were not anticipated by Prime Minister May, the process of withdrawal seems difficult to reverse. When the United Kingdom leaves the EU – by default, on March 29, 2019 unless the European Council unanimously accepts a request by the British government to extend membership[143] – the EU will need to look internally, and put its house in order. As explained above, a number of key EU provisions will need to be amended through a highly complex and politically demanding process. In this context, reforms in the EU institutional system – including more sweeping proposals to strengthen the EU executive through the establishment of a new President of the EU, as suggested in this chapter – may be taken up as part of a grand bargain between the remaining member states to enhance the form of government of the EU for good.

VI. CONCLUSION

The EU is at a crossroads. Over the last decade the EU has faced multiple crises, which in a crescendo have challenged the project of European integration. From the euro-crisis, threatening the survival of EMU, to the migration-crisis, threatening the survival of the Schengen free movement zone, the EU has increasingly been facing questions about its very existence. These crises have exposed important weaknesses of the EU institutional system, including the lack of an executive branch able to take effective and legitimate decisions. Under the current system of EU governance, the European Council, the body representing the heads of state and governments of the EU, has come to play a central role in the decision-making process. But this intergovernmental body has been the source of more problems than solutions. First, the European Council structurally fuels discord between the member states; and second, it unleashes domination by the larger member countries as a way to resolve inter-state disagreement. As the Greek crisis has revealed, such a decision making-regime will lead to measures which are perceived as illegitimate and which will ultimately fail to be effective. As this chapter has suggested in light of the Greek crisis, a union based on permanent negotiation between competing and parallel national democracies is inevitably bound to implode, undermining the achievements of more than sixty years of European integration.

As an alternative, this chapter has proposed a reform of the EU constitutional system that would institute an executive branch that is able to act effectively, and legitimately, in the interest of the EU as a whole. Specifically, the chapter has made the case in favor of creating a President of the EU, separated from the EU legislature, and controlled by it. The President should be vested with the executive powers of the EU, and elected through a democratic process that tempers pure majoritarianism with federalism-based election rules. Such an institutional figure could play a crucial role in channeling citizens' preferences, thereby creating a forum for

[143] See TEU, above n. 8, Art. 50 (saying that after a two-year period from notification of withdrawal, a country is out of the EU unless at the request of the withdrawing member state the European Council unanimously agrees to extend the negotiating period).

political contestation on the direction of the EU. Moreover, at a time of increasing disunity, such a monocratic executive office could act as an agent of unity – an integrative force taming disintegrative pressures. Reforming the EU institutional setup to establish a President of the EU would require a treaty amendment. Yet Brexit offers a major window of opportunity. With the United Kingdom on its way out of the EU, the remaining twenty-seven EU member states and the EU institutions will need to engage in sweeping constitutional changes. The EU treaties will have to be revised, and other constitutional acts (such as the rules on the EP composition and EU financing) have to be renegotiated. In this context, the possibility of redesigning the EU's institutional architecture conceivably could become part of a grand bargain that restructures the EU's institutional architecture.

On March 25, 2017, the EU celebrated the sixtieth anniversary of the Treaties of Rome, which in 1957 inaugurated the process of economic and political integration among the nations of Europe. The declaration signed by the heads of the EU institutions and twenty-seven leaders of the member states, however, was mostly focused on celebrating past achievements than on mapping the way ahead.[144] The absence of a clear vision for moving forward also can be seen in the stand taken by the European Commission, which in a White Paper published on March 1, 2017, was content to outline five alternative scenarios for the future of Europe, without taking a clear position on them.[145] But hesitation is not an option for the EU, and with the recent election of Emmanuel Macron as President of France, the èlan to address the deep structural flaws of the EU institutional system has returned on the agenda.[146] In fact, as the EP pointed out in February 2017, the project of European integration needs to be moved forward – not only by exploiting in full the potentials of the current EU treaties,[147] but also by appropriate constitutional reforms that will enhance the functioning of the EU institutions[148] and its resources.[149] It is therefore time for the EU member states which are willing and able to launch an ambitious reform initiative that can put the EU on track for another successful sixty years of integration.[150]

144 See Rome Declaration, European Council Press Release 149/17 (Mar. 25, 2017).

145 See European Commission White Paper on the Future of Europe, COM (2017) 2025 (Mar. 1, 2017).

146 See Emmanuel Macron, President of France, Speech at Sorbonne University (Sep. 29, 2017).

147 See European Parliament Resolution of 16 February 2017 on improving the functioning of the European Union building on the potential of the Lisbon Treaty, P8_TA (2017)0049.

148 See European Parliament Resolution of 16 February 2017 on possible evolutions of and adjustments to the current institutional set-up of the European Union, P8_TA (2017)0048.

149 See European Parliament Resolution of 16 February 2017 on budgetary capacity for the Eurozone, P8_TA (2017)0050.

150 See also Declaration by Germany, France, Italy and Spain after their informal summit in Versailles, 6 March 2017 (suggesting that Europe should move forward at different speeds, if not all member states are willing to participate).

IV

Implementing Austerity

12

The Constitutional Performance of Austerity in Portugal

Teresa Violante[*] *and Patrícia André*[†]

I. INTRODUCTION

The aim of this chapter is to analyze how a specific constitutional regime dealt with an impending financial emergency. To assess the constitution's constraining effects on the legislator's margin of choice within an economic crisis, we will focus on the Portuguese constitutional case law that has reviewed austerity measures.[1] For this purpose, we define "austerity legislation" as law that was adopted to cope with budgetary deficit reduction following the great recession and that affects individual rights and freedoms.[2]

We begin by briefly describing the domestic and international events that lead to the adoption of several packages of austerity and the formal financial rescue program. In section III, we go through the crisis constitutional case law. The Portuguese Constitutional Court (CC) has dealt with financial emergencies since its early days. After reviewing that initial jurisprudence, we analyze the case law on austerity which comprises not only legislation enacted before the bailout, but also the policies required by the formal program. In section IV we put forward a critical and global

* Research fellow at the Goethe-University Frankfurt a.M. and visiting research fellow at the Max Planck Institute for Comparative Public Law and International Law (Heidelberg).

† Researcher at CEDIS – NOVA Law School and DINAMIA'CET – IUL (Lisbon).

1 To grasp the intensity of the adjustment effort in other areas, particularly health, education, and private sector workers' rights, see: Miguel Nogueira de Brito, "Putting Social Rights in Brackets? The Portuguese Experience with Welfare Challenges in Times of Crisis." In Claire Kilpatrick and Bruno De Witte (eds), *Social Rights in Times of Crisis in the Eurozone: The Role of Fundamental Rights' Challenges*, EUI Working Papers (2014). Available at http://cadmus.eui.eu/handle/1814/31247 (Accessed November 16, 2017); Júlio Gomes, "Social Rights in Crisis in the Eurozone: Work Rights in Portugal." In Claire Kilpatrick and Bruno De Witte (eds), *Social Rights in Times of Crisis in the Eurozone: The Role of Fundamental Rights' Challenges*, EUI Working Papers (2014). Available at http://cadmus.eui.eu/handle/1814/31247 (Accessed November 16, 2017); Mariana Rodrigues Canotilho, Teresa Violante and Rui Lanceiro, "Austerity measures under judicial scrutiny: the Portuguese constitutional case law," *European Constitutional Law Review* 11: 155–83 (2015).

2 A similar definition was adopted in Canotilho, Violante, and Lanceiro, "Austerity measures under judicial scrutiny: the Portuguese constitutional case law."

review of the austerity case law. Bearing in mind that this is a complex object that recommends refraining from drawing over-simplistic interpretations, we argue the following main conclusions: first, that although the financial crisis required a judicial interpretation adjusted to the circumstances, the Court did not deny its role as the supreme guardian of the constitution; second, that the constitution (and its judicial enforcement) worked as strong constraints upon the political branches of power, as the "constitutional risks" subsequently identified by the international documents and institutions show; third, that the Court's discourse "nationalized" the crisis, thereby leading to an important misreading regarding the role of EU (European Union) law in the constitutional adjudication; fourth, that the Court failed to enter a productive dialogue with the legislature, thereby precluding the continuous development of the constitutional interpretation process, as shown by the fact that some of the attempted policies were left untouched ever since; finally, that the Court did not engage in real judicial activism, having instead kept a countermajoritarian role that matches its constitutional function.

II. THE 2008–16 ECONOMIC AND FINANCIAL CRISIS IN PORTUGAL

The financial collapse following the Lehman Brothers crash and the eurozone crisis were particularly harsh in Portugal, due to the country's already fragile situation. Increasing difficulties in the nation's financing forced the incumbent socialist cabinet to adopt several packages of measures aimed at lowering the budget deficit.[3] The first package was passed in March 2010 and envisaged a gradual reduction of the country's deficit to achieve the target of 2.8 percent of GDP by 2013. In May 2010, the government adopted a second package, introducing further public expenditure cuts, a VAT increase, the freezing of recruitment in the public sector, and a 5 percent pay-cut for civil servants and political office-holders. A third package was presented in September 2010 and included in the 2011 Budget which introduced pay-cuts for all public workers with monthly gross salaries above 1,500 euros. These austerity measures enjoyed the support of the main opposition party, the Social Democratic Party (PSD). However, the country's financial scenario continued to deteriorate, particularly the banking sector,[4] and the markets grew increasingly skeptical of the country's ability to repay its debt. As the risk of contagion ran higher, the government put forward a fourth austerity package. This time however the opposition parties withdrew their support. Backed by only a minority in parliament, the government resigned in March 2011.

On April 7, 2011, Portugal asked for financial assistance from the European Commission (EC), the European Central Bank (ECB), and the International

[3] Following the Excessive Deficit Procedure (EDP) initiated by Council Decision No. 2010/288/EU of 19 January 2010.

[4] In 2008, following Lehman Brothers' crash, Portugal bailed out two of its private banks. More recently, in 2014 (shortly after the assistance program ended) and in late 2015, two other banks were bailed out.

Monetary Fund (IMF). The agreement on the Financial and Economic Assistance Program (FEAP) was formally adopted on May 17, 2011. The rescue package took the form of a loan of 78 bn. euros[5] to be delivered in tranches between 2011 and mid-2014. The provision of further disbursements depended on positive interim quarterly evaluations of the conditions in the bailout agreements conducted by the Troika (IMF, EC, and ECB). These agreements were set out in three documents: (i) the Memorandum of Economic and Financial Policies, (ii) the Technical Memorandum of Understanding, and (iii) the Memorandum of Understanding on Specific Policy Conditionality (MoU).[6] The first two documents were sent as an attachment to a letter of intent written by the Portuguese State to the IMF's Executive Board. The third document, signed between the Portuguese State and the EC on May 17, 2011, detailed the general economic policy conditions as embedded in Council Implementing Decision 2011/344/EU of May 30, 2011, on granting European Union financial assistance to Portugal. This Decision was based on Council Regulation (EU) No. 407/2010 of May 11, 2010, establishing the EFSM. The documents were subject to several revisions following the quarterly reviews on which disbursement of the subsequent loan tranches relied.

The FEAP envisaged a sharp fiscal consolidation to achieve the fiscal deficit of 3 percent of GDP by 2013. At the same time, an ambitious program of structural reforms was designed primarily focusing on consolidating expenditures.

The legal nature of these agreements has been disputed. Some scholars claim that they are international agreements,[7] others refer to a mixed nature that joins a unilateral act (the IMF's declaration), a bilateral agreement (the framework agreement and the loan contract within the EFFS) and EU acts (on the EFSM, implemented by Council Regulation (EU) No. 407/2010).[8] Non-fulfillment of the conditions would in any case have consequences too hard to bear since Portugal had no other means to finance its needs. This will be a contentious aspect in the case law of the CC, as we will see below.

III. THE CONSTITUTIONAL CASE LAW OF THE CRISIS IN PORTUGAL

Portugal is a constitutional democracy with a written constitution entailing a detailed catalogue of both civil and economic and social rights that are judicially

5 The loan came from the IMF (26 bn euros, of which 12 bn euros were directed to the Bank Solvency Support Facility), the European Financial Stabilization Mechanism (EFSM) and the European Fund of Financial Stability (EFFS) (a total of 52 bn euros).

6 "Memorandos, Relatórios, Balanço E Outros Documentos Do Programa De Assistência Económica E Financeira." Available at www.historico.portugal.gov.pt/pt/o-governo/arquivo-historico/governos-constitucionais/gc19/os-temas/memorandos/memorandos.aspx.

7 Eduardo Correia Baptista, "Natureza jurídica dos memorandos com o FMI e com a União Europeia," *Revista da Ordem dos Advogados* 71: 477–88 (2011).

8 Francisco Pereira Coutinho, "Austerity on the loose in Portugal: European judicial restraint in times of crisis," *Perspectives on Federalism* 8 (2016). Available at http://on-federalism.eu/attachments/249_download.pdf (Accessed November 16, 2017).

enforceable. Article 204 of the Portuguese constitution grants all judges the power to disapply unconstitutional norms. Such decisions may be appealed to the CC under a constitutionality appeal. In these situations, the rulings of the CC are only binding to the parties in the concrete judicial disputes. But the CC may also assess the constitutionality of legislation at the request of several institutions (principally, the President of the Republic, the President of Parliament, the Prime Minister, the Ombudsman, the General Public Prosecutor, and one-tenth of Members of Parliament). In these cases, the review does not take place within a concrete judicial dispute. That is why it is called an "abstract review" and the CC has the exclusive power to perform it. Abstract review may take place before the legislative process has been completed (ex ante, a priori or preventive review[9]) or afterwards (ex post, a posteriori or successive review). Abstract review also comprises possible unconstitutionalities by omission, but this is a largely unused mechanism in Portugal.

Unconstitutionality rulings under ex post abstract review have general and binding force, whereas under ex ante review they have the mere force of a pronouncement for unconstitutionality, something that the legislator may overcome if a strengthened majority re-enacts the bill (to today, this only happened once in a case concerning regional legislation).

In this chapter, we exclusively consider abstract review because only in these proceedings the full constraining power of the Court upon the political process is exercised. Moreover, the case law delivered on concrete review will be assessed on a larger analysis of the Portuguese judicial reactions towards austerity.[10]

Fourteen decisions delivered by the CC between 2010 and 2016 match these criteria. We will however begin by reviewing the first cases dealing with financial emergency that date back to the early eighties.

1. *The Implicit Precedents: Decisions 11/83, 66/84, and 141/85*

In over forty years of democracy, Portugal has requested external financial aid three times: in 1978, 1983, and 2011. The first two loans did not give rise to significant constitutional litigation. In 1978, Portugal was still undergoing the transition process to democracy, and the competence for centralized judicial review of legislation was assigned to the Council of Revolution, a transitory body embedded with revolutionary legitimacy.

By 1983, when the IMF provided Portugal with its second grant of financial aid, Portugal already had in place the CC.[11] That same year, following the approval by Parliament of strong fiscal consolidation policies required by the IMF, an a priori review was requested of a bill that introduced an extraordinary tax on certain

9 These decisions must be delivered twenty-five days after the request.

10 Research project on *The Judicial Impact of the Crisis: An Analysis on Adjudication in a Context of Financial and Economic Crisis* promoted by the Francisco Manuel dos Santos Foundation.

11 The CC was introduced with the first constitutional revision (1982) and implemented in April 1983.

incomes that had been earned that year or the year before. This new tax was typical retroactive taxation, and particularly onerous to public workers.

The Court was thus confronted with an economic crisis scenario in the very first months of its existence (Decision 11/83).[12] The majority of the judges did not rule the tax unconstitutional, both because the constitution contained no explicit prohibition of retroactive taxation,[13] and because of the extraordinary and transitory nature of the tax. The extraordinary nature was linked to the financial crisis, a "notorious fact," in the judges' words, phraseology that was to be relied upon later in the Court's first decision concerning austerity measures following the Great Recession. What made the crisis notorious was the State's great difficulties in financing its needs. The Court concluded that the rule of law principle is not breached when urgent public interest reasons override legitimate expectations and legal security.

In Decision 66/84, the Court reviewed the same tax, but under an abstract successive review. The judges came to the same conclusion based on the very same considerations. A similar tax on companies' income was also validated by the Court on the same grounds (Decision 141/85).

2. *The Austerity Case Law*

(1) Before the Bailout (Decisions 399/2010 and 396/2011)

The Stability and Growth Pact (SGP) of 1997, based on Articles 121 and 126 of the Treaty on the Functioning of the European Union (TFEU), entailed, in its corrective arm, the EDP. In this framework, as mentioned, an EDP was initiated against Portugal that led to the adoption of several austerity packages. Some of them were analyzed by the CC but the judges swiftly cleared the restrictions from any constitutional censorship.

DECISION 399/2010. This case echoed the cases of 1984 and 1985. This ruling addressed two laws[14] that implemented a new bracket for income taxation of 45

12 All the decisions of the CC on the merits are available on its website. The collective decisions (delivered by any of the chambers or the plenary) are available at www.tribunalconstitucional.pt/tc/acordaos/. Some decisions have an English summary (sometimes extended), available at www.tribunalconstitucional.pt/tc/en/acordaos/ (all the case law on austerity legislation has an English summary available except for Decision 396/2011).

13 It was only introduced in the constitutional revision of 1997, Art. 103(3).

14 Laws are enacted by the parliament, whereas decree-laws are enacted by the government. Although legislative power is shared under certain grounds between these two organs, most of the reviewed legislation was enacted by the former at the proposal of the latter. In our context, this formal aspect is particularly important. In the proceedings, only the formal author is called by the CC to provide arguments to defend the constitutionality of the contested legislation and the Portuguese framework does not expressly allow *amicus curiae* briefings. However, in most cases the CC considers legal pieces

percent, that was to apply for the period 2010–13, and a general increase of the remaining tax rates.

The President of the Republic questioned the constitutionality of these measures based on their retroactivity and this decision became a landmark ruling, not only because it was the first assessing austerity legislation but mostly because it clarified the judicial interpretation of the prohibition of retroactive taxation clause (that disallows only genuine or authentic retroactivity, but not inauthentic retroactivity or retrospectivity).

The Court's ruling was extremely deferential to the legislator. The alleged breach of the principle of the protection of legitimate expectations was rejected by the Court because of the international economic and financial crisis. Given the prevailing economic trend, one could not argue that the measures could not have been reasonably and objectively expected nor were they intolerable nor unbearable for taxpayers.

When it assessed the international and economic situation, the Court took account of the "measures adopted in Member States of the EU in identical situation, such as Greece and Spain" (paragraph 12.1). In analyzing the tolerability of the restrictive measures, the Court took account of the public interest underlying the measures. In so doing, the Court treated the public interest as a factor that also enjoyed constitutional protection.

As in its findings in Decision 11/83, the Court acknowledged the crisis as a "notorious public fact," and even though it had only been referenced in the *travaux preparatoires* of one of the analyzed pieces of legislation, the judges relied on the notoriety of the crisis when they upheld all the restrictive measures.

DECISION 396/2011 (PAY-CUTS I). This followed at the request of a group of parliamentarians who challenged the constitutionality of legislation that cut the pay of public sector workers[15] and subsidies (or allowances) for magistrates. This decision was delivered *after* the bailout, but covered austerity measures that had been approved *before* the financial assistance request. However, the Court afforded particular relevance to the bailout rescue, stating that it provided a stronger formal binding to the budget deficit goals already applicable in the framework of the EDP.

The 2011 Budget included a general pay-cut for public workers, and a 20 percent cut in two subsidies paid to magistrates. The pay-cut took the form of a reduction of 3.5 percent to 10 percent in monthly gross salaries above 1,500 euros.

The Court began by determining that the pay-cuts were yearly applicable and not *cavaliers budgétaires*, thus requiring renewal each year they were to remain in force.

that are joined by third parties to the proceedings. That was the case for some of the austerity case law in which the Government joined the litigation with "technical notes" on the legislation under review.

15 Public sector workers are a broad category that comprises not only civil servants (who are generally protected from dismissal) but also temporary and permanent employees (who are subject to a regime similar to that which governs private employment relations).

The cuts of the magistrates' allowances, by contrast, were interpreted as permanent cuts. Though these permanent austerity measures[16] resulted in a significant reduction in magistrates' pay checks, they were easily upheld by the Court because, as subsidies, they were not considered to be salary, and thus fell outside the constitutional protection of the right to pay. The Court also considered that there were no legitimate expectations in their maintenance.

The general and temporary pay-cuts of public workers raised further constitutional difficulties. Although technically they were valid for that same fiscal year, the Court said that the goal they aimed to accomplish – the medium-term goal of a sharp deficit reduction by 2013 – proved they were part of a larger consolidation program such that there would be subsequent similar legislation until 2013. The Court thus took for granted that similar cuts would be enacted for the two years to follow and implicitly upheld these prospective restrictive measures.

The Court expressly acknowledged the financial emergency of the country that put the sovereign debt under strong stress. By mentioning that other countries were experiencing similar stress, and had implemented even more restrictive pay-cuts, the Court paved the way to rule *favor legislatoris*.

Importantly, the Court held that although the right to pay is a fundamental right, it only grants protection against *arbitrary* reductions. The Court then ruled that the right could be violated only by legislative action that breached the protection of legitimate expectations or the principle of equality.

Although there might be a legitimate expectation not to be subject to pay-cuts (fed by a continuous tendency to yearly raise the public salaries[17]), there had been no breach of that principle because of the *absolute exceptionality context* of sovereign debt crisis that had hit Portugal hard. The judges then applied a proportionality analysis and concluded that the measure was an adequate means to cope with a budgetary deficit and a financial crisis, and that the restrictions were not excessive since they were temporary, only applied to wages above 1,500 euros,[18] and amounted to no more than a 10 percent cut, a threshold below those enforced by other countries that were in a similar financial situation.

At this point, there is an important obiter dictum in the reasoning of the Court: it claimed that the option to reduce the budgetary deficit might be reached either through an increase in taxation – which means an increase in revenues – or a cut in public expenditure – such as cuts in wages of public workers. The judges argued that the principle of equality required the equality of citizens before public burdens, but gave no indication as to which option should be favored in light of the constitution. Moreover, the judges recognized that this is an area where the economic and political conflict is strong, and for the competence of the democratic legislature.

[16] These cuts were abolished in the 2018 Budget.

[17] In 2009, just before the general elections, the incumbent socialist cabinet had approved a raise of 2.9 percent in public sector wages, the biggest since 2001.

[18] The minimum monthly wage was then set at 485 euros.

They also expressly rejected a strict application of this parameter to the fiscal constitution, since it would mean that the fiscal consolidation, to meet the equality demands, would have to affect every citizen equally. Such a principle would have dire implications for tax policy. The Court instead held that determinations as to how fiscal demands are to be distributed among the population belong to the privileged domain of the legislature, and that a court cannot interfere unless the legislation is arbitrary. This is of great importance, for two reasons. First, it shows, together with the level of scrutiny applied, that the CC upheld a strong self-restraint in this holding. Second, this jurisprudence will be later tempered, with the judges claiming that, from a constitutional perspective, universal measures (i.e. taxation aggravations) should be favored over cuts in expenditure.

The Court then applied the lighter scrutiny of the principle of equality, and found the restrictions not to be arbitrary because they were transitory, applied only to relatively high wages, and aimed at producing sharp and swift results in line with the strong public interest of balancing the public finances.

Three judges dissented. They thought the legislature had failed to demonstrate that the cuts in public workers' salaries were the most "benign" measure. This line of reasoning, which afforded the legislature far less deference than the majority's approach, gained support over time.

(2) After the Bailout

As mentioned earlier, the initial relevant case law focused on legislation enacted under the framework of an EDP. From 2012 onwards, the jurisprudence focused on legislation enacted to comply with the bailout (FEAP) demands. The degree to which the content and details of such legislation were requested by the Memorandum varies: in some cases, the document set general ends to be reached and broad public policies to be adopted; in others, the degree of detail is more intense, and in a few cases, the MoU detailed the restrictions to fundamental rights that the national legislator should enforce. This distinction is fundamental: the official narrative, including the CC's narrative, is that the MoU, although binding, only entailed general goals to be reached, and thus the national legislator remained sovereign to choose the appropriate (and possibly unconstitutional) means. However, as we will see below, that was not always the case. By failing to acknowledge this distinction, the CC ignored the fact that in some cases the national legislation was derived directly from the international documents and, as such, a preliminary reference to the European Court of Justice (ECJ) should necessarily have been considered.

DECISION 353/2012 (PAY-CUTS II). The second updated version of the MoU laid down a new loan disbursement condition: the adoption in 2012 of a budgetary law that reduced wages and pensions expenditure by partially or totally suspending thirteenth and fourteenth monthly salary payments.[19] The measures that were ultimately adopted in the 2012 Budget Law were slightly different than what had been called for by the MoU, as the legislature raised the minimum pay threshold at which the suspensions would be triggered. A group of parliamentarians challenged these provisions, claiming breaches of the principles of the protection of legitimate expectations, equality, proportionality, and, regarding the cuts to public sector pensions, the right to social security (respectively, Articles 2, 13, 18(2), and 63(1) of the constitution).

Decision 353/2012 was the first ruling on policies adopted following the FEAP program. The Court found that the partial or total suspension of the Christmas and holiday allowances was unconstitutional because it breached the principle of equality understood as "proportional equality."[20]

The Court acknowledged the "binding force to the Portuguese State" of the FEAP, because it comprised documents that were legal instruments based on international and EU law. The Court went as far as to hold that the MoU was founded on Article 122 of the TFEU. However, it considered that the binding force[21] of the documents, including the ones that are EU law, was limited to the obligation to adopt public policies and legislation in order to balance public finances and reach financial stability over a minimum period of three years, covering 2012, 2013, and 2014.[22] Any other legal relevance of the MoU was sidestepped with the justification that the measures at stake were not foreseen in any of the documents: the Court explicitly stated that the MoU did not foresee the suspension of payments of Christmas and holiday allowances.

However, the MoU in its second revision version *did* expressly include the partial or total suspension of those allowances with even lower thresholds (i.e. even more restrictive). What could possibly explain this mistake? The 2012 Budget proposal was drafted by the government in October 2011, i.e., before the second MoU revision. This document was only updated after the Budget proposal was drafted (the Budget was approved in parliament on December 30, 2011). One

19 Holiday and Christmas allowances (see points 1.8. and 1.9. of the MoU).

20 This jurisprudence is influenced by the *neue Formel* developed by the German Federal Constitutional Court, and establishes that equality is breached if a specific group of individuals is treated differently and there are no relevant differences that legitimately ground the differentiation between that group and other individuals. For the sake of simplicity, although the Court's formulation varies over time, we just refer to the principle of "proportional equality."

21 The recognition of the binding character of the MoU in such clear terms was never repeated by the Court. In Decision 187/2013, the Court refers to the "more formally binding" nature of the MoU's obligations in respect of budgetary consolidation when compared to former austerity packages, phraseology that had already been adopted in Decision 396/2011.

22 The FEAP covered the period 2011–14. At first, the 3 percent deficit threshold was to have been reached by 2013, but the Troika later deferred that goal to the fiscal year of 2014, due to aggravation of recession.

reasonable explanation is that the Court may have ignored the revised version of the MoU.[23]

After denying any possible direct relevance to the nature of the MoU or its validity for the decision at hands, the Court reviewed the new pay-cuts within the framework of the principle of equality. It first noted that the legislature had opted to abolish some of its previous measures adopted to increase public revenues. It also noted that the legislature chose not to introduce a new extraordinary tax. Instead of a universal approach towards the crisis – as to the targets of the austerity sacrifices – the legislature chose, in the eyes of the judges, to aggravate the sacrifices imposed on public workers. The Court considered afterwards that the principle of equality of citizens before public burdens imposed limits as to the threshold of sacrifices requested from specific categories of individuals. The previous constitutional neutrality of this yardstick was gradually abandoned, as well as judicial self-restraint. As such, the Court introduced a new level of scrutiny, furthering the equality review beyond the rational basis test.

The Court ruled that the cumulative effects of the new cuts with the 2011 pay-cuts threshold that was kept in force, together with the freezing of public wages (applied since 2010), imposed a special burden upon public workers. The legislature had invoked, in the Budget law report, two main arguments to justify these measures. First, that there was an urgent need to reduce the budgetary deficit. Secondly, public workers enjoyed higher average wages and special job security, which together justified that they be temporarily subject to particularly restrictive measures. The Court rejected these justifications for additional differentiated treatment of public workers (bear in mind that the initial cuts were kept in force in 2012, although they were not challenged in these proceedings). The Court rejected that the average salary paid was a valid distinction, objecting that the State supports functions that are not covered in the private sector. The Court also rejected the argument that because public workers enjoy greater job security they should bear more of the burden of austerity than their private counterparts. The judges affirmed that the relevant comparison should be between workers who have a job, in either the private or public sector, considering the alternative possibility of applying cuts to both public and private-sector workers.

Although the Court thought it was permitted to require private and public workers to shoulder different levels of sacrifice, it considered that the intensity of these differences had to be scrutinized in accordance with the principle of "proportional equality." The Court calculated that the accumulation of austerity measures amounted to an average reduction of 14.3 percent of public workers' yearly wage, which was not "remotely matched by the sacrifice imposed on private workers and

23 Recently, Pereira Coutinho has reached the same conclusion. See Francisco Pereira Coutinho, "The Portuguese Bailout, Social Rights and the Rule of Law." In Alessandra Coli, Barbara Pacini and Elettra Stradella (eds.), *Policy, Welfare and Financial Resources – The Impact of the Crisis in the Territories* (Pisa: Pisa University Press, 2017), 86.

other income-earners." The Court acknowledged the threshold of the 2011 cuts, stating that the difference in treatment between public and private workers had been accepted as validating such a limit, but that the additional cuts were an *evident* violation of the threshold constitutionally accepted.

Though the Court ruled against the government's austerity measures, the crisis context ultimately appeared to play a crucial role insofar as the practical effects of the Court's ruling are concerned. This is because the Court prospectively suspended its declaration of unconstitutionality for the year of 2012. As a result, the pay-cuts called for in the legislation that had been successfully constitutionally challenged nonetheless were enforced in that year. Up to today, this has been the only time that the Court declared its power to suspend *pro futuro* the effects of its decisions.

DECISION 187/2013 (BUDGET LAW 2013). Constitutional challenges were asserted against several provisions of the 2013 Budget by the President of the Republic, some groups of parliamentarians, and the Ombudsman.[24] In a carefully reasoned, long, and complex opinion, the Court upheld many of the challenged provisions while finding others to be unconstitutional.

First, the Court scrutinized the pay-cuts thresholds that were first approved in 2011 and thereafter renewed in both the 2012 and 2013 Budgets. The 2011 cuts were again cleared by the Court based on its previous reasoning. But the 2013 Budget combined those pay-cuts with the partial or total suspension of the holiday allowance and a raise in taxation. The legislature provided two main justifications for these additional measures: first, the cuts should be framed within the constitutional principle of commitment to European integration, and second the measures were a result of Decision 353/2012 that prevented the cut of the two allowances and forced the legislature to find other alternatives.

Once again, the Court accepted the general principle that the financial crisis conceivably could justify the imposition of special sacrifices on public-sector workers but proceeded to carefully consider whether the 2013 Budget's particular provisions satisfied the limits imposed by the constitutional principles that protect legitimate expectations and demand equality and proportionality. The Court decided that the 2011 cuts did not violate legitimate expectations on grounds similar to its earlier 2011 decision. But in analyzing the principle of equality, the Court took account of the cumulative effects of the 2011 cuts along with the new reductions (the total or partial suspension of one of the allowances plus the increase in taxation). In the Budget law report, the legislature claimed that the new cuts design was the only available option left to guarantee both the maximum budget deficit allowed for that year (4.5 percent) and abidance with the 2012 ruling that had invalidated the total or partial suspension of both allowances. It also claimed that this option was in line

[24] The Ombudsman is an independent official appointed by the Parliament who is charged with addressing complaints on actions and omissions of public bodies.

with the Court's reasoning in Decision 353/2012, since the judges had *requested* more universal measures on the revenue side. However, the Court did not accept the legislature's arguments and considered that since the sacrifices imposed on public workers were not matched by equivalent sacrifices by other income-earners, there was an unequal treatment as to which the goal of reducing the public deficit did not constitute sufficient justification. Despite its previous arguments on Decision 353/2012, the Court didn't weigh the legislature's combined solution of adding to another cut to public workers' wages an increase in taxation that affected all citizens equally. Suspicions that the Court would not allow for an increase in the level of sacrifice imposed in 2011 were strengthened by the judges' failure to clearly articulate alternative options that might be available. However, this would later prove partially false when the Court accepted indirect slashes to public wages, such as the increase in working hours for no additional pay. At the same time, a political censorship shadows the Court's reasoning as it notes that other policies foreseen in the MoU targeting the State's and local government's management were still available and left unused by the legislature. A violation of the principle of equality, as "proportional equality," was found in line with Decision 353/2012.

Austerity provisions affecting retirees had mixed success. The Court found the partial suspension of the holiday allowance for pensioners to be unconstitutional. The judges paid special attention to the needs of pensioners, viewing them as being particularly vulnerable, since they could not readily find other resources. On the other hand, retired citizens were also affected by the extraordinary solidarity contribution ("CES"), which applied to monthly pensions exceeding 1,350 euros, with cuts ranging progressively from 3.5 percent to 10 percent.[25] The Court ruled that the CES was a temporary special contribution, rather than a tax, and that it was proportional and warranted by the context of financial and economic crisis, and therefore justified. In the eyes of the Court, cuts in both pensions and public wages were justified by the financial emergency context up to certain limits. Furthermore, an additional cut to monthly pensions exceeding 3,750 euros was cleared by the Court. This additional cut ranged from an extra 15 percent to 40 percent. Overall, the cuts in pensions above 3,750 euros could be subject to cuts of up to more than 50 percent. According to the Court, these cuts were validly grounded on the financial and economic emergency, and their temporary character prevented a constitutional sanction.

The remaining constitutional challenges likewise had mixed success. Contributions of 5 percent and 6 percent on sickness and unemployment benefits, although considered in line with the constitutional rights to social security and assistance in case of unemployment, work accident or sickness, were found to be in breach of the principle of proportionality and the constitutional right to a dignified life due to the absence of a

[25] CES was basically a transposition of the 2011 pay-cuts to pensions. A similar measure had first been applied in the 2011 Budget, which imposed a 10 percent contribution on pensions exceeding 5,000 euros.

safeguard clause that would prevent the reduction of the benefits to levels below the minimum threshold of resources legally guaranteed. On the other hand, the Court upheld a reduction in overtime payments to public workers, considering that these payments were not protected by the right to pay and because no legitimate expectations were breached. The Court also rejected the challenges against the personal income tax (IRS) chapter raised on the grounds of breach of the principle of progressive taxation. These challenges were discarded, considering that the system was still sensitive to differences in levels of income. An additional and progressive solidarity rate applicable to income subject to the marginal tax rates exceeding €80,000 was also accepted by the Court on the same reasons.

Reductions in, or elimination of, tax-deductible items were also upheld because the Court considered this to be a field where the constitution grants the legislature a wide margin of discretion. These measures were reviewed under the principle of the ability to pay taxes (a dimension of the principle of equality). The Court also found no breaches of the principles of the unitary and progressive nature of income taxes on the IRS surtax on account of its exceptional and transitory nature. The IRS surtax was first approved in 2011 and reintroduced in the 2013 Budget as an extraordinary surtax of 3.5 percent applicable to income that exceeded, per individual taxpayer, the annual minimum salary (6,790 euros). Since budget laws have a one-year force, and these provisions envisaged an immediate financial effect – the reduction of public expenses through a direct increase on the revenue side – they were qualified by the Court as transitory and exceptional and, as such, constitutionally permitted.

Decision 187/2013 was met with outrage by the government and sparked a political crisis. Two of the Cabinet's most prominent members resigned, including the Minister of Finance, one of the strongest supporters of austerity policies. Prime Minister Passos Coelho argued publicly in favor of a constitutional revision that might slim down the welfare state and allow for the cuts.[26] A renegotiation of the rescue program was set in motion to include supplementary policies to compensate for the cuts rejected by the Court which amounted to 0.3 percent of GDP. The seventh update of the MoU envisaged new measures that led to further constitutional case law. Some of those policies included the requalification of public workers (Decision 474/2013), a forty-hour working week in the public sector (Decision

[26] Available at www.economist.com/news/europe/21576144-court-ruling-could-force-portugal-seek-second-bail-out-constitutional-difficulties. A constitutional revision was never possible due to its two-thirds majority requirement. The Socialist Party never agreed to enter a constitutional revision process, which explains why the crisis did not spark any change to the constitutional text, namely to introduce the balanced budget rule. The political backlash was reduced to strong criticisms and a cut of around 200,000 euros in the CC's budget between 2013 and 2014. However, in 2015, the Budget raised the transfers to the Court, setting it at 6,115,000 euros, the highest level ever (4,649,869 euros for 2012, 4,809,374, 4,597,677 for 2014, and 6,115,000 euros for 2015). From the budget cut of 2014 we cannot conclude that a court-packing attempt was in track. It surely put the Court under financial stress during the year of 2014 though.

794/2013), and the convergence mechanism of the pensions system (Decision 862/2013).

DECISION 474/2013 (PUBLIC WORKERS REQUALIFICATION). This decision followed an a priori request by the President of the Republic on a bill that introduced a new framework that would have broadened the legal basis for firing public workers, both objectively (i.e. on the possible dismissal grounds) and subjectively (i.e. on the possible workers that might be subject to dismissal).

The new regime would have applied to all public workers, including those that in 2008 had seen their *appointment* bond (a definitive labor relationship, where dismissal was only possible in the case of disciplinary action against the worker) transformed into a *contractual* bond[27] (a regime where dismissal of workers is possible according to several other grounds). The bill introduced a further step in the *laboralization*[28] process of public administration by allowing the dismissal of workers on the grounds of budgetary reductions or management needs.

The government grounded this reform directly in the MoU, more specifically its seventh update (May 2013). The Court recognized that the MoU called for the adoption of a "Special Mobility Scheme" to simplify the procedures related with mobility of public workers and address the compensation due to affected individuals, but it also observed that the MoU did not detail a specific framework to be adopted by the domestic legislation. The Court furthermore held that the new bill had not only failed to provide sufficient grounds to justify requiring yet another sacrifice from public workers, but that the legislature had continually fed public workers' expectations that a regime reducing worker security would never be put into practice. After all, the legislature had spared the appointed workers from the mobility regime in 2008. Even more importantly, the legislature had repeatedly justified the pay-cuts and other austerity measure sacrifices on the ground that public workers enjoyed special work security benefits. For these reasons, though there is no general constitutional protection against dismissals in the public sector, the Court found that the bill would have breached the principle against dismissal without fair cause and, as to workers hired before 2008, the principle of the protection of legitimate expectations.[29]

It is important to stress that the legislature did not ground this bill directly on the financial crisis. Although the emergency situation was the permanent shadow behind the MoU, this reform was put forward as a structural amendment in light of the failure of previous legislation to provide an adequate framework for the

[27] In Decision 154/2010 the CC upheld new termination mechanisms if they did not apply to workers employed before 2008. They otherwise would have breached the prohibition of dismissal without just cause.

[28] A long process of convergence between the public and private sector labor regimes.

[29] To the present day, there have been no other legislative attempts to amend the legal framework to allow the dismissal of public workers for objective reasons. The requalification regime was abolished in 2017.

management and allocation of public workers. Furthermore, although the government joined the proceedings with a "technical note," the contents of this note were not disclosed in the reasoning of the Court – nor was this formally required.[30] The fact is that the Government's "technical note" was sent to the Court near the deadline for the ruling, and the judges were not reasonably required to take due notice of this document, not even in accordance with the principle of mutual and loyal cooperation. The Government's failure to properly ground this bill is inexplicable, particularly considering the successive warnings[31] of the judges as to the duty to provide sufficient grounds for restricting fundamental rights in light of the financial contingency of the country.

DECISION 602/2013 (LABOR CODE 2012). The MoU also requested changes in labor law which led to the approval, in 2012, of a significant revision of the Labor Code aimed at slashing labor costs and introducing changes regarding collective labor relations, namely through the legal suspension or invalidation of contractual clauses of collective agreements. The slashing of labor costs related to cuts in overtime work payment, an increase in the number of working days (by suppressing four public holidays out of the existing thirteen), and reductions in severance pay. Dismissals were also simplified.

Some of these amendments were brought for review by the CC by a group of parliamentarians. Where the amendments targeted the validity of previous collective agreements with more favorable regimes on compensatory rest for overtime work, the Court overruled them for breach of the fundamental right to collective bargaining. Similar legal effects on previous collective agreements on severance and overtime payments fell out of the scope of the protection of such right (which is defined in accordance to the law) and were cleared by the judges.

The Court also allowed provisions on the elimination of compensatory rest and the reduction in pay of supplementary work. Although directly affecting the right to pay, the right to rest and the right to reconcile work and family life, the Court considered that these were not intolerable restrictions of those social rights. This reasoning was founded on a combination of arguments: first, the legal framework was still sufficiently protective of the worker's right to refuse supplementary work; second, the new framework did not increase the legal limits, but rather slashed overtime payments; third, more favorable schemes could be reached through collective regulation.

The approval of flexible working time arrangements such as individual and group working hours pools (time banks) was recognized as compressing the individual rights of those workers that did not consent to such arrangements. Group time banks were considered essential to guarantee employers' directive powers, and that allowed

30 See n. 14.

31 These warning came first in the dissenting opinion of Judge Vítor Gomes to Decision 353/2012, and were strengthened in the reasoning of Decision 187/2013.

their mandatory nature with regard to all workers as long as at least 75 percent of them were in accordance with their establishment. Individual time banks were cleared because the Court considered that the legal framework still protected workers' rights to refuse the supplementary work.

The discretion afforded to the employer to choose the employees to be dismissed breached the principle of protection against unfair dismissal. This conclusion was also reached with regard to a measure that dispensed with the employer's duty to allocate workers to another workplace in the event of the redundancy of the original post. The new legislation abolished the employer's burden of providing evidence that the company had no other available working post in the event of dismissal due to a worker's inadequacy. It also allowed the employer to choose the criteria by which employees would be selected for dismissal and to discharge an employee due to his/her reduction in productivity. These changes were not accepted by the Court on the grounds of the constitutional protection against unfair dismissal.

DECISION 794/2013 (40-HOUR WORKING WEEK). A group of parliamentarians requested the review of a Parliament law that had been proposed by the government to introduce an increase in the working hours of public workers (with no additional pay). This legislation increased the normal working time of public workers from seven hours a day and thirty-five hours a week to eight hours a day and forty hours a week. As the report on the proposal stated, these measures were foreseen in the MoU following the seventh revision.[32]

The Court found that the new regime did not breach the prohibition of social regression because this principle only affords protection when the regression of social rights breaches other constitutional principles.

The Court also interpreted this regime as "another step in the *laboralization* process of Public Administration," thus rejecting any breach of the principle of the protection of legitimate expectations. Furthermore, it considered that there was a prevailing public interest underlying the new legislation, related to both the increase in availability of public services to the public and the reduction in expenditure on public wages as prescribed by the MoU, that justified the adoption. A violation of the right to pay was also rejected by the Court.[33] This decision was in line with the willingness of the Court to allow slashing of labor costs regarding both public and private sector workers.

DECISION 862/2013 (SOCIAL PROTECTION CONVERGENCE MECHANISM). Several provisions of a Parliament bill previously proposed by the Government were challenged under an a priori review requested by the President. These provisions would have

[32] May 2013 – see para. 1.5. requiring convergence of the public-sector work rules towards the legal regimes in the private sector, notably working hours and working time arrangements.

[33] These measures were abolished in 2016, and the public sector is currently back to the previous normal working periods: seven hours a day, thirty-five hours a week.

introduced a permanent 10 percent cut in the total amount of former public workers' pensions who had retired by December 31, 2005, as well as a recalculation scheme for pensions of public workers who had retired after that date. In both cases, these were pensions already in payment.

The legislature provided several justifications for this reform. The first was compliance with MoU obligations.[34] Second was that the intergenerational justice principle demands that the burdens of financial unsustainability of the system should not be imposed solely on the future beneficiaries. The third justification rested on the principle of financial self-sustainability of the pensions system. The government's final justification was that the public workers' pension system was far more generous than the pensions enjoyed by members of the general social protection system, and that reform was necessary to bring about a convergence between the two systems, a long-sought constitutional mandate entrenched in Article 63(2).

The Court acknowledged the constitutional relevance of the intergenerational justice and sustainability principles, as well as of the significance of reform. It noticed, however, in this regard, that the bill was partial and only dealt with a fraction of the beneficiaries since only the public system's pensions were affected and for those reasons it couldn't be qualified as a structural reform. While the Court also affirmed that the right to social security is a fundamental right, it provided two important qualifications. First, the legislative fulfillment of social rights is the responsibility of the legislature in accordance with the availability of resources, meaning that the constitutional requirement of safeguarding a minimum content does not imply an absolute rule of no regression. Second, the Court held that the constitutional right to pension does not protect against legal reductions of the paid amount, even as to those who presently receive pensions.

Nevertheless, the Court unanimously decided that the pensions reform measures were an unconstitutional breach of legitimate expectations for two reasons. First, the judges decided that any unsustainability of the current system had been intentionally created by the legislature when it closed the public pensions system to new subscribers,[35] thereby depriving it of additional revenue sources, and that the resulting burden therein should be borne collectively, through taxes. Second, that the cut in pensions that are already being paid has a retrospective character, and that expectations of no changes are very strong and can only be disappointed by a general and structural pension reform, not one limited to a subset of public workers.

34 Pensions reform was introduced in the MoU after the seventh update (May 2013). The MoU's eighth update (October 2013) set more precise guidelines on the reform and specific public expenditure savings.

35 Law 60/2005, of 29 December, provided that newly hired public workers could not join the public workers' pension system, but instead were to be part of the general social security system. This law was part of the longstanding effort to bring about a convergence between the special protection public workers system and the general social security system.

DECISION 413/2014 (BUDGET LAW 2014). 2014 would be the end of the FEAP. The financial pressure was still strong and overshadowed by the unconstitutionality ruling of Decision 862/2013, delivered on December 19, 2013. In another complex and long ruling, the Court reviewed several challenges against the 2014 Budget. This time, however, only one of the challenges failed, which shows the escalating process of affording the legislature less deference as time goes by. The ruling was delivered on May 30, 2014, two weeks after Portugal made a "clean exit" from the bailout program.

The Court was requested to review the constitutionality of some of the provisions of the 2014 Budget by two groups of parliamentarians and the Ombudsman. The ruling begins with a long transcript of both the Budget law report and the "technical note" presented by the government. The legislature basically argued that 2014 would be a transitional year between the FEAP and the new budgetary framework of the eurozone countries, particularly as to what concerns the SGP in its corrective arm as it allows for an EDP where government deficit and/or public debt exceed, respectively, 3 percent and 60 percent of GDP. The legislature also claimed that the new cuts should be framed as a preliminary step in a future reform of public sector wages, something repeatedly asked for by the Troika.

Despite the government's extensive report and technical note, the Court did not give much weight to the argument that it should analyze the law in light of a new framework. However, it recognized that budgetary goals set by the FEAP applied for the whole year even though the bailout program had formally ended in May 2014.

When ruling on the new pay-cuts, the Court stated that it would assess whether the level of sacrifice tolerated in 2011 had been complied with, or if the invalid level of 2012 and 2013 had been reached. This proved to be detrimental to the law, for the new legislation had wholly redesigned the system for determining pay-cuts by raising the maximum rate applicable and lowering the minimum wage threshold to which the reductions would apply. Instead of keeping the 2011 cuts threshold combined with additional measures (as it previously had done in 2012 and 2013), the 2014 law introduced a new cut, that varied between 2.5 and 12 percent, to all monthly wages above 675 euros. Whereas previously the cuts had been implemented through separate provisions, the legislator chose to address the Court's concern with a new technique consisting basically of an aggravation of the 2011 cuts. Although this may be justified as an attempt to find a legal option that might fully address the Court's concerns, the fact is that in the absence of formal or doctrinal mechanisms that allow for the severance of the unconstitutionality rulings, the Court was forced to strike down the cuts in their entirety (even the 2011 threshold, that would soon be allowed again for the period 2014–15 in Decision 574/2014).

First, the Court rejected the government's argument that the law should be viewed as a preliminary reform for two reasons: because the targets of the cuts remained the same (the broad category of "public workers" which included not only public servants but also temporary workers and holders of public offices), and also because its temporary nature pointed to the fact that no systematic reform concerns had guided its adoption. Second, the Court ruled that the overall reduction achieved by these new cuts did not substantially differ from the cuts that had been held unconstitutional in 2013 (with the accumulation of the total or partial suspension of the holiday pay with the 2011 cuts and the increase in income tax).

The 2014 Budget also tried to address a problem that the Court had found with the previous Budget.[36] The 2014 law re-enacted the 5–6 percent contribution on sickness and unemployment benefits, but this time included a break clause that was designed to safeguard the shortest possible existence. The Court ruled that the legislature had misinterpreted its prior ruling, and instead held that the new law was in breach of the principle of proportionality because of the particular vulnerability of these individuals. This reasoning, however, lacks consistency. The 2013 ruling expressly censored the absence of a safeguard clause that might shield individuals from cutting the unemployment or sickness benefits below the minimum threshold enforced by law. In fact, this was the only case in which the Court claimed that there was also a breach of the right to a dignified existence.[37]

Another provision of the 2014 Budget provided new methods for calculating pensions that reduced survivors' pensions. The new rules would have permanently reduced survivors' pensions in circumstances where the survivor was the beneficiary of another pension that in total amounted to more than 2,000 euros per month. The legislature justified this change on the basis of the emergency crisis and also the need to provide for the future sustainability of public finances and the pensions system. The Court concluded that the measure violated the principle of equality because it applied only to those survivors whose other income came from a retirement pension, and did not take account of those whose other monies came from other types of income.

The 2014 Budget also contained provisions that suspended the payment of pension supplements at state-owned business sector enterprises that had sustained net losses in the last three financial years. The Court ruled that these supplements were not included in the protection of the right to pay, and that the public interest related to budgetary balance was sufficient to set aside any violation of the protection of legitimate expectations.

36 In fact, the legislature had already addressed that problem previously, following the ruling on the 2013 Budget. An article of Law 50/2013, of 24 July (enacted to cope with the budgetary effects of Decision 187/2013), had already introduced the break clause to address the Court's rejection of this contribution. That provision was never brought to the CC for review however.

37 For the same interpretation of the 2013 ruling on this contribution, see Miguel Nogueira de Brito, "Putting Social Rights in Brackets? The Portuguese Experience with Welfare Challenges in Times of Crisis," In Claire Kilpatrick and Bruno De Witte (eds.), *Social Rights in Times of Crisis in the Eurozone: The Role of Fundamental Rights' Challenges*, EUI Working Papers (2014). Available at http://cadmus.eui.eu/handle/1814/31247 (Accessed November 16, 2017), 75.

In the assessment of these measures the importance of the crisis only allowed the cuts of pension supplements. According to the reasoning of the Court, the crisis context would have had enough weight to allow for another re-enactment of the 2011 cuts threshold, but not the new more aggravated one. As detailed above, the legal technique employed by the legislature in the 2014 Budget prevented the Court from expressly clearing the cuts up to the threshold previously ruled admissible.

Importantly, the Court invoked Article 282(4) of the constitution and ruled that all its constitutional decisions in this case would only have prospective effect. Because the decision was issued on May 30, this meant that the 2014 law's budgetary cuts that had been in force for almost half the fiscal year would not be retroactively altered. The fact that no suspension of effects was issued for the period after the Court's decision created a serious problem for the government, for it was forced to pay the entire wages subsequently until a new cuts scheme was put to force. The new cuts scheme would give rise to another a priori review request (Decision 574/2014). This ruling again met strong criticism from political actors. Prime Minister Passos Coelho, a few days after the ruling was made public, affirmed that the CC judges were "poorly chosen" and lacked legitimacy to strike down democratically adopted decisions.[38]

DECISION 572/2014 (EXTRAORDINARY SOLIDARITY CONTRIBUTION). The 2014 Budget maintained the Extraordinary Solidarity Contribution (CES).[39] This cut to pensions had been successively enforced since 2011, although the legal design was subject to several amendments. In 2014, CES was again enacted with another redefined design following Decision 862/2013: these new cuts were now applicable to monthly pensions above 1,000 euros, with rates that ranged from 2 percent to 40 percent. The cuts were temporary, mainly justified by the need to comply with the international obligation to reduce public debt and deficit and to attain short-term sustainability of the social security system. Consistent with its previous analysis on Decision 187/2013 (Budget Law 2013), the Court upheld the special contribution against a challenge that it undermined the principle of the protection of legitimate expectations. The judges justified their conclusion, claiming that the measures were temporary and necessary to comply with budgetary consolidation.

DECISION 575/2014 (SPECIAL SUSTAINABILITY CONTRIBUTION). This a priori review request envisaged the introduction of a *special sustainability contribution* on pensions paid by social protection systems as a legislative attempt to deal with the consequences of Decision 862/2013. The affected pensions were not clearly determined in the bill, and the Court concluded that it comprised pensions paid by three public entities, including the one responsible for paying lawyers and solicitors. The

[38] Available at www.tsf.pt/portugal/justica/interior/passos-coelho-diz-que-juizes-do-constitucional-tem-de-ser-mais-bem-escolhidos-3955293.html.

[39] Fully abolished under the 2017 Budget.

goal was to replace the CES (the mechanism that upheld the cuts for pensioners) by applying permanent cuts at lower rates. The government claimed that the mechanism was vital to the long-term sustainability of the social security system, was founded on intergenerational justice demands, and addressed commitments derived from budgetary discipline in view of EU law and eurozone demands.

The Court rejected a violation of the right to a pension and of the prohibition of regression, ascribing particular relevance to the economic and budgetary commitments arising from the adoption of public policies that were binding upon the Portuguese Republic, and to the intergenerational justice principle. However, the Court refused to consider the measure as part of a structural reform aimed at the fulfillment of the constitutional mandate for convergence of the pensions systems. Since it excluded private pension schemes, the Court qualified the new mechanism as a mere permanent cut.

Then the Court addressed the wider context of EU law and developed a thorough analysis of the EU framework on EDP. It also analyzed the formal nature of the Fiscal Stability Treaty, concluding that the Treaty is not EU law and, as such, is not governed by Article 8(4) of the constitution,[40] and that it is only valid as long as it is compatible with EU primary and secondary law. The Court also stressed the fact that Portugal was bound to reach a 2.5 percent deficit of GDP in 2015, in order to abide with recommendations made by the European Council under the EDP that was still pending.

Applying these principles, the Court concluded that such framework only detailed the final budgetary goals to be reached, and not the public policies that the legislature should adopt. So, the nature of the complex framework applicable, combining both EU and International law, had no consequence for the court's constitutional review. On the contrary,

> in a multilevel constitutional system, in which several legal orders interact, the national norms must necessarily conform with the Constitution (being the Constitutional Court's task to administer justice in legal constitutional matters – Article 221). Furthermore, EU law establishes the principle that the Union respects the national identity of its member states, reflected in their fundamental political and constitutional structures (Article 4(2) TEU). Finally, there is not even any divergence between EU law and Portuguese Constitutional law. In fact, the constitutional principles of the protection of legitimate expectations that have been the Constitutional Court's parameter to review national norms akin to those currently under appreciation are part of the legal common European patrimony, to which the Union is also bound.
>
> . . . we stress again that it is the indeclinable task of the Portuguese Constitutional Court to exercise its jurisdiction in accordance with Article 221 of the Constitution.

40 According to Article 8(4) of the Portuguese constitution, "The provisions of the treaties that govern the European Union and the norms issued by its institutions in the exercise of their respective competences are applicable in Portuguese internal law in accordance with Union law and with respect for the fundamental principles of a democratic state based on the rule of law."

After summarizing the operative principles that govern the interaction of Portuguese and EU law, the Court proceeded to the constitutional review of the challenged measures. It concluded that they were not part of any *structural reform* and that they generated savings gains akin to the *convergence system* that had been previously struck down in Decision 862/2013. The measure was not deemed adequate to solve any intergenerational justice problem since it was not framed within a consistent, coherent, and reliable reform. Furthermore, and in view of its particularly intrusive character since it affected pensions already in payment, the Court said that the legislature was under a special burden to justify the need to adopt such a harsh measure. Since it had not done so, the Court concluded that the protection of legitimate expectations had been breached.

DECISION 574/2014 (PAY-CUTS V. 1). This decision was delivered on the same day of Decision 575/2014 and was also based on a request for prior review. Following the Decision on the 2014 Budget, the government rapidly sought to find an alternative, since the Court had not suspended the effects of the unconstitutionality ruling. The new legislative proposal sent to the parliament included pay-cuts for public workers that closely mirrored the 2011 cuts that had been previously upheld by the Court. Full cuts were to apply until the end of 2014, after which only 80 percent of the reductions would go into effect for 2015. The cuts threshold for 2016, 2017, and 2018 were left to later determination.

The Court rejected the argument that the cuts would violate the principle of protection of legitimate expectations, since there were no reasonably grounded expectations of a full recovery of salaries by the end of 2014. The Court also restated the constitutional principles governing international and EU law that it had provided in Decision 575/2014.

The Court cleared the pay-cuts for the remainder of 2014 and 2015, considering that Portugal was under an EDP. However, these strict conditionalities would not justify a similar decision for the 2016/18 period where the emergency context would not apply, and the Court declared the norm partially unconstitutional, for violation of the principle of "proportional equality."[41]

DECISION 576/2015 (PAY-CUTS V. 2). A request filed by the Ombudsman challenged the constitutionality of the pay-cuts reviewed in Decision 574/2014 as applied to wholly or partially state-owned companies. The Ombudsman claimed that the cuts violated the proportionality principle insofar as there was no requirement that the employers deliver the savings owing to the cuts to the State. Taking account of the State Budget Reports, the Court concluded that the legislature had opted to allocate the savings derived from these measures to an increase in those companies' levels of financial self-sustainability. As such, the Court decided there was an

[41] The pay-cuts were fully abolished by the new Socialist government at the end of 2016.

adequate relationship between the pay-cuts and the goal underlying the restriction such that proportionality review was satisfied.

DECISION 3/2016 (LIFELONG ALLOWANCES[42]). At the request of a group of parliamentarians, the CC found unconstitutional the provision of the 2014 Budget that concerned lifelong monthly allowances awarded to former holders of political office. The provision would have suspended the allowance if the beneficiary earned another average monthly income above 2,000 euros, and diminished the allowance to the extent the sum of it and any other income exceeded 2,000 euros. The Court held that these allowances did not enjoy the protection of any fundamental right, but concluded that the provision breached the principle of the protection of legitimate expectations, since the legislature had fed legitimate hopes that these benefits – where they had already been ascribed – would not be eliminated, and the affected individuals had made their life plans accordingly. The financial crisis argument was easily rejected for two reasons: first, because in 2015 the FEAP had already been successfully concluded, notwithstanding the fact that an EDP was still pending; second, because the reduction in public expenditure achieved with the cuts was insignificant compared with the sacrifice imposed on the affected individuals.

IV. REVIEWING THE AUSTERITY CONSTITUTIONAL CASE LAW

It is now possible to provide a retrospective and global analysis of the case law. Extensive national and international literature has already dealt with this subject. However, none of the works has focused on the entire bulk of decisions from a critical perspective. Either by analyzing the case law relating to a specific topic (usually, pay-cuts for public workers), or by focusing on individual decisions, those contributions, although highly valuable, run the risk of missing the whole picture.

1. *Legal, Social, and Political Polarization*

The austerity period in Portugal was one of profound instability and social division[43] that reflected and certainly contributed to the increasing polarization of the constitutional case law, both internally and externally: internally, half of the decisions

42 A review request made by the Ombudsman on the constitutionality of permanent cuts to these allowances is still pending.

43 As in other countries, the crisis and the political responses to its demands sparked strong social mobilizations. Of a total of ten general strikes since 1974, four were held during this period (November 24, 2011; March 22 and November 14, 2012; and January 27, 2013). Large demonstrations also prevented the government from adopting some proposed austerity measures, such as an increase in the public and private workers' contribution to the social security system (TSU), matched by a decrease in the employer's contribution. Since the constitutional case law hindered some of the austerity policies, strong positive reactions to the Court's options were expressed during the demonstrations, some of them even contemplating stopping by its headquarters as a sign of gratitude.

have been adopted by the narrowest majority possible (seven to six majorities). This polarization was an extension of the societal and political instability and tensions. Externally, the case law sparked a much-heated academic debate that was not confined to the usual academia colloquia or writings.[44] Though the Portuguese CC began as a relatively unknown actor, it rose to stardom overnight, having made news on front pages across the world and receiving public attention not only within Portugal but internationally.[45]

Outside of its published opinions, the Court stayed mostly silent, though the tone of the decisions became more aggressive over time. Courts mostly speak through their holdings and legal reasoning, providing legal answers to the disputes in individual cases or procedures. But there are other formal contexts in which courts sometimes can communicate their views concerning outcomes or society's reactions to their decisions. Those contexts include judges' participation in legal debates or exchange platforms, which sometimes involve the drafting of reports that might provide relevant information regarding the matters, even if they do not, formally speaking, express the official position of the Court.

The report presented by the Court to the III Assembly of Constitutional Jurisdictions of Portuguese Speaking Countries in June 2014 is worth mentioning in this regard. When answering a question about whether pressures had ever been imposed on the Court by other state powers on the adjudication of fundamental rights, the Court alluded to "the creation of an environment akin to forcing the Court – rather than the executive or the legislature – to shoulder the burden of a possible non-compliance with the commitments foreseen in the international program of financial assistance."[46]

2. *The "Constitutional Risks" and Lack of Inter-Branch Dialogue*

The unconstitutionality rulings concerning some provisions of the Budgets for 2012 to 2014 created serious problems for the government. As regards the 2013 Budget, for

44 Gonçalo de Almeida Ribeiro and Luís Pereira Coutinho (eds.), *O Tribunal Constitucional e a Crise: Ensaios Críticos* (Coimbra: Almedina, 2014); Jorge Reis Novais, *Em Defesa do Tribunal Constitucional: Resposta aos Críticos* (Coimbra: Almedina, 2014).

45 Durão Barroso, then President of the EC, called upon the "responsibility" of all sovereign organs and the entire society. An internal memorandum of the EC that was leaked to the press dramatically raised the question: "Will the Constitutional Court put at risk the MOU implementation?," www.tsf.pt/storage/ng2823480.pdf (Accessed November 16, 2017). An unidentified member of the Eurogroup labeled the Portuguese Constitutional Court "activist," www.tvi24.iol.pt/economia–economia/constitucional-tc-eurogrupo-plano-b-chumbo-medidas/1497072–6377.html (Accessed November 16, 2017). International and national media described the CC, in general, as "activist" and a serious hazard to the country's ability to cope with the demands of the crisis.

46 See João Pedro Caupers and Bárbara Churro, *III Assembleia da Conferência das Jurisdições Constitucionais dos Países de Língua Portuguesa – Jurisdição constitucional e proteção dos direitos fundamentais*, "Relatório do Tribunal Constitucional de Portugal" (2014) 47. Available at www.tribunalconstitucional.pt/tc/content/files/conferencias/cjcplp_3_relatorioportugal.pdf (Accessed November 16, 2017).

example, the government was faced with the nullification of provisions aiming at reducing public expenditure in the middle of the fiscal year. This led to the inclusion of legal safeguards in the eighth and ninth updates to the MoU that were designed to avoid additional unconstitutionality decisions.[47] These preventive measures included justifying the legislation with the compliance of the Fiscal Compact and the principles of public/private sector and intergenerational equity, as well as the resort to general legislation (and not one-year budget laws). Although lacking legal teeth, as the MoU was considered a broad policy guideline document, these safeguards had a strong symbolic meaning. They were a direct reaction to the rulings on the 2012 and 2013 budgets, as well as on the imposition of dismissals and redeployments on the public sector.[48] The government, facing the difficulties raised by the CC's rulings, sought refuge in the lenders. The possibility of prior constitutional reviews to obtain clear and swift answers in case of constitutional issues was also advocated, and led to Decisions 574 and 575/2014.

The "constitutional risk"[49] was a contentious issue and it clearly became a visible element of the legislative and political dynamics. Indeed, the then Head of the IMF Mission, Subir Lall, allegedly claimed that if a second bailout were ever necessary, the country would seriously need to consider a constitutional amendment.[50]

The Court also displayed unwillingness to enter a productive dialogue with the legislator to reach acceptable expenditure reduction measures. Claiming that it was not its constitutional function to detail hypothetical effective measures that might comply with the MoU demands, the Court also provided unclear arguments, sometimes inducing the legislator into the wrong path. The most obvious example is the 2013 and 2014 Budget decisions on the contribution on sickness and unemployment benefits. Moreover, regarding the cuts, the legislature tried unsuccessfully to present acceptable designs to please the judges' demands. The persistent failure (as evidenced by the unconstitutionality rulings in Decisions 353/2012, 187/2013, and 413/2014) shows that, in fact, although the Court always claimed, in obiter dicta, that sacrifices imposed upon public workers were in general permitted, the maximum threshold of such sacrifices had already been reached by the 2011 cuts. The fact that it neither clearly admitted nor provided useful alternatives to the legislature (the Court only generally suggested a vague "special tax" or a stronger resort to universal

47 See paras. 9 and 7, respectively.

48 See Miguel Nogueira de Brito, "Putting Social Rights in Brackets? The Portuguese Experience with Welfare Challenges in Times of Crisis." In Claire Kilpatrick and Bruno De Witte (eds.), *Social Rights in Times of Crisis in the Eurozone: The Role of Fundamental Rights' Challenges*, EUI Working Papers (2014), pp. 70–71. Available at http://cadmus.eui.eu/handle/1814/31247 (Accessed November 16, 2017).

49 The "constitutional risk" was first elaborated by Almeida Ribeiro, who asserted that the case law was "unpredictable." See Gonçalo de Almeida Ribeiro, "Judicial Activism Against Austerity in Portugal," Int'l J. Const. L. Blog, Dec. 3, 2013. Available at: www.iconnectblog.com/2013/12/judicial-activism-against-austerity-in-portugal/.

50 At www.publico.pt/2015/03/05/politica/noticia/chefe-de-missao-do-fmi-pediu-revisao-constitucional-para-renovar-memorando-1688164 (Accessed November 16, 2017).

measures, something that was also rejected in 2013) signals a weak understanding of the role of constitutional adjudication arguments as dialogic-inducing mechanisms. The government was basically left to argue alone, facing a CC that remained intangible. This eventually led the government, in cooperation with the parliament, to draft a clarification request to the CC following the decision on the 2014 Budget.[51] The Court, however, found that request inadmissible, claiming that it was not its role to guide the legislature and the executive regarding the implementation of unconstitutionality rulings.[52]

3. *"Nationalization" of the Crisis and EU Law: "The Elephant in the Room"*

At the beginning of the financial assistance period, the bailout documents and the measures that implemented the loan conditionalities were perceived as national commitments, undertaken voluntarily by political forces. This is true not only for the Court, but also on a broader societal level. Several factors contributed to this "nationalization process," and the clear and explicit support of the newly elected coalition in 2011 to the bailout program was surely one of them. That was a crucial factor to shape the way austerity was perceived internally: it was mainly regarded as the result of internal options, and any rejection of those options should be blamed on national actors. This was also a crucial factor for the outcome of some of the CC's reactions: the conflict was always framed as a national matter, between the national legislature and the national court.

Undoubtedly, although the Court acknowledged the eurozone crisis, it always stressed the national character of austerity, and the margin of discretion of the national legislator to reach the memoranda's goals.

Furthermore, particularly in Decision 353/2012, as the Court considered the MoU to be founded upon Article 122 of the TFEU,[53] before ruling on the unconstitutionality of the national provisions, insofar as they translated the implementation into national law of positive obligations derived from an EU law act, there was only one of two paths for the Court to take:[54] first, to question the validity of the MoU under EU

[51] Allegedly pushed by the European Commission. See www.publico.pt/2014/06/04/politica/noticia/governo-forca-recurso-para-tc-com-artigo-que-preve-nulidade-do-acordao-1638590 (Accessed March 9, 2018).

[52] Decision 468/2014.

[53] The effective legal nature of the FEAP program and its documents is highly contested. However, the fact is that in Decision 353/2012 the Court recognized the MoU as EU law. The importance of EU law to the adjudication at stake was only sidestepped by the fact that the measures under evaluation were considered as purely national policies, exclusively decided by the national legislature. That is in line with the broader *nationalization of the crisis* that predominantly characterized the public discourses surrounding the bailout and its national consequences, at least in the first part of the program. That the austerity legislation implementing pay-cuts falls within the jurisdiction of the ECJ was later accepted by this court, although in the context of financial assistance for Member States not part of the eurozone, by the judgement of 13 June 2017, Case C-258/14, *Florescu* EU:C:2017:448. More recently, the ECJ accepted jurisdiction in a case of Portuguese austerity pay-cuts of judges but it avoided discussing whether or not these measures fell within the scope of EU law (judgment of 28 February 2018, Case 64/16, *Associação Sindical dos Juízes Portugueses* EU:C:2018:117).

[54] This was pointedly highlighted by Pereira Coutinho, "Austerity on the loose in Portugal: European judicial restraint in times of crisis," fn. X.

law before the ECJ on a preliminary reference order; second, to question the compatibility of the MoU with the Portuguese constitution (this jurisdiction would only be claimed by the Court much later, on the first two decisions delivered after the FEAP ended).

That the Court had not been expressly requested to rule on the compatibility of the MoU with the constitution – thus lacking jurisdiction to make such a judgment – cannot adequately explain why it did not do so. After all, the national budgetary provisions were expressly grounded on the FEAP. Furthermore, the Court is not limited to the arguments provided by the parties, according to the principle *iura novit curia*. Taking into account the normative connection between the Budget Law provisions and the MoU – since this document had, in aspects such as this, a parametric character in relation to the national norms (i.e. its content strongly induced and commanded the national policies that should be adopted) – the Court could have considered assessing the constitutionality of the MoU under Article 8(4) as long as the national norms were specifically determined by that document.[55]

This is the elephant in the room that was there all along, and whose presence the Court itself strengthened in its 353/2012 ruling: the role of EU law regarding austerity legislation and its relationship with national constitutional law. This elephant haunted the ensuing decisions in different ways. Decision 602/2013 is noteworthy, since the Court acknowledged the importance of the MoU as the inducer of the Labor Code revision of 2012 but made no reference to the nature of the memoranda, namely the MoU. If the Court's view on this matter had not been altered,[56] then it should have again contemplated either a reference to the ECJ or the consequences of dealing with Article 8(4) on the value of EU law regarding national constitutional law.

The Court has only expressly considered the relationship between EU law and the national legal order, particularly Portuguese constitutional law and the relevance of Article 8(4) of the constitution, in its review of austerity measures in the first two decisions delivered after the end of the bailout program (Decisions 574 and 575/2014). To this day, the Court has never effectively ruled on the relationship between EU law and national constitutional law in accordance with Article 8(4) of the constitution. And it remains one of the few European constitutional courts that has never ordered a preliminary reference to the ECJ. Yet these are all very basic, foundational questions that must be squarely addressed.

55 Recently, the CC recognized its own competence to rule on the validity of norms that, despite not having been included in the request, are in a parametrical relation to the object of the case (Decision 176/2017). This means that in these cases, although it had not been asked to review the constitutionality of the MoU, the Court's jurisdiction was confirmed as long as that document commanded the national legislation content. A further jurisdiction problem would be, then, the relation between EU law and national constitutional law that might prevent the Court from ruling on that issue, forcing the judges to refer a preliminary reference to the ECJ.

56 In July and September 2012, the composition of the Court was substantially changed.

This silent strategy may be regarded, ex post facto, as a wise move by the CC in preventing any possible clash between the national constitutional legal order and EU law (and, subsequently, between the CC and the ECJ).[57] It can also be claimed that the CC's case law had the paradoxical effect of shielding the national legislator from the growing demands of the creditors.[58] However, these retrospective analyses overshadow the fundamental fact that the Court qualified the austerity measures as *indeed* national options, adopted in a crisis context.

The fact that the Court only openly acknowledged the relevance of EU law after the FEAP was concluded gives credit to the interpretation that the Court was trying to avoid an open confrontation with the European judicial system. Consider the possible outcome of a preliminary reference order. The first possible outcome might be a rejection of the order based on its inadmissibility, e.g. on the basis that the case concerned exclusively national law and the EU law threshold was not met. Although this might have been an unlikely reaction from the EU court (as it would show a clear refusal to enter into dialogue with the supreme Portuguese court), the fact is that the ECJ, on a first moment, declined jurisdiction over austerity measures.[59] Another hypothesis is that the ECJ would have accepted the legislation by rejecting incompatibility with EU law, namely the Charter of Fundamental Rights and any of its social rights. That would put the Portuguese court in a perilous situation, trapped between a constitutional clause that enshrines superiority of EU law unless it violates a "fundamental principle of the democratic rule of law" and its shy legitimacy to stand up to an open confrontation with the ECJ.

This insulation feature is also noticeable regarding internal and external matters of fact that shaped the crisis' context, and its influence on how the Court dealt with the crisis as a de facto situation. In Decision 187/2013, the Court's deference to the legislator on the grounds of the economic and financial situation decreased, following the track of Decision 353/2012.[60] In the words of the Court, "the reasons [invoked by the legislator to ground the urgency of this type of measures] are now less

57 As Maduro, Frada and Pierdominici wrote, "the Constitutional Court may be trying to avoid an open conflict between what it itself understands to be the right interpretation of those principles under the national constitution and what it might be a different interpretation of the European Court of Justice." See Miguel Poiares Maduro, António Frada and Leonardo Pierdominici, "A Crisis Between Crises: Placing the Portuguese Jurisprudence of Crisis in Context," *epública Revista Eletrónica de Direito Público*, 4(1): 23 (2017).

58 As suggested in Roberto Cisotta and Daniele Gallo, "The Portuguese Constitutional Court Case Law on Austerity Measures: A Reappraisal." In Claire Kilpatrick and Bruno De Witte (eds.), *Social Rights in Times of Crisis in the Eurozone: The Role of Fundamental Rights' Challenges*, EUI Working Papers, 2014/05. Available at http://cadmus.eui.eu/handle/1814/31247.

59 ECJ 7 March 2013, Case C-128/12, *Sindicato dos Bancários do Norte and Others v BPN – Banco Português de Negócios SA* EU:C:2013:149; ECJ 26 June 2014, Case C-264/12, *Sindicato Nacional dos Profissionais de Seguros e Afins v Fidelidade Mundial — Companhia de Seguros SA* EU:C:2014:2036; ECJ 21 October 2014, Case C-665/13, *Sindicato Nacional dos Profissionais de Seguros e Afins v Via Directa — Companhia de Seguros SA* EU:C:2014:2327.

60 In the words of a former constitutional judge, "it was not the case law of the Constitutional Court that changed from 2011 to 2012; it was the austerity measures that became harsher." See Ana Maria Guerra

convincing than they were in earlier budgetary periods." The pressure upon the legislature to find other alternatives to cope with the adjustment program needs became stronger from 2012 onwards.

In fact, the Court seemed to claim for a better demonstration of the financial emergency: that same one that, in 2010 and 2011, and in relation to measures approved *before* the bailout, was a "notorious fact." This is at odds with the course of things at the European level, where 2011 and 2012 became known as *anni horribili* and a profound mutation of the European economic constitution was under way.

The Court's analysis in Decision 187/2013 failed to properly take account of changed facts on the ground. The main ground for unconstitutionality in this decision was the principle of "proportional equality," a test that, in the Court's words, can only be assessed within the concrete context. This context assessed the cumulating effects of the sacrifice level but was shy on the evaluation of the constitutional reality that induced a strong compression of the legislator's margin of discretion. In the EU, particularly in the eurozone, the situation was worsening, and Portugal had already ratified[61] the Fiscal Stability Treaty. Internally, the government faced serious social opposition to the approval of restrictive measures that carried a universal nature.[62] Externally, the eurozone was on the verge of collapsing. The Court's decision to ignore the well-known deterioration of the internal and external conditions was at odds with its previous willingness to assess the crisis context as a "public and notorious fact."

4. *Isolation of the Constitutional Case Law*

The isolationist posture of the Court is reflected in the fact that it hardly seeks inspiration for its decisions in the case law of other countries facing similar situations, and the fact that comparative law does not play any role in the judicial argumentation. This is in sharp contrast with the widely appraised generosity of the Portuguese constitutional case law to resort to comparative law whenever a hard case comes to play.[63]

In Decisions 399/2010 and 396/2011, the Court refers to similar or more severe measures adopted in other countries as a mere obiter dictum. However, by then some European constitutional courts had already ruled on temporary pay-cuts of

Martins, "Constitutional Judge, Social Rights and Public Debt Crisis – The Portuguese Constitutional Case Law," *Maastricht Journal of European and Comparative Law*, 22(5): 682 (2015). This shows that the Court's perspective was focused exclusively on the measures without balancing their aggravation with the worsening internal and external conditions.

61 Portugal was the first country to approve the Fiscal Stability Treaty. The golden rule was introduced in the Budgetary Framework Law which enjoys a special reinforced position with infra-constitutional value (Law 37/2013, 14 June).

62 See the TSU failure, n. 43.

63 See Teresa Violante, "A adjudicação constitucional e o direito comparado," *Teoria da argumentação e neoconstitucionalismo – Um conjunto de perspetivas* (Coimbra: Almedina, 2011), 337–59.

public workers at even higher rates.[64] For a country that stands from the crowd when it comes to including foreign elements and making use of comparative law in its decisions, this was an unexpected option that shows the isolationism underlying the case law.

5. *Real Judicial Activism?*

Several critics accused the CC of being activist through the employment of the principle of proportional equality, an alleged distorted version of the *neue Formel*. However, the adjudication of the crisis based on the equality principle did not have a positive effect on legislation, meaning there was no legislative creation therein, and that can be an indicator that the case law was not activist.[65]

The adjudication under the equality principle has made use of a stricter level of scrutiny that reduced the legislator's margin of discretion. Some scholars claim that this stricter level of scrutiny abandoned established jurisprudence on the adjudication under the equality principle.[66] It is arguably questioned whether the option for a more intense level of scrutiny is the best judicial option when the restrictive measures are explicitly temporary and there are sharp political divisions as to how states should cope with the financial crisis.

However, is the adoption of a stricter scrutiny level a truly distinctive feature of the Portuguese austerity case law? The Court showed more deference to the legislator's choices regarding universal measures (particularly tax rises), which is consistent with judicial implementation of the principle of equality regarding a fair share of burdens. This scrutiny involves a rational basis review that prevents the Court from undue intrusions on the legislature's choices. The Court has applied stricter levels of scrutiny in other areas, for example when reviewing measures that burdened certain categories of individuals. For the judges, the stricter scrutiny was justified either because of the vulnerability of the individuals at stake or the accumulation of sacrifices that fell on a particular category of workers.

The case law of the Court was, in fact, despite all the public attention, the typical exercise of countermajoritarianism by the constitutional jurisdiction, something that can hardly be labelled as spectacular or extraordinary. One thing is worth mentioning, though: as any court, the CC acts upon request, and some of the rulings

64 On June 25, 2010, the Romanian Constitutional Court accepted a 25 percent cut in public-sector wages. Three days earlier, the Latvian Constitutional Court had ruled a 15 percent cut on judicial wages unconstitutional, and suspended the effects of its decision until 1 January 2011.

65 Empirical analysis of the judicial behaviour of the Court during the crisis also found no evidence of any increased judicial activism. See Susana Coroado, Nuno Garoupa and Pedro Magalhães, "Judicial Behavior under Austerity: An Empirical Analysis of Behavioral Changes in the Portuguese Constitutional Court, 2002–2016," *Journal of Law and Courts* 5(2): 289–311 (2017).

66 See Ravi Afonso Pereira, "Igualdade e proporcionalidade: um comentário às decisões do Tribunal Constitucional de Portugal sobre cortes salariais no setor público," *Revista Española de Derecho Constitucional*, 98: 317–70 (2013).

were prompted by the President of the Republic, Cavaco Silva, a former leader of the main ruling party. It is clear that contestation of austerity was politically and socially broad and the government faced serious opposition even from its ideological side.

V. OVERALL CONCLUSIONS

From the description we have provided, it is fair to conclude that the Court's reaction to austerity legislation was complex and multi-tiered, and that the emergency crisis context was duly considered by the Court. However, that does not mean that it was either oblivious to the stringent pressures pending upon the legislature, nor that it declined its role as the fundamental guardian of the constitution. According to the typology developed by Contiades,[67] the Portuguese constitution, and its CC, *adjusted* to the requirements of the financial crisis: several restrictive measures encroaching on fundamental rights such as the right to pay or the right to a pension were allowed by the Court. This approval was twofold: on the one hand, the judges recognized the financial emergency context that demanded urgent and constricting measures to guarantee the country's solvability in the long run and the abidance with international commitments; on the other hand, the constitution was not suspended, nor was any unwritten state of financial exception developed or accepted by the case law. In fact, the Court easily allowed the legislature to slash labor costs, both directly and indirectly. That was visible concerning not only public workers (who were subject to both direct and indirect cuts) but also private workers (who mainly suffered indirect cuts).

The crisis context surfaces in the Court's jurisprudence mainly in three ways: (i) as a consideration relevant to its legitimate expectations analysis; (ii) as a demonstration of the notorious public interest underlying some restrictive policies and their adequacy to deal with a financial emergency context; and (iii) a justification for setting aside the usual *ex nunc* nullity that follows from the Court's unconstitutionality decisions under abstract review.[68]

The financial crisis demanded judicial interpretation adjusted to the circumstances; but it did not impose a continued deferential or self-restrained judicial attitude towards the legislature and the executive. The constitution kept its role as the supreme law of the land and the CC enforced its full jurisdiction as the main gatekeeper of fundamental rights. In a period where external pressure upon the Court was at its highest point in history, this is no small achievement. The fact that the Court not only kept but enhanced its social legitimacy all the way is perhaps the most remarkable aspect that fascinates commentators to this day.

This does not mean that criticism of the case law is unjustified. At some points the judges are to blame for failing to provide sufficient guidance to the legislature in times where the uncertainty was only matched in its intensity by the need to adapt

67 Xenophon Contiades, *Constitutions in the Global Financial Crisis – A Comparative Analysis* (Surrey: Ashgate, 2013), 5.

68 See Art. 282(1)(5) of the constitution.

and react swiftly to the increasing deterioration in the financial and economic scenarios. Constitutional judges are also to blame for a persistent refusal to engage in a productive dialogue with the legislature as the proper interpretation of the separation of powers should demand in a constitutional democracy. To their credit, the fact is that the government mostly opted to react to the case law by exerting external pressure on the Court, instead of focusing its energies on drafting the legislation "in such a way that it [might] withstand judicial evaluation."[69] That is evidenced by the late joining of the government's "technical note" during the proceedings for Decision 474/2013 (public workers requalification) or the executive's persistent failure to set in motion structural reforms of the pensions systems and the public administration's pay scheme.

The Court's unwillingness to enter dialogue with the legislature, along with the arguments on the binding character of the memoranda and the EU law nature of the MoU, at the same time that it affirmed its irrelevance due to the exclusively national character of the austerity measures,[70] together with the inability to assess the constitutional challenges in light of the aggravating national and European contexts, are perhaps the strongest criticisms to be made on the constitutional case law arising from the crisis.

For our purposes, however, a clear-cut conclusion should be put forward: even under a severe economic and financial crisis, the constitution has displayed a constraining force on the legislature's margin of political discretion, grounding the invalidation of several internationally negotiated or imposed measures and forcing the political branches to find alternatives to cope with the creditors' demands. It is not fair to say, however, that such context was irrelevant to the decision-making process: the fact remains that several temporary and permanent restrictions were cleared by the Court, precisely because of the crisis context, thus allowing for political reforms that would not have been possible otherwise.

69 Xenophon Contiades and Alkmene Fotiadou, "How Constitutions Reacted to the Financial Crisis." In Contiades, Xenophon (ed.), *Constitutions in the Global Financial Crisis – A Comparative Analysis* (Surrey: Ashgate, 2013), 12

70 Particularly evident in Decision 353/2012.

13

Constitutional Resilience and Constitutional Failure in the Face of Crisis: The Greek Case

Xenophon Contiades and Alkmene Fotiadou[*]

I. INTRODUCTION: CONSTITUTIONAL CHANGE AND FINANCIAL CRISIS

From the moment the global financial crisis broke out, the question of how constitutions respond to such crises has troubled constitutional scholars, especially in the countries most affected by it.[1] Two issues are central: are constitutions impacted by the financial crisis, and do they play a role in addressing it?

Constitutional change has occurred if one of three criteria is met: (a) formal constitutional change ranging from total revisions to modifications and adjustments, (b) informal change brought about by novel judicial interpretations of the constitution or by political practice, and (c) changes in the functions of the constitution affecting constitutional normativity and constitutional faith.[2] Among these, the detection of changes to the 'small-c' constitution through informal change is the most challenging. Tracking down such changes requires distinguishing between narratives of rule of law violation and genuine violations, and analysing jurisprudence in light of previous judicial doctrine. These tasks can only be performed with reference to the constitutional culture in place. Informal constitutional change often consists of subtle incremental changes that are quite difficult to monitor in real time.

The Greek constitution did not undergo any formal change during, or in the immediate aftermath of, the crisis. Early on, strong calls for constitutional reform emerged. The impression left at the time was that the chief impediment to such reforms were the strict amendment procedures, which impose a mandatory time

* Xenophon Contiades, Professor of Public Law, Panteion University of Social and Political Sciences (Athens, Greece) and Managing Director of the Centre for European Constitutional Law.
Alkmene Fotiadou, Dr.iur. and Research Associate at the Centre for European Constitutional Law (Athens, Greece).

1 X. Contiades (ed.), *Constitutions in the Global Financial Crisis: A Comparative Analysis* (Ashgate, 2013).

2 X. Contiades and A. Fotiadou, 'How Constitutions Reacted to the Financial Crisis' in Contiades (ed.), *Constitutions in the Global Financial Crisis* (n. 1) 9–59.

lapse between revisions. Constitutional revision in Greece is subject to very strict procedural limits set by Article 110 paragraphs 2–6 of the Greek constitution. It takes place in two phases, between which general elections are held. The revision process has no influence over the timing of general elections. During the first phase, the need for a constitutional revision is ascertained by resolution in parliament, adopted following the proposal of at least one-sixth of the members of parliament either by a three-fifths majority or by an absolute majority of its members in two ballots, held at least one month apart. This resolution specifies the provisions subject to revision. During the second phase, the next parliament amends the provisions specified by the previous parliament. If a proposal for amendment of the constitution receives an absolute majority of the votes of the total number of members, but not a three-fifths majority, the next parliament proceeds with the revision of the proposed provisions by a three-fifths majority of the total number of its members, and vice versa. Revision of the constitution is not permitted before the lapse of five years from the completion of a previous revision.

It thus appeared that due to the mandatory time lapse between revisions the revision process could not be initiated before May 2013. However, constitutional handcuffs[3] were not the problem. Even when the mandatory lapse date expired, no formal change was initiated. The amendment formula requires a degree of consensus that was difficult to achieve in conditions of polarization.

Thus, nothing happened until 25 July 2016, when the prime minister announced his intention to initiate revision of the constitution. The process he proposed for doing so included two innovations. First, the introduction of deliberative procedures, and, second, the potential for a constitutional referendum. A committee had already started to work on designing a deliberative process in December 2016. Although enhancing popular participation in constitutional amendment could bring the electorate closer to the constitution, rendering the participation provided for by the amendment mechanisms in place more meaningful, serious pitfalls exist. It is highly unlikely that the augmented consensus required by formal amendment rules shall be reached. There is thus a possibility of an impasse that will block formal change.

Another route to a constitutional revision put forward is to bypass the amendment formula. The possibility of a referendum on constitutional issues remains open. This route however is not provided for by the amendment formula that vests the amending power in parliament. The electorate takes part in the process through intervening elections; nonetheless, people in general elections vote taking into consideration a much broader political agenda than constitutional amendment proposals. Proclaiming a referendum on amendment proposals would lead to an unconstitutional constitutional amendment.[4] Such a development would be quite harmful to democratic institutions in a crisis-struck constitutional order and an environment of

[3] R. Albert, 'Constitutional Handcuffs' (2010) 42(3) *Ariz. St. L. J* .663.

[4] Y. Roznai, *Unconstitutional Constitutional Amendments: The Limits of Amendment Powers* (OUP, 2017).

deep political polarization, such as existed during and following the bailout referendum of July 2015. An unconstitutional amendment would be a clear indication of constitutional backslide.

As things stand in late 2017, the text of the Greek constitution remains unaltered. With respect to the first criterion of constitutional change, the answer is thus simple: the constitution endured. Nonetheless, the financial crisis induced a significant amount of informal constitutional change in Greece. Does such change qualify as a transition to a new constitutional order?[5] Is textual inertia a sign of constitutional resilience? Or is it the nature and substantive content of informal change that differentiates constitutional resilience from other constitutional responses to the stress-test of crisis?[6] Informal constitutional change triggered by the crisis affected different parts of the constitution. Throughout the financial crisis, a variety of actors applied, interpreted, by-passed, violated or changed structural provisions, the fiscal constitution, individual rights, social rights and general principles in different ways.

In this chapter, we provide an overview of the constitutional changes that resulted from the crisis in Greece. We focus on changes and shifts in the following areas: changes in jurisprudence and in the role of the judiciary, changes in the lawmaking process, and changes in the function of the political system.

II. THE FINANCIAL CRISIS JURISPRUDENCE: LITIGATION, BACKLASH AND THE ROLE OF THE JUDICIARY

1. *Judicial Review of Austerity Measures: From Self-Restraint to Judicial Activism?*

The Greek constitution includes numerous provisions referred to as the 'economic' and 'fiscal' constitution.[7] This made it inevitable that economic policies would be translated into constitutionality issues, and litigation would follow austerity measures.[8] Constitutional review was established in Greece earlier than in most European countries through two landmark cases of the Supreme Civil and Criminal Court, in 1871 and 1897, respectively. It was explicitly enshrined in the constitution of 1927. The current constitution provides for a decentralized system of constitutional review (Art. 93 para. 4 Gr. Const.), concentrated in practice to a great extent

5 M. Tushnet, 'Constitutional Hardball' (2004) 37 *J. Marshall L. Rev.* 523.

6 On the notion of 'constitutional resilience' see X. Contiades and A. Fotiadou, 'On Resilience of Constitutions: What Makes Constitutions Resistant to External Shocks?' (2015) 9(1) *ICL Journal* 3; X. Contiades and A. Fotiadou, 'The Resilient Constitution: Lessons from the Crisis' in A. Herwig, M. Simoncini (eds), *Law and the Management of Disasters: The Challenge of Resilience* (Routledge, 2017) 189–207.

7 See how such provisions often operate during financial crises in M. D. Rosen, 'Legislatures and Constitutions in Times of Severe Financial Crisis', Ch. 5 in this volume.

8 On the judicialization of austerity see R. D. Kelemen, 'Commitment for Cowards: Why the Judicialization of Austerity Is Bad Policy and Even Worse Politics', Ch. 8 in this volume.

(through jurisdictional mechanisms) in the three supreme courts (Art. 100 Const.). However, while there is a long history of constitutional review in Greece, the Greek judiciary had never taken the lead in constitutional change. Nonetheless, throughout the financial crisis, the judiciary was a key player in handling the strain posed by constitutional dilemmas.

The economic and fiscal provisions adopted in the constitution of 1975 are representative of an era when state interventionism was a still a prevailing trend in Europe, and fall within three basic categories:

a. Individual rights, such as the right to participate in economic life (Art. 5 para. 1), the right to engage in private economic initiative (Art. 106 para. 2), and the protection of private property (Art. 17).
b. Social rights, such as the right to work (Art. 22), freedom to unionize (Art. 23), the right to social security (Art. 22 para. 5), the right to health (Art. 21 para. 3), and the right to social welfare (Art. 21 paras 1, 2, 4). The 'welfare state principle' (enshrined in Art. 25 para. 1), and protection of human dignity (enshrined in Art. 2 para. 1), are also considered part of the Greek economic constitution.
c. The fiscal constitution, consisting of the constitutional principles governing the drafting and implementation of the state budget and fiscal laws (equality before public burdens enshrined in Art. 4 paras 1 and 5, and Arts 78–80, 98 and 102 para. 5).

The crisis jurisprudence in Greece can be roughly divided into two phases.[9] The first corresponds to the start of the financial crisis. During that phase, the constitutionality of international loan agreements was challenged, and judges were also asked to rule on the constitutionality of austerity measures. At this point, the judiciary – being reluctant to interfere in 'mega-politics' – demonstrated considerable self-restraint.[10] Decisions were carefully written to ensure that loan agreements were not put at risk. Judges made clear that it was the job of elected representatives to take fundamental decisions on how to respond to the crisis. Judgment 668/2012, which upheld the constitutionality of the first Memorandum of Understanding (2010), epitomises that tendency.[11]

The Council of State ruled that the first Memorandum was not an international treaty, but a political program that resulted from cooperation between the Greek government and the Troika, and that set targets to be achieved and policies to be implemented.[12] Therefore, the Court ruled, Article 28 of the constitution, which

9 For a comparative juxtaposition with Portuguese case law, see T. Violante and P. André, 'The Constitutional Performance of Austerity in Portugal', Ch. 12 in this volume.

10 See R. Hirschl, 'The Judicialization of Mega-Politics and the Rise of Political Courts' (2008) 11 *Ann. Rev. Pol. Sci.* 93.

11 To explore whether judicial self-restraint during crises is the expression of strong rather than weak courts, see M. Gulati and G. Vanberg, 'Financial Crises and Constitutional Compromise', in this volume.

12 X. Contiades and I. Tassopoulos, 'The Impact of the Financial Crisis on the Greek Constitution' in Contiades (ed.), *Constitutions in the Global Financial Crisis* (n. 1) 195.

regulates the transfer of sovereignty and competences following an international Treaty, was not applicable. The Council of State is competent to judge petitions for the annulment of administrative acts exercising ex post constitutional review in the context of a diffuse system of constitutionality review.[13] The Court indicated that it would decide on the constitutionality of specific measures taken toward implementation of the Memorandum upon enactment and went to review the specific measures brought before it, that is the cuts to salaries and allowances for employees in the public sector and the wider public sector and retirement benefits, introduced by Laws 3833/2010 and 3845/2010. According to the Court, measures taken in implementation of the first MoU are not disproportional, and do not violate the core content of the right to social security, legal certainty or Art.1 of the First Protocol to the ECHR. The Court held that the unexpected emergency, during which the measures were enacted, absolved the lawmaker from the obligation to conduct economic studies of their overall consequences and stressed that cuts were part of a broader program of fiscal adjustment and promotion of structural reforms of the Greek economy. In short, the Court showed deference to elected officials in its decision. Ruling differently would have signalled a remarkable departure from the Court's previous profile. With the exception of vigorous review in environmental cases, the Council of State had never been an activist court.

The second phase began when it became clear that the financial crisis was not merely an event, but a transition. Austerity measures would be challenged constantly, and the judiciary had to decide on the constitutionality of such measures. The courts began to play an important role in tackling the crisis, and much of this 'crisis' jurisprudence became a distinct feature of the constitutional response to the financial crisis. The fact that the Council had turned a corner towards a more activist role became apparent in Decision No. 1972/2012, which held that cutting of electricity to individuals who did not pay 'Special Property Contribution' constituted a violation of the right to property. In Decision No. 3354/2013, the Council of State held that the suspension of civil servants, if not decided in accordance with objective criteria, is an unconstitutional infringement on the principle of equality. In a judgment issued in May 2014,[14] the Council ruled that privatization of water in Athens was a violation of the constitutional right to health.[15]

Decisions dealing with pension and salary cuts were particularly sensitive, and have been subjected to severe criticism, including being inappropriately activist.

[13] On the Greek system of constitutional review, see X. Contiades and A. Fotiadou, 'The Hellenic Republic' in L. F. M. Besselink, P. P. T. Bovend'Eert, H. Broeksteeg, R. de Lange and W. Voermans (eds), *Constitutional Law of the EU Member States* (Kluwer Law International, 2014) 703–72.

[14] Judgment 1906/2014 of the Greek Council of State.

[15] The Council reversed the transfer of a controlling stake in the company from the State to the Hellenic Republic Asset Development Fund. According to the ruling, transferring water utilities from a state company to a private one, which does not operate on a non-profit basis, rendered the provision of accessible, high-quality water service too uncertain. Contiades and Fotiadou, see 'On Resilience of Constitutions' (n. 7).

In its case law with regard to public servants subject to 'special wage regimes' (including judges, diplomats, army and police personnel, and professors and teaching personnel of universities), the Court argued that the legislator should take into consideration the circumstances that justify categorization within a special payroll, and should not treat all categories alike without considering the special features of each. In Decision No. 2192/2014, the Court stressed that the discretion of the legislator to cut wages is limited by the principles of proportionality, equality in contributing to public expenditures, and respect for human dignity. In such decisions, the judiciary inevitably touched on distributional issues, that is, the question of who shall bear the burden of the austerity measures induced by the crisis.

In Decisions Nos 2287–2290/2015, the Council of State ruled that pension cuts introduced through laws implementing the second Memorandum[16] (2012) violated the fundamental right to social security. The Court decided that the constitution requires systematic analysis of the economic and social impact of cuts in supplementary pensions. As a result, the measures were found unconstitutional, because such analysis had not been conducted in advance. These decisions are characteristic of the turn toward judicial activism. The Court ruled that in the absence of an imminent threat of financial collapse, the pecuniary interest of the State is not the same as the general interest, that is the common good. This distinction, which appears often in the Court's crisis jurisprudence, holds that while the financial sustainability of the State can coincide with the common good during moments of acute crisis, the two concepts are distinct.

Another task for the Council of State was to find a way to abide by the rationale of the European Court of Human Rights (ECtHR) in *Meidanis* v. *Greece* (2008). In that decision the ECtHR had ruled that the different default interest rate applicable to public law legal entities and to individuals infringed on the applicant's right to the peaceful enjoyment of his possessions, enshrined in Article 1 of Protocol no. 1. According to the Court, 'the mere financial interest of a public corporation could not be considered as a public or general interest and could not justify the violation of a creditor's right to the peaceful enjoyment of his possessions caused by the impugned legislation'. The Council of State had to put forth a convincing rationale why financial interests could under specific circumstances fall within the notion of the general interest. It thus ruled that although mere financial interests do not qualify as the 'general interest', in extreme circumstances, where the danger of the state defaulting is imminent, financial interests may be considered as the general interest. In that sense the limitation of constitutional rights to serve financial interest can be justifiable. It must be noted that the ECtHR in *Koufaki and ADEDY (Supreme Administration of Greek Civil Servants Trade Unions)* v. *Greece* ruled that the reductions in salaries and pensions (made according to the first

[16] Available at http://ec.europa.eu/economy_finance/publications/occasional_paper/2012/pdf/ocp94_en.pdf.

Memorandum) are not in violation of the ECHR and are not disproportionate to the objective of handling acute fiscal crisis and the public financial reform in a way that will ensure the future.[17]

Crisis litigation is still unfolding. The Court's development of proportionality in novel directions may prove to be a resilient tool. A particular characteristic of the developing crisis jurisprudence is the elaboration of necessity as part of the exchange between lawmaker and judge. The necessity tier of proportionality acquired a life of its own, becoming one of the most basic tools for evaluating impugned measures. This new development links proportionality with a limited time factor, that is, the urgency of most measures, which left the lawmaker with limited time to consider their impact, and even less time for deliberation in parliament.

Still, the Court has insisted that the legislator is expected to pay due attention to the proportionality dictate of looking for alternatives that burden rights less. Courts demanded proof that the lawmaker studied, and took seriously, alternative measures and their potential impact. This rendered the second tier of proportionality a much more rigorous test, which created a specific obligation for the lawmaker to justify the choice of measures. Nonetheless, there may be pitfalls in decisions that repeatedly use the lack of detailed studies accompanying every piece of legislation. Becoming rule-like, this prerequisite could develop into a disguise for closet judicial activism. Thus, it is important for such rulings to include detailed and particularized use of proportionality, which can lead to narrow judgments.

Such ad hoc judgments, in the context of the financial crisis, limited rather than enhanced judicial discretion. This is the case because proportionality allowed the judiciary to exercise self-restraint by avoiding adoption of a predetermined stance in favour or against austerity measures. This was achieved through narrow, ad hoc holdings. This narrowness constitutes self-restraint, since the creation of rules in the context of a crisis would tie the hands of the lawmaker. Through the use of proportionality, judges chose to partner with the lawmaker in a dialogue, but refused to be the ultimate decision-maker. This potentiality of the necessity test is obvious in the aforementioned pension decisions that austerity legislation could be constitutionally permissible, provided such legislation included a detailed study of its impact, including actuarial calculations.

The ultimate criterion for resilient constitutional rights is whether they remain relevant during a crisis, and whether they bounce back in its aftermath. The key question is whether constitutional rights remain a basic consideration in the drafting of measures designed to address the crisis. Bouncing back entails the ability of the protective scope of rights to expand again after a crisis-induced shrinkage. Furthermore, if constitutional rights – despite their limitations or perhaps because of them – help to optimize constitutionalism during a crisis, they are resilient in

[17] *Koufaki Ioanna and ADEDY* v. *Greece* [2013] No. 57665 & 57657/2012. On the role of supranational courts during financial crises, see E. Brems, 'Protecting Fundamental Rights During Financial Crisis: Supranational Adjudication in the Council of Europe Context', Ch. 9 in this volume.

a sense. In that sense, mechanisms that add flexibility to constitutional rights are tools of constitutional resilience.[18]

2. *The TV Licensing Decision: A Case of Backlash-Consciousness?*

An important feature of the crisis case law is that it produced a backlash – a rather novel phenomenon in the Greek legal order. Backlash-consciousness thus became part of the judicial attitude toward the financial crisis. Apart from the jurisprudence dealing with the fiscal constitution and its multiple components, a seminal decision directly linked to the financial crisis, and the political developments it entailed, is the Council of State's decision striking down the law regulating the auction for television licences (Decision 95/2017). The case concerned the constitutionality of transferring competencies conferred by the constitution on an independent authority (the National Council for Radio and Television) to the executive branch (to the minister responsible for the media). This transfer was the result of a political impasse in appointing the members of the authority, as the necessary cross-party consent could not be reached. However, much more was at stake, since there were serious free speech implications in the power of the executive to control the media.

The landscape of TV regulation in Greece had been in a legal limbo for a long time. Private TV channels have operated in Greece with temporary licences that were issued in 1989, and extended since then by legislation or ministerial decisions. In 2015, a new law was enacted providing for a licensing procedure. Article 15 of the Greek constitution demands that 'Radio and television shall be under the immediate control of the State and shall aim at the objective transmission, on equal terms, of information and news reports as well as works of literature and art; the qualitative level of programs shall be assured in consideration of their social mission and the cultural development of the country'. A crucial constitutional issue was whether the National Council for Radio and Television is competent to decide licensing. Due to a political impasse in appointing its members, the power to issue licences was transferred to the ministry. The situation became more complicated as the government limited the number of TV licences to four, creating an intense controversy alleging attempts to limit media pluralism. The EU Commission also expressed concerns regarding the compatibility of the legislation with EU law.[19] The government, in the midst of a heated political debate, auctioned the licences for €246 million. The Court annulled the Minister of State decision 4297/1.3.2016, which transferred competences regarding the tender procedure for the provision of digital television licensing to the General Secretariat of Information and Communication and regulated the procedure. Subsequently parliament passed

[18] X. Contiades and A. Fotiadou, 'On Resilience of Constitutions' (n. 7).

[19] The EU was concerned that the law granted the Minister for Infrastructures, Transport and Networks control of an operator, as well as regulatory responsibilities in the same sector.

a legislative provision for the return by the State of the money paid by the media owners.

According to the Court's ruling, the role of the National Council of Radio and Television in the licensing procedure could not be overridden. The Court stated that the 'broadcast media must be organized in a way that ensures objectivity, impartiality and pluralism and prevent government and any unilateral influence that could affect the conditions of political antagonism to control the formation of public opinion'. Importantly, such independence should also be ensured during 'the step of administering licenses, a process which determines which broadcasters will operate in the future'.

The Court explained that while the constitution does not provide for an alternative mechanism for the selection of members of independent authorities, this does not imply that in case of an impasse in appointments, the competences of such authorities can be transferred by the legislator to other organs of executive power.

The TV licensing controversy brought the lurking antagonism between the executive and the judiciary to the fore. Throughout the crisis, the judiciary had demonstrated self-restraint. Nonetheless, on a case-by-case basis, judges had on occasion placed obstacles in the path of austerity measures favoured by the executive. This tension was inevitable, though the limits of polite conversation were never clearly overstepped.

After the ruling was issued, exchanges between the government and the judiciary took an unprecedented turn. The government spokeswoman, in a statement announcing that the government would introduce a new law, accused a narrow majority of judges on the Court of taking a decision that that would prevent an end to twenty-seven years of unaccountability in the television landscape. She accused the Court of upholding the constitutionality of bailout agreements that tore Greece apart, of closing down the state broadcaster, and of closing the PSI, which destroyed social security funds. While she acknowledged that judicial rulings are binding, she also argued that this does not mean that they cannot be judged. She also added that returning the down-payment on licensing fees would have serious consequences, including the loss of 15,000 kindergarten places, and an inability to hire an additional 4,000 hospital staff.

The associations of justices responded promptly. The Association of the Council of State Justices issued the following statement:

> With regard to political statements on the institutional role of the Council of State, we stress the following, which ought to be self-evident in a democratic state: 1) The Council of State exercises the judicial function which, according to Article 1 para 3 of the Constitution, derives from the people and is exercised in accordance to the Constitution. 2) the Constitution confers on the Council of State the authority to review the legality of administrative acts exercising constitutional review of impugned acts. 3) The Council of State has exercised its function throughout its long history, as the guardian of the rule of law and human rights respecting the

> fundamental principle of separation of powers and is composed of judges distinguished for their high academic training and ethos of independence. 4) Consequently, public discourse about the mission and role of the Court should take into account the above, be mindful of the way a democratic regime is organized and operates, and display a due degree of self-restraint.

The Union of Administrative Judges also issued a statement stressing that:

> the separation of powers is a fundamental feature of any democratic regime, provided for by the Constitution of our country. According to this principle, the legislative initiative is undoubtedly conferred upon the elected government. It is nonetheless correlated, in accordance with the above principle, to judicial review exercised by the judiciary. Calling into question the institutional role of the Courts in response to the decision of the Council of State, through derogatory comments made by representatives of the political power, is neither consistent with the constitutional order nor with the principles underlying the rule of law. This is not allowed by the Constitution and it is not institutionally tolerable.

Finally, the Association of Judges and Public Prosecutors also issued a harsh statement:

> The decision issued yesterday by the Council of State, in fulfilment of its function as guarantor of the rule of law conferred by the Constitution on the Judiciary, triggered once again unwarranted attacks by the government against the judiciary, made with unprecedented intensity, in a clear attempt to involve the judiciary in political rivalries. The Supreme Administrative Court was attacked for its decisions on the Memoranda, the 'haircut' on sovereign bonds, the destruction of social security funds, as if it is the Courts that legislate, and not governments that have imposed harsh measures. The Court was blamed for failing to take into consideration the consequences of ruling that the impugned Law is unconstitutional, because its ruling hinders the governmental fiscal policy. The fundamental obligation of judges is to consider cases in light of the Constitution without taking into account the expediency of contested measures and political aims. The administration of Justice in any other direction would be very dangerous for our democracy and for the rule of law. Financial planning, and finding the funds necessary for the functioning of state structures, is a governmental responsibility, while our task is to safeguard the Constitution. A conflict between the three branches is not acceptable in a democratic regime. The smooth functioning of the institutions presupposes understanding the distinct role of each power and that all branches abandon attempts to manipulate one another.[20]

This unusually heated dialogue between the executive and the judicial branch is indicative of the backlash that judicial decisions have triggered during the crisis. The backlash-consciousness that has resulted has induced a subtle transformation in the role of the courts.

[20] www.kathimerini.gr/881037/article/epikairothta/ellada/pyr-omadon-apo-dikastikes-enwseis-kata-gero vasilh (in Greek).

3. *Judicial Self-Awareness*

The way in which judges perceived their own part in handling the constitutional issues posed by the financial crisis is an expression of the dilemmas they faced. Different perceptions of the role of the judge underlie the different approaches expressed in judicial opinions (including dissenting opinions) in seminal decisions that are part of the crisis jurisprudence.

The thoughts expressed in public speeches and papers published by heads of the Council of State are useful for a deeper understanding of the crisis jurisprudence. The agony of judges regarding their own reputations is obvious, and expressive of the backlash suffered during the crisis. As a result, backlash consciousness is gradually becoming a factor that may influence rulings.[21]

Justice Panagiotis Pikramenos, former head of the Council of State (2008–12), argues that extraordinary circumstances, and the need to serve the pressing general interest, allow judges to decide whether a deviation from normal legality is justifiable, and therefore legally tolerable. Doing so, however, does not render them sovereign in the Schmittean sense, that is, they do not decide on the exception.[22] This is the case because judicial opinions are not arbitrary even though they may rely on ideological preconceptions, personal convictions, and a judge's world view. Judicial opinions must be methodologically sound, obey doctrine, recognize the wide discretion enjoyed by the political authorities given their popular legitimacy, and rely on generally accepted legal concepts and principles such as human dignity, equality and proportionality. The longstanding development of these concepts by the courts has resulted in a strictly limited normative content that leaves no room for arbitrariness. The judge can neither be the sovereign nor absent. The judiciary has the important constitutional mandate to delineate the limits of the wide decision-making discretion enjoyed by the political authorities. During crises this mandate acquires extra importance because wrong choices may have detrimental consequences.[23]

The thoughts expressed by Sotirios Rizos, former head of the Council of State (2013–15), express a different approach to the role of the judge. According to Justice Rizos, governmental institutions have attacked judicial decisions by arguing that courts go beyond their role when they intervene in economic policy. According to Justice Rizos, it is true that the administration faces severe economic problems, but even in that context, constant criticism by the government of judicial decisions, arguing that the courts intervene unduly in fiscal policy, conveys the sense to litigants and judges that the rule of law is eroding. Justice Rizos concludes that

21 N. Garupa and T. Ginsburg, *Judicial Reputation: A Comparative Theory* (University of Chicago Press, 2015).

22 C. Schmitt, *Political Theology. Four Chapters on the Concept of Sovereignty* (1922) (George Schwab tr., University of Chicago Press, 2005).

23 P. Pikramenos, 'Public law in extra-ordinary circumstances: a view from the aspect of judicial Review', (in Greek) (2012) 2 *Θεωρία και Πράξη Διοικητικού Δικαίου [Theorie et Pratique du Droit Administrative]* 97.

Greek judges are aware that the constitution is not a mere piece of paper, isolated from reality:

> We are aware of Lassale's conceptualization. Nonetheless, as judges, we work with a rich legal document, the Constitution, and possess a range of highly developed interpretative methods for approaching it. We rely on information, our study of legal texts, dialogue with other judges, the arguments of the litigants, and external advice; we attempt to ignore propaganda, and leave aside personal political party preferences: this is how we approach each case in the hope of taking a fair decision.[24]

According to the head of the Council of State, Nikolaos Sakellariou (2015–18), technocrats and experts are central to decision-making in the contemporary era, and there is a mere pretence of parliamentary control and judicial review. According to Justice Sakellariou, the period of severe economic crisis is characterized by the systematic erosion of the rule of law and of the social state. Systematic attempts are made through the invocation of the so-called financial general interest and the threat of socio-economic collapse to bypass the constitution by curtailing constitutional review of financial measures. Justice Sakellariou concludes that what is needed more than ever is judges who do not give in to pressure, but perform their duties with a heightened sense of responsibility, determination, and cautiousness but also audacity when necessary.[25]

The perspectives of these three judges who served consecutively during the financial crisis as heads of the Council of State (the court largely responsible for constitutional review of austerity measures) are quite different. Beneath the similarities on matters of judicial ethos lie different conceptions of self-restraint, and distinct notions of the nature of law production during financial crisis. These differences correspond to competing understandings of the role of the judge, which underpin the ongoing battles that take place within courts, and are expressed in concurring and dissenting opinions as the crisis jurisprudence matures.

III. INCREMENTAL AND EPISODIC CHANGE: LAWMAKING, POLITICAL SYSTEM AND THE BAILOUT REFERENDUM

1. *Changes in the Modes of Lawmaking*

Change in the modes of lawmaking is an ongoing transformation triggered by the crisis. When the economic crisis erupted, emergency narratives began to be used

[24] S. A. Rizos, 'The Council of State between the constitutional model of the Social State and the political claim "I can't pay, if I haven't got it"', (in Greek) (2015) 4 *Θεωρία και Πράξη Διοικητικού Δικαίου [Theorie et Pratique du Droit Administrative]* 289.

[25] N. Sakellariou, 'The Personal Liability of the Judge and his Importance to the Rule of Law' (in Greek) (2015) 12 *Θεωρία και Πράξη Διοικητικού Δικαίου [Theorie et Pratique du Droit Administrative]* 1089.

frequently. Although a state of emergency was never officially declared, the notion of emergency was elaborated in two directions. First, as a judicial standard in court rulings, and second as a criterion for fast-track legislation. Gradually, the central element became the need for immediate action, since the notion of unexpectedness became more difficult to invoke after several years of crisis.

Notwithstanding the clear constitutional ban on introducing bills containing provisions that are not related to the main subject matter of the bill (art. 74 para. 5), most laws include such provisions. In the period between 1975 and 1995, 61 percent of laws contained such irrelevant provisions.[26] The crisis exacerbated this problem of 'patchwork legislation', but did not cause it.

Ever since the financial crisis broke out, the role of parliament has undergone change. The executive took the lead in lawmaking, and the deliberative role of parliament gave way. The executive plays a major role in the production of legal rules, while the participation of the legislature is frequently limited to the ex post approval of such rules. It is true that speed is often necessary to respond to a financial crisis. It is also true, however, that the need for last-minute legislation is in part a function of the negotiation tactics used by governments, and not the result of unexpected events. Furthermore, at the beginning of the crisis, the abuse of the constitutional path of fast-track legislation was central to the political narratives. Before winning the election and forming a coalition government, SYRIZA had criticised harshly the use of fast-track legislation by the ND–PASOK coalition, depicting it as a blatant violation of the rule of law, only to adopt the same practice when it came to power. Fast-track thus gradually became the path followed by all governments, irrespective of their political affiliation.

This (often unconstitutional) practice marked a shift in the traditional relationship between the parliament and the executive branch. This occurred because of the extensive and repeated use of fast-track lawmaking. Although most constitutions provide for the use of decree laws when urgent legislation is needed, the way such laws are being used during the crisis has acquired permanency, becoming almost the default form of lawmaking. This is a side-effect of overusing the notion of emergency to suggest haste, and quite different from an official declaration of a state of emergency, in which case it is clear that the executive will take over legislative powers for a limited time.[27]

By contrast, an undeclared emergency, which is used as a justification for the substantive content of legislation, for the process by which measures are adopted, and also as a judicial standard for their evaluation, is still an unfamiliar tool. It is possible that it expresses a more permanent change in the role of parliament. In several crisis-stricken countries, there are signs of recovery, and parliaments

26 See data available at www.dianeosis.org/research/polynomia-kai-kakonomia/.

27 On the concept of emergency and the difficulty of addressing in an effective manner through the use ordinary governmental actions see J. Ferejohn, 'Financial Emergencies', Ch. 2 in this volume.

appear to be regaining their role.[28] However, this is not the case in Greece. The crisis is still unfolding in unknown directions, impacting the role of parliament, the interrelation between the three branches, and the political system as a whole.

2. *The Impact of the Crisis on the Political System*

The impact of the financial crisis on the established party system was strong.[29] Following the restoration of democracy in 1974, and a short period during which the remnants of the pre-dictatorship years were expressed in a multiparty system, a polarized two-party system emerged. From 1981 until the crisis broke out, political power was monopolized by the two major parties, the centre-right New Democracy (ND) and the centre-left social democratic party (PASOK). This political configuration expressed the traditional left-right cleavage.

Since 1974, the electoral system has provided for 'reinforced proportionality', giving the plurality party an absolute majority of seats in parliament, provided its nationwide percentage of the vote was approximately 40 per cent. When this electoral system was briefly changed to introduce pure proportional representation (June 1989–April 1990), political polarization was further increased, and two short-lived coalition governments were formed.

The financial crisis put an end to the alternation in power of the two major parties. During the first crisis period, a coalition government of the two major parties (originally with a smaller party that subsequently withdrew) formed under a technocrat prime minister (November 2011). This government was formed to ratify and implement decisions taken by the eurozone countries and the IMF, despite the fact that the centre-left PASOK party still held the majority of seats in parliament.

The most important consequence of the crisis has been the fragmentation of the party system. In the election held in October 2009, five political parties entered parliament. Before the end of the parliamentary term in April 2012, six new parties had been formed with the participation of MPs who had abandoned the party they were elected with. The two major parties split, as their populist factions either created new parties (such as the right wing populist party Independent Greeks), or turned toward other parties of the left spectrum. Another development was the rise of the radical right, nationalistic and xenophobic Golden Dawn party. Finally, PASOK's political hegemony in the centre-left came to an end as the radical left party SYRIZA steadily transformed itself into a new political force.

28 On the impact of the crisis on national parliaments see C. Fasone, 'Taking Budgetary Powers Away from National Parliaments? On Parliamentary Prerogatives in the Eurozone Crisis' (2015) *EUI Department of Law Research Paper No. 2015/37*.

29 See X. Contiades and I. Tassopoulos (n. 12) 209; A.-I. Marketou and M. Dekastros Report on Greece in 'Constitutional Change through Euro Crisis Law' (*Eurocrisislaw.eui.eu*, 16 January 2014) http://eurocrisislaw.eui.eu/greece/.

In the elections of May 2012, the fragmentation of the party system was confirmed with the entry of seven political parties in parliament, none of which received more than 20 per cent of the vote. It is noteworthy that this thoroughly novel picture emerged notwithstanding the 3 per cent threshold required to achieve parliamentary representation.

On 8 December 2014, Prime Minister Samaras announced that a presidential election would take place a few months before they were due. The next day, he announced the candidacy of an ND politician jointly supported by the ruling ND–PASOK coalition. According to the constitution, if no super-majority is achieved after three ballots, parliament is dissolved within ten days, and new elections are called. This provision is intended to ensure that the head of state is elected with significant support. In practice, it provides a weapon to opposition parties for triggering premature elections.

On 29 December 2014, after failing to elect a President of the Republic in the third round of voting with the required 180 votes, parliament was dissolved. Elections were held in January 2015. The Coalition of the Radical Left (SYRIZA) won. It was the first time that a radical left party had won an election in Greece. With 149 of 300 seats, SYRIZA was two seats short of an absolute majority, and its populist leader Alexis Tsipras was sworn in as prime minister on 26 January 2015, forming a coalition government with the populist right-wing Independent Greeks. The next general elections were held on 20 September 2015. This was a snap election following the snap referendum held in July 2015. With the lowest turnout since the restoration of democracy in 1974, SYRIZA won again. Failing to achieve an absolute majority, it once again formed a coalition government with Independent Greeks (ANEL). The far-right Golden Dawn remained the third political force in the country, rising slightly to 7 per cent.

Despite major changes in the political and party system induced by the crisis, it is important to remember that these changes took place by way of free and fair elections. No doubts were ever cast on electoral results, and changes in government took place smoothly.

3. *The Snap Bailout Referendum: A Symptom of the Financial Crisis?*

On 5 July 2015, Greek citizens went to the polls to vote in the so-called Grexit referendum, although it is far from clear what the question they were called to answer was about.[30] The referendum was free and fair, nonetheless it did not fulfil

[30] The analysis on the referendum of July 2015 is based on the following texts: X. Contiades and A. Fotiadou, 'The Greek Referendum: Unconstitutional and Undemocratic' (*Eurocrisislaw.eui.eu*, 7 July 2015), http://eurocrisislaw.eui.eu/news/the-greek-referendum-unconstitutional-and-undemocratic-by-xenophon-contiades-and-alkmene-fotiadou/ and A. Fotiadou, 'The role of the people in constitutional amendment in Greece: Between narratives and practice' in X. Contiades and A. Fotiadou (eds), *Participatory Constitutional Change. The People as Amenders of the Constitution* (Routledge, 2017) 156.

the prerequisites of a democratic referendum. The referendum question was ambiguous, and open to multiple interpretations. Furthermore, the referendum could not produce a binding result.

The events leading up to the vote involved a series of oddities. The announcement of the referendum took place on Friday, 26 June, after midnight. The Greek prime minister stated that a referendum would be held on Sunday, 5 July. Citizens would be called on to vote on the 'reforms for the completion of the current program and beyond' and on the 'preliminary debt sustainability analysis', which represented the latest offer by the international lenders. The referendum was officially declared by the President of the Republic on 28 June, following a parliamentary vote held on 27 June. The proposals on which citizens would vote became available on 28 June, when the European Commission published them in English 'in the interest of transparency and for the information of the Greek people'. On 28 June, several pre-existing rules regarding referendums were changed by legislation. The government proclaimed a bank holiday effective as of 28 June, and also imposed capital controls that still remain in place (although they have been relaxed). The first official translation of the two documents was made public on 29 June. It contained a mistake, and was replaced by the corrected version on 30 June. On that day, the current offer by international lenders expired, which meant that the proposals on which citizens would vote were no longer on the table. Subsequently, Greece did not pay its dues to the IMF. On 3 July, the Supreme Administrative Court unanimously rejected a complaint against the constitutionality of the referendum, arguing that the referendum was a governmental act not subject to judicial review.[31] On 5 July, the referendum was held with a 62.5 per cent turnout. The 'no' vote prevailed, with 61.31 per cent. On 8 June, three days after the 'no' vote, Greece officially requested a three-year bailout agreement, and on 13 July, the Greek government accepted a bailout package containing severe austerity measures.

A lack of experience with referenda had the effect of creating an awkward combination of direct and representative democracy. The prime minister campaigned for 'no', and implied that he would resign if 'yes' prevailed, adding an extra parameter to the referendum dilemma.[32] It was difficult to know whether citizens were answering the question posed, or giving a more general mandate to the freshly elected government. Voting in a referendum was a novel experience for voters, and many citizens felt empowered by participating in a democratic procedure. The absence of an independent electoral committee to elaborate the question and to monitor the campaign seemed like trivial legal technicalities compared to the opportunity of popular expression. And yet, lack of a clear question and lack of time for deliberation created fertile ground for elite manipulation.

[31] Decision 2767/2015 Council of State which ruled on the constitutionality of the referendum.

[32] See A. Trechsel, 'The Greek Referendum: How Democratic is it?' (*Eurocrisislaw.eui.eu*, 4 July 2015), http://eurocrisislaw.eui.eu/news/the-greek-referendum-how-democratic-is-it/.

A possible way to treat the bailout referendum is to consider it a symptom of the financial crisis, and to place it within the context of the impact of the crisis on constitutions. One characteristic of the financial crisis has been that it accelerated lawmaking.[33] The question is whether the importance and urgency of the matter can be used as an argument in favour of holding a hurried referendum, in the same manner as decree-laws that are used to speed up lawmaking at the cost of deliberation in parliament. The campaign lasted for five days only, and was doomed to focus on narratives rather than information. The amount of time available for reflection did not allow the making of rational choices based on information. Closed banks and the imposition of capital controls were an unprecedented experience that imperilled sober reflection and debate.

German chancellor Angela Merkel and French president Francois Hollande announced that the result of the referendum would be respected. Subsequently, Greece submitted a request for a third bailout. This was agreed upon at the eurozone summit on 12–13 July, a few days after the referendum, and was finalized following further negotiations in August. The ambiguous referendum question did not only allow contrasting interpretations with regard to its true meaning before the vote, but in the aftermath as well. Whether the result of the referendum was respected appears open to multiple interpretations. Given that the 'no' vote had won a sweeping victory, the signing of the new bailout meant that in the event that the 'no' victory really meant 'no to the eurozone', the result was not respected. By contrast, if 'no' meant merely 'no to the particular measures but acceptance of other bailout measures', focus should be placed on the differences between the measures rejected and the new measures. To answer whether the deal taken had better or worse terms requires economic analysis. Still, the two deals appear to have striking similarities, suggesting that creditors were not ready to respect a win for an anti-austerity 'no'. Pension cuts and tax increases were part of the new bailout package.

A narrow reading of the referendum dilemma could suggest that any difference between the two bailout agreements is sufficient to support the conclusion that the outcome of the referendum was respected. Given the ambiguity of the question posed implied that the result was open to interpretation and manipulation. Narratives about the referendum dilemma were replaced by narratives about whether the will expressed by the people had been respected. These narratives are no longer central to the political discourse, which swiftly moved away from the referendum to focus on the new bailout terms.

In retrospect, this peculiar referendum provides an important case study for various reasons. Held before the Brexit referendum, it is now part of EU referendum history, and offers lessons on polarization and resentment. Being the only referendum held under the current constitution, it will shape the future practice of

33 X. Contiades and A. Fotiadou (n. 2), 14–17.

referenda in Greece, as well as discussions about enhancing their use. This referendum may have longstanding consequences for the way citizens perceive referenda. It also leaves a disquieting question. If the first Greek referendum is interpreted as not having posed the question of Grexit, can a second Grexit referendum be held in the near future? If the bailout referendum is considered as precedent rather than bad practice, it could open the way for a second referendum, and future referenda could also be snap referenda.

At the moment, deliberations regarding potential amendment of the constitution are unfolding. It is doubtful whether these deliberations will be successful, and whether they are consistent with the required amendment process. One possibility is that a referendum might be used to amend the constitution, and to bypass the constraints set by formal amendment rules. One aspect of such constitutional revision is the suggestion of enhancing direct democratic procedures. The only referendum experience Greece has had in forty-three years should be revisited and scrutinized, and not swept under the carpet.

IV. FINANCIAL CRISIS, CONSTITUTIONAL RESILIENCE AND CONSTITUTIONAL RETROGRESSION

The following notions provide useful conceptual lenses for understanding subtle, crisis-induced constitutional change.

1. The notion of constitutional resilience – that is, 'the ability of a constitution not only to withstand a severe shock, but also to enable the legal order, whose ground rules it sets out, to seek recovery within the constraints of these ground rules'.[34]
2. The notion of constitutional retrogression – that is, 'subtle, incremental erosion that happens simultaneously to three institutional predicates of democracy: competitive elections; rights of political speech and association; and the administrative and adjudicative rule of law'.[35]
3. The notion that the rule of law may be eroded through the mutual agreement of legal professionals. Mark Tushnet suggests that 'the rule of law, such as it is, is stabilized by the historically contingent agreement among well-socialized legal professionals that certain behaviours are consistent with the rule of law, and others not . . . that agreement can erode when well-socialized legal professionals begin to disagree about whether particular behaviours are or are not consistent with the rule of law'.[36]

[34] X. Contiades and A. Fotiadou, 'On Resilience of Constitutions' (n. 7).

[35] A. Huq and T. Ginsburg, 'How to Lose a Constitutional Democracy', https://ssrn.com/abstract=2901776.

[36] M. Tushnet, 'Oakland, Brigadoon, and the Rule of Law' (*Balkin.blogspot.gr*, 6 June 2016), https://balkin.blogspot.gr/2016/06/oakland-brigadoon-and-rule-of-law.html.

The third notion is perhaps the most disquieting, because it departs from the fixity of the rule of law as a reference point, and renders it fluid. There is a thin line between resilience and inertia, and qualitative criteria are necessary to distinguish between the two. Erosion of the rule of law may be a slow process, in which case it is difficult to pin down signs of its occurrence. Retrogression requires the simultaneous erosion of three basic premises of democracy. Nonetheless, the erosion of two out of three, or detectable signs of deterioration that do not amount to erosion, or attempts to intentionally impair them, may indicate significant constitutional change.

During the first years of the financial crisis, distinct types of constitutional reaction towards the crisis became conspicuous. These constitutional reactions took a variety of forms: the occurrence of formal constitutional change (ranging from total revisions to modifications and adjustments), transformations of the party system, informal change effected through novel judicial interpretations of the constitution, and changes in the functions of the constitution affecting constitutional normativity and constitutional faith.[37] The four main constitutional reactions towards the crisis were adjustment, submission, breakdown, and stamina. Constitutions confronted with the crisis either adjusted to the new circumstances, became submissive but still went on living, suffered breakdown, or managed to remain intact.[38] As the crisis unfolded, the original reactions to the shock evolved into more permanent features of the constitutional order.[39]

Constitutional developments in crisis-struck Greece have been on the edge between normality and backslide, between constitutional crisis and constitutional hardball, between resilience and retrogression. Throughout the crisis, constitutional narratives were caught in the divide between pro- and anti-Memoranda rhetoric. This polarized debate reached its high point at the time of the Grexit referendum.

It is clear that the three criteria of retrogression are not satisfied in the Greek case. Free and fair elections are held, freedom of speech exists, and rule of law guarantees are in place (although often under serious strain). Nonetheless, there are clear marks of erosion, and there were moments when the possibility of violation became quite strong. The referendum was free and fair, but it was an undemocratic, sham referendum. Had the result of the referendum been a sudden Grexit along with a default on Greek debt, it is hard to imagine that such a transition would have occurred without a constitutional backslide. The TV licensing incident is also

37 X. Contiades and A. Fotiadou (n. 2). See also the application of the Contiades and Fotiadou typology of constitutional reactions toward the financial crisis in the Asian context in B. Dressel, 'Liberal Democratic Constitutions During Severe Financial Crisis: Perspectives on East and Southeast Asia', in this volume.

38 X. Contiades and A. Fotiadou (n. 2).

39 The adoption of a balanced budget rule within constitutions is a sign of adaptation and adjustment to the requirements of the crisis. Nonetheless, the symbolic power of such a constitutional rule appeared stronger than its actual efficacity. On the efficiency of the constitutionalization of the balanced budget rule see T. Ginsburg, 'Balanced Budget Provisions in Constitutions', Ch. 4 in this volume.

characteristic. The transfer of competencies from an independent authority to the executive poses serious questions of media freedom.

Whether there has been a backslide in the rule of law is a complex question. Undoubtedly, the rule of law has been in retreat as a result of the financial crisis. Legal certainty with regard to economic and social rights has weakened. Fast-track lawmaking provides a good example. At the beginning of the crisis, the overuse of fast-track legislation was generally seen as an unconstitutional practice, and it was condemned strongly and frequently by the opposition.[40] But when the opposition came into power, it continued these practices, de facto accepting them as normal. A pragmatic approach would have recognized the clear need for fast-track lawmaking routes that do not violate or circumvent the constitution, and would have provided for such powers through a consensual amendment to the constitution. However, because polarization made this option unavailable, these practices came to be tacitly accepted as consistent with the rule of law.

One question that emerges is whether the acceptance of such fluidity with regard to the rule of law is the result of faulty institutional design. For example, the normalization of unconstitutional fast-track lawmaking results, in part, from the fact that there is no institutional way to control it. According to longstanding judicial doctrine, the existence of emergency and of urgent and unforeseen necessity is not subject to judicial review. Left unchecked, political actors tend to exploit such opportunities to avoid the limitations set by constitutional provisions.

It is still not clear what the result of the ongoing pre-amendment process will be. As a government-initiated process, it can hardly be described as a bottom-up process of constitutional reform. If it is confined to a dialogue that aims to raise awareness of the need for constitutional revision, it could be a positive step. The formal amendment process involves the electorate only through a general election that follows after the amending process has been initiated. However, given that citizens typically do not cast their vote in general elections on the basis of constitutional issues, it is a positive step to render their role more meaningful. By contrast, if the current process is used to bypass the amendment formula in a way that results in an unconstitutional amendment, the consequences will be unpredictable.

The incumbent government is composed of the radical left-wing party SYRIZA, which won the general elections of September 2015 with roughly 35 per cent of the vote, and its populist right-wing partner, the 'Independent Greeks', who secured just under 4 per cent of the vote. The current political landscape as reflected in parliament does not suggest the wake of constituent power. The conditions for a constitutional revolution do not seem to exist. Thus, bypassing formal amendment rules will result in the first unconstitutional constitutional amendment after the restoration of democracy.

40 See criticism of the rule of law critique during crises in E. A. Posner, 'Rule-of-Law Objections to the Lender of Last Resort', Ch. 3 in this volume.

Greece has a history of unconstitutional constitutional amendments. Due to the cumbersome amendment procedures, these procedures were not followed, despite the fact that the constitutions of 1911, 1952 and 1975 were enacted by assemblies self-proclaimed as 'revisional', and the amended constitutions were in continuity with the constitution of 1864. This practice is linked to the turbulent political history of Greece before the restoration of democracy in 1974.[41] The symbolic significance of abiding by the amendment formula throughout the forty-three years of uninterrupted democracy is not easily replaceable. An unconstitutional constitutional amendment in times of economic crisis and deep political polarization could have major unpredictable consequences.

V. CONCLUSION

How a constitution responds to a severe crisis depends on multiple intertwined internal and external factors. The first set includes constitutional design, constitutional and political culture, the system of constitutional review, judicial and political culture, and the constitutional amendment model, whereas the second entails the type and severity of the crisis, and the nature of the political system.

Faced with crisis, constitutions may adapt (changing formally or informally), become irrelevant, or crumble. The strengths and weaknesses of a constitution are revealed under the pressure exerted by a severe crisis. Informal constitutional change has so far been the main constitutional response to the financial crisis, consisting of legislation passed to tackle the financial crisis and the jurisprudence that has dealt with the constitutionality of such measures. Moreover, the roles of the three branches have shifted as a result of the financial crisis, producing tensions and bringing forth pre-existing institutional malfunctions. Informal constitutional change is incremental change, which corresponds to the conceptualization of crisis as a transition.

Apart from such slow-moving incremental change, there were distinct moments during the crisis when there was the possibility of change in the course of events. What if the first Memorandum of Understanding between Greece and its international lenders had been found unconstitutional in 2010? What if Greece had exited the eurozone after the snap referendum of 2015?

The Greek constitution did not undergo formal change during the financial crisis. The constitution endured and continued to perform its basic functions in setting the rules of the game. The three criteria of retrogression are not met, at least not to an extent that would indicate constitutional backslide. Still, signs of erosion are conspicuous in all three areas, and there were crucial occasions when the possibility of backsliding was high. The amount of informal change and textual constitutional inertia do not signify constitutional resilience.

[41] X. Contiades and A. Fotiadou, 'The Hellenic Republic' (n. 13).

In July 2016, the initiation of a constitutional revision process was announced, and an experimental deliberation process is currently unfolding. Nonetheless, it is hard to predict whether it will succeed to enhance popular deliberation, or lead to an attempt to bypass formal amendment rules with unpredictable consequences, or result in a political impasse that fails to produce much awaited constitutional reforms.

V

The Effect of Crises on Constitutions

14

Economic Crises, Political Fragmentation, and Constitutional Choice

The Agenda-Setting Power of Presidents in Latin America

Gabriel L. Negretto

By the end of the nineteenth century the vast majority of Latin American constitutions had presidents with a relatively high degree of autonomy from congress in the operation of government, reactive legislative power, and little or no power to promote legislative change. This design has changed radically; gradually in the early decades of the twentieth century, and more rapidly after the expansion of electoral democracy in the region since the late 1970s. One salient feature of this transformation is that whereas the government powers of presidents have generally decreased, their powers in the legislative arena, in particular to promote legislative change, have increased.

This chapter argues that, under certain political conditions, economic crises had an impact on how institutional reformers allocated legislative powers during processes of constitutional change. In particular, it proposes that in a fragmented political environment, economic crises that demanded prompt policy shifts provided reformers with an incentive to strengthen the agenda-setting powers of the president at the time of replacing or amending the constitution. This argument is supported with a statistical analysis of the determinants of constitutional choice in eighteen countries of Latin America from 1900 to 2014 and a comparative study of the cases of Mexico and Argentina between 1982 and 1994.

The chapter is organized as follows. Section I discusses the concept of presidential power and the evolution of its different dimensions from 1900 to 2014. This is followed by the presentation of a theory of constitutional choice based on the assessment of the past performance of the constitution and the distribution of partisan power at the time of change. Section III offers a statistical analysis of the determinants of the design of executive policy-making powers in Latin America. Section IV provides a comparative analysis of economic crisis, political fragmentation, and constitutional choice in Mexico and Argentina. A brief conclusion follows.

I. PRESIDENTIAL POWER IN LATIN AMERICA

As many scholars and observers have noted over time, Latin Americans adopted presidential systems that concentrate too much power in the executive branch.

Compared to the US presidential regime, based on a model of co-equal branches of government sharing powers, Latin American presidents have usually had considerably more powers than their North American counterparts to enact or change legislation, interfere with judicial functions, and suspend the constitution in emergency situations (see Negretto 2003; Cheibub, Elkins, and Ginsburg 2012). While this comparison is generally correct, three problems affect any general appraisal of presidential power in Latin America.

In the first place, it is not always clear whether the assessment refers to de jure or de facto executive powers. In some countries, such as Chile or Colombia, the formal powers of presidents in the areas of government, legislation, and emergencies have historically been very strong. In practice, however, these powers did not always prove to be effective. By contrast, in countries such as Mexico or Venezuela, or even in the United States at some historical junctures, presidents have enjoyed more influence on legislation and policy-making than one would expect from the formal prerogatives listed in the constitution. This is due to the fact that the actual power of presidents results from a complex interaction between their formal prerogatives, unwritten constitutional conventions, the distribution of partisan power, and the strength of other institutions.

In addition, and more importantly for the purposes of this chapter, the power of presidents cannot be conceived as a set of prerogatives that can simply be added along a single dimension. Presidential power is a multidimensional concept. It encompasses the authority of the president in her different roles as chief of party, chief of government, and co-legislator. As chief of party, the power of the executive refers to the capacity to command a cohesive partisan majority in the legislature, as chief of government to the power to appoint and remove cabinet ministers and other high officials in the administration and the judiciary, and as co-legislator to the authority to participate in and have influence over policy-making. The first dimension refers to partisan powers, the second to government powers, and the third to legislative powers.

One final factor that affects debates about the powers of the executive in Latin America is that they have varied both across countries and over time. For instance, toward the second half of the nineteenth century, most presidents in the region had strong formal powers in emergency situations. However, whereas the 1844 constitution of Paraguay established no limits to this power, the 1853 constitution of Argentina placed substantial restraints to it. At the same time, while by the end of the twentieth century the vast majority of presidents in Latin America acquired strong legislative powers, important variations persist across countries. Whereas presidents in Costa Rica have almost no agenda powers, presidents in Argentina or Brazil have the power to make legislative changes by decree.

Keeping these conceptual challenges in mind, I now turn to a more systematic analysis of the evolution of the legislative and non-legislative powers of presidents. Specifically, I focus on the scores of the formal legislative and non-legislative powers of presidents that followed constitutional revisions in eighteen Latin American countries between 1900 and 2014. These revisions include all new constitutions and amendments enacted during authoritarian and democratic years that had the potential to affect or that actually altered the legislative and non-legislative powers of the executive.[1]

I have assigned scores to each dimension of presidential power using a categorical principal component analysis (CATPCA), which allows the researcher to combine qualitative judgment in the coding of each variable with a weighting method that reflects the relative importance of each variable in explaining variation within a particular dataset.[2] To facilitate the analysis and use of the indexes, the original CATPCA scores for each variable were transformed to an ordinal scale ranging from 1 to 100.[3] As we will see, the comparison of scores over time shows general trends, but also reveals that these trends are not consistent across all dimensions of executive power.

Legislative powers include both reactive and proactive powers. The first refer to the capacity of the executive to prevent legislative change through the use of a veto, including both the traditional veto that allows the president to oppose a bill in its entirety, and the line-item veto that enables the president to oppose part of a bill while promulgating the rest.[4] Proactive or agenda-setting powers allude to the authority of the president to constrain the set of policy alternatives from which the assembly may choose, or the timetable according to which these choices must be made, or both (Carey and Shugart 1998: 6; Negretto 2004). The main powers in this category are those that provide the executive with (1) exclusive authority to introduce bills on important economic and financial issues; power to (2) set the budget, (3) introduce bills that must be voted on in Congress within a time limit, (4) issue decrees of legislative content, and (5) submit approval of bills to popular referenda.

Figure 14.1 shows changes in the overall legislative powers of presidents. Figures 14.2 and 14.3 illustrate these changes in the two main components of reactive

1 The analysis of legislative powers is based on 122 observations of constitutional revision and the analysis of non-legislative powers on 132.

2 For a description of the technique and the variables included in the analysis of legislative and agenda-setting powers, see Negretto (2013).

3 The original scale has both negative and positive scores, with a mean of 0 and a standard deviation of 1. The indexes can be downloaded from http://la-constitutionalchange.cide.edu/.

4 The traditional veto (also called "package" veto) allows the president to oppose a bill in its entirety, so that the latter cannot be passed unless legislators reach the necessary, usually qualified, majorities to override the veto. Using the same procedure, since the nineteenth century some constitutions in Latin America had allowed the president to veto only parts of a bill. This power, however, was greatly expanded during the twentieth century when the president was invested with the explicit authority to veto portions of a bill *and* promulgate the rest if congress did not reach the necessary majorities to override the partial objection. The first constitutions to create this power explicitly were the 1949 Argentinian constitution and the 1967 Uruguayan constitution. Other Latin American innovations that have also expanded the legislative powers of presidents are what Aleman and Tsebelis (2005) call "amendatory observations," which allude to the capacity of the president to amend a bill while using a veto. This power, however, stands in a gray area between veto and agenda powers.

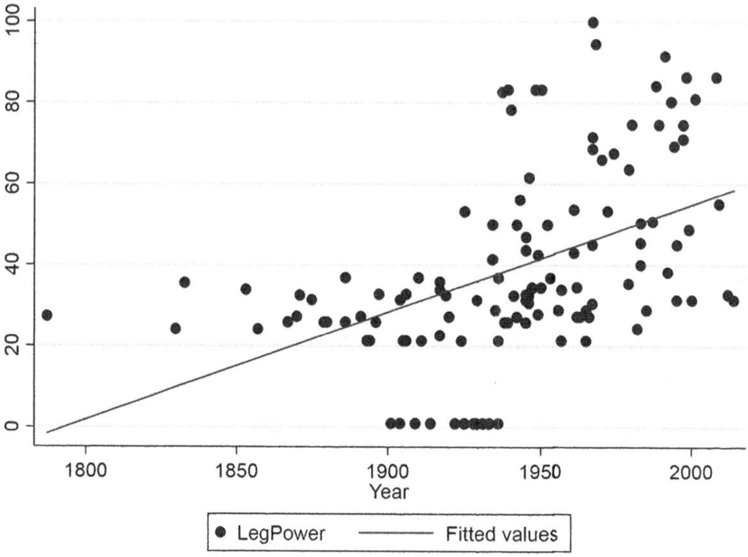

FIGURE 14.1 Presidential legislative powers in Latin America, 1900–2014

and proactive legislative powers. As one can see, all these powers have increased over time. However, the increase in reactive powers is not only more moderate, but also more limited in range than the increase in proactive powers. This is confirmed in bivariate correlations. Whereas the correlation between the year in which the constitution was adopted or amended and the scores of legislative presidential powers and agenda-setting powers is equally strong (0.47; $p < 0.001$), the correlation between year of adoption and the score of veto powers alone is much weaker (.19; $p < 0.05$).

Non-legislative powers include the powers of presidents to appoint and remove cabinet ministers, high officials, members of the judiciary, and local executives; the powers to declare and regulate emergencies; and the powers to deal with inter-branch conflicts. Figure 14.4 shows temporal changes in the overall non-legislative powers of presidents, while Figure 14.5 shows shifts in their government (or appointment) powers. As these figures illustrate, the trend over time is negative, meaning that these powers have generally decreased. In both cases the correlation between the year of adoption of the constitution or amendment and the score of these powers is negative and statistically significant (−0.30; $p < 0.001$).

The positive trend toward strengthening the legislative powers of presidents while weakening their non-legislative powers can be observed before and after the last wave of democratization in Latin America, initiated in the late 1970s. In a sense, this presents a puzzle. The decline in non-legislative powers is

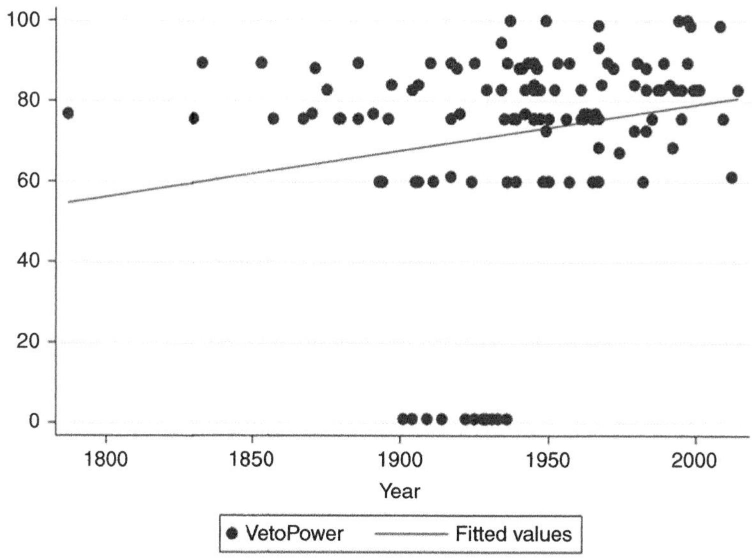

FIGURE 14.2 Reactive legislative powers in Latin America, 1900–2014

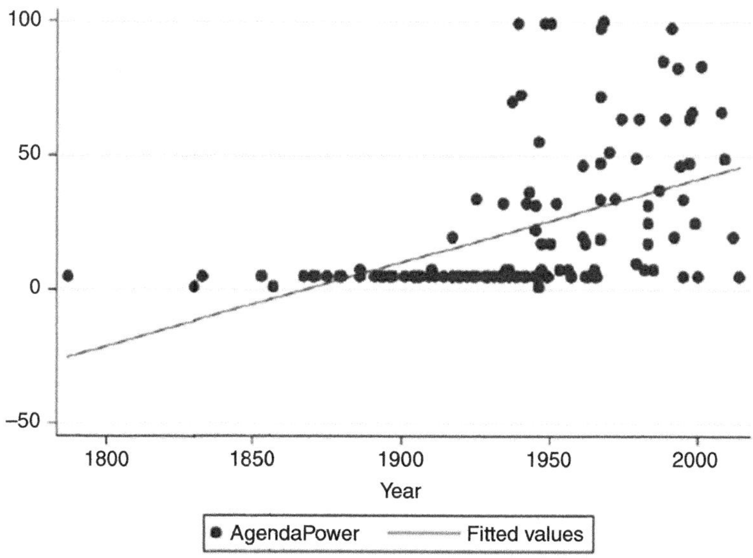

FIGURE 14.3 Proactive legislative powers in Latin America, 1900–2014

consistent with a new political environment that stressed the rule of law and the separation of powers as democracy expanded in the region. But the strengthening of the legislative powers of the executive does not fit easily with this narrative. Even reforms that reduced the legislative powers of presidents after 1978 – Brazil in 1988

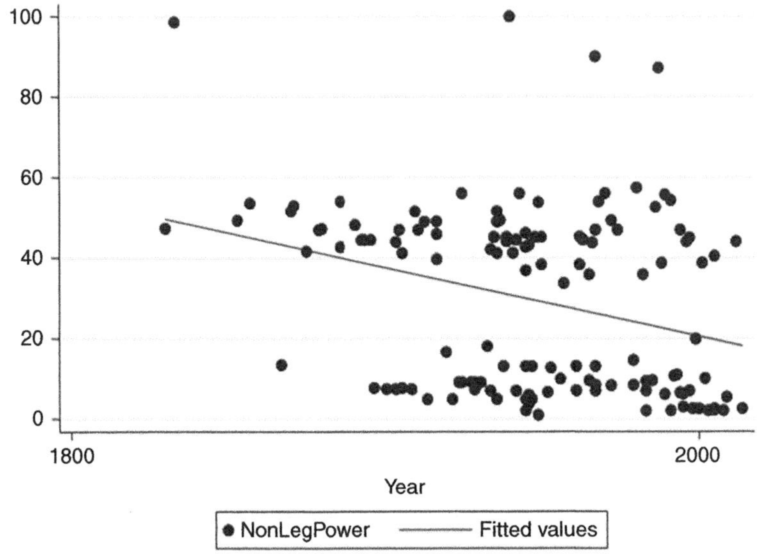

FIGURE 14.4 Non-legislative powers of presidents in Latin America, 1900–2014

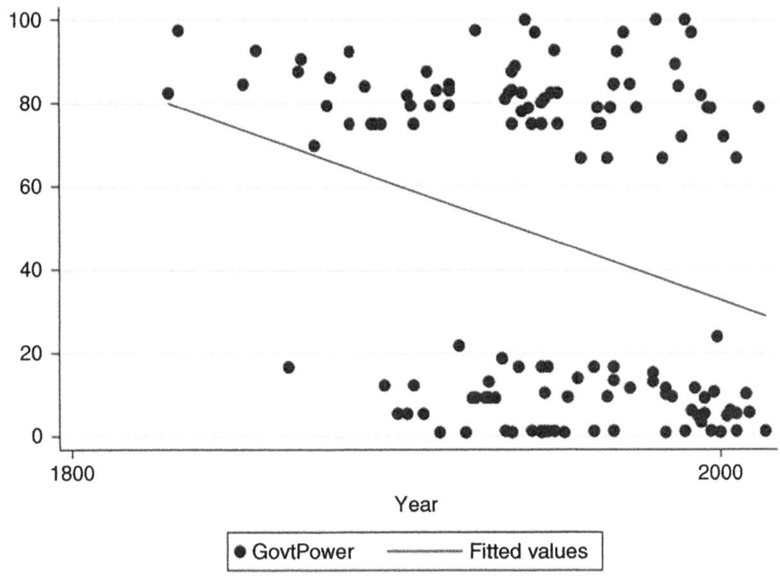

FIGURE 14.5 Government powers of presidents in Latin America, 1900–2014

and 2001, Colombia in 1991, Nicaragua in 1987, and Paraguay in 1992 – left presidents with legislative powers that are still quite strong in comparative terms. What explains the pressure to maintain or strengthen the influence of democratic presidents over policy-making?

II. EXPLAINING THE AGENDA-SETTING POWERS OF PRESIDENTS

Constitutions are formally amended or replaced when the costs of maintaining and implementing existing institutional arrangements are higher than the costs of revising them. As I have argued elsewhere, this is likely to occur in cases of deep political transformations at the state or regime level, sudden balance-of-power shifts among political actors, and institutional crises that stem from the dysfunctional performance of the existing constitutional regime (see Negretto 2012, 2013). Although we may on occasion trace the origins of specific provisions back to the event that triggered constitutional revisions, there is an important distinction between the general decision to initiate a process of constitutional change and the adoption of a particular set of institutions during that process.

For instance, although regime change is a common factor triggering the adoption of new constitutions or comprehensive amendments, the actual content of the institutions selected as a result of those processes might vary widely depending on the effects that reformers anticipate from the implementation of new institutions in different contexts. Both Brazil in 1988 and Honduras in 1982 adopted new constitutions as a key instance in their transitions from authoritarianism to democracy. Yet there is a sharp contrast between the legislative powers of the president in these two constitutions. The diverse environments from which these constitutions emerged explain this contrast.

Constitutional choice is determined by two types of assessments that reformers make at the time of replacing or amending a constitution. The first is a retrospective evaluation of the performance of the constitution in response to the challenges that governments face in a given historical juncture. At this level, constitution-makers take a relatively impartial stance that intends to justify the reform and elicit consensus about the need for introducing substantive changes. This stage sets the menu of reform options available. The second assessment consists of a prospective calculation of how alternative designs are likely to affect the power and influence of reformers over collective decisions. At this level, constitution-makers take a partisan position that inevitably generates political conflict. Given this conflict, final choices are usually explained by the distribution of power resources among the actors (see Negretto 2011, 2013).

Whereas these assessments account for the logic of constitutional choice in a wide variety of settings, the actual substance of reforms depends on specific historical constraints. Except at foundational moments, constitutional provisions change within the limits of an inherited constitutional regime whose basic structure remains unaltered. For instance, only rarely do reformers shift from a presidential to a parliamentary regime, or vice-versa. Even mixed regimes are generally stable.[5] This means that some basic institutional structure will shape future paths of reform

[5] For the evolution of constitutional regimes across the world, see Cheibub (2006).

and, in interaction with the political environment where choices are made, the direction of change.

In the case of Latin America, the adoption of a presidential regime in all the countries of the region by the second half of the nineteenth century is a crucial point of departure to understand general patterns of constitutional choice over time and across countries. This regime was initially based on the checks-and-balances model proposed by the American Federalists and adopted in the 1787 US constitution.[6] This model can be characterized as separate institutions sharing powers for the purpose of mutual control. The executive veto and bicameralism are typical examples of powers of mutual control in the legislative arena. Given this design, when separate institutions such as the executive and the legislature, or the lower and upper house of the assembly are placed under the control of different political interests, changing the legislative status quo is difficult and when it occurs, incremental (see Tsebelis 1995, 2002; Haggard and Shugart 2001).

The early model of separation of powers adopted in Latin America typically invested the president with a strong reactive power – a veto subject to a qualified majority override in each chamber of a bicameral congress – but deprived him of any specific power to change the legislative status quo. This arrangement does not prevent the executive from responding to pressures for policy reform if he has the support of a cohesive majority or near majority in congress. It becomes a liability, however, when a sharp deterioration of the legislative status quo demands prompt policy shifts and the president is unable to muster this support.

In this situation, presidents that have or expect to have insufficient partisan support in the legislature are likely to use every opportunity in which possible constitutional reforms are debated to demand the strengthening of their powers to induce or implement policy change. Members of the president's party have an obvious incentive to favor such change because in the absence of a cohesive legislative majority of their own, their only way to influence lawmaking is through executive action. In a fragmented political environment, parties that oppose the executive at the time may have the capacity to veto these proposals. Yet they are usually willing to compromise because they want concessions in other dimensions of design, or because they hope to control the presidency in the future but know they will lack a legislative majority to influence policy.

This discussion suggests that two factors are likely to explain whether a Madisonian model of separation of powers is likely to be altered during a process of constitutional revision to provide the executive with agenda-setting powers. The first is a deterioration of the status quo that demands rapid policy change, such as when the economy experiences a sharp downturn. The second is a fragmented political environment in which the president is unlikely to have the

6 James Madison provides the classic analysis of the checks and balances model adopted by the American constitution. See Federalist Papers 47 to 51, in Madison, Hamilton, and Jay ([1788] 1987: 302–22).

support of a cohesive majority to implement the required policy change. These two factors are likely to interact, in the sense that pressures for shifting from a reactive to a proactive role of the president in the legislative arena should be lower if economic conditions are good or if being critical, the president is able count on the support of a cohesive legislative majority.

The literature on economic crisis and policy reform in Latin America has already suggested the existence of a correlation between critical economic conditions, in particular inflation and fiscal crisis, and the use of exceptional presidential powers to stabilize the economy (Przeworski 1991; Haggard and Kaufman 1995). Some authors have also pointed out the importance of the structure of political institutions and the rules of the political game to account for the timing and type of policy reform (Nelson 1990; Kaufman 1990). This type analysis, however, has not been used to explain the link between economic crisis, the political environment, and constitutional choice in Latin America.

III. DETERMINANTS OF THE DESIGN OF EXECUTIVE POLICY-MAKING POWERS IN LATIN AMERICA

To evaluate this argument, I collected data on the determinants of the design of executive policy-making powers in Latin America between 1900 and 2014. The selected observations consist of new constitutions and constitutional amendments enacted by popularly elected civilian parties, in force during years where the executive and the legislature were elected, and more than one independent party competed in elections. Given these requirements, the revisions include all instances of constitutional replacement and all amendments in which institutional designers revised the allocation of legislative or non-legislative constitutional powers between presidents and assemblies. A total of fifty-seven observations were gathered according to these criteria.[7]

These observations allow us to determine the type of institutions reformers selected once the decision was made to adopt a new constitution or to amend the previous one. The dependent variable under analysis is thus the score of presidential powers observed after the constitution is replaced or amended. It is important to note that in each episode of constitutional change reformers may maintain, reduce, or increase previous scores of presidential legislative powers. Specifically, the sample includes twenty-five observations in which the preexisting legislative powers of presidents were maintained, ten where those powers were curtailed, and twenty-

7 The observations included are Argentina 1949 and 1994; Bolivia 1961, 1995, 2005, and 2009; Brazil 1946, 1988, and 2001; Colombia 1910, 1936, 1945, 1968, 1986, 1991, and 2003; Costa Rica 1949; Chile 1943, 1970, 1991, 1997, and 2005; Dominican Republic 1963 and 1966; Ecuador 1946, 1983, 1998, and 2008; El Salvador 1983; Guatemala 1945, 1965, and 1985; Honduras 1957, 1965, and 1982; Mexico 1917, 1994, 1996, and 2012; Nicaragua 1987, 1995, 2000, and 2005; Panama 1946; Paraguay 1992; Peru 1979, 1993, and 2002; Uruguay 1917, 1942, 1952, 1967, and 1997; Venezuela 1947, 1961, 1989, and 1999.

two where they were increased. In other words, the observations were selected due to the importance of the formal change, not because a particular outcome occurred. All new constitutions during the period under consideration are included because in these cases reformers are supposed to consider all aspects of the constitution. Similarly, the database includes as observations all cases of comprehensive amendments in which reformers revised some aspect of the distribution of powers between presidents and assemblies. In both situations, however, reformers may decide to keep or transform the specific powers of the president in the legislative dimension.

1. *Dependent Variables*

Two different outcomes of constitutional choice will be analyzed: the aggregate legislative powers of presidents, and their agenda-setting powers. As explained in section I of this chapter, whereas the former includes both reactive and proactive powers, the latter refers specifically to the power of presidents to induce or decide legislative change. Both have been measured using an index that ranges from 1 to 100 derived from categorical principal component analysis.[8]

2. *Independent Variables*

As explanatory factors for the substantive change in the policy-making powers of presidents, I have included two variables (INFLATION and GDP GROWTH) that measure economic conditions at the time of replacing or amending a constitution. The first is a direct measure of economic crisis and indicates the average rate of inflation during the last five years before a constitutional change takes place.[9] The second variable captures relative economic performance through the average GDP per capita growth, also during the last five years before a constitutional change takes place.[10] Since amending and even more replacing a constitution takes considerable time, it seems implausible that politicians would react immediately to critical economic conditions.

I use different variables to measure the level of fragmentation of the political environment at the time of deciding constitutional change. I first use two separate variables intended to capture the number of significant parties operating in the system and the level of internal unity of these parties. For the number of parties, I created

[8] Note that the indexes were constructed based on a larger database of presidential powers using new constitutions and amendments adopted and implemented during both democratic and authoritarian years. See n. 1.

[9] Annual rates of inflation were calculated based on the consumer price indexes from 1900 to 2010 for all Latin American countries provided by the Moxlad database (http://moxlad-staging.herokuapp.com/). Since rates of inflation varied widely both across countries and across time, the variable used in the statistical analysis is the natural logarithm of the original variable to avoid undue influence from extreme values.

[10] This variable is calculated based on the yearly gross domestic product (at purchasing power parity) in 1990 US dollars and population data provided by the Moxlad database (http://moxlad-staging.herokuapp.com/).

an ordinal scale (MNP) indicating the minimum number of parties necessary to pass constitutional changes according to the decision rule. Its actual range goes from 1 to 5. For party unity I use a dummy variable (PARTY DECENTRALIZATION), coded as 1 when members of the constituent body are elected in open lists, flexible lists, or multiple closed lists, and 0 if they were elected in single closed lists. Although there is no perfect measure for the level of internal unity of parties, several authors have argued that it is when legislators are elected in single closed lists that the party label matters most and parties tend to act as unitary actors (Carey and Shugart 1995; Cox and McCubbins 2001: 44–5).

I have also combined the number of parties needed to pass a reform and their level of internal unity into a single ordinal variable (fragmentation) that attempts to capture the degree of inter and intra-party negotiation needed to make collective decisions at the time of constitutional change. This variable is coded as 0 when a single centralized party is able to adopt the reform unilaterally, 1 when one decentralized party or more than one party is needed to pass the reform, and 2 when a multiparty coalition is required to pass constitutional changes and parties have a decentralized organization. Since this is a rank-ordered variable that seeks to measure power dispersion both across and within parties, I will report how results change when the full scale is used and when the minimum level of power fragmentation works as a baseline category for comparison.

As I have argued, the incentive of reformers to increase the policy-making powers of the president is likely to be stronger when governments must respond to critical economic conditions in the context of a fragmented political environment. To facilitate the interpretation of this interaction I will use the aggregate scale of political fragmentation to examine whether the impact of critical economic conditions is significant at low or high values of this variable.

Three control variables will be used.[11] The first is the lagged value of the dependent variable (DV t-1) before a constitutional change takes place. Since substantive constitutional change is usually incremental, it is important to assess to what extent the choice of presidential powers is determined by a previous path of design or is the product of other factors. It could also be argued that younger parties, where the influence of personal leadership is stronger, are more likely to demand strong legislative powers for the executive. I have thus used a party age variable, which measures the age in years of the largest party in the constituent body from its foundation to the time when a constitution is being replaced or amended.[12] Finally, it is possible that non-centrist parties are more likely to support presidents with strong lawmaking powers in the expectation that their policies would be opposed in congress. For this reason, I included a variable (PARTY POLICY) that captures whether the platform of the largest

[11] For the sake of simplicity, I have not presented here the results when other control variables, such as diffusion, are used. Results, however, do not diverge from those discussed here. For a discussion of the impact of diffusion on constitutional choice, see Negretto (2013).

[12] The concept of institutionalization of both parties and party systems has several components, but the most important are the age of parties and the stability of voting patterns across elections. See Mainwaring and Scully (1995: 4–6).

party in the constituent body has an extreme policy position. This variable ranges from 0, when this party has a centrist policy position, to 2, when it has a clear left or right position. Parties that combine positions from either side of the ideological spectrum receive an intermediate score of 1.[13]

3. *Regression Analysis*

I used an OLS regression with robust standard errors clustered by country to estimate the determinants of legislative and agenda-setting powers of presidents. Table 14.1 shows the results for the determinants of the legislative powers of presidents. Models 1 to 3 test the influence of the economic and political environment, and Model 4 tests the interaction between the two.

Model 1 includes the key economic and political variables and the lagged value of the dependent variable as a control. It shows that inflation has a substantive and statistically significant impact on how reformers allocate legislative powers between presidents and assemblies during processes of constitutional revision. In particular, it suggests that when constitutions are replaced or amended against a background of high inflation reformers tend to increase the legislative powers of the executive. GDP per capita growth has no discernible effect on this decision and the impact of inflation remains the same after excluding this variable. This suggests that, at least for the Latin American context, inflation is the main indicator of economic performance that affects constitutional choice.

As for the political environment, this model indicates that constitution-makers are likely to strengthen the legislative powers of the president when the number of parties making up the reform coalition increases. Party decentralization also has a positive and significant effect on the selection of presidential legislative powers, showing that constitution-makers are more likely to strengthen these powers when parties have a decentralized organization. The lagged score of executive policy-making power has an expected positive and statistically significant effect on subsequent choices, suggesting that constitution-makers either maintained previous scores or moved gradually toward higher scores. The small size of the coefficient, however, indicates that the impact of institutional inertia is in reality weak compared to the economic and political variables. Model 2 shows generally the same results as Model 1 after including the rest of the control variables.

Model 3 uses fragmentation as an aggregate measure that captures both the number of parties with control over constitutional change and their degree of internal unity, and confirms that the legislative powers of presidents tend to increase as political fragmentation grows. It is important to note that if in this model we use a single centralized party able to adopt the reform unilaterally as a baseline category, the results (not shown) indicate that it is only when a multiparty coalition is required

[13] Results do not change, however, if they are coded as centrist or extreme.

TABLE 14.1 *Determinants of the legislative powers of presidents*[a]
Dependent variable: legislative powers of presidents[b]

Independent variables	Model 1	Model 2	Model 3	Model 4
INFLATION (ln)	3.361 **	3.558***	3.212**	1.919
	(1.212)	(1.173)	(1.181)	(2.506)
GDP P/C GROWTH	.619	.751	. 835	.759
	(.500)	(.560)	(.482)	(.489)
MNP	5.108**	4.828**	———	———
	(1.823)	(1.745)		
PARTY DECENTRALIZATION	16.359 ***	15.029**	———	———
	(4.404)	(5.172)		
FRAGMENTATION	———	———	13.097***	10.195*
			(3.583)	(4.916)
INFLATION* FRAGMENTATION	———	———	———	1.171
				(1.468)
LAGGED DV (t-1)	0.431 **	. 417***	.444***	.452***
	(.148)	(.126)	(.108)	(.113)
PARTY AGE	———	.096	.077	.081
		(.063)	(.063)	(.066)
PARTY POLICY	———	3.313	4.662	4.956
		(3.428)	(3.651)	(3.841)
Constant	3.215	2.275	.3067	2.208
	(5.354)	(7.017)	(6.179)	(6.292)
Adjusted R^2	0.66	0.68	0.69	0.69
N	55	55	55	55

[a] OLS
[b] Continuous variable ranging from 1 to 100
Numbers in parentheses are robust standard errors clustered by country.
* $p < 0.1$; ** $p < 0.05$; *** $p < 0.01$

to pass constitutional changes and parties have a decentralized organization (i.e., when fragmentation = 2) that political fragmentation has a substantively and statistically significant effect on the strengthening of the legislative powers of presidents.

Model 4, finally, tests whether the impact of the economic environment on constitutional choice is conditional on features of the political environment. The interactive model explicitly shows this conditionality. When the level of political fragmentation is at its lowest, that is when a single unified party controls constitutional change (fragmentation = 0), inflation has a positive but not significant impact on the design of the legislative powers of presidents. On the other hand, significance tests derived from the model indicate that as inflation increases, the legislative powers of presidents tend to be strengthened in a systematic way when one

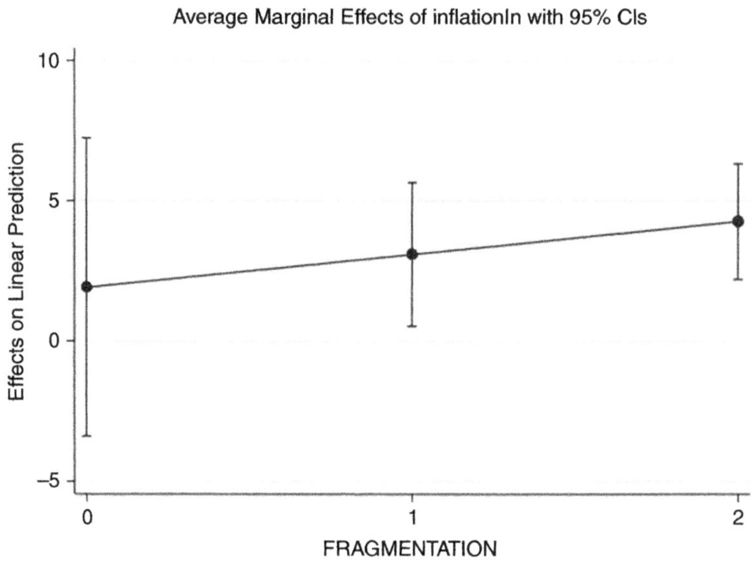

FIGURE 14.6 Marginal effects of inflation at increasing degrees of political fragmentation

decentralized party or more than one party is needed to pass the reform (fragmentation = 1) and when a multiparty coalition is required to pass constitutional changes and parties have a decentralized organization (fragmentation = 2). Figure 14.6 illustrates the marginal effect of inflation at different degrees of political fragmentation.[14]

As indicated in the analysis of long-term trends of constitutional change, the systematic increase of the legislative powers of presidents over time is largely due to the strengthening of their agenda-setting powers. If this correct, we should observe that the same factors that account for the overall legislative powers of presidents should also account for their agenda-setting powers specifically. This is indeed what we observe in Table 14.2, with one important difference to note in the interactive model, namely, that political fragmentation does not cause a significant increase in the agenda-setting powers of the president at the lowest possible level of inflation (i.e., inflation = 0). This suggests that although the degree of political fragmentation still has the stronger independent effect on substantive constitutional change, it may not account for a significant increase in the agenda powers of the executive in isolation from the general conditions of the economy.

Overall, these results indicate that while bad economic conditions, such as high or rising levels of inflation, may enter into the evaluations of reformers to

[14] The lines represent the upper and lower bounds of 95 percent confidence intervals. Lines above the 0 line indicate a statistically significant effect.

TABLE 14.2 *Determinants of the agenda-setting powers of presidents*[a]
Dependent variable: agenda-setting powers of presidents[b]

Independent variables	Model 1	Model 2	Model 3	Model 4
INFLATION (ln)	3.935 *	4.229**	3.910 **	2.224
	(1.897)	(1.858)	(1.828)	(3.713)
GDP P/C GROWTH	579	767	883	790
	(.559)	(.659)	(.614)	(.603)
MNP	6.055 **	5.714 **	———	———
	(2.718)	(2.627)		
PARTY DECENTRALIZATION	15.823 **	13.999 **	———	———
	(5.670)	(6.579)		
FRAGMENTATION	———		13.936**	10.168
			(5.172)	(5.918)
INFLATION* FRAGMENTATION	———		———	1.529
				(2.104)
LAGGED DV (t-1)	539***	521***	523***	531***
	(.125)	(.104)	(.092)	(.094)
PARTY AGE	———	(134)	.112	117
		(.105)	(.102)	(.107)
PARTY POLICY	———	4.997	6.362	6.756
		(4.229)	(4.502)	(4.817)
Constant[2]	12.042	20.457	17.023	13.488
	(7.632)	(10.475)	(9.538)	(9.458)
Adjusted R^2	0.63	0.65	0.66	0.66
N	55	55	55	55

[a] OLS
[b] Continuous variable ranging from 1 to 100
Numbers in parentheses are robust standard errors clustered by country.
* $p < 0.1$; ** $p < 0.05$; *** $p < 0.01$

change existing institutions, the actual decision to strengthen the legislative powers of the president becomes more likely only when the political environment is fragmented. In other words, how much deteriorating economic conditions lead to an increase in the formal legislative powers of presidents during processes of constitutional revision ultimately depends on how capable governments are to produce policy shifts with reliable legislative support. As I show in section IV, the cases of Mexico and Argentina illustrate this mechanism well.

IV. COMPARATIVE ANALYSIS OF MEXICO AND ARGENTINA

A comparison between Mexico and Argentina between 1982 and 1994 is ideal to flesh out how critical economic conditions may affect the formal agenda-setting powers of presidents, depending on the level of political fragmentation.[15] By the early 1980s, Mexico and Argentina shared similar constitutional structures, which followed the essential tenets of the checks-and-balances model of separation of powers. Both had a federal state, a bicameral congressional structure, and an executive invested with a strong veto but no authority to promote or implement legislative changes. At the same time, from 1982 to 1991, each of these countries experienced several years of high inflation, low or negative economic growth, and large fiscal deficits that called for important policy reforms. Tables 14.3 and 14.4 show economic indicators for both countries.

In both Mexico and Argentina, political actors adopted important constitutional amendments at the time of or immediately after the economic crisis. However, whereas Mexico maintained the model of a president invested with only reactive legislative powers, presidents in Argentina acquired new and extremely powerful agenda-setting powers. These powers were first used de facto, and later incorporated into the constitution via formal amendment (see Negretto 2004, 2013). The different political environments that governments faced in implementing economic policy changes in these countries explain the maintenance or reform of the initial distribution of legislative powers between presidents and assemblies.

At the beginning of the debt crisis, in 1982, Mexico was still an authoritarian regime in which the ruling party was able to control a qualified majority of seats in both the lower and upper chamber of congress. By the end of the period under consideration, in 1994, political competition and party pluralism had increased and a process of slow and gradual transition to democracy was already visible.[16] Throughout these political transformations, however, the government party not only maintained a majority in both chambers of congress but also a strongly centralized organization that guaranteed very high levels of legislative discipline (see Weldon 1997; Nacif 2002).

Governments in Argentina faced a different political environment. In 1983, the country had its first democratic election since 1973. Since that date, the party of the president consistently lacked an absolute majority of seats in both chambers of congress. In addition, although the main parties in Argentina were disciplined, their levels of cohesion on economic policy were not always high, particularly within the PJ (see Negretto 2004). Tables 14.5 and 14.6 show the seat share of the president's party in both countries during the period under consideration.

As students of economic reforms in Latin America have argued, the highly concentrated system of executive authority in Mexico was crucial in establishing the basis for the implementation of a tough austerity program to fight inflation

15 If we conceive of critical economic conditions and political fragmentation as causal factors that have independent effects and the strengthening of the legislative powers of the president as an outcome that is present or absent, the comparison between these two cases approaches a most-similar design method of case analysis (see Gerring 2008).

16 By 1988 the government party lost control over its qualified majority in the lower chamber. Opposition parties, in turn, increased their share of seats in the lower chamber from 20 percent in 1982 to 40 percent in 1994.

TABLE 14.3 *Mexico, economic indicators 1982–93*

President	Party	Year	Inflation rate[a]	GDPPCGROWTH[b]	Fiscal Deficit[c]
Miguel de la Madrid	**PRI**	1982	29.7	-2.7	−1,309,000
		1983	46.6	-6.1	−1,246,000
		1984	56.1	1.6	−1,975,000
		1985	62.4	0.6	−3,964,000
		1986	74.1	-5.5	−10,157,000
		1987	88.6	0.1	−26,020,000
Salinas	**PRI**	1988	91.1	-0.5	−39,808,000
		1989	82.0	2.4	−24,739,000
		1990	75.8	3.2	−18,820,000
		1991	63.1	2.4	−69,000
		1992	39.8	1.8	10,990,000
		1993	18.9	0.1	2,870

a Annual rate of inflation based on variations in the consumer price index ([CPI year 2- CPI year 1)/CPI year 1] * 100).

b Annual rate of GDP per capita growth ([(GDPPC year 2- GDPPC year 1)/GDPPC year 1] * 100) estimated in purchasing power parity, using 1990 US dollars.

c Difference in central government revenues and expenditures, expressed in millions in local currency unit.

Source: Montevideo-Oxford Latin American Economic History Data Base (MOxLAD), http://moxlad-staging.herokuapp.com/home/en

TABLE 14.4 *Argentina, economic indicators 1983–95*

President	Party	Year	Inflation rate[a]	GDPCGROWTH[b]	Fiscal deficit[c]
Alfonsín	UCR	1984	626.7	0.5	−102,000
		1985	672.0	−8.3	−1,100
		1986	90.2	5.6	−800
		1987	131.3	1.1	−2,900
		1988	200	−3.3	−17,000
		1989	3,300.0	−8.3	85,000
Menem I	PJ	1990	2,325.50	−3.2	−123,300
		1991	171.7	9.1	−4,566,000
		1992	24.9	8.2	561
		1993	10.6	4.3	1,098
		1994	4.2	4.5	−895
		1995	3.4	−4.0	−4,457

[a] Annual rate of inflation based on variations in the consumer price index ([CPI year 2- CPI year 1)/CPI year 1]* 100).
[b] Annual rate of GDP per capita growth ([(GDPPC year 2- GDPPC year 1)/GDPPC year 1]* 100) estimated in purchasing power parity, using 1990 US dollars.
[c] Difference in central government revenues and expenditures, expressed in millions in local currency unit.
Source: Montevideo-Oxford Latin American Economic History Data Base (MOxLAD), in http://moxlad-staging.herokuapp.com/home/en

TABLE 14.5 *Mexico, government party's share 1982–94*

President	Party	Period	Chamber of Deputies	Senate
Miguel de la Madrid	PRI	1982–85	80.4	1982–88 98.4
		1985–88	73.0	
Salinas	PRI	**1988–91**	**52.0**	1988–91 93.8
		1991–94	64.0	1991–94 95.3

TABLE 14.6 *Argentina, government party's share 1983–95*

President	Party	Period	Chamber of Deputies	Senate	Convention
Alfonsín	UCR	1983–85	50.8	**1983–86 39.1**	
		1985–87	51.6	1986–89 39.1	
		1987–89	45.4		
Menem I	PJ	**1989–91**	**47.2**	**1989–92 56.3**	
		1991–93	45.1	1992–95 62.5	
		1993–95	49.4		
Menem I	PJ	1994			45.0

during the 1980s (see Kaufman 1990). Several constitutional amendments were adopted in this country between 1990 and 1996, and two of them (in 1994 and 1996) explicitly affected the allocation of powers between presidents and assemblies.[17] None of these reforms, however, altered the preexisting powers of the president in the legislative arena. Presidents relied on their parties to muster sufficient legislative support to shift economic policy.

By contrast, in the absence of cohesive majority support in the legislature, presidents in Argentina used de facto decree powers to implement stabilization measures from 1985 to 1990. In 1990, a Supreme Court ruling constitutionalized these powers, provided that a "serious social danger" existed and that Congress "does not adopt decisions different from the decree on the issues of economic policy involved."[18] Finally, a deep constitutional revision enacted in 1994 with the agreement of the two parties that had occupied the presidency in the previous years, formalized the power of the executive to issue decrees with the immediate force of law in cases of urgency and necessity (see Negretto 2004, 2013).

[17] Both amendments altered the appointment powers of the president.

[18] See the *Peralta* case, in *El Derecho*, 1991, Vol. 141, pp. 519–48.

V. CONCLUSIONS

In spite of the expansion of electoral democracy during recent decades in Latin America and the adoption of several reforms intended to moderate or reduce the traditional non-legislative powers of the executive, the legislative powers of Latin American presidents (in particular the power to promote legislative change) have remained strong or increased. As this chapter has argued and supported with comparative empirical data, this result is due, at least in part, to the impact of economic stress. When economic crises demanded prompt policy shifts, but the political environment provided presidents with insufficient partisan support to implement legislative changes through congressional action, a typical response was the strengthening of executive powers in the legislative realm.

The persistent trend toward maintaining presidents with strong legislative powers, or even strengthening these powers, suggests that most countries in Latin America that experienced cycles of economic crises during the 1980s and early 1990s (or later) faced a political environment more similar to that of Argentina than Mexico's. This is indeed the case. With some exceptions, party system fragmentation has increased in Latin America since the 1980s, and parties have become less cohesive and disciplined. From this perspective, it is not coincidental that it was not until 2012 that a constitutional amendment in Mexico increased the formal agenda powers of the president. This transformation occurred without an economic crisis but after experiencing two successive minority governments.

The strengthening of the executive agenda-setting powers may not be a phenomenon restricted to Latin America. It is also observed in several parliamentary regimes in Western Europe. Yet the pressure to do so is likely to be stronger in presidential systems that face economic crises in a fragmented political environment. Most parliamentary regimes have built-in mechanisms that enable governments to obtain disciplined parliamentary support even in situations of multipartism and decentralized party organization. In a separation-of-powers system, by contrast, a president invested with strong agenda-setting powers may be necessary to provide the government party with influence over policy if it lacks the support of a cohesive legislative majority.

15

Constitutions, Crisis, and Regime Change: Perspectives on East and Southeast Asia

Björn Dressel[*]

I. INTRODUCTION

What happens to liberal democratic constitutions during a severe financial crisis? How does such an event affect their nature, their practice, and their enforcement, particularly where such constitutions are relatively new? In this chapter, I seek answers to these questions through empirical analysis of the experience of the states in Southeast and East Asia over the last quarter century (1990–2013), eliciting both quantitative and well-rooted qualitative evidence.

Though highly challenging, Asia is particularly suitable terrain for this kind of empirical exploration. While the political and constitutional diversity of the region make broad generalization problematic – many states in the region are so far from the normative liberal-constitutional ideal they might best be described as hybrid-nominal constitutional orders[1] – it is also true that the severe impact of the Asian financial crisis (AFC, 1997–98) and to a lesser degree the recent global financial crisis (GFC, 2008–09), has provided a unique opportunity to explore the nexus between liberal constitutional practice and financial crisis – and to test the claim that 'constitutionalism has significantly broadened and deepened its reach in Asia in modern and contemporary times.'[2]

Given such fertile ground, it is somewhat surprising to note that the question before us is so far largely unexplored in Asia. It may be, perhaps, that such questions have traditionally fallen between disciplines. For instance, while a number of

* I would like to thank Syed Hasan for excellent research assistance in preparation for this chapter. Thanks also go to Mathias Sinning, Tomoo Inoue and participants of the Lisbon workshop on 'Liberal Constitutions during severe Financial Crisis' (22 May 2017) for constructive feedback and thoughtful comments, which greatly improved this chapter.

[1] Albert Chen, 'The Achievement of Constitutionalism in Asia: Moving Beyond "Constitutions without Constitutionalism"' (2014); Björn Dressel and Marco Bünte, *Contesting Constitutionalism: Constitutional Politics in Southeast Asia. Politics and Constitutions*. Abingdon: Routledge, 2016, 1–22.

[2] Albert Chen, 'Pathways of Western Liberal Constitutional Development in Asia: A Comparative Study of five Major Nations', *International Journal of Constitutional Law* 8(4): 884 (2010).

economic scholars have explored the roots and dynamics of both financial crises in the region, and even debated the consequences for regulatory reform,[3] they have generally done so with little regard to the constitutional architecture itself. Similarly, political scientists have studied the political roots and consequences of the financial crisis in Asia[4] and shown how the crisis led to pressures for changes in political institutions and regime structures, but they have now engaged much with actual constitutional dynamics. Finally, while legal scholars have certainly studied legal change and constitutional practice in the region, their work has generally relegated economic shocks at best to a background condition.[5] In short, what has emerged is a series of separate scholarly debates, all of which lack a clear political-economy perspective on constitutional change in East and Southeast Asia.

How, then, should we think about the nexus between economic or financial crisis and constitutional change? A closer look at some contributions in this volume suggests that the answer is far from straightforward. In fact, rather than assuming a simple uniform relationship, it might perhaps be best to think about it in terms of a conditional effect – one in which crisis reveals inadequacies in the constitutional structures, which then could prompt demands for constitutional change. In other words, the relationship is conditional on the crisis demonstrating the limits of the current constitution; conversely, where the constitution can deal adequately with a crisis, it will not generate constitutional change.[6]

And yet, this only prompts further contextual and political questions. For instance, it has been suggested, based on the European experience during the GFC, that perhaps the pattern is more nuanced, should go beyond the binary of constitutional change/no change to encompass more subtle subtypes of change (e.g., breakdown and adjustment) and lack of change (e.g., submission and stamina) – which deserve analysis in their own right.[7] Others, like Negretto,[8] have specifically drawn attention to the impact of crisis on legislative and executive powers as part of the constitutional change that has taken place in Latin America.

3 William Hunter, George Kaufman, and Thomas Krueger (eds). *The Asian Financial Crisis: Origins, Implications, and Solutions*. Heidelberg: Springer Science & Business Media, 2012.

4 Karl Jackson, 'Asian Contagion', *Singapore: ISEAS* (1999); Haggard, Stephan. *The Political Economy of the Asian Financial Crisis*. Peterson Institute, 2000; Gregory Noble and John Ravenhill (eds). *The Asian Financial Crisis and the Architecture of Global Finance*. Cambridge: Cambridge University Press, 2000; Andrew MacIntyre, *The Power of Institutions: Political Architecture and Governance*. Ithaca NY: Cornell University Press, 2003.

5 Wen-Chen Chang, Li-ann Thio, Kevin YL Tan, and Jiunn-rong Yeh. *Constitutionalism in Asia: cases and materials*. London: Bloomsbury Publishing, 2014; Chen, *Constitutionalism in Asia in the Early Twenty-First Century*.

6 See Negretto, Ch. 14 in this volume.

7 Xenophon Contiades, 'Constitutions in the Global Financial Crisis'. A *Comparative Analysis*. Surrey: Ashgate, 2013, 177–90.

8 See Ch. 14 in this volume, and Gabriel Negretto, 'Replacing and Amending Constitutions: The Logic of Constitutional Change in Latin America'. *Law & Society Review* 46(4): 749–79 (2012).

It is against such broader discussion that this chapter uses both cross-regional quantitative analysis to describe and test for the effect of crisis on constitutional change and comprehensive qualitative analysis of selected case studies to explore more nuanced dynamics of change (or the apparent absence thereof), as laid out by Contiades.[9] Since in Asia the 1997 AFC was a far more severe event than the 2008 GFC, I emphasize the former – though a certain constitutional vigor in the latest crisis also prompts reflection on constitutional learning and adaptation in the region.

My analysis finds little evidence to suggest that severe financial crisis has directly influenced constitutional change to the point of generating new versions, or even amendments. Instead political variables (e.g., type of political system) offer a much more powerful explanation of the changes (or the lack thereof) we observe – thus supporting the conditional effect. The case studies also suggest that crisis may have stimulated informal change to constitutions through changes in other laws and judicial interventions – sometimes with direct consequences for how the constitution is applied.[10] However, rather than being a transferable pattern, this might also simply reflect a uniquely Asian context – one where the crisis events were perceived as not only external but also transitory; the recentness of constitutional changes may have helped to legitimize existing constitutions.

To elaborate this argument, first, I describe and analyse patterns of financial crisis and constitutional change in Asia over the last four decades, with particular attention to 1990–2013. Based on simple regressions using a linear probability model (LPM), I present inferential findings on the nexus between severe crisis and constitutional change. Second, I use case studies to illustrate the more nuanced dynamics of constitutional reactions to crisis. The intent is to illustrate causal pathways and pressures exerted on the constitution. The chapter concludes with theoretical and empirical reflections on the findings, especially as they relate to the future of constitutionalism in the region.

II. SURVEYING FINANCIAL CRISIS AND CONSTITUTIONAL CHANGE IN EAST AND SOUTHEAST ASIA

Before we focus on constitutional dynamics in times of crisis, it might be helpful to survey regional patterns of financial crisis and constitutional change over time. We first compare the 1997 AFC and the 2008 GFC, which had regional impacts of differing types and severity: the former emanated from the region to have global consequences, the latter was a global crisis with consequences for the region. We then look at patterns of constitutional changes, first generally for 1945–2013, and then more narrowly for the period during which both crises occurred (1990–2013). The goal is to provide the foundation for the analysis that follows.

[9] Contiades, 'Constitutions in the Global Financial Crisis'.

[10] See for similar insights Ch. 6 by Cushman and Ch. 7 by Gulati and Vanberg in this volume.

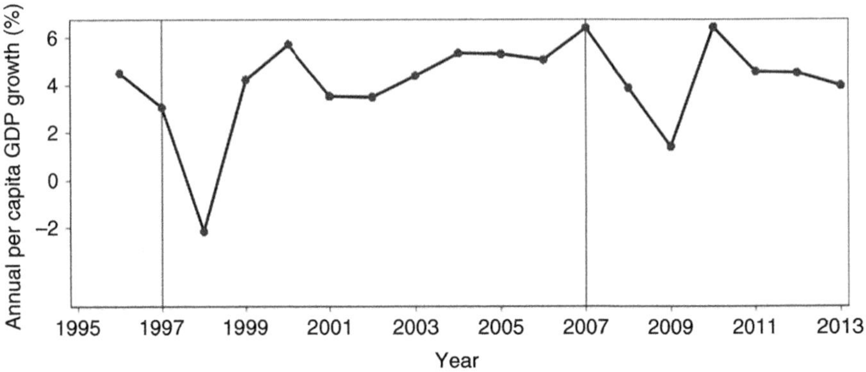

FIGURE 15.1 Annual per capita GDP growth in East and Southeast Asia (%)[11]
Source: WDI database

1. *A Tale of Two Financial Crises*

While individual states in Asia had experienced financial crises before (e.g., Thailand in 1983 and the Philippines in 1983–84), the AFC that began in 1997 stands out for both its regional concentration and the severity of the impact for the states in the region (Figure 15.1, e.g., demonstrates the impact on per capita GDP growth for the countries in our region of interest).

That crisis unfolded in several overlapping phases, beginning with the collapse of the Thai baht in July 1997 due to a lack of foreign currency reserves and a high burden of foreign debt. This event infected neighbouring Southeast Asian countries, East Asia, and even the BRIC economies beyond the region.[12] Indonesia, South Korea and Thailand seemed to been most affected, but the pain of rapid withdrawal of short-term capital, currency devaluation, and systemic bank failures was also felt to varying degrees in Malaysia, Singapore, the Philippines, Taiwan, and China.[13]

By early 1998, not just the financial sector but also the real economy that produces actual goods and services was feeling the AFC effects, as the region began to suffer from a loss of demand and confidence. The economic and social consequences were severe: economies in Southeast Asia and South Korea contracted by 7–13 percent in real terms. In some countries, unemployment tripled, and national poverty rates shot up, almost doubling in Indonesia and South Korea.[14] Eventually the IMF stepped in

[11] Annual per capita GDP growth (%), averaged for selected countries in our data set (e.g., Brunei, Cambodia, China, East Timor, Indonesia, Japan, North Korea, South Korea, Laos, Malaysia, Mongolia, Myanmar, Philippines, Singapore, Taiwan, Thailand, and Vietnam).

[12] Morris Goldstein, *The Asian Financial Crisis: Causes, Cures, and Systemic Implications*. Washington, DC: Institute for International Economics, 1998.

[13] Yunpeng Zhu and Hal Hill (eds). *The Social Impact of the Asian Financial Crisis*, Vol. 129. Cheltenham: Edward Elgar Publishing, 2001.

[14] Eddy Lee, *The Asian Financial Crisis: The Challenge for Social Policy*. International Labour Organization, 1998; M. Ramesh, 'Economic Crisis and Its Social Impacts'. *Global Social Policy* 9 (1): 79–99 (2009).

with a $40 billion program to stabilize the economies affected, and further support from international and bilateral donors followed.[15]

There was considerable debate about the sources of the crisis and the subsequent interventions.[16] Eventually, there was growing acknowledgement that the interventions stimulated a gradual recovery of the Asian economies from what was then considered one of the most severe financial crises since the Great Depression.[17] In fact, by 1999, growth was returning in most states, though for many countries the macroeconomic and above all political consequences were felt far beyond that date (Figure 15.1).

As Figure 15.1 illustrates, the 2008 GFC, by contrast, had far less severe effects on states in Asia.[18] With the GFC rooted in the subprime mortgage market in the United States and subsequent deleveraging by global financial institutions that were involved in highly complex financial transactions, the effects were largely felt in Asia through the synchronized global slowdown that began in the second half of 2008. The GFC caused fewer problems for Asian financial sectors, which had only limited exposure to subprime and related products.[19]

Hence, transmission of the GFC in Asia occurred principally through trade and financial channels, which increased output volatility and overall economic vulnerability, particularly in countries closely linked to international markets. The impact differed, though, depending on the degree of dependence on external demand and credit, which meant that export-dependent countries like South Korea and many Southeast Asian countries experienced a noticeable slowdown in export demand (down by 13–22 percent in 2009) that had serious spillover effects on their domestic sectors. Growth abruptly decelerated in 2008 for some countries. Nevertheless, with the exception of Thailand, most continued to grow throughout the GFC. Furthermore, backed by solid fiscal positions (e.g., fiscal deficits of less than 5 percent of GDP), governments could pursue several aggressive and timely responses, such as fiscal stimuli that ranged from 6 percent of GDP in South Korea to 17 percent in Thailand, and specific measures to safeguard the stability of the banking sector.[20] As a result, credit continued to flow normally and by 2009 growth rates were almost back to pre-crisis levels.

15 Barry Eichengreen, 'The International Monetary Fund in the Wake of the Asian Crisis'. In G. W. Noble and J. Ravenhill (eds), *The Asian Financial Crisis and the Architecture of Global Finance*. Cambridge: Cambridge University Press, 2000, 170–91.

16 Some blamed macroeconomic and exchange rate mismanagement; others the volatility of international financial markets, self-fulfilling speculative attacks and contagion; and a third group regulatory and structural problem, such as rapid growth in lending growth, high corporate leveraging and excessive risk-taking often linked to corruption, nepotism and cronyism in government–business relations. See Haggard, *The Political Economy of the Asian Financial Crisis*.

17 Sara Hsu, *Financial Crises, 1929 to the Present*. Cheltenham: Edward Elgar Publishing, 2017.

18 Rajah Rasiah, Kee Cheok Cheong, and Richard Doner, 'Southeast Asia and the Asian and Global Financial Crises'. *Journal of Contemporary Asia* 44(4): 572–80 (2014).

19 Asian Development Bank, *Asian Development Outlook*. Manila: ADB, 2009.

20 Asian Development Bank, *Asian Development Outlook*. Manila: ADB, 2010.

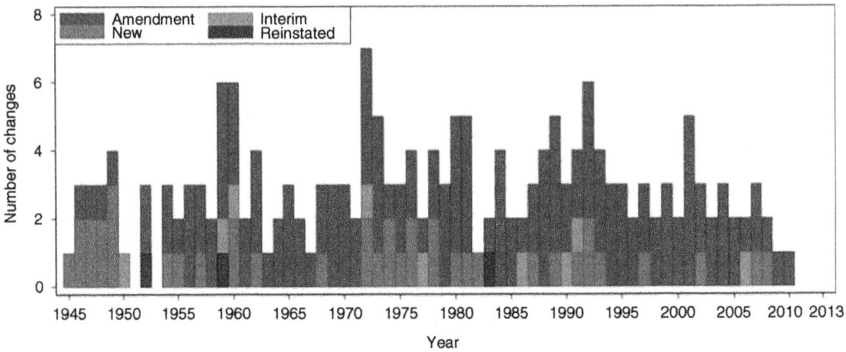

FIGURE 15.2 Constitutional change (by type), 1945–2013
Source: Comparative Constitutions Project Database (2014)

In short, setting aside effects on the real economy, there were dramatic differences between the AFC and the GFC in terms of their geographical origins, regional exposure, and how prepared states in Asia were for the financial crisis event. As a result, both events not only differed in terms of the severity of their impact on states in the region, but also in terms of how much the impact was rooted in, and transmitted by, financial sectors in the region. Consistent with the 'severe financial crisis' theme, our analysis will focus principally on events related to the 1997 Asian crisis, though not forgetting the 2008 global crisis.

2. *A Changing Constitutional Landscape*

A quick survey of constitutional reform in the region over the last sixty-five years suggests a region in constitutional flux (Figure 15.2).[21] The activity of constitution-making coincided roughly with two transitions: the departure of European colonial powers and the decolonization process that took place in its aftermath (1945–1970s), and the post-1989 era, when Thailand (in 1991, 1997, 2006), Mongolia (1992), Cambodia (1993), East Timor (2001), Nepal (2007), and Bhutan (2008) drafted constitutions as part of political transitions, or on becoming independent.[22]

Other constitutional changes occurred via reinstatement (e.g., Indonesia 1959; Thailand 1953, 1983), or in Thailand as interim constitutions, often linked to military coups (e.g., 1959, 1960, 1972, 1977, 1991, 2006). However, most change post-1989 has occurred through constitutional amendments – especially in Malaysia and Singapore, which together account for 50 percent of amendments between 1990 and 2013.

[21] Countries covered by the analysis are Brunei, Cambodia, China, East Timor, Indonesia, Japan, North Korea, South Korea, Laos, Malaysia, Mongolia, Myanmar, Philippines, Singapore, Taiwan, Thailand, and Vietnam.

[22] Kevin Tan, 'The Making and Remaking of Constitutions in Southeast Asia: An Overview', *Singapore Journal of International & Comparative Law* 6: 1-41 (2002).

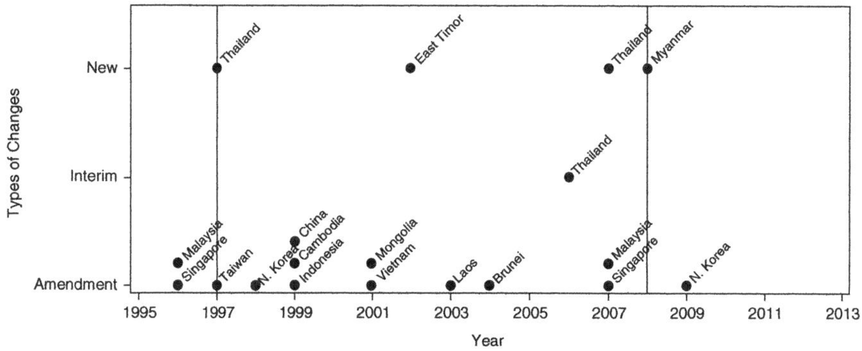

FIGURE 15.3 Financial crisis and constitutional change, 1996–2013
Source: Comparative Constitutions Project Database (2014)

A closer look at the constitutional change processes within two years before or after each of the two major financial crises reveals few additional insights, at least at first glance (Figure 15.3). While social and economic crisis is widely considered a trigger for constitution-making,[23] Thailand and Myanmar seem to be the only countries that adopted a new constitution in close temporal proximity to the crisis, although Indonesia's protracted amendment process (1999, 2000, 2001, 2002) might be added to the list because the changes were so comprehensive.[24] The majority of changes in patterns (81 percent) relate to constitutional amendments, which may not be directly related to either financial crisis.

Yet perhaps equally noteworthy is the absence of any change within a small number of states (e.g., South Korea, Philippines, Japan), which suggests that rather than being generalizable, the relationship between crisis and constitutional change is marked by subtle national nuances that require a more contextual understanding.

Indeed, any analysis of the nexus between financial crisis and liberal constitutions, needs to consider both situations – crisis-induced change and no change – plus the more nuanced dynamics within each of these two types. Following the typology of constitutional reactions suggested by Contiades,[25] these might include two scenarios of change: one of *breakdown*, which is marked by constitutional replacement, total revision, or the establishment of a new constitutional order, and one of *adjustment*, which is marked by formal and informal change as the constitution adapts to keep up with what is happening in the society. Similarly, a non-change scenario might be further subdivided for analytical purposes into cases of *stamina*, where the constitution is able to confront the financial crisis and remain intact, and *submission*, where the new demands overwhelm the constitution, and thus its

23 Chang et al. *Constitutionalism in Asia*, 58.
24 Donald Horowitz, *Constitutional Change and Democracy in Indonesia*. Cambridge and New York: Cambridge University Press, 2013.
25 Contiades, 'Constitutions in the Global Financial Crisis'.

function may be eroded, with the effect that while formally the constitution remains unchanged, it will undergo lawmaker-driven informal change.[26]

It is with these concepts in mind that we turn to analysis of the data, which will proceed from (a) a broad statistical exploration of constitutional change in our regional sample, to (b) a more detailed analysis of constitutional dynamics within each of the ideal types just described. Ultimately, we hope to generate insights into how liberal constitutional frameworks in Asia responded to severe financial crisis.

III. DATA AND METHODS

To perform the quantitative analysis, we rely on several different sources in constructing the regional data set.[27] The dependent variable in our analysis, Constitutional Change, is a binary variable generated using the *evnttype* variable in the Characteristics of National Constitutions data set. It takes the value of 1 for any type of constitutional change (e.g., amendments, interim, new, reinstated), and 0 if there is no change.

To capture the effect of financial crisis on constitutional change, we relied on an indicator variable for *financial crisis* and several other important variables associated with constitutional change:

Financial Crisis – an aggregate indicator variable was created relying on the data set developed by Laeven and Valencia.[28] It takes the value of 1 if any type of financial crisis (e.g., systemic banking crisis, currency crisis, and sovereign debt crisis) occurred, 0 otherwise.

Five-year moving average of GDP Growth (%)– taken from the World Development Indicator (WDI) data set.

Five-year moving average of CPI Inflation (%) – taken from the WDI data set.

Five-year moving average of Total Unemployment (% of total labor force) – taken from the WDI data set.

We also added several political control variables that may be important for explaining constitutional change:

Democracy, which assumes the value of 1 if the polity2 variable of the Polity IV data set takes a value of 6 or more, and 0 otherwise.

Parliamentary, which, relying on the dpi system variable in the Quality of Government data set, takes the value of 1 if the system is parliamentary, and 0 if not.

Length, measuring the length of the constitution (in number of words) derived from the Characteristics of National Constitutions data set.

[26] Ibid. at 46–53.

[27] The databases used were Characteristics of National Constitutions (Comparative Constitutions Project) 2014, PolityIV 2016, the Quality of Government (QoG) Basic Data set 2017, World Development Indicators (WDI) 2017 and the Systemic Banking Crises Database developed by Laeven and Valencia (2012).

[28] Luc Laeven, and Fabian Valencia, 'Systemic Banking Crises Database: An Update'. IMF Working Papers (No. 12/163) (2012), 1–32.

These variables are derived from the literature: for instance, it has been suggested that democratic regimes are better able than others to resist institutional breakdown in times of crisis, because their institutions are more flexible, dissent has an outlet, and legitimacy is broad-based. In authoritarian regimes, on the other hand, institutions depend to a considerable degree on economic performance.[29] Parliamentary regimes, particularly those of the Westminster type, can be expected to engage more easily in constitutional changes due to clear majorities and fewer veto points, though the amendment rules of a given country may make a difference.[30] Ginsburg and Melton[31] suggest, too, that the length of a constitution may be correlated with willingness to amend, because its specificity may create more pressure and opportunity for change.

Restricting the data set to 1990–2013 due to the limited availability of a number of important variables, we started with seventeen countries in Southeast and East Asia but decided to drop Brunei, East Timor, Laos, Myanmar, and North Korea because for most of the period they could not be considered liberal constitutional regimes. Taiwan was dropped because there were no data on GDP growth, CPI inflation and unemployment. Our sample thus forms an unbalanced panel of 221 observations from eleven countries. Summary statistics for the dependent and independent variables are presented in Table 15.1.

For the analysis, we employ a simple linear probability model (LPM) to examine the effect of financial crisis on constitutional change:

$$Y_{ct} = \beta_0 + X_{ct}\beta_1 + Z_{ct}\beta_2 + u_{ct}$$

where, for each country c and year t, Y is the indicator for constitutional change, X is a vector of independent variables, Z is the control for financial crisis (including lags) and u is the error term. The explanatory variables include dummies for democracy, parliamentary system, (log of) length of constitution, GDP growth, CPI inflation and unemployment rate. Thus, the coefficient vector β_2 captures the effect of financial crisis on constitutional change.

Given the limitations of linear probability models,[32] we also check robustness by repeating the analysis using Probit models. However, since the marginal effects in

29 Stephan Haggard and Robert Kaufman, *The Political Economy of Democratic Transitions*. Princeton NJ: Princeton University Press, 1995.

30 Bjorn Rasch and Roger Congleton, *Amendment Procedures and Constitutional Stability. Democratic Constitutional Design and Public Policy: Analysis and Evidence*. Cambridge MA: MIT Press, 2006, 319–25; George Tsebelis, 'Constitutional Rigidity: A Veto Players Approach'. Working Paper (2016).

31 Tom Ginsburg and James Melton. 'Does the Constitutional Amendment Rule Matter at all? Amendment Cultures and the Challenges of Measuring Amendment Difficulty', *International Journal of Constitutional Law* 13(3): 686–713 (2015).

32 Two specific disadvantages are that predicted probabilities can fall outside the 0–1 bound, and that the partial effect of any linear explanatory variable remains constant. Wooldridge, J. M. *Econometric analysis of cross section and panel data*. Boston: MIT Press, 2010.

TABLE 15.1 *Summary statistics*

Variable	Mean	Std.Dev.	Min	Max
Constitutional change	0.150	0.357	0	1
Financial crisis	0.068	0.253	0	1
Parliamentary system	0.419	0.494	0	1
Democracy	0.667	0.472	0	1
Length of constitution (no of words)	19,793	18,382	1,802	64,080
Unemployment rate (%)	4.291	2.435	0.100	11.900
GDP growth (%)	5.491	4.217	−13.130	17.290
N	234			

LPM and Probit models are similar around mean values of other explanatory variables, we rely on the former because LPM results are easier to interpret.

For the qualitative country-specific analysis, we have selected cases that emerged from the quantitative analysis as interesting illustrations for the ideal types Contiades[33] described (breakdown, adjustment, submission, stamina). To explore the cases in detail, we mainly relied on legal and socio-political scholarship, such as descriptions of economic and constitutional reforms, landmark constitutional cases, and commentary from legal and political actors in those countries. Comparative case and material collections complemented the descriptions.[34]

IV. FINDINGS

Table 15.2 presents our main findings: Column 1 shows the results given by equation (1) but with financial crisis dummies that have three lags and no other control variables; the results indicate that financial crisis does not induce changes in constitutions (all tests are conducted at the 5 percent level of significance). We next model constitutional change on GDP growth, CPI inflation and unemployment rate, as those variables can influence people's attitude to the ruling government and thus trigger changes in constitution. Again, we find that neither has a significant impact on constitutional change (Column 2). Employing them together with indicators for financial crisis (with lags) also finds no significant effect of any variable on the dependent variable (Column 3). Furthermore, the R^2 value for all three models indicates that the models have very little explanatory power.

In contrast, modelling constitutional change on political control variables suggests that, as we expect, democracy and the length of constitutions affect the

[33] Contiades, 'Constitutions in the Global Financial Crisis'.

[34] Chang et al. *Constitutionalism in Asia: Cases and Materials*.

TABLE 15.2 *Financial crises and constitutional change in Southeast and East Asia*

	(1)	(2)	(3)	(4)	(5)
Financial crisis	−0.033		−0.045		0.009
	(0.098)		(0.098)		(0.092)
Financial crisis in previous year	0.062		0.062		0.091
	(0.104)		(0.104)		(0.097)
Financial crisis two years earlier	−0.012		−0.002		0.025
	(0.104)		(0.104)		(0.098)
Financial crisis three years earlier	0.116		0.140		0.163*
	(0.098)		(0.098)		(0.093)
GDP growth (%) 5 yrs MA		0.008	0.011		−0.000
		(0.008)	(0.008)		(0.012)
CPI inflation 5 yrs MA		−0.000	0.000		0.000
		(0.001)	(0.001)		(0.001)
Unemployment (%) 5 yrs MA		−0.020*	−0.020*		0.015
		(0.010)	(0.010)		(0.013)
Parliamentary				0.075	0.128*
				(0.050)	(0.071)
Democracy				−0.161***	−0.209***
				(0.046)	(0.067)
log(length)				0.072**	0.062**
				(0.028)	(0.029)
Constant	0.135***	0.184**	0.159**	−0.489*	−0.483*
	(0.026)	(0.076)	(0.078)	(0.263)	(0.277)
R sq.	0.01	0.03	0.04	0.14	0.17
F	0.48	2.09	1.29	11.98	4.23
N	221	221	221	221	221

Standard errors in parentheses.
* $p < 0.10$, ** $p < 0.05$, *** $p < 0.01$

likelihood of constitutional change (Column 4). Their effects remain statistically significant when we add the financial crisis indicator (with lags), GDP growth, and the unemployment rate (Column 5).[35] In the last and our preferred model (Column 5), although not statistically significant, all other variables also appear to have an expected effect on constitutional change. For example, financial crisis, inflation and unemployment positively affect the dependent variable, while the opposite is true for GDP growth. Importantly, a parliamentary system increases the probability of constitutional change. This appears to be consistent with the common observation that a parliamentary system – particularly the Westminster type with a clear electoral

[35] Note however that, while not statistically significant, the coefficients of financial crisis indicate that the financial crisis increases the likelihood of a constitutional reform as shown in model 5. Our findings also remain largely unaffected with the inclusion of unemployment rate in these models (results not presented).

majority, as in Singapore and Malaysia – might best be able to meet supermajority requirements and thus promote constitutional change through amendment. Also, in our model, a democratic system is less likely to experience a constitutional change – perhaps because the regime may be considered more legitimate and less dominated by authoritarian leadership personalities, whose fate is often linked to economic performance. Validating the observations of Ginsburg and Melton,[36] the length of a constitution also has a positive effect on constitutional change, perhaps because longer constitutions tend to offer more opportunities for change than shorter ones. In general, the explanatory power of our models significantly increases with political controls; about 17 percent of the total variation in the dependent variable is now explained by our preferred model, model 5.[37]

The quantitative analysis thus confirms some intuitive expectations arising from consideration of the data. In Southeast and East Asia, at least, financial crisis seems to have little effect on constitutional changes. However, many of the political control variables are statistically significant and have the expected direction, which suggests some interesting sub-dynamics in both the democratic–authoritarian and the parliamentary–presidential divides.[38] That calls for further exploration into how crisis provokes the need for structural change in different political-institutional arrangements – an aspect Negretto explores in this volume in terms of legislative and executive powers. Unfortunately, the limitations of the dataset prevent comprehensive analysis here.

My findings may also not be catching far more nuanced and complex dynamics that may be playing out as a result of financial crisis – dynamics that cannot be properly accounted for in regression models that lump various forms of change into a single variable. In fact, the quantitative analysis may fail to capture the dynamics within countries where there is no evidence of formal change but where informal change may have been induced by law-makers and judges that affect rights and principles as well as allocation of state powers. That is why a more qualitative treatment of selected cases is necessary.

V. UNDERSTANDING COUNTRY-LEVEL DYNAMICS

Drawing on the ideal types of constitutional reaction to crisis, we present here selected narratives consistent with the Contiades typology.[39] Again, the AFC period

36 Ginsburg and Melton. 'Does the constitutional amendment rule matter at all? Amendment cultures and the challenges of measuring amendment difficulty'.

37 Using annual values of GDP growth, inflation and unemployment do not affect our results; nor does dropping from the model either the indicators of financial crisis or the other economic variables.

38 A potential concern about our analysis can be the idiosyncratic differences between countries, which were not controlled for. The reason is the low variation within countries over time. However, when considered, country fixed effects have been found significant in all our models. Thus they indicate that examination by country may be a good way to focus light on this issue.

39 Contiades, 'Constitutions in the Global Financial Crisis'.

is the principal concern, though recent-GFC related events are also considered where relevant.

1. *Breakdown: Thailand and Indonesia?*

Severe financial crisis may provide the context or trigger for replacement or comprehensive revision of a constitution, particularly when it may have lost its uniting symbolic power or is perceived as unable to contribute to overcoming the crisis. At first glance, Thailand (1997) and Indonesia (1999, 2000, 2001, 2002) might be considered exemplars of such a situation. Both countries were severely affected by the AFC, and also changed their constitutions comprehensively in temporal proximity to the crisis itself. But the dynamics are often not as clear-cut as might be expected.

Take, for instance, Thailand's 1997 'People's Constitution', which is generally considered a watershed event in Thai constitutional history. Though it was enacted by parliament in October 1997 at the height of the unfolding financial crisis, the crisis was hardly the trigger for it. Instead, this change is best understood as the culmination of a decade-long reform process by liberal elites that emanated from dissatisfaction with the poor functioning of Thai democracy, and the rise of money-based electoral politics.[40] Nevertheless, the crisis likely affected the timing of the change, because reformers benefited from a weakened political class and public support for a comprehensive overhaul of the political architecture. As a result, they were able to ensure passage of the draft despite considerable resistance from established politicians, and civilian and military bureaucracies.[41]

Similarly, in Indonesia, amendment of the 1945 post-independence constitution (which was from the beginning considered to be provisional) had been widely debated in academic and reformist circles since the 1980s. President Suharto's New Order regime attempted to defer demands for constitutional change through a decree in 1983, and a law in 1985 that set exceedingly strict criteria for any constitutional change (e.g., both a 90 percent turnout and approval in a public referendum). However, with the fall of Suharto, and accelerated by public protests and a loss of legitimacy in light of the impact of the AFC,[42] these restrictions were removed and a four-stage revision process was launched with the People's Consultative Assembly. This process was helped along by a sense of urgency that resulted from the economic impact of the crisis.

40 Borwornsak Uwanno and Wayne Burns, 'The Thai Constitution of 1997: Sources and Process'. *University of British Columbia Law Review* 32: 227–47 (1998).

41 Prudhisan Jumbala, 'Thailand: Constitutional Reform Amidst Economic Crisis'. *Southeast Asian Affairs* (1998): 265–91; Suchitra Punyaratabandhu, 'Thailand in 1997: Financial Crisis and Constitutional Reform'. *Asian Survey* 38(2) 161–67 (1998); Connors, 'Framing the "People's Constitution"'. In D. McCargo (ed.), *Reforming Thai Politics*. Copenhagen: NIAS, 2002, 37–55.

42 Aspinall, *Opposing Suharto*.

In short, in both cases, the financial crisis was neither a necessary nor a sufficient condition for the breakdown, but arguably helped remove road-blocks, and facilitated passage of a new, though often contested, constitutional framework.

This is not to say, however, that the crisis had no impact on the constitutional dynamics in both countries. For instance, the impact of the crisis may have been reflected in the phrasing of provisions in both constitutions. In Thailand, as perhaps more broadly elsewhere,[43] this meant emphasis on a strong executive (Chapter VII) and provisions intended to promote transparency and accountability (Chapter X) in the 1997 constitution, and more recently requirements for financial and fiscal responsibility in the 2008 and 2017 constitutions.[44] In Indonesia, where drafting started only after the crisis, several provisions might have emanated directly from that experience – for instance, the effort in the fourth amendment to set both central and regional education spending at 20 percent of GDP (in combination with the Law on National Education, No. 20/2003), and to use new financial management laws to introduce new transparency standards and spending constraints.[45] This includes a maximum budget deficit of 3 percent of GDP and a cumulative loan ratio of 60 percent of GDP (similar to the Maastricht treaty).

Perhaps even more interesting, the crisis also induced important informal changes in the judiciary through the new political architecture prompted by the crisis itself. Here the Thai case is particularly instructive. One of the first decisions of the new Constitutional Court in 1999 was the constitutionality of four executive decrees that the Chuan administration issued under Art. 218/219 to deal with the economic crisis. Asked to rule on whether the royal ordinances were 'cases of emergency and unavoidable necessary urgency', the Court went beyond the petition to validate the ordinances – a line it held against eight more attacks on economic policy measures.[46] Later, the Court would also reject a submission to impeach PM Leekpai and his finance minister for signing a fifth letter with the IMF, arguing that it did not constitute an international treaty that would require approval from the National Assembly. The Court also sanctioned the government's State Enterprise Corporatisation Bill (50/2542), which was meant to help liquidize state assets for the government.[47]

Hence, through judicial intervention, executive powers over the economy were interpreted broadly, and often at odds with powers specified in the laws – a stance

43 See Negretto's chapter on Latin America.

44 See Art. 84 Sec. 3 of the 2007 constitution and the expanded Art. 62 of the 2017 constitution – although both might also be seen as a reaction to financial improprieties under the Thaksin government.

45 Laws nos 17/2003 State Financial Law, 1/2004 Treasury Law, 15/2004 Financial Auditing and Report Law.

46 Borwornsak Uwanno, 'Economic Crisis and Political Crisis in Thailand: Past and Present'. *NTU Law Review* 4(3): 142–98 (2009).

47 See James Klein, 'The Battle for the Rule of Law in Thailand: The Constitutional Court of Thailand'. In Amara Raksasataya and J. R. Klein (eds), *The Constitutional Court of Thailand. The Provisions and the Working of the Court*. Bangkok: Constitution for the People Society, 2003, 34–90.

that was reversed only later under the Thaksin government.[48] The 2007 constitution explicitly states that parliament must approve treaties that have an 'impact on the country's economic and social stability'.[49] Indonesia exhibited similar dynamics though there the court several times ruled against laws passed by parliament or the executive. After several warnings, the court even struck down the 2008 budget as unconstitutional (though not with immediate effect) because it contradicted a constitutional provision that the 'education budget' should at least be 20 percent of the total annual budget (Art. 31(4)).[50]

In short, while in both cases crisis was not a necessary condition for constitutional breakdown, where forces were already poised and mobilized it certainly facilitated political liberalization, and eventually democratization. This paved the way for constitutional reforms guided by a new set of actors, which triggered major informal changes to constitutional practice, as evidenced by the growing role of an empowered judiciary.

2. *Adjustment: Malaysia and Singapore?*

Malaysia and Singapore are outliers in the region in terms of the frequency with which they have amended their constitutions since independence – Malaysia over fifty-seven times and Singapore fifty times.[51] They might therefore be considered approximations to an 'adjustment' scenario, where through a mix of formal and informal changes, the constitution adapts to new developments. There are political and legal reasons for this situation: for instance, both countries are dominated by single parties (UMNO and PAP, respectively), so it is relatively easy for the government to meet parliamentary supermajority rules for constitutional amendments.[52] Also, courts in both countries have regularly rejected the basic-feature doctrine, which would limit the power of parliament to amend the constitution.[53] A leading constitutional scholar has claimed that in Singapore it is parliament, rather than the constitution, that is supreme.[54]

A close look at the amendments also makes clear that linking them to financial crisis is not easy, because formal amendments made around the crises have generally

48 Case No. 3–5, 2550 (2007), July 8, 2007. See, e.g., the. *Preah Veah* case.

49 Art. 190, 2007 constitution (now repeated in Art. 178 of the 2017 constitution).

50 Court decision 013/PUU-VI/2008.

51 For Malaysia, see *Malay Law Review*; for Singapore, see 'legislative history section' of the Constitution of the Republic of Singapore.

52 Singapore requires a two-thirds parliamentary majority, and some provisions pertaining to state sovereignty require a two-thirds majority in a popular referendum (Art. 5). In Malaysia, on the second and third readings, a bill to amend the constitution must have the votes of not less than two-thirds of the total number of members thereof (Art. 159).

53 See for Malaysia *Phan Chin Hock Public Prosecutor* [1980] 1 MLJ 213; see for Singapore *Teo Soh Lung* v. *Minister for Home Affairs* (1989) 1 Sing. L.R. 499 (HC), *Teo Soh Lung* v. *Minister for Home Affairs* [1990] 2 Malayan Law Journal, 129 (Sing. CA).

54 Harding (1983).

had little to do with the financial crisis event.[55] A crisis may occasionally inform parliamentary debate, as was shown in Singapore with attempts to enhance revenues and thus reserve requirements by constitutional amendments in 2008[56] – a debate also shaped by GFC experience.[57] But for the most part the impact of the crisis was felt politically, as in Malaysia, where it gave rise to a split between then PM Mahathir and his deputy PM Anwar Ibrahim – a split that still complicates political dynamics today.[58]

It still might be argued that the crisis has triggered informal changes, as in the decision of Malaysia's Federal Court (FC) in *Danaharta Urus Sdn Bhd* v. *Kekatong Sdn Bhd*.[59] The case emanated from the Danaharta Act (1998) that after the AFC established a national asset management company (Danaharta) charged with buying non-performing loans (NPLs) from financial institutions. Here, the FC was dealing with a Court of Appeal decision that had declared unconstitutional section 72 of the Act – which provides that courts cannot give an order preventing, compelling, stopping or restraining the powers or any action taken by Danaharta or any committee or officer of Danaharta. The Court of Appeal had reasoned that section 72 was unconstitutional because it infringed Article 8(1) of the Federal Constitution, which declares all persons equal before the law and entitled to the equal protection of the law.[60] It therefore held that the provision in the Act elevated Danaharta above the law, and hence was unconstitutional. For many, this was a remarkable decision, not only for its broad interpretation of Article 8, but also for what many saw as an attempt by the judiciary to reassert their independence and stop executive infringement after the constitutional crisis in 1988.[61] However, the FC bench overturned the ruling in deference to parliamentary supremacy.[62]

Similarly, in Singapore, the Court of Appeal rejected attempts by Reform Party Chief Kenneth Jeyaretnam to block a $4 billion loan from the Singapore government to the International Monetary Fund (IMF) in the wake of the GFC, based on

55 Malaysia made three amendments in 2001, and two in 2009. Singapore made one amendment in 1997, four in 1998, and one in 1999. No amendment in either country responded directly to economic issues.

56 See Act 27 of 2008 – Constitution of the Republic of Singapore (Amendment) Act 2008.

57 MP Mr Gautam Banerjee argued '[that] this very important Bill is taking place today when we are in the midst of a global financial crisis of unprecedented proportions is entirely a coincidence. However, the financial meltdown we have experienced over the past few weeks will inevitably influence the discussion and debate we will have in this House during the Second Reading of this Bill.', http://sprs.parl.gov.sg/search/topic.jsp?currentTopicID=00073078-ZZ.

58 William Case, 'Malaysia: New Reforms, Old Continuities, Tense Ambiguities'. *The Journal of Development Studies* 41(2): 284–309 (2005).

59 [2004] 2 MLJ 257.

60 [2003] 3 MLJ 1.

61 See Malaysian Bar, 'The God-provision', www.malaysianbar.org.my/constitutional_law/the_god_provision.html?date=2016-03-01.

62 The majority opinion was written by CA judge Augustine Paul (who sat on the FC bench pursuant to Art. 122(2)) – a judge suspected of close government ties after presiding over the sodomy cases of opposition leader Anwar Ibrahim in 1998.

the claim that the loan contravened Article 144 of the Constitution because it would require parliamentary and presidential approval; the court ruled that Jeyaretnam did not have standing because he did not have any public or private rights to protect.[63]

In both countries, there is little evidence that the constitutional amendments were linked to the financial crisis, though the crisis may have triggered subtle informal changes by judges or lawmakers that might occasionally bear on practices related to the constitutions, though few can be considered of far-reaching importance. Rather, the political structures in place, as well as the limited impact of the crisis itself, have allowed the political class to manage the impact of the crisis well. That could also be seen as a good predictor of constitutional resilience.

3. *Stamina: Philippines and Taiwan?*

The AFC, and even the GFC, had only limited impact on the Philippines and Taiwan, because the Philippines had little exposure and Taiwan had sufficient reserves.[64] Therefore, it should perhaps not be surprising that both constitutions were virtually unchanged by the crises. Not that Taiwan is a stranger to constitutional amendments – there have been seven since democratization in 1987 – but none was in response to the regional crisis; all were driven by political dynamics.[65] Thus both cases are good illustrations not only of stamina – where the constitution was able to meet the demands of the crisis and remain intact – but also of a more general resistance to change, despite ever-present pressures for change.

Consider, for instance, the Philippines and its 1987 post-Marcos 'Freedom Constitution', which has seen several attempts at amendment via petitions for a public plebiscite under Article XVII Sec. 2 of the constitution. These were thwarted by the Supreme Court in 1997 and 2006 on technicalities.[66] However, that has not stopped debates about constitutional change – ranging from calls for a parliamentary system to recent calls for a federal structure – though these have often faced stiff opposition from civil society groups, which have suspected a hidden executive agenda to extend the presidential term limit, based on the country's experiences under Marcos.[67] Perhaps most notable, though, are the challenges to nationalist economic provisions in the constitution. These require the state to develop 'a self-reliant and independent national economy effectively controlled by Filipinos' (Art. II section 19) and also grant privileged rights for the national

63 *Jeyaretnam Kenneth Andrew* v. *Attorney-General*, www.singaporelaw.sg/sglaw/laws-of-singapore/case-law/free-law/court-of-appeal-judgments/15402-jeyaretnam-kenneth-andrew-v-attorney-general-2013-sgca-56.

64 Haggard, *The Political Economy of the Asian Financial Crisis* (2000), 126.

65 Chien-Chih Lin, 'Taiwan: A Patchwork Constitution' (2015).

66 See, People's Initiative for Reform, Modernization and Action (PIRMA), G.R. No XX (1997); G.R. No 174153 (2006).

67 Dante Gatmaytan-Magno, 'Changing Constitutions: Judicial Review and Redemptions in the Philippines'. *Pacific Basin Law Journal* 25(1): 1–24 (2007).

economy. Among these are protection against foreign competition, and a provision requiring Filipino ownership or a 60 percent majority for joint ventures related to ownership of land (e.g., mineral resources), educational institutions, and media organizations (Art. XII secs 1, 2, 10).

These provisions have repeatedly been questioned whenever the country's economic performance was poor and during fiscal crises. For instance, as recently as 2006, lawmakers sought to include economic amendments in the charter change debates during the Aquino III presidency,[68] and similarly in 2004 the Supreme Court reversed its earlier narrow interpretation of the Philippines Mining Act,[69] thus loosening the prohibition on foreign participation, with direct reference to the 2003 fiscal crisis.[70] The latter paved the way for further liberalization in the Mineral Resources Act of 2012.

Similarly in Taiwan, since the 1990s there have been regular calls for a comprehensive overhaul of the constitution – though efforts by President Chen Shui-bian in 2003 faced severe political resistance, and the idea was eventually shelved.[71] Meanwhile, the Constitutional Court began to push back against constitutional amendments – especially when these were perceived as self-aggrandising efforts of the National Assembly – and to insist on strict compliance with adherence to the formal constitutional process.[72] As a result, constitutional amendments have been quite rare since 2005.

There have been few court cases related to either financial crisis. One exception occurred in 1998, when the Court was asked to decide on the constitutionality of the government's take-over of two small banks under Article 15 of the constitution – a request the Court granted, but with strict limits.[73] Faced with the impact of a severe earthquake in 1999, the Court also declared constitutional many extraordinary measures in the emergency decree issued by the President, thus providing room for executive action during times of economic emergency.[74]

In sum, while the constitutions of both countries did show resilience during the AFC and the GFC, they also illuminate the continuing pressures for change, although some have been induced or blocked by judicial and legislative actors.

68 www.gmanetwork.com/news/story/317020/news/nation/house-bill-pushes-for-cha-cha-to-change-phl-form-of-govt.

69 *La Bugal-B'Laan Tribal Association, Inc.* v. *Ramos* G.R. No 127882; (see also related *Manila Prince Hotel* v. *Government Service Insurance System)* G.R. No X.X.

70 See reference to fiscal crisis by C. J. Panganiban, who was the ponente in this case. For a thorough analysis, see Cienca Jr., A. N. (2010) 'The Philippine Supreme Court and the Mining Act Ruling Reversal'. Doctor of Philosophy in Political Science, University of the Philippines.

71 These included a proposed amendment bill to reform the Legislative Yuan and abolish the National Assembly, see Chu, Y.-H. 'Taiwan's Year of Stress.' *Journal of Democracy* 16(2): 34–57 (2005).

72 See, JY Interpretation No. 314 (1993).

73 See JY Interpretation No. 488 (1999) and No. 489 (1999).

74 JY Interpretation No. 543 (2002).

4. Submission: South Korea?

Though South Korea was one of the countries most deeply affected by the AFC (Heo and Kim 2000), there have been few changes to the constitutional document itself. However, given comprehensive revisions to other legislation, South Korea might be considered a case of submission, where the 'constitution appears immobilized in the face of the crisis, unable to offer either institutional support or some sort of catharsis through change, and is subordinated to informal interventions made by the law-maker in accordance with commitments by loan agreements.'[75]

At first glance, this may be a good description of what happened in South Korea in 1997–98. Within just twelve months, the government was able to pass or revise over twenty financial reform acts and two major laws (dealing with corporate composition and corporate reorganization), driven in part by the IMF rescue package.[76] Most of the reform legislation, which was designed to enhance the transparency and accountability of business–government relations with regard to the chaebol conglomerates and the financial sector, was passed under new President Kim Dae Jung (1998–2003), who despite his narrow victory, was able to enjoy unusual executive and legislative authority because he benefited from a disruption of Korea's traditional policy patterns and practices, and because of the crisis, was able to draw on widespread public as well as political support to make sweeping reforms.[77] Even from the Constitutional Court, the guardian of the constitution, there was little resistance to these changes, despite its earlier involvement in constitutional tussles over the presidential choice of the prime minister and occasional resistance from lawmakers, who challenged the reform legislation in the Court.[78]

Yet there is still a question of whether South Korea's is actually a 'submission' scenario. While it is certainly true that the AFC eroded trust in the political class and raised questions about the ability of the institutional architecture to provide enough oversight to prevent the financial crisis, it is not entirely clear that the loss of confidence extended to the constitution itself, perhaps because amendments made during the political transition ten years earlier were popular. The strict amendment procedures, requiring two-thirds majorities in parliament and a public referendum within thirty days after passage, might also explain why most of the changes have been legislative. And while it might be interesting to investigate whether some specialized laws or their revisions (e.g., Labor Standard Acts, Employment Adjustment Act) might be at odds with social provisions in the

[75] Contiades, 'Constitutions in the Global Financial Crisis', 49.

[76] See overview of legislation in Haggard (2000: 100).

[77] Mo, 'The Politics of Economic reform'. In C. E. R. Network (ed.), *The Politics of Economic Crisis in Asia: Consensus and Controversies*. Washington, DC: Carnegie Endowment for International Peace, 1999, 53; Haggard, *The Political Economy of the Asian Financial Crisis*, 101.

[78] Tom Ginsburg, *Judicial Review in New Democracies. Constitutional Courts in Asian Cases*. Cambridge: Cambridge University Press, 2003, 232.

constitution, they were never challenged in the Constitutional Court, whose landmark decisions have often been found in other issue areas.[79]

While the Korean cases certainly evidence elements of a 'submission' scenario, Korea might be best viewed as a resilient state in which political actors used the crisis to implement far-reaching reforms that made it possible to more quickly globalize the economy. The constitution held up because it was young and legitimate, and – only a decade after Korea's transition to democracy – there was little appetite for regime change. The outcome might have been very different under a military regime, but such a counterfactual exercise is difficult to evaluate – though it may well prompt further reflection on how crises might play out differently depending on the timing of earlier regime change.

VI. CONCLUSION

In this chapter, we have sought to investigate how severe financial crisis has impacted liberal constitutional regimes in Asia. This study, which combines quantitative and qualitative evidence from the region over the last quarter-century, found little evidence of a direct impact of the Asian and global financial crises on constitutional change in the region if measured in terms of amendments or new constitutions. Instead it appears that in Asia, the effect of crisis depends on the underlying political-institutional structure, and on the informal dynamics created by other laws and judicial interventions in reaction to the crises – at times, however, with major consequences for national constitutional practice.

To what extent are these findings surprising? Given the severity of the AFC crisis in 1997 (and to a lesser extent the GFC 2008), and the amount of constitutional change the last two decades have seen in the region, the findings may indeed be unexpected.[80] And yet, precisely because change has been so regular a feature in the region, the amount of constitutional change is similar, both before and after the crises; nor is it possible to discern markedly different *patterns* of change after financial crisis. In fact, with states returning to high growth often within two years, it should not be surprising that the effects were felt largely through intermediate political variables – whether because liberal democratic regimes were able to resist constitutional changes, perhaps because their legitimacy was less tied to an authoritarian compact, or parliamentary regimes were more effective in adjusting to the crisis by amendments and other legal changes, or that longer and thus more rigid

79 See e.g. Tom Ginsburg, 'The Constitutional Court and the Judicialization of Korean Politics'. In A. Harding and P. Nicholson (eds), *New Courts in Asia*. Abingdon: Routledge, 2010, 145–57.

80 The mean size (in words) of the constitutions (for seventeen countries, between 1990 and 2013) was 17,536, with considerable variations (standard deviation 16,709, minimum 1,802 and maximum 64,080).

constitutions were more prone to change – our findings are generally consistent with the political economy scholarship on the crisis.[81]

However, some crisis effects have played out in the constitutional realm. Based on what they learned in adapting to the exigencies of the AFC, several states inserted fiscal rules in their constitutions and lawmakers were quick to pass supportive laws – the dynamics of which might have helped mitigate the effect of the 2008 GFC in many countries in the region. Equally important, during these exceptional events courts have increasingly shaped the nature of executive prerogatives and constitutional rights – thus giving new direction and meaning to some constitutional norms and language as part of the broader regional trend to judicialize politics.[82] Still, as shown here, the impact of some of these decisions has often been less than momentous.

Clearly, the region does offer interesting insights for wider debate. While we find much that is useful in the work of Contiades in Europe, Asia also offers some unique dynamics that a more developed Europe did not experience. There, as the cases demonstrate, the patterns generated by crisis have been closely intertwined with regime change, facilitating social mobilization and offering new focal points for political and constitutional reforms. The remarkable mix of regime types in the region compared to other regions also allows for a unique perspective on how such reforms come about – whether by drawing attention to the nexus between crisis and political resilience across political systems, or by recognizing the variations in the impact of a crisis depending on its severity or its timing relative to reform initiatives already underway and earlier regime change.

But what does our study imply for the future of constitutionalism in Asia? The answer is far from obvious. It may be tempting to see constitutional resilience, legal adaptation, and judicial interventions as part of a gradual move within the region towards normative liberal constitutional orders. Yet it is questionable whether financial crisis has been a true test case for such assumptions, because the shocks were relatively short-term and the crises often perceived as externally induced. In fact, the crises seem to have revealed an almost automatic reflex to empower the executive at the expense of other institutions and individual rights – which is consistent with the regional legacies of executive dominance. An exclusive focus on the financial crises also deflects from the continuing contestation around several constitutional flashpoints (e.g., drafting, human rights, military, judiciary) that are currently shaping constitutional practice in the region.[83]

A more fruitful intellectual engagement might emerge from closer study of the nexus between economic changes and constitutional practice in the region. For instance, rising inequality and the higher performance expectations engendered by

81 Haggard, *The Political Economy of the Asian Financial Crisis*; MacIntyre, *The Power of Institutions*.

82 See for a thorough evaluation of the judicialization phenomenon in Asia, Dressel, B. (ed.), *The Judicialization of Politics in Asia*. Abingdon and New York: Routledge, 2012.

83 Bünte and Dressel, *Politics and Constitutions in Southeast Asia*.

years of high growth might have powerful effects in the years to come, which are perhaps prefigured by the current turn in some countries to authoritarian populism and democratic regression, often with direct support from middle-class constituencies. Questions are also emerging about some traditional assumptions derived from modernization theory and its liberal constitutional correlates. In short, rather than providing definitive answers, our chapter spells out a future research agenda. As Asia's importance continues to rise globally, what is happening there can provide valuable information about the future of liberal constitutionalism, not just in the region but well beyond.

Index